D0966324

50-11

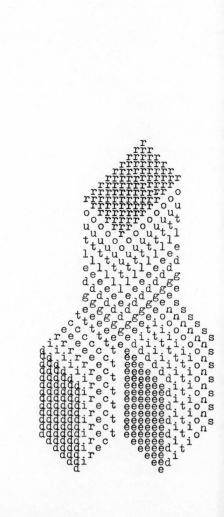

GERMAN FOREIGN POLICY, 1871-1914

IMANUEL GEISS

ROUTLEDGE DIRECT EDITIONS

ROUTLEDGE & KEGAN PAUL
London and Boston

First published in 1976
by Routledge & Kegan Paul Ltd
Broadway House, 68-74 Carter Lane
London EC4V 5EL and
9 Park Street,
Boston, Mass. 02108, USA
Manuscript typed by Jacqueline Bayes
Printed and bound in Great Britain
by Unwin Brothers Limited,
The Gresham Press, Old Woking, Surrey
A member of the Staples Printing Group
© Imanuel Geiss 1976
No part of this book may be reproduced in
any form without permission from the publisher,
except for the quotation of brief passages
in criticism

ISBN 0 7100 8303 3

DD
221.5
.G42

To Fritz Fischer

CONTENTS

LIBRARY
ALMA COLLEGE
ALMA, MICHIGAN

Part four THE COMING OF WAR, 1909-14   119

12 'ENCIRCLEMENT' AND GERMANY'S SELF-ISOLATION   121

13 GERMANY'S POLITICAL OFFENSIVE AGAINST
    'ENCIRCLEMENT', 1909-12   128

14 THE DECISION TO GO TO WAR, JANUARY TO 8
    DECEMBER 1912   139

15 PREPARING FOR WAR, DECEMBER 1912-JUNE 1914   146

Part five GERMANY'S WAR OF AGGRESSION AND CONQUEST   161

16 GERMANY'S WAR OF AGGRESSION: THE CRISIS
    AND THE OUTBREAK OF WAR, 28 JUNE-4 AUGUST 1914   163

17 GERMANY'S WAR OF CONQUEST: GERMAN WAR
    AIMS, 1914   173

    DOCUMENTS   182

    NOTES   219

    BIBLIOGRAPHY   245

    INDEX   253

INTRODUCTION

By German foreign policy during the forty-three years before the
outbreak of the First World War is to be understood the foreign
policy of the German Empire in that period. The foreign policy of
Austria-Hungary is discussed only when it affected directly that of
the German Empire, in particular in 1878-9, 1909-9 and 1914.   The
author has tried not to overwhelm the reader with a flood of diplomatic details.   Instead, it is his hope to explain the character
and results of German foreign policy.   The basic idea of the book
is to demonstrate the interplay of domestic and foreign factors in
the making of the foreign policy of the German Empire.   In order
to do this, the economic and political structure of the German
Empire from Bismarck to Wilhelm II had to be sketched, and the
structural changes and their political effects explained, which
also affected the aims and motivation of diplomatic action.
   The reader, therefore, should not expect a strictly narrative
account of German foreign policy between 1871 and 1914, evenly
spread over more than four decades.   The author has tried rather
to concentrate on the crucial stages of German foreign policy at
the time, seeing them also in the light of the general character
of the German Empire and interpreting them with the help of key
passages from key diplomatic documents.   It seemed to be more
enlightening to set out the alternatives and dilemmas with which
German statesmen were confronted than to indulge in elaborate psychological portraits of Germany's leaders.   It might also be helpful to explain why one alternative became official policy, while
others remained academic, only to be found in speeches and articles
of the opposition or in confidential memoranda of the ruling
circles.
   The first period of what can be justly called 'German' foreign
policy in modern times is identical with a span of forty-three
years between two major wars - the Franco-Prussian War of 1870-1
(called in German the 'Germano-French War') and the First World War
of 1914-18.   The period was one of peace for Germany and most of
Europe, but it was also the time when the tensions accumulated
which produced the conflict in 1914.   It was a period full of diplomatic crises, great and small, revolutions and local war in the
Balkans and outside Europe.   During that period we also have to

take into account the colonial expansion of Europe and the United
States, in particular the establishment of European colonial rule
over Africa.

The new German Empire, which emerged from three local wars
against Denmark, Austria and France (1864, 1866, 1870-1) played an
increasingly important part in the chain of events that led from
one great war to an even greater one. A survey of German foreign
policy between those two wars will necessarily have to bring out
the dynamics of the German Empire. Between its foundation in
1871 through war and its downfall in 1918 at the end of war, its
turn from a predominantly continental policy to the new concept of
imperialist 'Weltpolitik' in 1897-8 occupies a central position,
because the decision for 'Weltpolitik' made world war almost inevitable. Modern research, initiated by Fritz Fischer in Germany,
no longer denies the leading part of the German Empire in causing
the First World War. (1)

One possible misunderstanding, however, has to be cleared up at
the beginning: even if Germany, as will be explained in the following chapters, had a predominant share in the outbreak of the First
World War, this does not mean that German statesmen were bent on
war all the time. Although certain mechanisms were at work to
produce tensions and to convert tensions into conflict, there
always existed from 1871 to July 1914 rational alternatives to the
official policy, which might have preserved peace.

Many monographs and publications of documents see the period
before 1914 only as the background to the outbreak of the First
World War. But they vary, according to the point of view adopted,
in the dates taken as a point of departure: both the German and
the French official documents on the origins of the First World War
begin with 1871,(2) the British with 1898, (3) the Austrian with
1908, (4) the Russian with January 1914. (5)   Of all the authors,
Luigi Albertini goes farthest back - as far as 1867, seeing in the
constitutional compromise between Germans in Austria and Magyars
leading to the Austro-Hungarian Dual Monarchy, the starting point
leading to Sarajevo and war in 1914. (6)   Since the present author
sees the time between the founding of the new German Empire and the
outbreak of the war that initiated its downfall only four years
later as one distinct period of German foreign policy, he also
begins with 1871.

The documentation and literature on the whole period in general,
and on German foreign policy in particular, is enormous in quantity
and varying in quality. With their help the author has tried to
give a coherent picture of German foreign policy between the
Franco-German War of 1870-1 and the First World War of 1914-18.
Most recent research is being done in Germany again, as it should
be. In a way, the following analysis is also a kind of summary of
modern research on the period. Nevertheless, older accounts have
still proved invaluable. They provide a general framework and/or
treat many problems in greater detail than can be done here. For
the period until 1902 the two massive volumes by William L. Langer
are still indispensable. (7)   For the period until 1914 the first
volume of Luigi Albertini's master-work has often been referred to.
The final years from 1911 to 1914 are most extensively covered by
Professor Fritz Fischer's latest book. (8)   For the last two

chapters his first book on the subject will always remain
important. (9)

   In spite of the many shortcomings, its prejudiced selection and
presentation, the official publication of German documents on
foreign policy, 'Die Grosse Politik', is still the main source on
Germany's foreign policy.   If used with circumspection and a
critical mind, the 39 volumes are still an indispensable mine of
information, although recent research has confirmed how biased and
manipulated the whole work is.   There is in existence a condensed
selection in four volumes of the 'Grosse Politik' in English. (10)
One hesitates to recommend them, because both the selection of
documents and its translation into English are unsatisfactory.
But since the volumes are there, even reprinted recently, they
should at least be mentioned here.   Very helpful on the Bismarck
period are two recent publications, one in English, (11) the other
in German. (12)

   Whenever possible, the author has made use of existing transla-
tions into English.   Where he did not know of any he has ventured
to translate German quotations into English himself, both in the
text and in the documents.

   Parts of the chapters on July 1914 and German war aims 1914 are
taken from the present author's contributions to Purnell's 'History of the Twentieth Century', by kind permission of Purnell.

   Dr Peter-Christian Witt and Dr John C.G. Röhl have been critical
and helpful readers of most of the German and English versions of
the manuscript.   The gratitude for their help also includes their
acquittal of any errors in facts or judgment.
Bremen   I.G.

ACKNOWLEDGMENTS

The author and publishers would like to thank the following for
permission to reproduce copyright material:
Edward Arnold for Documents 5 and 6, from W.N. Medlicott and
D. Coveney, 'Bismarck and Europe' in the series Documents of
Modern History edited by A.G. Dickens and Alun Davies; B.T.
Batsford for Documents 10 and 19, from J.C.G. Röhl, 'Germany
without Bismarck', and Documents 20-24 from I. Geiss, 'July 1914';
Cambridge University Press for Documents 8 and 18, from 'The
Historical Journal' vol. VII, I, p. 147, 1964 and vol. XII, 4,
pp. 661-2, 1969 respectively; Chatto & Windus, London, and W.W.
Norton, New York, for Document 26, from Fritz Fischer, 'Germany's
Aims in the First World War', pp. 103-5; HMSO for Documents 11
and 25 from vols 3 and 11 respectively of 'British Documents on
the Origins of the War 1898-1914', edited by G.P. Gooch and
H.W.V. Temperley; Musterschmidt Verlag, Göttingen, for Document 9
from 'Der Kaiser', edited by W. Görlitz; and Phoebus Publishing
for extracts from Professor Geiss's contributions to 'History of
the Twentieth Century'.

Part one

THE GENERAL FRAMEWORK: THE REICH AND EUROPEAN DIPLOMACY

Chapter 1

THE SECOND GERMAN EMPIRE-HISTORICAL BACKGROUND AND SOCIAL STRUCTURE

Before discussing German foreign policy from 1871 to 1914, the historical background of the Second German Empire, and its economic and political structure have to be explained. Bismarck's Empire was the successor to the (First) Medieval Empire, which had been founded with the pretence of restoring the Roman Empire, but was ruled by dynasties of German emperors. (1)   In its struggle with the Pope, it adopted the addition 'Holy' to its official name in the thirteenth century and at the beginning of the sixteenth the addition 'of the German Nation'.   Originally a cover for the claims of German tribes or their leaders to a kind of hegemony over Christian Europe, the Empire degenerated, from the second half of the thirteenth century, into a kind of loose confederation of minute, small, some middle-sized and two great states - Austria and Prussia - both of whom had part of their territories lying outside the official boundaries of the Empire.   The Empire, the regional and the lesser local dynasties preserved the feudal structure in Germany more than the great national monarchies in the West, in particular Britain and France. (2)   The growth of modern capitalism on the basis of overseas trade in general, the transatlantic Slave Trade and slavery in the New World in particular, from the late fifteenth century onwards, relegated Germany for centuries to the background of economic development, which, in its turn, helped to stabilize the traditional structures of feudalism and monarchy. (3)

THE CONSEQUENCES OF THE FRENCH REVOLUTION

Only the shattering effects of the French Revolution, executed by Napoleon I, put an end to the century-long agony of the 'Holy Roman German Empire of the German Nation' in 1806.   After a short period of confusion, the Congress of Vienna constructed the German Confederation ('Deutscher Bund') as a kind of provisional substitute without a formal sovereign at its head.   Two hegemonial German powers dominated the 'Bund' - Austria the greater, with an emperor of her own, and Prussia the lesser, having only a king.   The rivalries of both powers largely dissipated whatever strength had remained in the Old Empire during the eighteenth century.   After

3

defeating Napoleon, the heir of the French Revolution, Austria and
Prussia carried on their rivalries in the German Confederation as
the question arose how to organize the German power into a more
definite form.   The Revolution of 1848-9 tried to create a new
German Empire through a combination of pressure from below, from the
liberal middle classes, and action from above, the princes and dynasties of Germany. (4)   The driving force behind the liberal clamour
for another Reich was the economic interest of the emerging industrial bourgeoisie who wanted a wider common market in Germany,
secured by a greater degree of political unity than offered by the
German Confederation.   The German Customs Union of 1834 ('Zollverein') in fact foreshadowed the later German Empire of 1871.   It
also pointed to the final decision as to who would be dominant in
the coming German 'Reich' - Austria or Prussia.   The Zollverein
had been introduced by Prussia as early as 1818 to further Prussia's
economic and political interest in Germany.   By acquisition of the
Rhine Province in 1815, Prussia was to become the leading industrial state in Germany in the nineteenth century. (5)

The ideology, corresponding to the political interests of the
middle classes was, apart from free trade and liberalism, a roman-
tic patriotism which idealized the medieval Empire through the
restoration of its glory and power by the resurrection of 'Kaiser
and Reich'.   The Revolution of 1848-9, for all its failures,
decided two issues: first, Austria would not be the dominant factor
in the new Empire.   Austria's ruling class, an aristocracy headed
by the Austrian Emperor, was unwilling to accept the new political
structure without the inclusion of the predominantly peasant provinces of non-German population, because they were their traditional
source of strength.   The liberal movement in Germany, however, only
wanted to include the Austrian Germans in the new Empire and not the
many non-German nationalities.   The first German parliament, assem-
bled in Frankfurt's Paulskirche, offered the German crown to the
King of Prussia, not to the Emperor of Austria.

The second issue was closely connected with the first: King
Friedrich Wilhelm IV refused the crown offered by a deputation of
the 'revolutionary' parliament.   He made it clear that another
German Reich would be created only by the ruling classes, not in
cooperation with the middle classes.   There was no doubt as to
where the seat of political sovereignty would be in such a Reich -
with the crown and not with the people or its spokesmen.   The
Second German Empire, therefore, would mean the creation of economic and military power on the one hand and the crown on the other,
using the liberal movement as a welcome propaganda force only as
long as its demands for a constitution could be made to coincide
with the more authoritarian concepts of the ruling Junkers, the
landed Prussian gentry.   This rigidly conservative ruling class,
with the support of Tsarist Russia, had broken the backbone of the
Revolution in Prussia.   Aristocratic and monarchical Prussia had
been the champion for conservatism and counter-revolution in 1848-9
in Germany.   From the late 1850s onwards, Prussia became the great
champion of German unification, first in its short-lived phase of
a sham-liberal renaissance with the 'New Course' of 1859, then
after 1862, with the coming of Bismarck, in its more enduring
phase of military preparation and military conquest.   Bismarck's

statecraft largely consisted of combining two contradictory elements: the threat or use of military force inside and outside
Germany to suppress or domesticate revolutionary or progressive
elements, and the fulfilment of political demands of the liberal
classes - unification and a constitution.

BISMARCK AND THE CREATION OF THE NEW GERMAN EMPIRE

Bismarck had been called to power in 1862 as Prussian Prime Minister
at the height of the prolonged constitutional crisis between the
liberal majority in Parliament and the crown.   The crown insisted
on streamlining and expanding the army under the exclusive command
of the crown.   The new King, Wilhelm I, had even considered a
military coup to subdue parliament.   Bismarck's coming to power,
however, spared him the risks of a military coup and made a
civilian form of the same policy possible: Bismarck eliminated
parliament by openly flouting the Prussian Constitution and reorganized the Prussian army to become a force capable of waging offensive
wars.   From now onwards, Prussian politics, later to be the politics of the German Empire, stood under the shadow of threatening
'coup d'état' from above. (6)
    Bismarck's first political move in the field of foreign policy
was to persuade Russia not to abandon Russian Poland as a reaction
to the last Polish revolt of 1863.   This he did through the
Alvensleben Convention.   It meant that Prussia, later the German
Empire, would cling to its part of Poland, restored to Prussia in
Vienna 1815, at any cost.   If Russia had given freedom to her
Poles under liberal pressure or under the pressure of resurgent
Poles in Russian Poland, the position of Prussia in its predominantly Polish provinces would have become impossible in the long run.
Bismarck made it clear that there would be no coexistence between a
free Polish national state and Prussia, with serious consequences
for the existence of monarchical and feudal Prussia.   Bismarck's
Prussia was more vitally interested than Austria-Hungary or Russia
to keep Poland divided and to preserve the conservative solidarity
for the partitioning powers against the Poles.   With the help of
the Alvensleben Convention, Bismarck also succeeded in neutralizing
Russia in the coming struggles ahead for German unification.   It
was with great justice that a conservative German historian, Egmont
Zechlin, saw the Alvensleben Convention as Bismarck's starting
point in laying the foundations of Germany's position as a great
power. (7)
    Bismarck's next step was the first of the three short wars which
led to the creation of the new German Empire.   This war waged by
Prussia and Austria against Denmark, in 1864, gave Prussia the
greatest immediate advantages.   By embroiling Austria in the hopeless maze of the Schleswig-Holstein question, Prussia not only
gained Schleswig immediately and Holstein a little later, but also
acquired an instrument to put pressure on Austria.   The squabble
over Holstein, which was administered by Austria after Denmark's
defeat, connected with the reform of the German Bund in the interest
of Prussia, furnished the immediate cause of the Prussian war of
1866 against Austria and nearly all of the remaining German states

(in particular Saxony, Hanover, Hesse, Baden, Württemberg, Bavaria).
The battle of Sadowa in July 1866 decided Prussia's hegemony in
Germany and finally broke the backbone of German liberalism. Most
of the liberals made their peace with Bismarck and supported him
through the National Liberal Party, founded in 1867. In the same
year, Prussia, enlarged by the annexation of Hanover, Northern
Hesse, and Frankfurt, founded the North German Confederation with a
Reichstag based on universal and equal (male) suffrage. (8)
Bismarck was now halfway to achieving the future Empire, the
southern German states still remaining outside. By incorporating
the Poles in the eastern provinces of Prussia who had not formed
part of the old Empire into the North German Federation, and through
the protest of their spokesmen in parliament, it was decided that
the new German Empire would also be burdened with the liability of
the partition of Poland. Austria was thrown out of Germany and,
in reaction to her defeat, was reorganized in 1867 under pressure
of the Magyars by means of a constitutional compromise ('Ausgleich')
to form the Dual Monarchy Austria-Hungary.

By cleverly manipulating the liberal and constitutional movement
in Germany and by superior diplomacy, Bismarck succeeded in manoeuvring France into isolation and a position of appearing to be the
last enemy left to stop German unification. The Franco-Prussian
War, finally, was decided by numerical superiority in manpower
provided by all German states, including those of southern Germany,
by more efficient organization and strategic leadership of the
united German armies. After the defeat of Napoleon III at Sedan,
Prussia made the Germans carry on with the war against the French
Republic, with the aim of annexing Alsace-Lorraine. The German
Empire was officially proclaimed in a ceremony full of symbolic
implication at Versailles, the seat of the old French monarchy, on
18 January 1871, exactly 170 years after the coronation of the
first King in Prussia at Königsberg, i.e. on territory outside the
old German Empire. The Second German Empire was founded and proclaimed on the foreign soil of conquered France. (9)   Bismarck
meanwhile managed to neutralize Austria-Hungary, thanks to the
looming threat of Russian intervention on behalf of Prussia and the
emerging German Empire. (10)

THE SECOND GERMAN EMPIRE

With the founding of the Second German Empire the Germans, or at
least their majority, had a common state of their own for the first
time in modern history. The lesser German solution ('klein-
deutsch') had materialized, as had first been hinted at by the
Paulskirche parliament in 1848-9. It was not the product of a
successful revolution or of a democratic movement and it was not
based on the principle of the sovereignty of the people. To
employ the word 'national' is misleading, if taken in the strictest
political sense; it can only be loosely applied to the German
Empire to describe the highest political level in the state, in
contrast to the regional or local level. (11)

The constitution of the German Reich was an extension and adap-
tation of the North German Constitution of 1867. The new Empire

was officially a Federation or League ('Bund') of the German princes
and three free Hanseatic Cities (Hamburg, Lübeck, Bremen).   The
Kingdom of Prussia was by far the largest and most powerful of the
federal states.   The other states preserved a large degree of internal autonomy, and the largest of them, i.e. the kingdoms of
Bavaria, Württemberg and Saxony had preserved a few special rights,
among them the privilege of having an army of their own in peace-
time and of maintaining ministers of their own in the important
capitals of Europe.   The character of a federation was stressed by
the fact that all German states kept ministers in Berlin, which
formed part of the diplomatic corps there in the capital of Prussia
and the new German Reich.
     The seat of sovereignty lay with the German princes and Free
Cities, and the King of Prussia was officially no more than the
permanent President of the Federation, although having the title of
Emperor.   As the monarchical head of the Empire, he had the power
to rule through the Chancellor of the Reich.   Constitutionally,
the Chancellor was not obliged to have a majority in the Reichstag,
the central parliament of the Empire.   The confidence of the
Emperor was enough to keep him in power.   As a matter of fact, all
Chancellors were interested in having a majority.   In all the
changes of majorities over the decades one principle emerged: the
very structure of the German Empire and German society made it
impossible for a Chancellor to rule while seeking Socialist
support, at least not in peacetime.
     The Constitution gave the Reichstag more the appearance than the
substance of political power: universal and equal suffrage (while
in the individual federal states unequal franchise still existed,
e.g. the three-class franchise in Prussia) and budgetary rights were
the only attributes of modern parliament granted to the Reichstag.
It had no direct influence on the composition of governments, could
not elect or overthrow a Chancellor, could not even, on its own
initiative, debate on foreign policy or vote on a declaration of
war.   It could only indirectly influence the course of the government by its vote on the budget and was a general rostrum for the
expression of public opinion.   But in both respects the Reichstag
was open to manipulation from the government, who tried to relegate
the Reichstag to a rubber-stamping and acclamatory body.   The main
political function of the Reichstag consisted in giving an outlet
to political forces in Germany, to represent and articulate public
opinion in a specific form, on the strength of the various political
parties and the speeches made in parliament and during election
campaigns.
     Prussia in the nineteenth century had been a bulwark of conser-
vatism, and the new Reich as an extension of Prussia was even more
so.   But the economic development of Germany, especially after
the founding of the new Reich, created serious discrepancies
between the economic foundation, the social structure and the political institutions of the Reich.   Germany witnessed a remarkable
coalescence of feudal-monarchical elements with industrial power.
Prussia had originally been a predominantly agrarian monarchy, run
by a military-minded lower gentry, the Junkers, east of the River
Elbe.   Their economic basis was fairly small manors, the
Rittergüter, which they ran more in the manner of agrarian entre-

preneurs than as typical feudal landlords.   In 1815 Prussia
acquired the valuable Rhine Provinces, where the industrial revolution was just beginning.   The growing industries in the west
(Rhineland, Westphalia, Saar) and the secondary industrial district
in the east (Upper Silesia) provided the economic and material
basis for Prussia's emergence as the founding and hegemonial
state of the new German Empire in 1871. (12)
     Yet, Prussia's Junker class was threatened by Revolution and
Liberalism.   The Crown's triumph over the Revolution of 1848-9 and
Liberalism in 1862-6 consolidated the leading political position of
the junkers in Prussia and also indirectly in the new Reich.   The
army, the bureaucracy, in particular the diplomatic service and the
courts, but also schools, universities and the churches were the
strongholds of the conservative elements in Bismarck's Germany.
They were dominated either by members of the aristocratic classes
themselves or by members of the middle classes who had conformed
to the political and social standards set up by the ruling junkers
or their southern German counterparts.   By the late 1870s the
last remnants of liberal interludes since 1848 had been purged or
quietly dropped for reasons of age. (13)

THE IMPACT OF INDUSTRIAL REVOLUTION

Between the wars of 1870-1 and 1914-18, however, Germany advanced
to become the most powerful industrial state of the Continent,
having the most modern industry in all Europe, including Britain.
By 1914 Germany had even surpassed Britain, the motherland of the
Industrial Revolution, in key sections, i.e. the production of
steel or chemicals and the electrical industries. (14)   The founding of the Reich in 1871 brought about a unification of the German
market by unifying currencies, weights and measures, the legal
system and through a common representation abroad.   The five
milliards francs paid by France to Germany as reparation were an
additional incentive to a powerful boom, which ended abruptly in
the great crash of 1873.   The following period up to 1895 is now
known as the 'Great Depression', owing to the slow recovery of the
economy and reduced economic growth. (15)   From 1896 to 1914
economic expansion was the characteristic trait, apart from a few
oscillations.   In particular, the last two decades of peace saw
the hectic, even breathtaking rise of German industry with serious
political, social and psychological consequences.
     One of the immediate consequences of industrialization was the
rapid increase in population.   Emigration, in particular to
America, was drastically reduced in the 1880s and more Germans
found work and relative prosperity in the new German industries.
The German population rose from 41 million in 1871 to 64 million.
Germany by far surpassed France, traditionally the largest nation
in Europe since the Middle Ages.   The French population in the
same inter-war period rose only from 38 to 40 million.
     In the last pre-war years, however, Germans were impressed and
frightened by a corresponding rise of population further to the
East.   In the last few years before the war the population increase
became an additional justification of political expansion both in

Europe and overseas, sought by the Reich.   Even Kurt Riezler,
the political aide of Chancellor Bethmann Hollweg and in many respects the most liberal of Germany's Establishment, could write in
1914, immediately before the outbreak of the war: (16)

But the young German Empire pushed out into the world.   Its
population grows yearly by 800,000 to 900,000 people, and for
the new masses food, or what amounts to the same and work must
be found.... German economy by its interests and achievements
penetrated the world.   In some branches it has conquered the
first place, in others a second or third.   The economic interest
had to be followed by the political.   The enormous economic
achievement of a rising nation propels the young Empire into
'Weltpolitik'.

The new Reich thus was the product of traditional Junkers east
of the Elbe and of modern industrialists near the Rhine, of Krupp's
cannons and old-Prussian bayonets, of neo-Prussian machiavellism
and traditional German idealism for the Reich.   The same combination determined both the social structure of the Reich and its
foreign policy.   Industrialization upset the traditional balance
of power in German society and produced dangerous instabilities
and tensions. (17)   The rise of German industry, however, welcomed
for 'national' or modern prestige reasons, made the proportion of
national income derived from agriculture steadily dwindle.   From
the 1870s onwards Germany could no longer be fed by agricultural
products from its own soil.   Food had to be imported for the
rising population in the rapidly growing industrial and urban
centres.   The massive imports from Russia, America, later also
from Australia, produced a permanent and sharpening crisis in German
agriculture.   While millions of peasants or farmhands left the
provinces and moved into the industrial centres, the Junkers,
being able to control Prussia and the Conservative parties, outwardly managed to hold their position.   They remained practically
tax-immune and were protected in many forms by the monarchical
state, whose chief social foundation they were, with high tariffs
to protect German agriculture from America and Russia's cheap
grain, the near monopoly of lucrative jobs in the army, at Court
and in the diplomatic service.   Intermarriage with new-rich
families of the emerging industrial and financial bourgeoisie and
far-reaching rationalization of their own holdings east of the River
Elbe could not help in the long run, because of the increasing rate
at which economic emphasis within Germany itself was shifting from
agriculture to industry.   Urbanization also meant that fewer people
were directly or indirectly subject to the Junkers who clung to
their social privileges and political positions to the very end of
the Second Reich.   In the end they even succeeded in winning the
allegiance of the middle classes and the peasantry, as long as the
Reich seemed to be successful.

The working alliance of aristocracy and most of the middle
classes in the German Empire can be explained by their common
interest in German economic and political power as well as their
feeling of being threatened by a common enemy - socialism.   The
middle-class strongholds were industry and business, the universities and schools.   They were also penetrating traditionally aristocratic sectors, such as the army and the diplomatic service, just

before the war.   Men such as Ludendorff and Groener, practically
Chiefs of Staff of the German army from 1916 to 1919, were the more
reactionary and more liberal-moderate variants of the middle-class
officers who could make brilliant careers by adapting themselves to
the given political structures: always in the service of a more
powerful Reich. 'From 1849 and 1866 the middle classes were, on
the whole, satisfied to leave political power where it was - with
the aristocracy and the Crown.   Instead, they preferred to concentrate their activities on the economic and educational spheres.
They managed to create and to officer the most modern weapon of the
new Reich, the navy.

The battle fleet, built from 1898 onwards, was the most imposing
expression of Germany's new industrial power.   It was more than
just the whim of a notoriously vain and immature monarch or of an
apparently a-political technical expert - Wilhelm II and Admiral
von Tirpitz.   The battle fleet was the pride of most of the German
middle class and of the academic community.   In contrast to the
army, the Imperial navy fell under the direct competence of the
Reich.   Most of its officers came from the middle classes, its
rank-and-file from the working classes.   The battle fleet was,
furthermore, a substantial economic investment for German heavy
industry. (18)   The need to protect growing German commerce overseas and the establishment of German colonies were additional
reasons put forward by the naval propagandists.   They in turn,
were organized and largely financed by Krupp whose economic interest
in the battle fleet was evident.   Its numerical and qualitative
strength by far exceeded defensive purposes and was from the outset
clearly directed against Britain. (19)

Farmers and peasants in Germany, both Catholic and Protestant,
were predominantly conservative in their political allegiance.
Catholic farmers and peasants were one of the mainstays of the
Catholic Centre Party.   Protestant farmers and peasants east of
the River Elbe voted mostly for the Conservative Party, often led
by their local Junker to the polls 'en masse' and being subject to
heavy social pressure from him.   The Junker also controlled the
Landrat, the highest representative of State bureaucracy in the
Landkreis, the equivalent to the county.   In some regions west of
the River Elbe, e.g. in the depressed parts of Hesse, Protestant
peasants tended to vote for early antisemitic groups, the forerunner
of Fascism in Germany.

The working-class population rapidly grew parallel to the expansion of industry and cities.   They organized themselves in 'free'
trade unions, which meant that they inclined to the Social Democratic Party, and in 'Christian' trade unions, which were predominantly
Catholic.   Trade union politics and party politics followed the
same lines: most protestant workers voted SPD, most Catholic
workers the Centre Party.   Both parties, originally were treated
by Bismarck as 'enemies of the Reich' ('Reichsfeinde').   After
Bismarck made his peace with the Centre Party by liquidating his
struggle against the Catholic Church ('Kulturkampf') in the 1870s,
the Centre Party reached a pivotal position between Conservatives
and right-wing Liberals ('Nationalliberale') to the Right, and
left-wing Liberals ('Fortschritt' and 'Freisinn') and Socialists to
the Left.   From 1880 onwards, the Centre Party supported the

official policy of the Reich, however grudgingly, after initial misgivings or even opposition at times.   The Socialists, however, were
persecuted between 1878 and 1890 by special laws ('Sozialisten-
gesetz')   and were kept in political isolation to the outbreak of
the First World War, although by 1912 the SPD had become the largest
parliamentary group in the Reichstag, winning nearly one third of
all seats. (20)

NATIONAL MINORITIES IN GERMANY

Other political elements, marginal geographically, but important
for German foreign policy, were the various national minorities in
the German Empire - the French in Alsace-Lorraine, the Danes in
northern Schleswig, the Poles in Prussia's eastern provinces, especially in Posen (Poznan).   The predominantly Catholic Poles had
been one of the main factors in the launching of Bismarck's
'Kulturkampf' against the Catholic Church, because by hitting Cath-
olics in East Prussia, he could also take steps against the unwanted
Polish nationality.   His policy of germanizing the Prussian Poles,
by combining administrative and social pressure, backfired and
became one of the sources of constant friction within the German
Empire. (21)   By the discrimination against second-class citizens
in the Reich, Bismarck managed to make peaceful coexistence between
a free Polish national state and the German Empire impossible.
His harsh measures of discrimination made Germany and Prussia at
least in the East increasingly unpopular.   The presence of a substantial Polish minority - in 1910 about three million - in the
border provinces of the Reich also governed German policy towards
Russia.   In times of peace the common partnership in partitioning
Poland could serve as a constant appeal to solidarity against democratic revolution.   In war, however, the Poles could be used to
blow up the Tsarist Empire.
      The annexation of Alsace-Lorraine against the clear wishes of
the population into the new German Empire in 1871 for ideological
and strategical reasons turned out to be another liability for the
German Empire.   The historical experience of the population of
Alsace-Lorraine, though mostly German in language and culture, had
made them French politically ever since the French Revolution.   But
Alsace-Lorraine remained in the abnormal position of a 'Reichs-
land', governed directly by Berlin through an Imperial Governor at
Strasbourg and without the full constitutional rights of a German
federal state, such as Württemberg or Saxony.   A timid attempt to
normalize the situation by granting a limited constitution to
Alsace-Lorraine in 1911 came too late.   Alsace-Lorraine made France
a natural enemy of the Reich, even more so, since German foreign
policy, due to a feeling of guilt and fear, always tried to isolate
France as long as possible. (22)
      The problem of the Danish minority belongs in the same context.
By refusing to hold the plebiscite in northern Schleswig on the
question as to whether the population preferred to belong to Denmark
or to Prussian Germany - although Prussia in the 1866 Peace Treaty
of Prague had promised to do so - German policy was a constant re-
minder that the principle of national self-determination was well

known even in the second half of the nineteenth century and that
the very existence, structure and policy of the Reich was in open
contradiction to that principle.   The policy of petty discrimination against the Danes ensured that, together with the Poles and
the French in Alsace-Lorraine, they were never interested in staying
within the German Empire.
   The three major non-German nationalities amounted to roughly one
tenth of the Empire's population.   They lived on politically sensitive borders.   Although annexed to increase the power of the German
Empire, they were in fact a liability, because they weakened
Germany's position morally and politically.   It is no historical
coincidence that the denial of national self-determination or self-
government by one of the Central Powers, was to become the immediate cause of war in 1914: Austria-Hungary, supported by Germany,
denied her southern Slavs politically autonomy and took the outrage
at Sarajevo as an excuse for trying to subdue the recalcitrant
Serbs. (23)

THE GENERAL CHARACTER OF GERMAN FOREIGN POLICY, 1871-1914

Given Germany's territorial size, its central position in Europe,
the weight of its population, its economic and military power and
its crushing victories over three of its neighbours (Denmark,
Austria, France), the new German Empire even in 1871 was more than
a traditional European Great Power, but less than a World Power,
such as Britain and her Empire, or Russia.   Germany's position, in
fact, amounted to one of a latent hegemonial power in Europe,
whether it knew it or not, whether it wished it or not.   This
state of affairs was bound to create new suspicions and tensions.
The future depended on Germany.   Either it yielded to the temptation of converting its latent hegemony into an open one, or it
remained satisfied with its present position as one of the Great
Powers in Europe.
   The unification of Germany by conquest, however, sharpened the
permanent dilemma with which Germans had been confronted during
their national existence - unification of all Germans into one
powerful central state was impossible because it would lead to
German domination over Europe.   Since Europe never accepted hegemony of any European power the Germans thus came into conflict whenever they tried to organize themselves into a powerful Empire,
claiming to unite, if possible all Germans.   Bismarck's Empire was
a delicate compromise, which was in 1871 just tolerable as the
unification of all Germans in one state had not been absolutely
achieved.   Germans in Austria and German minorities in eastern and
southeastern Europe remained outside the Lesser German Empire
('kleindeutsches Reich').
   The Reich enjoyed a position of relative hegemony, not of open
and absolute hegemony.   Absolute unification of Germans in one
state would almost automatically lead to absolute German power over
Europe and would provoke the massive resistance from the other
Great Powers in Europe.   The inevitable conflict abroad would, in
the case of German defeat, reactivate all internal tensions, which
had been superficially hidden by the victorious and dazzling estab-

lishment of the Second German Empire.   If the attempt to increase the power of the German Reich were to fail, the combination of a defeat abroad together with internal conflicts would threaten the very existence of the German Empire.

It is only thus that Bismarck's formula is to be properly understood, that Germany was 'satiated' after 1871.   On the one hand he certainly wanted to appease Germany's suspicious neighbours.   Their feelings were expressed by Disraeli's warning in the House of Commons on 9 February 1871. (24)   On the other hand, Bismarck's formula was intended to serve as a warning to German chauvinists who pressed for even more expansion by including, if possible, Germans in Austria and the Baltic Provinces.   Bismarck saw that his achievements 'could only be jeopardized by pressing for further expansion of German power'. (25)   In his time as Chancellor, however, Bismarck failed to educate the German public sufficiently so that at least the ruling circles in Germany would have understood and accepted his realistic insight.   Instead, he allowed himself to be pushed into a German imperialism overseas in the 1880s. (26)   After his fall as Chancellor in 1890, he partly tolerated and partly encouraged the emerging Pan-German movement to use him as the 'Iron Chancellor' for a policy of expansion and chauvinism, which was bound to produce the very constellation he knew would be fatal for the German Reich. (27)

Today one may doubt whether any German leader, however gifted and 'titanic', would have been able to hold back the dynamic or even expansive forces within German society.   Two elementary factors of the present and future and one of the past made Germany's drive into the world and the collision at least with Europe difficult to avoid.   These were rapid industrialization and the population increase on the one hand, the idea and reality of the 'Reich' and of the German Empire, in contrast to the normal national states of other nations, on the other.

The German Empire stood for a maximum of power concentrated in the traditional and new ruling classes in Germany, the aristocracy and industrial bourgeoisie.   Bismarck's Empire was built on the solidarity of the two ruling classes, who, by common interests against Democracy and Socialism and by intermarriage were on their way to becoming one class.   But the combination of the two classes also produced a remarkable paralysis inside and outside Germany. This paralysis could be seen behind the glittering façade of economic expansion and political dynamism, after the breakdown of the Reich, by the historian.   In domestic policy the two main wings of Germany's ruling class balanced each other through their economic interests and in foreign policy they cancelled each other out in a curious way, which must be explained in more detail. (28)

The agrarian sector declined economically, but maintained its position of political power, while the industrial sector advanced by leaps and bounds.   The overall result inside Germany was one of almost perfect stagnation.   There were two important changes – the rise of the trade unions and of the Socialist Party to a kind of unrecognized unofficial opposition and the rise of middle-class individuals into the ruling circles just before the war, e.g. Ludendorff and Groener in the army, Zimmermann and Riezler in the diplomatic service, Erzberger in parliament.   Neither the increase

in force behind the working class nor the individual rise of members
of the middle class into the ruling class seriously modified or even
challenged the character of the German Empire.   The ruling classes
interested in conserving the 'status quo' were strong enough to keep
themselves in power, while the democratic elements were too weak to
challenge the 'status quo' more than verbally.

There was no real or readily visible development in the precarious balance between the Reich and its various components, neither
in the direction of parliamentary democracy nor of a caesarian-
totalitarian dictatorship.   Both possibilities germinated in the
Second Empire and both became reality for about twelve years after
1918 - parliamentary democracy after the breakdown of the Second
Reich and the caesarian-totalitarian dictatorship after the breakdown of the Weimar Republic in the form of the Third Reich.   It was
only the First World War which, after Germany's defeat and the fall
of the dynasties, set free those conflicting forces which have al-
ternately dominated ever since.   During the period under considera-
tion, however, the German Empire remained in position between the
older industrial states in the West, organized as liberal and parliamentary democracies, and Tsarist Russia in the East.   Russia was
still predominantly agrarian in her structure, but had experienced,
in the last decade before the war, a sharp rise of industrialization, concentrated on a few cities, i.e. St Petersburg, Moscow and
some industrial regions to the South.

Similarly, divergent economic interests and ideological traditions blocked each other in foreign policy, preventing a clear
option between Britain or Russia.   It was easy enough to appeal to
the unity of the 'nation', i.e. of the ruling classes against their
domestic common enemy - democracy and revolution - but it proved to
be impossible to find a common strategy for increasing the power of
the Reich.   Both wings of Germany's ruling class - agrarian and
industrial - worked themselves into a hopeless dilemma over their
economic interests and ideological inclinations, only to produce a
foreign policy that agreed with their short-term economic interests
but clashed with their ideological inclinations.   The agrarians
and especially the Prussian Junkers were interested in high grain
tariffs, once Germany's agriculture could no longer feed the growing urban population by its own production.   These high tariffs to
keep out cheap grain from abroad meant high prices of food for
Germany's urban population who had to finance the Junkers' efforts
to preserve their privileged social and political positions in
Prussia and within the Empire.   These high tariffs happened to hit
the Junkers' traditional friend, Tsarist Russia, hardest.   Russia
urgently needed the income derived from the export of grain to
finance her own efforts toward industrialization and in order to
feed the masses set free by the abolition of serfdom in 1861 after
the defeat of the Crimean War.   Although Tsarist Russia was also a
bulwark of feudalism and monarchy against democracy, parliamentar-
ism and revolution, for Germany's agrarian Conservatives their
immediate bread-and-butter interests clashed with their traditional
sentiments and preferences.   Their policy of high grain tariffs
(after 1879) and closing the German finance market for Russian loans
(1887) finally drove Russia into the arms of France.

Similarly, German commerce and industry were originally liberal

(by German standards) and looked traditionally to Britain, the
motherland of industrial capitalism.   Since the beginning of the
Great Depression of 1873, however, they pressed for protective
tariffs to keep out cheap British industrial goods from the German
market.   The overall anti-British economic interest gradually
developed into an anti-British foreign policy, culminating in 'Weltpolitik' and the building of a great battle fleet. (29)
   The economic interests of agriculture prevented an understanding
with Tsarist Russia; the economic interests of industry, later also
of the shipping industry, prevented an understanding with liberal
Britain.   Ideological preferences in each sector with regard to
their economic foreign competitor or enemy furthered these misunder-
standings.   The two most powerful wings of Germany's ruling class
worked at cross purposes not only with each other, but also with
their domestic partners.   The political leadership of the Reich
never succeeded in finding a satisfactory solution for this twofold dilemma resulting from the structure of the German Empire and
its society.   As German statecraft failed to coordinate the divergent forces pulling the Reich in opposite directions, it was
impossible to work out a concept of constructive and peaceful
foreign policy.   The mistrust of the new Empire, stemming from the
three wars, was serious enough, even as long as the Reich remained
the way it was in 1871.   Any German ambition of advancing to the
level of a global World Power meaning hegemonial power inside
Europe, would inevitably provoke at least passive hostility throughout the world.   This could only be partially overcome if Germany
decided whether it wanted to become a world power with the help of
one of the existing world powers, either Britain or Russia, however
different their structures.   Its constitutional inability to
settle for either of them resulted in provocation on both sides.
   The inherent defect of German foreign policy was only brought
into the open when Germany entered a phase of imperialism in 1897-8.
Bismarck's continental policy of keeping his options to the West or
East as long as he possibly could, carried on to the level of 'Weltpolitik', resulted in an unrealistic and suicidal policy of imperial
claims on all sides.   The birth of German 'Weltpolitik' also
brought a third weakness of German foreign policy to light: the
uncertainty of German society regarding its status in the world.
The population increase and an increase in economic power after the
founding of the German Empire soon raised the question of whether
Germany would remain in its precarious position of being more than
a Continental Power but less than a World Power.   The new German
'Weltpolitik' made a definite answer to this question seem more
urgent than ever, once the aim of foreign policy had become to
achieve the status of a world power.   Yet right from the beginning
of this new 'Weltpolitik', German society (and, for that matter,
German historiography until recently) was not sure whether pre-war
Germany was already a world power or not.   Claims differed according to the political situation or interest behind them.   This uncertainty itself produced a dangerous emotional and political instability.   Germany was not sure of itself, of its own strength
and status or of its limitations and weaknesses.
   Since German society and statecraft proved unable to define
Germany's position in the world, to lay down priorities of German

foreign policy and properly coordinate and channel its growing
forces for peaceful purposes, German foreign policy gave the impression of aiming at a hectic, boundless and uncontrollable expansion in all directions at the same time.   This expansion was
sought peacefully through economic and diplomatic methods before
the war; by military conquest, political rule and economic penetration once war had broken out.   Germany's unpredictable zigzag
course in its phase of peaceful 'Weltpolitik' was logically followed
by Germany's failure in the First World War to concentrate its
military forces on one front and to make peace on the other.   The
military failure in the West and East resulted from the lack of
definite decisions between the priorities of agrarian or industrial
interests.   Germany's political leadership, composed of both elements and constantly exposed to conflicting counsels and pressures,
could not make up its mind and was thus condemned to muddle through
to a catastrophe based on the very structure of the Reich, whose
power and glory the leaders wanted to enhance through their efforts.
The proud German Empire can best be compared with a coach where
the horses are harnessed in opposite directions, or, less charita-
bly, to the famous two asses bound together in opposite directions
and each being offered a bundle of hay.

The second German Empire had been founded on a complex of
tensions and potential conflicts: (i) the discrepancy between a
modern economic structure through industrialization and the continuing leadership of the more traditional agrarian élites; (ii) the
paralysing tension between divergent economic interests and divergent aims in foreign policy of the industrial and agrarian wing of
Germany's ruling class; (iii) tensions between formally democratic
suffrage in the Reichstag and the political weakness of democratic
forces; (iv) the dilemma created by the German problem - the incompatibility of absolute national unity and power on the one hand,
of German hegemony and the balance of power in Europe on the other.
Bismarck's Empire was, therefore, as its first Chancellor knew only
too well, a delicate compromise which would be endangered the very
moment it tried to exceed its boundaries.   Behind the façade of
his official optimism, Bismarck was deeply pessimistic about the
future of the Reich.   Only one year after the proclamation of the
new German Empire he confided to one of his Prussian ministers: 'I
cannot find rest when I sleep.   I continue in dreaming what I
think while I am awake, if I sleep at all.   Recently, I saw a map
of Germany in front of me.   One rotten blot after another appeared
on it and peeled off.' (30)   Bismarck's vision came true in less
than a century.   One of his leading political opponents, Wilhelm
Liebknecht, gave a shorthand analysis and prognosis of the Reich:
'Born on the battle-field, the child of 'coups d'état', of war and
of revolution from above, it must restlessly hurry from 'coup
d'état' to 'coup d'état', from war to war, and it must either break
down on the battlefield or submit to the revolution from below.
This is a law of nature.' (31)

Chapter 2

THE PATTERN OF EUROPEAN DIPLOMACY, 1871-1914

Even a rapid glance at the diplomatic situation in Europe at the beginning and the end of the period in question reveals an important difference between 1871 and 1914: at the beginning, the Great Powers in Europe faced each other in isolation, without alliances with each other or with smaller powers. Germany, France, Britain, Austria-Hungary, Italy - all lived in a kind of diplomatic anarchy. In order to achieve short-term aims they formed short-lived alliances in diplomatic actions, where practically all Powers made alliances with each other and against each other. Even France and Germany were allies occasionally, although Germany at that time had one overriding aim, that of keeping France in isolation after her defeat as long as possible, while France naturally tried to escape the isolation imposed by Bismarck's Germany. The rapid changes in diplomatic constellations during the first two decades of European diplomacy after 1871 tend to blur the great lines of political development. It may be summed up by the remark that during the period of diplomatic anarchy Europe was spared further war among its Great Powers. There were tensions, to be sure, but actual conflicts shifted from the centre to the periphery of Europe, to the Balkans, or even overseas, once the scramble for power in Africa had started in the early 1880s and the period of Imperialism proper in the late 1890s.

In 1914, however, Europe was divided into two great blocks: the Triple Alliance, made up of Germany, Austria-Hungary and Italy, and the Triple Entente, consisting of France, Russia and Britain. The hard core of the Triple Alliance were Germany and Austria-Hungary, who formed the Dual Alliance in 1879, Italy joining in 1882 as an always uncertain partner. (1)   Provoked by the forming of the Dual and Triple Alliance, France succeeded in breaking out of her involuntary isolation by making an agreement with Russia in 1892, known as the Franco-Russian Dual Alliance, which came into force in January 1894. The Dual Alliance was enlarged in 1904 by the 'Entente Cordiale' between Britain and France and the Anglo-Russian Agreement of 1907, thus constituting, not formally, but in effect what was called the Triple Entente. (2)   The existence of the two power blocs, originally hailed as a safeguard for European peace, actually turned out to be one of the essential preconditions of the First World War.

GERMANY AND THE GREAT POWERS

After the founding of the Reich in 1871, the overriding aim of
German foreign policy was consolidating and maintaining the enormous
increase of power accumulated within the new German Empire.
Bismarck's ideal was to conserve a constellation in Europe without
alliances as long as possible.   He wanted to balance and play off
the European Powers against each other so that they would be dependent on Germany, while the Chancellor tried to keep in his hands all
the strings of European power politics.   His 'idée fixe' was to
keep all the other Powers from concluding an alliance with France.
When this concept failed in 1892-4, Bismarck's successors tried to
prolong this idea by trying to keep the French-Russian alliance isolated.   In his famous memorandum, which he dictated at Kissingen
in 1877, Bismarck himself concurred with the opinion of a French
paper which had spoken of Germany's 'cauchemar des coalitions', and
he continued:

> This kind of nightmare will long (and perhaps always) be a legi-
> timate one for a German minister.   Coalitions can be formed
> against us, based on the western powers with the addition of
> Austria, even more dangerous perhaps on a Russo-Austrian-French
> basis;   great intimacy between two of the last-named powers
> would always offer the third of them a means of exerting very
> effective pressure on us. (3)

It was in this context that Bismarck sketched his ideal 'of a political situation as a whole, in which all the powers except France
had need of us, and would thus be deterred as far as possible from
coalitions against us by their relations with each other'.
Bismarck, apparently, saw himself in the role of another 'Europe's
coachman', just as Metternich had seen himself before 1848.   This
was not a very promising symptom of Bismarck's faith in his own
conservative policy.   At the same time, Bismarck claimed to be
Europe's 'honest broker'.   There was an obvious discrepancy
between the two concepts.   Without pressing words too much, one
may detect behind the figurative speech - 'coachman', 'broker' -
indeed the basic alternatives open to the new German Empire:
either Germany refrained from further increase of power and strove
to be no more than a disinterested mediator between the other
Powers, its only interest being the preservation of peace in the
service of an essentially cautious foreign policy;   or Germany
tried to become the directing Power in Europe, using its geographically central position, which would lead it, sooner or later to a
more expansionist foreign policy.

It was obvious that Bismarck's original ideal of a Europe without alliances was only possible if Germany itself were to refrain
from entering into alliances and from pursuing an expansionist
foreign policy.   Even if Germany were to remain strictly on the
defensive, the constellation most advantageous to it could not be
preserved 'ad infinitum'.   The day came, sooner than Germany's
leading statesmen could wish, when Germany saw itself committed to
one of the existing Powers.   Once the options were closed, it lay
in the nature of the European power system that the other Powers
would sooner or later follow suit in grouping themselves around
France.   Bismarck himself had made France through the annexation

of Alsace-Lorraine and his policy of isolation almost automatically the nucleus of an alliance confronting any combination Germany
might enter.   France, therefore, had become in a negative way the
hinge of German foreign policy under Bismarck.   His policy of
isolating France explains the tortuous way of German diplomacy
towards the other Powers, i.e. Russia, Austria, Italy and Britain.
   While France remained a negative constant in German foreign
policy almost throughout the entire inter-war period from 1871 to
1914, German relations with the other Powers underwent remarkable
changes.   Russia had been a positive constant ever since the partition of Poland, because she served as a prop for Prussian conservatism, especially during the crisis in the Napoleonic era and in
1848-9.   By 1914 Tsarist Russia had wandered from the positive pole
to the negative pole within the field of German foreign policy, even
serving as the 'pons asinorum' to drive the German Socialists into
the war.
   Austria-Hungary developed in the opposite direction.   Since the
eighteenth century, Austria had been Prussia's great rival, and it
was only in reaction to common danger from abroad, in this case the
French Revolution and its heir, Napoleon, that Prussia had joined
forces with Austria in 1792 and 1813-15.   In 1866 Prussia had even
defeated Austria, throwing her out of the German Confederation and
the new German Empire and producing a serious internal crisis which
could only be resolved by the factual division of the Habsburg
Empire into Austria and Hungary by the Compromise ('Ausgleich') of
1867.   Within the thirteen years after Sadowa, however, Austria-
Hungary was to wander from the historically negative pole to the
positive pole of Germany's foreign policy.   For reasons both domestic and foreign, Germany chose Austria-Hungary as its partner to
help preserve the Dual Monarchy at all costs.   It is, therefore,
no historical coincidence that the First World War broke out over
the question of preserving the Habsburg Monarchy in the ferment of
national self-determination in the Balkans, symbolized by the murder
at Sarajevo.
   Germany's position vis-à-vis Italy had been ambivalent from the
start.   A wave of anti-Italian feeling had swept Germany in 1859
during Austria's war to defend her Italian provinces against the
'Risorgimento', particularly as Piedmont was allied with Bonapartist
France.   On the other hand, after 1871, there was a definite feeling of sympathy for Italy, the other latecomer on the scene of
national unification.   This feeling was strengthened by sympathy
of an ideological kind.   Italy, in spite of her liberal elements,
remained a monarchy.   When Italy joined the Dual Alliance in 1882
to make the Triple Alliance, it was done mainly for power politics
and ideological reasons, in order to strengthen the monarchy.   But
Italy remained an ally of doubtful value, even more so when she
felt her imperialist ambitions in North Africa coming into conflict
with those of Germany in the Middle East and Austria-Hungary's in
the Balkans. (4)   At the same time, the rise of nationalism in the
Balkans reactivated the radical heritage of the 'Risorgimento' to
such a point that Italy had more affinity to Serbia in July 1914
than to Austria-Hungary or Germany, and left the Triple Alliance in
1915 to join the Triple Entente.   Italy, thus, moved from a rather
negative pole in 1859 to a mildly positive one in 1882 and back to
a negative one by the outbreak of the First World War.

Germany's relations with Britain were no less complex; Britain
was, for different reasons, also interested in preserving a situation in Europe without alliances, because they could become the
basis of a continental hegemony of one Power or the other.   In
order to prevent being excluded from Europe, Britain tried to preserve the balance of forces from the periphery, relying on her sea
power and colonial empire overseas, while Germany tried to come to
terms with the new balance of power for its own advantage, from its
central position as the formidable military Power on the continent.
Longer than the German Empire, Britain stood by her traditional
policy of keeping her options open, under both liberal and conservative governments.   While Germany tried to prevent the forming of
alliances among the European Powers, it tried again and again to
establish some kind of diplomatic cooperation with Britain, after
the conclusion of the Dual and Triple Alliances in 1879 and 1882
even with the new alliance under Germany's leadership.   Germany,
however, was never prepared to pay an adequate price for the tremendous advantage of having Britain's constant cooperation or even
partnership in a common alliance.

After the end of the nineteenth century the price to be paid
would have meant forgoing ambitions to challenge Britain's supremacy
at sea and accepting a position of a junior partner under Britain
in the German effort to raise Germany's status to that of a fully-
fledged World Power.   In 1870-1 Britain had taken a neutral position, being both benevolent and critical at the same time.   After
some oscillation, Britain drifted from her ambivalent, but not indifferent position to a negative position, once Germany's imperialist real ambitions showed that they could only be satisfied at the
expense of the British Empire.   Even in the formative years of the
European system of alliances, Britain remained longest outside the
whole system.   When she joined France and Russia, it was in the
form of loose arrangements formalized only at the beginning of the
First World War by the Treaty of London, concluded on 4 September
1914.   Up to the actual outbreak of war, Britain always tried to
bridge the differences between the two power blocs.   Through her
offers of mediation in the Balkan Wars and in the crisis of July
1914, however, Britain only created illusions in Berlin that she
might remain neutral in the case of a continental war.   Once the
illusion had finally been destroyed, Germany was shaken by an
explosion of hatred and anti-British feelings, which were to remain
in the German mind for decades to come.

Spain and Turkey, the old Empires of early modern history, no
longer counted as great powers.   They had become more (Turkey) or
less (Spain) objects of modern imperialism themselves.   The USA
and Japan were beyond the horizon of European diplomacy in the
nineteenth century, but they slowly emerged as potential World
Powers by their entrance into the imperialist sphere.   In 1904-5
Japan even defeated one European Great Power in the Far East -
Russia - with repercussions on the European scene.(5)

CAUSES FOR WAR: ALLIANCES AND THE REJECTION OF NATIONAL SELF-DETERMINATION

It took almost half a century until European Powers clashed again in 1914, not because of a lack of tensions between them, but because they succeeded in directing their tensions to the periphery of Europe and overseas, e.g. 1875-82 in the Balkans. (6)   The scramble for Africa made Africa one of the chief theatres of operation. (7) After colonial penetration of North Africa had been completed, and when Germany recognized the French protectorate of Morocco (1911) and the Italian conquest of Libya (1911-12), tensions returned to the Balkans and thus to the Continent.   It was in the Balkans that tensions sparked off the conflagration known as the First World War.

If Europe, thus, was divided in 1914 by two power blocs, in marked contrast to the situation in 1871, those blocs were never so rigid as many contemporaries then thought.   Britain, France and Russia had been driven together mainly by fear or mistrust of Germany, and Britain's comparative aloofness forced France and Russia to renew, as it were, their links with Britain in any major diplomatic crisis up to July 1914.   Italy's uncertainty was obvious, because of divergent interests in North Africa and her ideological sympathy for the south Slav 'Risorgimento' in the Balkans.   The alliance system replaced the chaotic balance of the individual powers only by another - no less precarious - balance of power grouped in two alliances confronting each other in Europe. It was theoretically possible that a conflagration of the kind which actually broke out in 1914, could also have taken place in the pre-alliance phase of European diplomacy in 1859, 1866, 1871, 1875 or 1878.   The mechanism of power interests could have worked, once set into motion, without formal alliances.   In fact, during the wars and diplomatic crises during the years in question, the outbreak of a major conflagration was always feared and was averted only by the restraint of one or the other power not to intervene. The way in which the First World War began in 1914, however, suggests that the existence of hostile alliances in Europe was perhaps not a necessary condition, but at least one that helped to make a great war inevitable, once a great power from one camp was directly engaged with one from the opposing camp.

In any case, the stages of the formation of the alliance system were also the stages of the accumulation of tensions which were to explode at the outbreak of the First World War:

i   the 'war-in-sight' crisis of 1875;
ii   the eastern crisis of 1875-8, which was solved for the time
     being by the Berlin Congress of 1878 and, amongst others, by
     the annexation of Bosnia-Herzegovina by Austria-Hungary;
iii the Dual Alliance of 1879;
iv   the Triple Alliance of 1882;
v   the Franco-Russian Dual Alliance of 1892-4;
vi   the Anglo-French Entente of 1904;
vii the Anglo-Russian Agreement of 1907.

At the beginning of the diplomatic regrouping of the Powers, came the Dual Alliance between Germany and Austria-Hungary in 1879;   at the end the agreement between Britain and Russia of 1907.   The forming of the European system of alliances was thus provoked by

Germany, because it took the initiative in forming the Dual and Triple Alliance, which in its turn, a generation later, provoked the formation of the Triple Entente. The German Secretary of State, Jagow may have accused 'this damned system of alliances, which is the curse of modern times' as the real cause of the World War on 1 August 1914. (8)   It was in fact the German Empire that had been responsible for creating it, while the other powers only more or less reacted to Germany's actions.

But Germany's overall responsibility for the creation of tensions leading to the First World War is not limited to the rather formal aspect of alliances. Germany's 'Weltpolitik' made world war inevitable sooner or later by provoking Britain.   Per-haps a more subtle reason for the outbreak of the war was Germany's self-chosen role as the chief bulwark of conservatism and monar-chism against democracy and national self-determination which made a peaceful settlement in the Balkans impossible. In July 1914 Germany drove Austria-Hungary into repressing the south Slav nationalist movement by trying to crush Serbia, the south Slav Piedmont.

German foreign policy may be understood as that of a politically conservative power reacting against the social and political conse-quences of the industrial revolution, i.e. democracy and national self-determination. The reaction abroad was the same as at home - the use of power and violence to suppress mass movements which would endanger the privileged positions of the ruling classes, both old and new, in the German Empire.

The new German Empire had been founded as a measure against the forces of radical Liberals and Socialists and by the military defeat of France that had taken a liberal turn under Napoleon III in 1869, to become a republic after Napoleon's defeat at Sedan and Metz. The Reich included, as mentioned above, substantial national minorities who had been absorbed into Germany against their wishes. Germany's foreign policy from 1871 to 1914 was dic-tated by hostility towards the principle of national self-determi-nation. In this respect, the decisive events coincided with the great crises that led up to July 1914: the Oriental Crisis of 1875 was sparked off by the revolt of the south Slavs in the Turkish provinces Bosnia and Herzegovina. By occupying the two provinces in 1878 and annexing them in 1908, Austria-Hungary, with the support of Germany, incorporated the critical mass of politically explosive matter, which led directly to the outrage of Sarajevo in June 1914.   This also produced the great crisis of 1908-9 which confronted Austria-Hungary and Germany on one side and Russia on the other. The problem grew worse and was even sharpened by the Austrian threat to intervene in the Balkan Wars of 1912-13.   Under the onslaught of complications created by the First Balkan War, Germany's leaders finally resolved to go to war as soon as it was technically possible. (9)   The outrage of Sarajevo and the conse-quent steps Germany insisted on taking must be seen in the same context. Germany's ruling class felt threatened by the rising forces of democracy and national revolt, while Germany's last reliable ally, Austria-Hungary, was threatened even more by the same forces and looked to the more powerful German Reich for help. (10)

Part two

GERMAN FOREIGN POLICY IN THE PRE-IMPERIALIST ERA, 1871-95

Apart from the brief outburst of colonial activities under Bismarck between 1883 and 1885, Germany entered its imperialist phase, strictly speaking, only after the introduction of German 'Weltpolitik', the German contribution to the universal phenomenon of Imperialism around 1900.   It is, therefore, justifiable to consider the period between 1871 and 1895 as one great unit, as far as German foreign policy is concerned.

Chapter 3

FROM THE FOUNDING OF THE GERMAN EMPIRE TO THE CONGRESS OF BERLIN, 1871-8

AFTERMATH TO VICTORY OVER FRANCE

The founding of the new Empire in the midst of a war on foreign
soil, the victory over France that had just taken a liberal turn
even under Napoleon III ('L'Empire libérale'), the victory over
republican France after Napoleon's abdication in early September
1870, together with the annexation of Alsace-Lorraine against the
clear wishes of the majority of the population, were all liabili-
ties for the young Reich. (1)   Mistrust of Prussian militarism
was widespread in Europe, probably because it had proved so successful.   The impression created by the new concentration of power in
the centre of Europe was a strong one.   For centuries Europe had
been used to having a centre that was weak or paralysed by internal
rivalries.   Sensitive minds outside and even inside Germany itself
saw and feared serious consequences inevitable for Germany and peace
in Europe: Germany would be militarized through Prussia's military
success and politically hegemony.   The new imperial chauvinism
would sooner or later provoke an alliance between France and Russia.
The Swiss conservative historian Jacob Burckhardt, Friedrich
Nietzsche, Friedrich Engels and Karl Marx, together with many others
saw for different ideological and political reasons, mostly negative
results coming from the founding of the Reich.   In a letter of 27
September 1870 Burckhardt warned, even before the founding of the
Reich, that Germany, by humiliating France, would endanger European
peace in the future:

> Oh, how much the German nation errs if it thinks it will be able
> to put the rifle in one corner and turn to the arts and the
> happiness of peace!   They will be told: above all you must con-
> tinue your military training!   And after a time no one will
> really be able to say what is the purpose of living.   For soon
> the German-Russian war will loom on the horizon. (2)

Benjamin Disraeli, then speaking for the Conservative Opposition, articulated similar misgivings in his famous speech of 9
February 1871, in the House of Commons.   His conclusions may have
seemed alarming then and were, to a certain extent, exaggerated.
They testified, however, to the deep shock brought about by the
emergence of the new Reich through a series of wars:

It is no common war.... This war represents the German Revolution, a greater political event than the French Revolution of
the last century.... What its social consequences may be are in
the future.... You have a new world, new influences at work, new
and unknown objects and dangers with which to cope.... The
balance of power has been entirely destroyed, and the country
which suffers most, and feels the effects of this great change
most, is England.' (3)

The balance of power in Europe had not been destroyed by the
emergence of the German Reich, but it was deeply disturbed.   It
would take some time for a new balance of power to assert itself
with the powerful Reich as the new centre.   All powers, great and
small, saw their positions changed and had no option but to adjust
to the new situation.

The necessity of finding a new balance of power, advantageous to
Germany, easily explained Bismarck's new peaceful policy.   It has
been unduly idealized by patriotic historiography in Germany.   In
fact, after 1871 Bismarck had a natural interest in securing peace,
after he had gained such a tremendous success through his reckless,
but clever war policy since 1864.   His 'love of peace' after 1871
is best explained against the background of his preceding warlike
period, just as Friedrich II of Prussia was 'peace-minded' after
conquering and defending Silesia in a series of three wars between
1740 and 1763.   As a matter of course Bismarck now tried to avoid
wars which could only have jeopardized all the gains of the preceding wars.   In a new war Germany would have to fight against a
Europe aroused by the coups of 1864, 1866 and 1870-1.   Bismarck
proclaimed Germany to be 'satiated' after 1871.   But once it had
digested its tremendous successes, the question arose as to what it
would do if it were to become war-hungry again.   Bismarck, thus,
had not miraculously turned pacifist after 1871; but a policy of
consolidation was normal in the situation.   Bismarck remained as
prepared as ever to go to war or to threaten to do so whenever he
thought it was in the interest of the Reich.   But war was not the
overriding preoccupation of the Reich in its pre-imperialist phase,
as it had been Prussia's between 1862 and 1871 and was to become
again in the age of 'Weltpolitik'.   There was at least a theoretical chance that the German 'peace-mindedness' for tactical reasons
after 1871 might have changed into one based on reason and conviction.   This change did not take place, and one of the aims of our
analysis is to explain why the theoretical chance was not seized by
Germany's ruling class.

Within given reality inside and outside Germany, there were three
alternatives open for the conduct of German foreign policy.   They
have been clearly defined by a German scholar recently: (i) Germany
could seek arrangements with the other Great Powers at the cost of
small and medium-sized states in Europe.   (ii) Germany could try
to hold down potential rivals on the Continent by a series of rapid
preventive wars against them, as they turned up one after the
other, a concept suggested by the elder Moltke.   (iii) Germany
could play off the other Powers against each other and try to divert
tensions from Europe to overseas. (4)   In fact, Germany under
Bismarck followed the third alternative with some success on the
level of Continental policy but failed when it tried to apply the

same policy on the level of imperialist 'Weltpolitik'.   With its
decision to go to war at the end of 1912, Germany then fell back
on the second alternative, while in the war itself German war aims
came nearest to the first alternative, when German leaders envisaged
the possibility of a compromise separate peace on one front, which,
necessarily, would have led to an arrangement with one Great Power
to the cost of small and medium-sized Powers in Europe.

GERMANY AND FRANCE, 1871-5

After 1871 a policy of consolidation made it necessary to redefine
Germany's position vis-à-vis the two Great Powers beaten by Prussia-
Germany in the last five years - France and Austria-Hungary.
Bismarck's policy attempted to keep France, then allegedly Germany's
'arch enemy', in political quarantine.   In spite of his monarchist
convictions, Bismarck was only too pleased that the French had returned to the uncertainties of the (Third) Republic after the
defeat of Sedan.   In a Europe which was still overwhelmingly monarchical, a French Republic was almost automatically isolated if
only for ideological reasons.   After the Paris Commune had been
crushed in the spring of 1871, Bismarck was confident that he could
control the domestic repercussions of the French Republic on
Germany through a combination of formal concessions (universal and
equal suffrage in the Reichstag) and repression if he felt it to be
necessary.   Bismarck's reasoning worked for two decades.   Then the
weight of power politics began to override ideological divergences
between Republican France and Tsarist Russia.
    Bismarck's sudden calculated 'kindness' towards the French after
the Peace of Frankfurt, concluded in March 1871, produced the first
major clash within Germany's political structure.   The Arnim case,
for a long time the 'cause célèbre' of European foreign policy, is
more interesting for the political problems behind it than the
'chronique scandaleuse' before 1914 seems to suggest. (5)   Behind
the apparently personal intrigues about divergencies in diplomacy
between the first Chancellor of the Reich and his first Ambassador
to Paris in the early 1870s some of the structural problems that
beset the Reich from the beginning of its existence can be seen.
    A group of staunchly conservative Prussian Junkers who were sus-
picious of Bismarck's apparent flirt with the Liberals in his domestic policy were also against Bismarck's tactical opportunism towards
the French Republic.   Count Arnim, considered to be Bismarck's
rival, made himself the spokesman of this group.   As German Ambassador to France from 1871 to 1873 he tried to influence German
policy in the opposite direction: he recommended that the monar-
chists in France should be encouraged to help to overthrow the
Republican regime. (6)   Bismarck remained victorious after a
bitter struggle in 1873.   While defeating the ultra-conservative
Fronde, in the person of Arnim, Bismarck also decided two important
issues for German foreign policy: (i) a German ambassador was subordinate to the Auswärtiges Amt (Foreign Office), i.e. to the
Chancellor, and he had no right to influence policy by appealing
directly to the head-of-state, the German Emperor.   (ii) The
German policy of isolating France by ideological means - keeping

her a Republic - was continued. (7)   Bismarck's total victory over
Arnim, however, was changed by the course of history into a curious
draw: from a short term point of view, Bismarck was proved right.
Prolonged instability kept France weak and unattractive as a partner
in foreign policy for almost two decades.   But in the long run,
Bismarck was proved wrong, as Germany could not keep France forever
in diplomatic isolation.   On the other hand, it is more than doubtful as to whether Arnim's policy of making an alliance with France,
once she had turned monarchist, could have worked indefinitely.
It might have provoked another Republican outburst, with the same
net result as Bismarck's policy.   The only other alternative, being
radically different from official policy, never had a chance in the
German Reich, i.e. the conclusion of an alliance with Republican
France on the basis of restoring Alsace-Lorraine and the acceptance
of democratic or republican repercussions in Germany.

Sooner than Bismarck had expected, France recovered from the
shock of military defeat.   Under Thiers, the conservative interim
President, France succeeded in paying Germany the sum of five
thousand million francs, a tremendous sum for the time, in 1873.
German occupation troops were withdrawn sooner than expected, with
the result that France recovered full sovereignty over her own
territory.   The French army recovered quickly as a fighting force
to be reckoned with.   In 1875 the French Republic was consolidated
by the final defeat of all monarchist ambitions, even if only by
default, because the three rivalling monarchist factions - legiti-
mists, Orléanists and Bonapartists - could not make up their minds
to support one single candidate.   Bismarck himself encouraged
France to pursue a more active colonial policy in order to divert
her attention from Alsace-Lorraine.   His plan was successful for a
short time, but in the long run colonial expansion, beginning with
the protectorate over Tunis in 1881, restored self-confidence to
the French.   After the Boulanger crisis of 1885-8 was over, the
Third Republic remained unchallenged for more than half a century.
Only a few years after the final consolidation of the Third Republic, in 1892-4, France succeeded in breaking through the isolation
imposed by Bismarck's Germany, when France and Russia concluded the
Dual Alliance.

France's military and political recovery made Germany surpris-
ingly nervous.   The 'war-in-sight' crisis, called after an article
in the German conservative paper 'Post', was the first major crisis
in Europe after 1871.   Field-Marshal Moltke, Germany's Chief of
Staff, even pressed for another preventive war against France,
before her military power was fully restored.   French measures to
round off military reorganization and consolidation in early 1875
were answered by Germany in a combination of alarmist press
articles and diplomatic pressure on Paris to reduce French armaments, going as far as to threaten France with 'preventive war' on
21 April 1875. (8)

France, alarmed by the threat from Germany, informed Russia and
Britain, who unmistakably warned Germany that they would not endure
a repetition of 1870-1.   The constellation of 1914 began to take
shape as early as 1875: Britain and Russia were trying to prevent
another French defeat at the hands of the German Empire, which was
already overwhelmingly powerful in Europe.   Austria-Hungary and

Italy did not take part in the diplomatic intervention against Germany, but Italy in 1914 remained neutral and joined the 'Entente Cordiale' in 1915.

Bismarck, shaken by the spectre of German isolation in the event of another war against France, quietly beat a retreat and tried to cover up his defeat through peaceful speeches in the Reichstag and ironical remarks in his memoirs.

THE SPECTRE OF THE HOLY ALLIANCE - THE THREE EMPERORS' ATTEMPT TO FORM A COMMON FRONT, 1872-3

The sobering experience of the 'war-in-sight' crisis had the effect of raising the problem of alliances in a serious form for Germany for the first time.   Although Bismarck would have preferred the constellation in Europe without alliances, he now felt uncomfortable in his self-chosen isolation in the centre of Europe.   Even before 1875 Bismarck had taken first tentative steps to rebuild an alliance of the three great conservative monarchies - Germany, Russia, Austria-Hungary.   Its common basis would have been the conservation of the monarchical principle and the feudal structures against demo-cratic trends of socialist and nationalist character.   The common partnership in the Partition of Poland and the tradition of the common fight against the French Revolution and Napoleon I must have given additional plausibility to Conservative minds.   In 1872 the three Emperors met in Berlin, and in the next year a series of bi-lateral agreements between the three powers culminated in the Three Emperors' Agreement of 22 October 1873.   Its aim was to fight 'any revolutions from whatever side they may come' through active soli-darity of the monarchies. (9)   Formally a defensive alliance, it could have imposed a conservative structure on most of Europe, if it had been realized and would probably have lasted for some time.

Political and social realities, however, proved stronger than the vain attempt to build castles in central and eastern Europe by conjuring up the spectre of the Holy Alliance.   The discrepancies in the structures of all three conservative Empires and the diver-gencies in their political interests abroad defeated any such attempt.   While Germany entered its illiberal phase in 1878, re-sulting in the conflicting economic and political aims of agricul-ture and industry, (10) Russia felt the consequences of the reforms under Tsar Alexander II, beginning with the emancipation of peasants in 1861.   The liberal bourgeoisie, who were more French than German orientated, gained considerable influence behind the façade of autocratic Tsarism.   The liberal forces pressed for an alliance with France and they supported, in the first upsurge of Pan-Slavism in Russia, the aspirations of the national minorities in the Balkans against the Ottoman Empire.   The traditional expan-sionist ambitions of Tsarist Russia were thus justified by another ideological element: the defence of Orthodox Christians in the Balkans.   This more traditional factor now began to coincide with the support of nationalist liberation movements against the rule of out-dated empires, i.e. Turkey. (11)   But once she was defeated, Austria-Hungary with her south Slav and other Slav nationalities remained as the next object of national revolt.

Russia was thus to come into conflict with Austria-Hungary directly and indirectly with Germany, once the latter committed itself on the side of the Dual Monarchy.   Her ruling classes - Germans in Austria, Magyars in Hungary - had to look around for backing abroad against the threatening upsurge of democratic or even revolutionary nationalism at home.   Their natural ally in Europe was Germany who by reason of its own internal structure was hostile to any victory of democratic and revolutionary nationalism for fear of its position vis-à-vis its own national minorities and socialist opposition. (12)   Once Germany's imperialist ambitions were to be directed to the Ottoman Empire, Germany would also be interested in gaining control of the Balkans as a vital geographical link to Constantinople.

Interests of power politics and ideology clashed between Austria-Hungary and Germany on the one hand and Russia and the Balkan national movements on the other.   The divergence of interests was strong enough to erode, in the course of time, the traditional partnership of the past, culminating in the Holy Alliance of 1815 and the defeat of the Revolution of 1848-9.   This is why the League of the three Emperors of Germany, Austria-Hungary and Russia of October 1873 was no more than an empty frame.   Even a German-Russian military convention of May 1873, which stipulated reciprocal military assistance in case Germany or Russia were to be attacked, (13) remained on paper.   The 'war-in-sight' crisis of early 1875 demonstrated the ineffectiveness of the League of the three Emperors as an instrument of foreign policy.   It was destroyed by the first oriental crisis after 1871 - in 1875-8.

The crisis was provoked by the revolt of the south Slav population in the Turkish provinces Bosnia and Herzegovina in 1875 and was resolved through the Congress of Berlin in 1878 - with memorable consequences: Germany was forced to leave its self-chosen position of avoiding alliances and to reappraise its relations both to Russia and Austria-Hungary.

Austria's defeat in 1866 had been the final culmination of traditional antagonism between Prussia and Austria.   After the founding of the Reich, Bismarck sought to reconcile Austria-Hungary with the new German Empire.   The Austrian Foreign Minister, Count Beust of Saxon origin, represented the anti-Prussian tradition, and he was prevented from intervening in the Franco-German War in 1870 only by Russia's threat.   Count Andrássy, representing the Magyar aristocracy, whose only wish was to preserve their dominant position against the Slav nationalities who formed the majority in Hungary, looked to Germany, especially to Prussia, for support.   Their class interest coincided with that of the German aristocracy and the bourgeoisie in Austria.   It was logical that Beust, after two visits of the German Emperor to his Austrian colleague Franz Joseph in Austria in 1871, was dismissed in the same year and replaced by Andrássy.   The Magyar ex-revolutionary and aristocrat prepared the foreign policy of his country which culminated in the Dual Alliance of 1879.

THE ORIENTAL CRISIS, 1875-8, AND THE BERLIN CONGRESS

One of the important stages of the Dual Alliance was, once the 'war-in-sight' crisis had passed, the oriental crisis of 1875-8. (14)
The general revolt of the south Slav population in Bosnia and Herze-govina had been an indirect consequence of the international econo-mic crisis of 1873.   The Turkish authorities had demanded higher taxes, which hit hardest the Orthodox Serb peasants at the end of the social hierarchy.   The revolt spread to Bulgaria and found, on 30 June 1876, the military support of the two small independent south Slav monarchies, Serbia and Montenegro.   On 8 July 1876 Austria-Hungary and Russia tried to coordinate their conflicting interests at the informal meeting at Reichstadt.   If Serbia and Montenegro were to remain victorious, they could be allowed to annex parts of Bosnia and Herzegovina, while the rest were to be annexed by Austria.   Russia should re-annex Bessarabia, which had been Russian until 1856. (15)
The defeat of Serbia and Montenegro, however, provoked the first upsurge of Pan-Slavism and propelled Russia into a war to defend the Christian south Slav states.   Russia's crushing victories in the Russo-Turkish War of 1877-8 upset the agreement of Reichstadt and threatened to establish Russian hegemony in the Balkans, thus thwarting any Austrian ambitions in southeast Europe.   The Treaty of San Stefano, concluded on 3 March 1878 between Russia and Turkey, read like a fulfilment of the Pan-Slav programme, enlarging Serbia and Montenegro, Bulgaria and Roumania, while reducing European Turkey to a small area west of Constantinople.   Austria-Hungary felt both deceived and threatened by Russian expansion under the guise of south Slav states in the Balkans.   In January 1878 Austria pressed for a European Congress.   On 6 March 1878, after consultation with Berlin and St Petersburg, Andrássy invited the Powers to a Congress to be held in Berlin. (16)
The question had now been put to Germany to decide its position between Russia and Austria-Hungary, the two partners of the League of the three Emperors, although they all had conflicting aims and interests.   Even in the summer of 1876, after the Reichstadt agreement, war with Austria-Hungary had been a possibility, if Russia were to intervene against Turkey.   In autumn 1876 Russia asked Germany how it would act in such a contingency, reminding it of Russia's part in neutralizing Austria-Hungary in 1870. (17)
Bismarck was not pleased at the idea of having to choose between Russia and Austria-Hungary and he tried to solve the problem by broaching the idea of a European Congress.   He may not have dis-liked a war between Russia and Austria-Hungary or, for that matter, between Russia and Britain.   But he saw that the perennial orien-tal question was bound to enlarge any war between the Powers mentioned into a continental war, in which Germany could not remain neutral and might endanger the gains made in 1870-1.
Germany had, at that time, no direct interest in the Balkans (18) and was really only concerned with keeping Austria-Hungary intact. On the other hand, it had to face the reality that any of the two Powers who did not feel satisfied by Germany's part as a mediator, would turn against Germany in the long run by approaching France. Bismarck tried once more to avoid any commitment, however indirect,

by working closely together with Britain and stressing his intentions of having an equally good relationship with Russia and
Austria-Hungary.   At St Petersburg he made it clear that Germany
would not tolerate an attack on the integrity of Austria-Hungary.
(19)   Thus, three years before the Dual Alliance between Germany
and Austria-Hungary, Bismarck indirectly and cautiously opted for
Austria-Hungary.

At the same time, the constellation of 1914 continued to take
shape: after the 'war-in-sight' crisis of 1875 had demonstrated
how the mechanism of power interest could work even without formal
alliances, the oriental crisis of 1875-8 began to provide the fuse
for the future explosion.   The revolutionary potential behind the
principle of national self-determination would bring the major
powers into conflict, with Germany trying to defend Austria-Hungary
against any revolutionary disturbances.   Pan-Slavism in revolutionary action against the Turkish Empire was supported morally,
politically, financially and militarily, first by Serbia and Montenegro, then by Russia.   It represented a direct and massive attack
against the conservative principles upon which the German and the
Habsburg Empires were based.   In Russia, Bismarck saw that only
the Romanov dynasty and a small group of aristocratic conservatives,
many of them German Baltic barons, still supported the alliance
with Germany.   Since the oriental crisis and Russia's intervention
in the Balkans for Pan-Slav reasons, he saw Tsarist autocracy
threatened by a revolution at home from the Russian liberal bourgeoisie who tended more to the French side than to the German one.
Russia, with possible revolution at home and supporting the south
Slav independence movement in the Balkans against Austria-Hungary,
became a less reliable partner to dynastic and conservative Germany
than Austria-Hungary. (20)

Apart from such considerations, the military and political
developments in the Balkans, culminating in the preliminary peace
of San Stefano, made a European congress necessary to prevent a
European conflagration.   Britain, in February 1878, opposed
Russia's military advance on land by sending a fleet into the Mar-
mara Sea to protect Constantinople.   Bismarck, for all his misgivings, came round to the idea that a Congress would be the lesser
evil, since through the role of a mediator between Austria-Hungary
and Russia he hoped to be able to put off the question of open
alliances once more.   The Russian Chancellor Gorchakov, however,
hoped to push Bismarck into opting for Russia.

The Berlin Congress of 1878, seen superficially, was the
brilliant climax of Bismarck's career as a European statesman and
confirmed Germany's central position in European affairs.
Bismarck's mediating role as 'the honest broker', as he formulated
it himself in a speech in the Reichstag on 19 February 1878,
stressed the importance of the new German Empire.   The Congress
was, indeed, a short-term success, as it avoided a major conflagration in 1878, mostly at Turkey's expense.   But by its failure to
solve any of the long-term problems involved in the oriental crisis
of 1875-8, the Congress of Berlin helped to prepare the conflict
that was only postponed for one generation: Russia's dynamism was
blocked for the moment, because the ring of smaller south Slav
states in the Balkans was not allowed full national sovereignty and

freedom of action.   Serbia and Montenegro remained small, receiving none of Bosnia and Herzegovina;   Bulgaria remained divided into an autonomous Principality and the province of Eastern Rumelia. Macedonia and the coast of Thracia became Turkish again.   The occupation of Cyprus by Britain as a stepping stone to the Suez Canal opened up the possibility of modernising the island after 300 years of neglect under Turkish rule.   But the loss of domination created new problems for the Turkish minority, which were to explode only after the formal independence of Cyprus through a bloody civil war in our days.

One particular stipulation of the Congress created new tensions one generation later, resulting in the conflict of 1914 - the occupation of Bosnia-Herzegovina by Austria-Hungary.   The south Slav Orthodox population of the two Turkish provinces had, in their revolt of 1875, opted for a union with Serbia.   When, on 28 June 1878, the Congress of Berlin formally decided that Austria-Hungary should be allowed to occupy Bosnia-Herzegovina, they did so in total disregard of the wishes of the population, and for purely egoistic reasons.   In particular, Austria pressed for compensation for the losses she had incurred in 1866 when she had lost most of her possessions in northern Italy to unified Italy.   She also wanted to prevent the creation of one unified south Slav state, which might have attracted south Slavs in Austria-Hungary - in Croatia, Slovenia and Dalmatia.   By way of compromise, Austria-Hungary was only allowed to occupy the two provinces so that they technically remained under the sovereignty of the Ottoman Empire. Once Turkey was to reclaim actual sovereignty, which happened in 1908 after the Revolution of the Young Turks, a new conflict would arise. (21)

Another source of conflict was heralded by the reaction of the south Slav Orthodox population to their occupation by Austria-Hungary.   They had not risen in arms against Turkish rule only to change it for undesired Austrian rule.   They took to arms again and, supported by the Muslim element, fought Austrian authority, which had to be imposed by a bloody campaign.   It took an Austrian army of 200,000 men three months of bitter fighting, culminating in the conquest of Sarajevo after violent street-fights. (22)

Bosnia-Herzegovina, thus, was not merely occupied territory, it was also conquered territory, with a tradition of armed resistance and guerilla warfare against unwanted conquerors, whether they were Turkish or Austrian.   This tradition was carried on, a generation later, in the movement of 'Young Bosnia', where the modern revolutionary elements of a rising young intelligentsia were combined with older traditions of peasants' guerilla resistance.   The sentimental value of Sarajevo as the symbol of armed resistance can also be better understood when seen against the background of the historic tradition in Bosnia and Herzegovina. (23)

The occupation of Bosnia-Herzegovina through military conquest in 1878 had far-reaching consequences for Austria-Hungary: this was the last piece of territory to be acquired by the Habsburg Monarchy. By occupying the two provinces, the Dual Monarchy had incorporated the critical mass of additional political conflict, which was to bring about the deadly explosion in 1914-18.   Bosnia provided the real fuse for the First World War, through the murder at Sarajevo, because occupation meant rule in Bosnia and Herzegovina without consent of the population.   The net result was a hardening of the ruling oligarchies in Austria and Hungary.   The way was now blocked for the only alternative solution to revolutionary nationalism, i.e. the transformation of the Dual Monarchy into a Trialism, including the south Slavs, and later into a truly federated system where all nationalities would be on an equal footing.   All theoretical attempts to achieve this foundered on the interests of the ruling classes in Austria and Hungary who tried to prevent any peaceful moves towards a free and democratic Danube Federation, as these would have ended their rule. (24)

Finally, Russia was disappointed by the results of the Congress of Berlin and blamed Germany for having betrayed her to Austrian and British interests.   Russia thus reacted against Germany, which, in its turn, opted for solidarity with dynastic and feudal Austria-Hungary.   Germany became entangled in the dialectics of national revolution and the conservation of the 'status quo'.

The Congress of Berlin, superficially the last triumph of the Concert of Powers in Europe, really helped to found the new system of European Powers forty years later.   The flagrant disregard of a population's wishes brought about a solution which seemed to ensure peace and calm for the time being.   However, it only provoked new tensions and conflicts within the space of a generation.   The aspiration towards national self-determination continued to grow even more strongly in the new generation for whom the history of the revolt in Bosnia and Herzegovina in 1875 and its bloody suppression, first by the Turks, then by the Austrians, was more than an echo of history;   it was an example to do better next time.

Chapter 4

DUAL AND TRIPLE ALLIANCE, 1879-82

GERMANY BETWEEN RUSSIA AND AUSTRIA-HUNGARY

The long-term indirect consequences of the Congress of Berlin were only to be felt in the unknown future, but one direct and short-term consequence changed the scenery of European diplomacy: Russian resentment over Germany's blocking Russia's advance in the Balkans drove Germany and Austria-Hungary together and provoked the formation of the Dual Alliance in 1879. One year after the Congress of Berlin Alexander II complained about Bismarck in a sharply worded letter to Wilhelm I. He personally blamed Bismarck for having abandoned Russian interests and warned about serious consequences to both countries. (1) Bismarck interpreted the warning at least as an oblique threat of war and reacted accordingly. Germany might have stomached Russian resentment as such; further provocation, however, provided by the oriental crisis and the principle of national self-determination underlying it, led to the break with Russia and destroyed the League of the Three Emperors for good. In 1879 Bismarck was returning to domestic policy on a conservative basis, culminating in protective tariffs for agriculture and industry. At the beginning of his struggle with the Socialists, Bismarck saw the structure of the Reich threatened if, under such circumstances at home, he condoned a policy of supporting revolutionary elements abroad, if only in the Balkans, and if only indirectly by opting for Russia.

Also for reasons of sheer power politics, Germany was now confronted with choosing between Russia and Austria-Hungary. After all that had happened at the Congress of Berlin, Germany really had no choice at all. Austria-Hungary would have to be chosen for her structural, historical and ideological affinities with Germany. The Habsburg Monarchy, after all, could be interpreted as an offspring of the old Holy Roman Empire of German Nations, although the Habsburgs had been thrown out of Germany in 1866, making them turn towards south-east Europe.

The link between Russian disappointment over the Congress of Berlin and Germany's Dual Alliance with Austria-Hungary can be seen from the logical sequence of events. Bismarck also testified that he had pleaded with Emperor Wilhelm I for an alliance with Austria-

Hungary.   Bismarck tried then, as he did later, to define the
structural, historical and ideological affinities between Germany
and Austria-Hungary.
    The letter of the Tsar complaining about Bismarck's stand at the
Congress of Berlin was dated 15 August 1879.   Bismarck's first
memorandum to his Emperor, replying to the Tsar's letter, was dated
24 August.   In a second memorandum on 31 August, Bismarck openly
pleaded for an alliance with Austria-Hungary as the only adequate
reaction to Russia's move.   Further memoranda were sent on 5 and 7
September. (2)   Bismarck travelled to Vienna, at the end of September, to complete the Treaty of Alliance on 7 October.   The two
Emperors ratified it in the same month.   Thus, in less than two
months after the Tsar's letter to Wilhelm I, the Dual Alliance
between Germany and Austria-Hungary had become reality, and the
Tsar's letter was constantly referred to in the process as the
starting point.   The pace of events was remarkable, not only for
the time.   The reasons Bismarck gave are no less remarkable,
because they confirm our analysis of the German Empire: domestic
reasons for German foreign policy clearly pointed to the defence of
the social and political 'status quo' as it had developed by 1871.
(3)
    In his first memorandum to Emperor Wilhelm of 24 August 1879,
Bismarck explained that, when choosing between Russia and Austria in
the past, he had been biased towards the Russian position, because
he thought that 'Russia's backing ['Anlehnung'] had been more
secure' than Austria's.   But now, apparently, the situation had
changed, as Bismarck continued:
    With Austria we have more in common than with Russia.   German
    kinship, historical memories, the German language, the interest
    of the Hungarians for us - all that makes an alliance with
    Austria more popular, perhaps also more enduring in Germany than
    an alliance with Russia.   Only dynastic links, in particular
    the personal friendship of Tsar Alexander, were more favourable
    in Russia and decided in favour of Russia.   Once this advantage
    of the Russian alliance, if it did not disappear, at least
    became uncertain, I deemed it imperative that the policy of Your
    Majesty should cultivate our relations with Austria even more
    intensely than before. (4)
    Bismarck's new passion for Ausgria was so strong that he would
have liked to have gone to Vienna to conclude the treaty of alliance
immediately, although it would have meant breaking his holiday in
Bad Gastein.   The reason for Bismarck's haste can be explained by
Andrássy's pending retirement from the Foreign Ministry.   Bismarck,
as a Prussian Junker, thought that he would quickly find a common
denominator with the Magyar aristocrat.   Andrássy's successor was
still unknown.   Soon after his first memorandum to Emperor Wilhelm,
Bismarck, on 27 and 28 August, agreed with Andrássy in principle on
a defensive alliance between Austria-Hungary and Germany. (5)   In
three further memoranda to his Emperor, Bismarck expounded his
reasons for the new turn in German foreign policy.   In contrast to
his former policy of keeping a free hand, Bismarck now thought it a
matter of course 'that we, situated in the centre of Europe, must
not be exposed to isolation'. (6)   The alliance with Austria was
to prevent such isolation.   It was a kind of substitute for the

links with Austria in the form of the German Confederation, which
Bismarck himself had destroyed in 1866.   Bismarck now claimed that
even at Nikolsburg, after the Prussian victory in 1866, he already
had this political vision.   While the dynastic links to Russia
still functioned, he had postponed the idea.   Alexander's letter
had destroyed the dynastic links from a traditional point of view.
To secure peace an alliance with Austria was inevitable;   because
Russia would not attack the two Empires.   On the other hand,
Andrássy's retirement might result in Austria's orientation towards
France which could easily be enlarged by Russia's accession to the
kind of European constellation that Prussia had to fight in the
Seven Years War.   Bismarck still hoped that Russia would join
Germany and Austria-Hungary, as she had joined Prussia and Austria
in 1866.   Britain might also be attracted by 'the alliance of the
two mid-European Empires' to seek firmer links with them. (7)
      In his memorandum of 24 August Bismarck had already hinted at
his idea that, behind the façade of Tsarism, revolutionary forces
were at work in Russia and that they regarded the League of the
Three Emperors as a formidable obstacle. (8)   In his third memorandum of 5 September Bismarck further developed this idea by unfavourably contrasting Russia's internal structure with that of
Austria-Hungary: Tsar Alexander, either wrongly assessing Russia's
power or becoming an unwitting tool of his revolutionary advisers,
would make Russia 'an uncalculable factor', in any essentially conservative policy.   'Austria, in contrast, is not [incalculable] to
the same degree.'   Austria could not conclude an alliance with
Russia against the wishes and constitutions of her people or even
wage a war against Germany.   In Russia, however, war was possible
any time.   Furthermore, Austria needed Germany, which Russia did
not.   Bismarck's reasoning culminated in the classical argument:
   Austria's social structure is perhaps the soundest of all great
   powers, and the rule of the dynasty is firmly founded with all
   nationalities.   As for Russia, no one knows what eruptions of
   revolutionary elements may suddenly happen in the interior of
   the great Empire. (9)
      Bismarck apparently thought that his sovereign had not yet been
convinced by his arguments.   In his fourth memorandum in two weeks
on the same subject sent from his holiday resort, Bad Gastein,
Bismarck further elaborated the theme of the Russian Tsar as an
instrument of the Pan-Slav revolution.   He explained the Tsar's
turn against Germany by 'placing the Russian policy and the Imperial
power into the service of the Slav revolution and conducting diplomacy in that sense'.   The Tsar, even during the Congress of Berlin,
had consciously made himself a partner.
   We cannot come to an understanding with the elementary power of
   that Slav revolution.   It is inconceivable that the Tsar or his
   successor will be able sufficiently to emancipate himself from
   such influences to oppose the hatred of Germans by his subjects,
   artificially produced by his government.... The apparent change
   of Russian policy for the moment must not deceive us: the same
   ambitious Slav elements are stronger than the Tsar's power of
   resistance, and they may, perhaps in months, perhaps in years
   ahead, produce again the same kind of atmosphere, which led to
   the Tsar's attempt at blackmailing us in the first half of this
   August. (10)

One year later and in a different context, Bismarck returned to the
subject and warned that Russia was threatened by revolution from
within by furthering the Slav revolution abroad.   In his important
instruction on 7 November 1880 to all German diplomats on German
policy in the eastern question, especially towards Greece, Bismarck
wrote:

> Pan-Slavism with its revolutionary aims is dangerous to both
> Germanic Powers, to Austria more than to us, most dangerous to
> the Russian Empire itself, including its dynasty.   The Slav
> world in revolution, with or without the Russian Emperor at its
> head, will always be the ally of Republican elements not only in
> France, but also in Italy, Spain, perhaps also in Britain.   In
> Britain the beginnings can be seen in Gladstone's doctrine. (11)

Bismarck may have exaggerated his fear of incipient Pan-Slavism
and revolution in Russia to scare his Emperor into accepting the
alliance with Austria-Hungary, but his analysis of 1879 was a remarkable mixture of truth and error.   He proved to be wrong in the
narrow field of diplomacy and foreign policy, as neither Russia nor
Britain joined the Dual Alliance in the long run.   The Dual
Alliance did not prevent Germany's world-wide isolation, once it
entered world politics in the age of Imperialism. (12)   Bismarck
was half right and half wrong in the more fundamental question of
social structures and revolutionary trends.   He was right in assum-
ing that Russia, for reasons mentioned above, had become an unreliable partner for any conservative foreign policy, because for
domestic reasons she was propelled into supporting the south Slav
movement in the Balkans, which was contradictory to the structure
of feudal and monarchic Tsarism in Russia.   But Bismarck proved
hopelessly wrong when judging Austria-Hungary.   It was a remarkable
illusion, perhaps more the product of conservative wishful thinking
than of anything else, to assume that Austria-Hungary would be a
more stable partner to Bismarck's conservative foreign policy, only
because there were, at the time, no revolutionary forces in sight.

This illusion of social stability reflected his plea for allying
with a social and political structure that was closest akin to that
of the German Empire.   Bismarck's nomenclature by calling Germany
and Austria-Hungary 'German' and 'mid-European' synonymously, indicated another trend in German foreign policy which continued into
the twentieth century;   the attempt to establish even closer links
than those created by an international treaty.   'Mid-Europe'
('Mitteleuropa') in the First World War, and the 'Greater German
Empire' ('Grossdeutsches Reich') from 1933 to 1945, were the two
phases of German foreign policy which brought Bismarck's idea of
1879 to its logical conclusion by having the Dual Alliance confirmed
in the constitutions of the two Empires.   Andrássy, however,
opposed this idea and the Austro-Hungarians managed to avoid any
closer 'mid-European' links until 1918.   The Dual Alliance remained a normal international treaty, without any further attempt
to confirm it by constitutional law.

THE DUAL ALLIANCE, 1879, AND THE PROBLEM OF ALLIANCES

The preamble of the treaty stresses its defensive character. (13)
Articles I, II and IV make it clear that it was motivated by fear
of a Russian attack against either empire.   As a result, the two
governments agreed to support each other 'with all the military
power of their Empires' and only to make peace together (Art. I).
If Russia were to support the attack of another Power against
Germany or Austria-Hungary (Art. II) they would still support each
other.   The treaty was to be kept secret;   communications with
other Powers were only to be carried out by special agreement (Art.
IV).   Wilhelm I informed Tsar Alexander II, the Foreign Ministry
in Vienna and the British Foreign Office in London.
      The text of the treaty itself did not refer to the ideological
motives of the Dual Alliance, as outlined by Bismarck in his memoranda to the Emperor, in particular the fear of Russia's latent
revolutionary potential with repercussions in the Balkans. (14)
      Some months before, in January 1879, Austria-Hungary had agreed
to suspend Article V of the 1866 Treaty of Prague, which had envisaged a plebiscite to be held in the predominantly Danish districts
of northern Schleswig. (15)   By doing this, Austria-Hungary antici-
pated the alliance with Germany by six months, as a plebiscite of
this kind would have been contrary to all principles of the German
Empire.   It would further have amounted to conceding to the
principle of national self-determination, which would probably have
resulted in encouraging other national minorities within the Reich
to clamour for the application of the same principle.   By 1879,
Austria-Hungary could easily fulfil Germany's wish to suspend
Article V of the Peace Treaty of Prague, as she was even more
hostile to the principle of national self-determination than
Germany and because a check to the principle in far-distant northern
Schleswig was of little interest to her in the Balkans.
      This detail, largely ignored by Germany, sheds an instructive
light on the internal structure of Germany and her main ally,
Austria-Hungary, and shows the inherent weakness of the two conservative Powers, which only came into the open during the First World
War.
      The conclusion of the Dual Alliance reopened the problem of
alliances in Europe.   Bismarck had hoped to group other Powers
around the Dual Alliance, in order to isolate Russia, because he
thought her to be more dangerous in her first phase of Pan-Slav
agitation than an isolated French Republic.   As the relationship
between Britain and Austria had always been good, Bismarck hoped
that 'Austria will carry Britain' into his camp. (16)   As Bismarck
feared that a possible result of the Dual Alliance would be Russia's
declaration of war against Germany, he tried to secure Britain's
backing.   Germany's cautious sounding out of Britain's position
was answered at the end of September 1879 by Disraelis' equally
cautious reply.   He stated that Britain would keep France and Italy
neutral in case of a war between Germany and Russia over the oriental question, if Germany were to support Britain there. (17)
      This was not exactly what Bismarck had expected from Britain.
When the Russian ambassador, a few hours after hearing about the
British reply, came to Bismarck with accommodating proposals of re-

newing the League of the Three Emperors of 1873, Bismarck no longer
felt Germany depended on British support.   When Disraeli became
more forthcoming and offered an alliance with Germany against Russia,
two weeks later, Bismarck apparently did not even bother to reply.
He hoped that Germany would be able to cope with both Russia and
France without British support. (18)   Bismarck's hesitation was
explained by his fear that the Liberals under Gladstone would win in
forthcoming General Elections.   If Gladstone returned to power it
would be improbable that Britain would join an alliance against the
French Republic for the conservation of Turkey, since Gladstone was
attacking Turkey in his election speeches.   In March 1880 a Liberal
majority government under Gladstone returned to the House of Commons,
thus confirming Bismarck's fears.   The possibility of Britain joining Germany or the Dual Alliance in one form or another was thus
forestalled for the foreseeable future.

Happier perspectives, however, seemed to be opened by offers
made by Russia in Berlin on 27 September 1879, to renew the League
of the Three Emperors, which had just been shattered by the oriental crisis.   After prolonged negotiations to overcome Austria's
reluctance to come to terms with Russia, the old relationship of
the three conservative Empires was superficially reconstructed on
18 June 1881 by another Treaty of the Three Emperors.   Bismarck
had recommended this to his Emperor with three arguments: (i) peace
between the three great monarchies would be secured for years,
because Tsar Alexander III who succeeded his father after the
assassination of Alexander II, was known to be reliable, and a
rupture between the three monarchies 'would considerably shake the
strength of the monarchical principle in Europe vis-à-vis the revolutionary one; (ii) the 'danger of a Franco-Russian coalition
would be completely eliminated and France's peaceful disposition
towards us will be virtually ensured'; (iii) the 'attempts of the
anti-German war party in Russia to influence the decisions of the
young Tsar' would be foiled by the pledges given by Alexander III.
(19)   For Bismarck the new treaty made by the three conservative
monarchies restored an ideal constellation.   The two 'German' or
'mid-European' Empires were, compared with the first League of the
Three Emperors, attached to each other with special links, i.e. the
Dual Alliance.

The Treaty of 1881 was not an alliance, but contained only the
agreement to remain neutral in the case of an attack by a fourth
power and to try and settle all problems concerning the Balkans and
Turkey.   An additional protocol specified further points: Austria-
Hungary reserved the right to annex Bosnia-Herzegovina at a suitable
time.   Russia was prepared to concede to Austria-Hungary the right
of occupation, not of annexation of the Sanjak (district) of Novibazar.   The three powers had nothing against a future unification
of Bulgaria with East Rumelia, but not with Macedonia (20) a delicate compromise between Russia and Austria.   The special protocol
mentioned the points which would lead to future crises in the
Balkans: Bosnia-Herzegovina, the Sanjak of Novibazar, Bulgaria
and Macedonia.   The treaty was shattered by the Bulgarian crisis
of 1885 and lasted no more than four years.

After the restoration of the League of the Three Emperors closer
links with Britain were improbable due to the presence of Russia.

The idea of extending the Dual Alliance would only be possible if
medium and smaller-sized Powers were to join it.   Bismarck did not
actively encourage new allies, but several candidates came forward,
e.g. Roumania in 1880 and Turkey and Italy in 1881.   After the loss
of Bessarabia to Russia at the Congress of Berlin, Roumania feared
that Russia wished to create direct territorial communications with
Bulgaria by the annexation of the Dobrudja.   Roumania wanted to protect herself against such a loss by joining the Dual Alliance.
During the negotiations leading to the Treaty of the Three Emperors
in 1881, Bismarck hesitated to commit himself, but promised the
support of the Dual Alliance if Roumania were threatened by Russia.
The dynastic links with the Catholic line of Hohenzollerns on the
Roumanian throne and the chance to block direct territorial communications between Russia and Bulgaria with Roumania's help were good
enough reasons to work together with Roumania.   It was only in
October 1883 that Roumania was allowed to join the Dual Alliance.
(21)   The political effect of this move, however, proved to be
marginal in the long run.   In 1914 Roumania remained neutral, for
the same reasons as Italy, and entered the war on the side of the
Entente in August 1916.

Applications from Italy and Turkey were more difficult to handle.
Turkey was weakened through her internal structure and the danger
of being attacked from outside.   When the Turkish government asked
Berlin for help to fight against France in North Africa in December
1881, Bismarck refused promptly and energetically.   He told the
Turks he 'was firmly convinced that France harboured no designs on
Tripoli'. (22)   Even when the Turkish Empire became highly attractive to German 'Weltpolitik' after 1895-6, Germany did not enter
into a formal alliance with Turkey until 2 August 1914, when the
German government was desperately trying to pick up allies wherever
they could be found. (23)

THE TRIPLE ALLIANCE, 1882

Bismarck's mixed feelings about the link between Italy, Germany and
Austria-Hungary stemmed from different reasons, one of them being
Italy's long coastline which made her vulnerable to attack by sea.
A more fundamental reason was Germany's ambivalent position towards
Italy for historical and ideological reasons. (24)   Although Italy
had achieved national unity only a few years before Germany and although she had been a direct ally to Prussia in 1866 and an indirect
one in 1870, Bismarck did not think Italy worthy of becoming an
ally of the German Empire because of her liberal character and parliamentary structure.   Bismarck did not believe in the future of
the Italian monarchy and he feared that 'an Italian Republic would
go together with the French Republic'. (25)   When the Italian
Ambassador to Berlin formally asked to be accepted into the Dual
Alliance on 31 January 1882, Bismarck pointed out that Italy's parliamentary constitution was an obstacle to be overcome.   Giving
Britain as an example, Bismarck explained that such a parliamentary
structure would not guarantee a continuously conservative foreign
policy.   Bismarck also stressed that 'Italy offered ... the
spectacle of cabinets drifting continuously to the Left'.   When

the Ambassador assured him that his king could firmly rely on the
army to pursue a policy acceptable to Bismarck, the German Chancellor pushed his conservative flippancy so far as to 'allow himself',
as he put it, the ironical 'hint that a Monarch who is wearing
civilian clothes does not do everything in his power to keep in
contact with his army'. (26)   It was difficult for the German
military monarchy where not only the Emperor but even his first
ministers often appeared in military uniform in public, to place
confidence in a liberal and parliamentary monarchy, with a king at
its head who preferred civilian clothes to military uniforms.

Bismarck was not completely hostile.   After humiliating the
Italian ambassador Bismarck passed on the Italian request to
Vienna.   Because of the Italian irredenta in Austria (Trentino) and
competing interests on the Adriatic Coast and in the Balkans, Italy
and Austria-Hungary had to be organized before the Dual Alliance
could be enlarged.   Bismarck saw the strategical advantage of
having Italy allied against France, while Italy was anxious to join
Germany and Austria-Hungary for reasons of foreign and domestic
policy. (27)

The Triple Alliance Treaty was signed on 20 May 1882, without
great enthusiasm on the part of Austria-Hungary and Germany.   The
Triple Alliance would, however, give Germany more power and prestige than the Dual Alliance, which remained intact.   Bismarck's
mistrust of democratic trends in Italy and the wish of the Italian
monarchy to strengthen its position at home through close contact
with the Dual Alliance, explain why the ideological motivation was
mentioned in the official text.   The preamble to the treaty explicitly states that the three monarchs wished 'to increase the
guarantee of general peace, to strengthen the monarchical principle
and to keep intact by that the social and political order of their
states'. (28)   The Triple Alliance was made to defend the social
and political 'status quo' in the three monarchies and perfectly
reflected Germany's conservative foreign policy at this time.

The partners were forbidden to enter into alliances or agreements
with any other partner (Art. I).   In the case of France attacking
Italy or Germany without provocation, the country that was not under
attack was pledged to give military support (Art. II).   The 'casus
foederis' was only to be invoked if one or two partners were
attacked simultaneously by two or more Great Powers, without having
been provoked by any of the partners in the Triple Alliance (Art.
III).   If any partner of the Triple Alliance should be forced into
a preventive war, the other partners were pledged to remain neutral
and were expected to give their partner military support at a later
date (Art. IV).   Any threat to security was to be met by agreeing
to military cooperation, if this was thought to be necessary.
Armistice and peace were only to be decided upon by all three partners and separate decisions were ruled out (Art. V).

Until now, German historians have always interpreted the Triple
Alliance as being defensive.   It may have been defensive at the
beginning, but Article IV could be turned into an instrument of
aggression: an 'unprovoked attack' on one of the partners of the
Triple Alliance could always be camouflaged by an alleged threat
from outside. (29)   The First World War, indeed, broke out in 1914
without a clear 'casus foederis' stated in the Triple Alliance.

Austria-Hungary was not attacked by two or more Great Powers, and provocation came from Austria-Hungary. Neither Austria-Hungary nor Italy were obliged to assist Germany, if it chose to interpret the situation of July 1914 as one to justify a 'preventive war'. In this case, other partners could have remained neutral. Even Article I of the Dual Alliance did not cover the situation, because neither Austria-Hungary nor Germany were attacked in 1914 by Russia 'against the hope and the sincere wish of the two contracting parties'. Russia was provoked into mobilizing against the Dual Alliance by Germany and Austria-Hungary. (30)

The direct consequence of these alliances was that after the Reich was founded in 1871, a new concentration of power in central Europe under German leadership came into being. When the Reich tried to make the Triple Alliance the basis for Germany's 'Welt-politik', this action almost inevitably provoked an alliance between the Great Powers in eastern and western Europe. (31)

Chapter 5

COLONIAL EXPANSION AS A FIRST STEP TOWARDS IMPERIALISM, 1882-5

The Triple Alliance, broadening Germany's position on the Continent, had scarcely been concluded when the 'Scramble for Africa' opened a new phase of international Imperialism. Germany was asked indirectly if it wanted to join the colonial adventure or not, and it did, in a wave of enthusiasm for colonial expansion. The facts are clear enough, (1) but varying motives for colonial expansion have been attributed to Bismarck. The personal ideas of the German Chancellor are, of course, not irrelevant in explaining German foreign policy, but in the final analysis, they remain of secondary importance. From a certain point onwards, the German Chancellor had to conform to dominating trends in German society, whatever his personal views may have been. It is more than a coincidence that in 1882 the first political pressure group with a kind of mass appeal was founded, the 'Deutscher Kolonialverein'. It propagated colonial expansion and was certainly instrumental in promoting it to a considerable degree.

More important than Bismarck's subjective outlook, which was probably overridden by collective trends in German society at this period, was the state of German society in the early 1880s. Certain economic, political and psychological factors were at this time strong enough to render colonial expansion not only possible, but from the standpoint of Germany's ruling classes even necessary. Industrial expansion in Germany created increasing demands for raw materials and markets for industrial goods. A feeling of power and pride after the founding of the Reich made for increased self-confidence. Finally, the necessity was felt to divert the attention of the emerging working class from domestic tensions and problems by a spectacular foreign policy abroad. All of those factors were used to justify German 'Weltpolitik' after 1896. The importance of the comparatively short spell of German colonial expansion must not be judged by the modest size of colonial territories occupied, but by its function as a kind of dress rehearsal for the actual 'Weltpolitik' more than a decade later. (2)

When searching for Bismarck's motives for his colonial policy, several explanations have been offered: a favourable constellation in foreign policy; domestic policy; a socio-economic factor connected with emerging Imperialism. (3) Taking Bismarck's complex

character and his tactical flexibility into account, we may presume
that a combination of all three factors influenced the Chancellor in
his final decisions.   One interpretation, however, may be excluded
as definitely wrong - the idea that Bismarck had wanted colonies for
a long time and was only waiting for the best moment to secure them
in a bold diplomatic action. (4)

OVERSEAS INTERESTS BEFORE IMPERIALISM

The last two explanations taken together give the most satisfactory
answer to the question of German motivation for colonial policy.
They also allow us to go beyond the search for Bismarck's personal
views and to look for more collective and substantial reasons, which
are to be found in the structure of German society in 1880.
Prussia's first colonial adventure around 1700 had demonstrated the
futility of participating in expansion overseas without a sufficient
territorial basis, without adequate harbour facilities (the small
port of Emden was not large enough) and without a seafaring population at home.   Above all, Brandenburg-Prussia had become a 'colonial power' in 1683 only with the help of Holland, who sublet, as
it were, territory on the Gold Coast and in the West Indies enabling
Brandenburg to take a share of the transatlantic slave trade and of
the lucrative plantations in the West Indies which were run on
African slave labour, recruited from West Africa. (5)   The second
phase of colonialism was characterized - after the abolition of the
slave trade and slavery - by the actual seizure of territories in
Africa by European Powers, starting in 1874 with the conquest and
annexation of Ashanti.   Germany thought it was entitled to share
in the possession of colonial territories.   In contrast to Brandenburg-Prussia two centuries earlier, it was by now one of the Great
Powers in Europe, with a considerable coastline and seafaring population.   Germany was now in a position to deal with other colonial
Powers on an equal footing.
    The first tentative moves towards colonial expansion before 1871
only show that Prussia's geographical and economic basis was still
too weak, before the Reich was founded.   In 1859 Prussia had
played an active, but modest part in the pro-imperialist policy of
the 'open door' towards China, followed by a Prussian expedition
to the Far East one year later.   Early in 1871 war aims were ten-
tatively formulated with a view to demanding territories for
Germany in Indochina. (6)   After 1871 the trading interests of the
individual firms, based mainly in Hamburg and Bremen, were as a
rule closely linked with shipping lines - Hapag in Hamburg and
Norddeutscher Lloyd in Bremen - originally founded to carry emi-
grants from Germany to America.   After 1871 they followed the
development of trade into the Pacific (Samoa, New Guinea) and
Africa.   Hamburg's material interest in the colonial trade was
mainly concerned with exporting the cheapest kind of spirits to
West Africa.   British humanitarian groups, in the tradition of the
Abolitionists, promptly organized their famous 'Anti-Liquor
Campaign' to protect Africans against the devastating effects of
that alcohol, known as 'Fusel' in Germany.   Its main source was
the potato 'schnapps', produced by many Junkers east of the River

Elbe, (including Prince Bismarck himself) who in this way acquired
additional liquid capital to ward off the worst consequences of the
permanent structural crisis in German agriculture. (7)

German individual interests overseas had grown, in the age of
free trade, without direct protection or aid from the state.   This
is why German overseas interests up to 1870 had, as it were, sought
the protection of the British flag.   As long as Free Trade ruled
supreme there was no need for direct intervention or protection by
the German Empire.   The Empire could, on the contrary, rather disturb established patterns and structures than actually strengthen
them.   The situation changed, however, when Germany introduced its
system of agrarian and industrial protective tariffs in 1879.
German commercial interests overseas soon developed the tendency to
seek for intervention of the new German state into the economic
process not only at home, but also abroad.   The partition of the
globe into spheres of indirect influence, commercial penetration
and colonial possessions through emerging Imperialism also provoked
German merchants overseas to ask for a clear definition and protection of areas where Germany, i.e. they themselves, would be able to
enjoy paramount influence.   The modern state became one of the most
important instruments for securing and consolidating private economic interests.   In Germany, as in other Imperialist countries, the
state acted as a powerful agent for Imperialism, always in the name
of increased welfare and prestige for the whole nation, although
only small capitalist groups profited directly from colonial expansion.

Even increased pressure from the comparatively marginal economic
interests overseas would probably not have been strong enough to
overcome Bismarck's scepticism as to the value of colonies for
Germany.   He was perhaps convinced by the class argument, which
the spokesmen for colonial expansion never failed to mention.
Even in 1858 Bismarck was impressed by the argument that activities
of the state overseas would enhance Prussia's prestige and would reduce discontent at home. (8)   What may have been true for Prussia,
which was then in uncertain rivalry with Austria, must have been
even more true for the powerful German Empire with an increasing
industrial population, increasing social problems and a disconten-
ted, growing, working-class movement.

In July 1879, the same month in which the protective tariffs
were passed by the Reichstag, (9) Bismarck for the first time took
an interest in pro-colonial activities through his sponsorship of
the Samoa Bill.   The Chancellor pleaded for a takeover of the
plantations and settlements from the then bankrupt Hamburg firm
Godeffroy in Samoa.   Bismarck wanted to save the vested interest
of a private firm by using funds from the Reich in order to uphold
German trade through private initiative.   The Samoa Bill was rejected by the Reichstag in 1880.   The opponents to the Bill were
mainly the Liberals, who opposed colonial adventures.   However,
during the struggle for the Samoa Bill, a colonial movement in
Germany began to crystallize.   Even the 'Norddeutsche Allgemeine
Zeitung', the semi-official mouthpiece of the Imperial government,
called the Samoa Bill of April 1880 a 'prelude' to German colonial
policy. (10)

But even then, Bismarck still opposed the establishment of

regular German colonies overseas.   By the end of 1880, he decided
against supporting a new project to be financed by the 'Disconto
Gesellschaft', one of the leading German banks, in New Guinea.   On
the other hand, Bismarck introduced a Bill in the Reichstag to sub-
sidize a German shipping line to the Far East, following the precedents of other European countries with colonial interests.   The
Bill failed in 1881, but was reintroduced and passed in 1885.   By
then the radical change in official colonial policy had already
occurred and found its formal expression through Germany's seizure
of several colonies, mainly in Africa.   In 1881 even the Hamburg
merchants had been against the principle of subsidies from the
Reich for the shipping line to the Far East.   By 1885 they came
round to accepting financial support from the Reich, after the long-
term effect of the Great Depression after 1873 had reduced their
former confidence in Free Trade.

GERMANY'S PART IN THE 'SCRAMBLE FOR AFRICA', 1884-5

After industry had gone over to protective tariffs in 1879, it was
also more responsive to appeals from colonial enthusiasts who organized the 'Deutscher Kolonialverein' (1882) and the 'Gesellschaft für Deutsche Kolonisation' (1884).   They succeeded in
mobilizing a wave of colonial enthusiasm within Germany and in en-
listing financial support from business circles as founder members
of the two organizations.   Their main argument was that German
economy would be able to break through the long-term relative
stagnation only by securing sources for raw materials together with
markets for Germany's industrial finished goods.   For domestic
consumption they had in the years of the Anti-Socialist Laws an
additional argument on hand, which had even impressed Bismarck
twenty-five years earlier, i.e. that colonial expansion abroad
would release pressure at home.   The colonial lobby adroitly
appealed to national ambition and vanity when pointing out the
fact that other nations were carving up the world and that the
German Empire could not be excluded from such a movement.
    In 1880 the 'scramble for Africa' began in earnest. (11)   France
advanced from the Senegal to the Niger, established her Protectorate
over Tunisia one year later and began French colonial expansion from
the Congo to Central Africa in 1882.   In the same year Britain
occupied Egypt.   Leopold II of Belgium established, by means of a
private company concerned with furthering for his own private
interests, the Congo Free State. (12)   By this time, precedents
abroad were powerful enough for Germany's ruling class to decide to
take their share in carving up the colonial world.   Wherever possible, the model of the Godeffroy-Samoa Bill was applied.   Claims
by German private or corporate interests were placed under the
'protection' of the German Empire.   Another variant was to send
Imperial commissioners into African territories which had not yet
been claimed by a European power as its colonial possession, but
where German explorers had left at least a shadow of plausibility
for German claims of sovereignty.
    Between April 1884 and May 1885, Germany took over its most im-
portant colonial possessions. (13)   In April 1884, Lüderitz Bay

was placed under Imperial 'protection'; the Bremen merchant
Lüderitz had 'purchased' a strip of land from the Nama tribe under
false pretences. He spoke about 'miles' and implied that he meant
English miles. It was realized too late that he meant German miles
which were about four times longer. German South-West Africa, now
known as Namibia, developed from this fraudulent transaction. (14)
In July 1884 the German explorer Gustav Nachtigal returned to Togo
and the Cameroons, not only in the interest of some Hamburg firms,
e.g. the Woermann shipping line, but also as German Consul-General,
with the Imperial flag and a mandate from Bismarck to place the
territory under German sovereignty. He had travelled through this
part of Africa as the first European 'explorer'. (15)   In February
1885 German East Africa, now Tanzania, was 'acquired' by the German
Empire. Carl Peters, probably the shadiest character of all German colonial 'pioneers', had 'acquired' large tracts of land a year
earlier from tribal chiefs with the help of fraudulent 'treaties'.
Carl Peters's record of treating the Africans brutally was so bad
that, under pressure from the Socialist members of the Reichstag,
he was recalled from his post as first Governor of German East
Africa.   (After his recall, he offered his semi-private colonial
empire to the Reich who gladly accepted it throught its Chancellor.) (16)
    Finally, in May 1885, the Reich took over the north of New
Guinea, where the 'Disconto Gesellschaft' had been active earlier
at their own risk and initiative. (17)
    Wherever German colonies developed out of private colonial com-
panies, e.g. Tanganyika or New Guinea, comparisons can be made with
the 'Chartered Companies' of the Mercantilist era, which were
characteristic of Dutch colonial expansion in the seventeenth century, of British in the seventeenth and eighteenth centuries, but
also in early British colonialism around 1900 (Cecil Rhodes's
chartered companies). The case of Carl Peters, the German Rhodes,
shows the difference between British and German colonial rule, at
least in Africa. The other German colonies in Africa were
'acquired' through no less doubtful methods than German East Africa,
but by less disreputable people than Carl Peters. Nachtigal in
particular enjoyed high prestige as an explorer and the first
Imperial Commissioner to Togo and the Cameroons.
    The sudden spurt of German colonial expansion in 1884-5 was only
made possible by favourable conditions at home and abroad. In
1884 Germany's domestic policy was still influenced by the effects
of the changeover from Free Trade to Protective Tariffs and the
resulting split between the National Liberals and the struggle
against the Socialists. Bismarck was interested in uniting the
reliably patriotic parties, the Conservatives and right-wing
National Liberals, against the left-wing Liberals and the Socialists.
The new enthusiasm for colonial policy could be ideally exploited
as a form of agitation against the domestic 'enemies of the Reich'
and to produce a majority in the Reichstag, consisting of Conservatives and right-wing National Liberals. This idea materialized
in the Reichstag elections of 1884, as Bismarck had hoped. Some
contemporary observers were so surprised by Bismarck's sudden con-
version to colonial expansion that they suspected him of using the
colonial question merely as an election stunt against the left

wing.   This tactical manoeuvring may certainly have played its part, but it also fitted into the concept of what has recently been called somewhat misleadingly 'Social Imperialism'. (18)   There were no contradictions between trying to direct internal tensions abroad and strengthening those political parties who were anxious to help Bismarck in fighting political discontent at home.

Another precondition of colonial success in 1884-5 was, of course, a favourable situation in foreign policy.   Just as in 1870-1, the other powers, who could have prevented German colonial expansion, had either neutralized themselves through rivalry or had exposed themselves through colonial activities to such a degree that they even became susceptible to pressure from Germany.   This was particularly true of Britain, the potential chief rival and opponent to Germany's colonial expansion.   Normally Britain could have blocked any German colonial activity by veto or, if necessary, with the help of the Royal Navy.

The occupation of Egypt in 1882 and rivalry with France over colonies in Africa, and with Russia in Asia, had absorbed British forces with the result that Britain was not interested in additional frictions or conflicts with Germany over comparatively unimportant matters.   Bismarck brazenly raised the spectre of British isolation in the colonial question.   At the Berlin Conference of 1884-5 which formally decided and legalized the partitioning of Africa among the Imperialist Powers, Germany ostentatiously allied itself with France against Britain. (19)   This had the additional advantage for Germany that French wounds inflicted by the Alsace-Lorraine question would be healed by encouraging France's colonial ambitions under the leadership of Jules Ferry, the Prime Minister. The only other Great Power who could have blocked German colonial expansion was Russia.   Russia, however, was engaged in Asia against Britain and was therefore in no position to block Germany in Africa, especially as the renewal of the Treaty of the Three Emperors in 1884 had, for the time being, reaffirmed favourable conditions for Germany.

After conditions at home and abroad for German colonial expansion had sufficiently matured, Bismarck was forced into action more through the growing colonial movement in Germany than through his own enthusiasm.   Bismarck was able to seize his chance to found the German colonial 'Empire' without any direct serious complications.   Divergences with Britain over the colonial question remained unimportant.   They were later reactivated and contributed to resentment and rivalry on both sides of the Channel.

THE GERMAN COLONIES SEEN IN PERSPECTIVE

The material effect of German colonies remained marginal throughout the period of the Second Reich.   Investments in the colonies were slight because the colonies were expected to pay their own way. Most of what Germany invested were payments for the establishment of the military and of infrastructure, e.g. railways, which were important for strategical reasons.   German colonial methods were a combination of paternalism, inexperience, arrogance, exploitation and racism, which naturally led to large-scale revolts among the

African population in all the German colonies except Togo.   The
most famous revolts shook German South-West Africa and East Africa
around 1890 and 1904-6.   They were suppressed with singular bru-
tality, culminating in the attempted genocide of the Herero people
in the Kalahari Desert by Admiral von Trotha in 1905. (20)

Revolts in German colonies brought the scandalous methods of
German colonial administration and German settlers to light.
After complaints in the Reichstag, reforms were introduced in 1907
by the first Secretary for the colonies, von Dernburg.   Although
investments in the colonies were slightly increased, they still remained an economic failure.   They neither supplied raw materials
in sufficient or expected quantities - the discovery of large dia-
mond fields in South-West Africa in 1907 was the only exception up
to 1914 - nor could a sparse African population, exploited, disci-
plined and decimated by roughshod colonial methods, be expected to
become consumers for German industrial goods to a degree which
would make additional investments in the colonies worthwhile.
Colonial lobbyists in Germany probably did not believe in the
illusions of economic prosperity in the colonies being profitable
to the German Fatherland.   Colonial propaganda and traditional
German historiography continued to spread the myth of benevolent
German colonial rule to justify Germany's colonial expansion and
claims to recover colonies lost at Versailles at a time when the
truth about German colonial methods and their effects on Africans
were well known outside Germany. (21)

The real significance of the short period of colonial acquisition between 1884-5 for German foreign policy was that the German
'Weltpolitik' in the following decades received a material basis
through colonial possessions.   Although the colonies were small
and scattered when compared to the British or French colonial
empires, they remained marginal in their economic importance.   The
colonies constituted a constant challenged to German 'Weltpolitik'
in future to enlarge and unify the geographically scattered and
comparatively poor colonies into one solid block.   German colonial
propaganda had even invented a name for it - 'Mittelafrika' - the
colonial equivalent to 'Mitteleuropa', the territorial basis of
'Weltpolitik' on the European continent itself.   'Mittelafrika'
became therefore, implicitly or explicitly, the overall aim of
German 'Weltpolitik' and colonial expansion before 1914 (22) and
became one of Imperial Germany's official war aims in the First
World War. (23)   One of the most important and most coveted
prizes was the Belgian Congo, or rather Katanga, with its rich
copper mines.   The Portuguese colonies in Africa were thought
necessary to round off and consolidate Germany's colonial empire in
Africa.

If the acquisition of German colonies in 1884-5 did not create
special problems at the time in the field of foreign policy, the
colonial question could always be used later as a diplomatic lever
against Britain or France.   France could be diverted from Alsace-
Lorraine;   later on German ambition for colonial compensation in
the Congo region in 1911 created tension between France and Germany. (24)   Pressure on Britain over Egypt or an attempt to reach
an understanding with Britain over the division of Portuguese colonies in Africa between Germany and Britain could be used either to
blackmail or to neutralize Britain. (25)

After the initial burst of colonial enthusiasm in Germany was over, and when it became clear that they would not become an econo- mic Eldorado, German colonies were the ruins of a more grandiose scheme and a permanent challenge to fulfil the great project of 'Mittelafrika'.   They also served as an additional pretext for building a strong fleet and the acquisition of naval bases all over the world.

In the First World War German colonies were lost fairly quickly: Togo, Kiaochow, New Guinea and Samoa in 1914, German South-West Africa in 1915, Cameroons in 1916, and German East Africa in 1917. What remained was the myth of model German colonial rule and German society's resentment over the loss of colonies, which was legalized at Versailles in 1919.   Between the two World Wars this resentment was articulated by constant demands from Germany to have the moral right to colonies and to have them restored to the Fatherland. (26)

Chapter 6

THE TANGLE OF ALLIANCES, 1885-90

Bismarck's last five years as Chancellor have traditionally been thought of as the climax of his achievements as a European states- man. His system of alliances for the consolidation of Germany's position as a latent hegemonial power was completed in 1887 by the Re-insurance Treaty with Russia and the Mediterranean Entent between Britain, Italy and Austria-Hungary. In reality, Bismarck desperately tried to juggle with new treaties in order at least to postpone the breakdown of his whole concept, as the alliance between Russia and France became a more and more threatening possibility.

CRISES ON TWO FRONTS - BOULANGER AND BULGARIA, 1887

The alliance between France and Russia could be considered normal according to the rules of power politics, first formulated by Machiavelli: Your neighbour's neighbour is your natural ally. The Franco-Russian alliance had been foreseen in 1871 as a logical consequence of France's defeat and loss of Alsace-Lorraine. (1) It was also logical, because France and Russia had no common fron- tiers, no serious clash of interests. On the contrary, they matched each other in their economic structures almost ideally. As a half-industrialized society France had accumulated surplus capital which was crying out for investment, while Russia, in the early stages of industrialization, needed liquid capital very badly for building factories and railways for economic and military reasons. Ideological considerations and constitutional differences remained secondary to economic considerations and political aims from 1892 onwards.

Neither Bismarck nor an even greater political genius at the head of German foreign policy could probably have prevented the elementary change on the European scene - an alliance between Russia and France. The price would have been drastic moderation or even a complete change in foreign policy and the structure of the new Reich - something unthinkable for the official spokesmen of the ruling class in Germany. Thus Bismarck failed in his short- term aim of isolating France and keeping her from entering into an alliance with Russia, not only because of the foolishness of his

successors, but also because of the very structure of the German
Reich. His failure became even more serious, as German foreign
policy after Bismarck proved unable to adjust itself to the new situation after the Franco-Russian Dual Alliance of 1892-4.
Bismarck's foreign policy between 1885 and early 1890 was thus dictated by the need to ward off his 'cauchemar des coalitions', (2)
the coalition between Tsarist Russia and Republican France.

Germany's position after the conclusion of colonial expansion in
May 1885 appeared stronger than ever before. In November 1884 a
meeting of the three Emperors at Skiernewice renewed the Treaty of
1881 for another three years, thus consolidating the alliance
between the three great conservative monarchies in central and
eastern Europe in an impressive manner. In July 1885 the Liberals
under Gladstone were defeated by the Conservatives under Salisbury,
thus presenting an opportunity for a better relationship with
Britain. Two months after the change of government in Britain,
however, Bismarck's system of alliances suffered heavy blows, both
in East and West.

In September 1885 Bulgaria and East Roumelia united in a kind of
Bulgarian 'Risorgimento', destroying an important stipulation of
the 1878 Congress of Berlin. (3) The war between Bulgaria and
Serbia in 1885 resulted in Russia's support of Bulgaria and Austria-
Hungary's support of Serbia. The confrontation between the two
rival Great Powers in the Balkans finally and irreparably destroyed
the solidarity of the three conservative monarchies. Neither
Russia nor Austria-Hungary were willing, after tensions caused over
Bulgaria in 1885, to renew the Treaty of the Three Emperors in 1887.
The Berlin-Vienna-St Petersburg axis was broken, never to be re-
paired. Russia left the front of conservative empires and was
therefore free for other alignments. Germany could only try to
arrange for short-term bilateral understandings, i.e. the Reinsurance Treaty in 1887 (4) and the attempted alliance of Björkoe in
1905. (5)

Six months before the Bulgarian crisis erupted, the ministry of
Jules Ferry was defeated in France, in March 1885. Ferry's defeat
ended a short spell of diplomatic understanding between Germany and
France over colonial questions, and gave more freedom of action to
more chauvinist elements, in particular organized by the French
'Ligue des Patriotes'. Their demand for revenge against Germany
was combined with a conservative or even authoritarian programme at
home. The champion of this cause was, between 1886-7, the French
War Minister, General Boulanger. The ensuing crisis was settled
in May 1887 by the victory of saner Republican elements, culminating
in Boulanger's resignation. The heated agitation of French chauvinists made Bismarck pretend in autumn 1886 and early 1887 that he
feared the outbreak of another war between Germany and France. In
France public opinion became more conscious than ever that an
alliance with Russia would mean an end to the isolation imposed by
Bismarck's Germany. It was the eastern crisis which brought the
real threat to peace - war against Russia. (6)

The continuation of the Bulgarian crisis in 1886 brought Germany
into the position of having again to choose between Russia and
Austria-Hungary. When it was feared that Russian troops would
occupy Bulgaria, Vienna and London demanded a pledge from Berlin to

oppose the Russian advance in the direction of the Straits.
Bismarck was confronted by an awkward dilemma: if Germany decided
against Russia in the Bulgarian crisis, Bismarck would more or
less provoke the coalition of Russia and France.   On the other
hand, Bismarck did not wish to see Germany relegated to the position of Britain's agent on the Continent against Russia.   Bismarck,
on the contrary, was interested in Britain blocking the Russian
advance in the Balkans.   In this way he would not risk a final
break with Russia, driving her into the arms of France, and leading
to a war against Russia and France, while Austria-Hungary was militarily weaker than Germany. (7)

This was the complicated situation in Europe which gave rise to
the completion of Bismarck's complex system of alliances - the Reinsurance Treaty with Russia and the Mediterranean Entente in 1887.
Bismarck dealt with France in his usual manner: he met the
alleged threat of a French war of revenge (which, however, did not
materialize after Boulanger's fall in May 1887) by ostentatiously
strengthening the German army in March 1887 and by spectacular
military manoeuvres in Alsace.   The Chancellor accompanied the
display of military power by his assurance in parliament that he
had always opposed the idea 'to wage a war because later on it
might become inevitable and would have to be waged under less
favourable conditions'. (8)

His verbal rejection of preventive war did not stop him, however,
from announcing that, if war with France was inevitable and if
Germany were to emerge victorious, Germany would try to 'render
France incapable of attacking us for thirty years and to enable us
to guarantee our security against France for at least one generation'. (9)   In the first of his famous speeches in the Reichstag
on the military budget, on 11 January 1887, Bismarck aired several
subjects of German policy, which later became relevant in 1914:
preventive war, the elimination of France as a Great Power for a
generation and 'securities' for Germany. (10)   It is conceivable
that Bismarck's position of strength had a sobering effect on the
French bourgeoisie and may have helped to solve the Boulanger
crisis.   In the long run Bismarck's display of military power had
devastating effects on Germany itself.   His boasts about German
efficiency and military superiority in a speech on 6 February 1887,
together with his pride in the better 'material' of his officers
and noncommissioned officers, culminating in his slogan 'We Germans
fear God, but after that nothing in the world!', helped to create a
powerful arrogance which became so characteristic of the German
mentality from Bismarck's time into the second half of this century.

While Bismarck hoped to protect the German Empire against France
by relying on German military power alone, he mobilized all his
forces of diplomatic finesse against Russia, the potential enemy of
the dreaded war on two fronts.   On the one hand he refused to give
Britain and Austria-Hungary a pledge that Germany would intervene,
if Russian troops were to occupy Bulgaria. (11)   On the other hand
he sought to contain Russia by two moves: after the Treaty of
Three Emperors expired in 1887, Germany established a special bilateral link with Russia and encouraged an indirect coalition of
other powers against Russia.   The Reinsurance Treaty with Russia
and the Mediterranean Entente, so highly praised as the summit of

Bismarck's statesmanship, were nothing more than desperate stop-
gap measures to prolong and safeguard Bismarck's concept of conservative foreign policy.

CONTAINING RUSSIA: THE MEDITERRANEAN AGREEMENT AND THE REINSURANCE
TREATY; BAN TO LOANS FOR RUSSIA AND THE DEMAND FOR PREVENTIVE WAR,
1887

The Mediterranean Entente, which came into force before the Reinsurance Treaty, was not the result of German initiative, but
fitted neatly into Bismarck's whole concept and was encouraged by
him to show the other powers concerned that Germany could be counted
on as a sleeping partner in the arrangement.   Technically, the
Mediterranean Entente only consisted of an exchange of notes between
the Italian and British governments on 12 February 1887.   This
exchange was joined by Austria-Hungary in a similar form on 24
March the same year.   The Powers were united in their wish to preserve, if possible, the 'status quo' not only in the Mediterranean,
but also in the Aegean and the Black Sea.   If changes were unavoidable, the Powers wanted to be able to consult and support each
other.   Italy was concerned with British policy in Egypt and
Britain was interested in Italian policy in Tripoli and Cyrenaica.
The arrangement was primarily directed against Russia, but also
against France. (12)   The diplomatic barricade against Russia's
plans for Constantinople was fragile indeed, as the Entente did not
take the form of a treaty of alliance.   The British government
still refused to join an alliance, because parliament was against
the ratification of firm commitments.   Britain's government kept to
this policy up to 1914 and so influenced German foreign policy
during the same period by creating or preserving the illusion of an
Anglo-German entente. (13)
     Although Bismarck agreed with the intentions of the Mediterranean
Entente, he managed to weaken it even more by his Reinsurance Treaty
with Russia. (14)   This was the most disputed link in Bismarck's
chain of alliances.   It amounted to no more than a desperate
attempt to replace the 'constellation à trois' (Berlin, St Petersburg, Vienna) by an 'arrangement à deux' (Berlin, St Petersburg) for
as long as possible.   Bismarck did not want to break his communications with Russia because by doing so he would finally drive her
into an alliance with France.   The Reinsurance Treaty, concluded
on 18 June 1887, had a text similar to that of the 1881 Treaty of
the Three Emperors.   The two Powers reassured each other their
benevolent neutrality and their efforts to localize any conflict,
an exception being Germany's unprovoked attack on France and an
attack on Austria-Hungary by Russia. (15)   Germany thus avoided a
collision with obligations towards its ally Austria-Hungary, while
Russia considered future obligations towards her potential ally,
France.   In Article II Germany recognized Russia's position in the
Balkans and especially in Bulgaria.   Both Powers promised to allow
changes in the 'status quo' in the Balkans only after consultation
and agreement.
     So far, there was nothing problematical about the treaty.   But
in a strictly secret protocol to the treaty, which remained undis-

closed until the First World War, Germany and Russia formulated less defensive aims.   In the first point Germany pledged to support Russia against reinstatement of the Prince of Battenberg as Prince of Bulgaria.   In the second and last point Germany gave Russia a free hand to take over the Straits, if it was necessary for the defence of her interests. (16)   Resulting from this second point, the whole Reinsurance Treaty came into conflict with the Dual and Triple Alliances.   It also clashed directly with the aims of the Mediterranean Agreement, of which Germany, of only through its allies - Austria-Hungary and Italy - was an indirect partner.

The Reinsurance Treaty was the culmination of Bismarck's desperate juggling with powers, alignments and alliances in order to stave off the consequences of the founding of the Reich by military conquest, of the annexation of Alsace-Lorraine and of the formation of the Dual and Triple Alliances.   For Bismarck's loyal admirers the Reinsurance Treaty became an unerring secret weapon, rather like the Schlieffen plan twenty years later.   Because of its doubtful moral qualities, the Reinsurance Treaty was unable to prevent a 'rapprochement' between Russia and France.   Even after the conclusion of the secret treaty, tensions between Germany and Russia increased.   A press campaign in Russia against the background of the continuing Pan-Slav movement was a constant source of irritation to Germany.   More serious, however, was the escalation of measures taken by the governments against each other.   After the Prussian law for the settlement of Germans in the province of Posen in 1886, which was clearly directed against the Poles, the Russian government followed suit in May 1887 by banning all foreigners from buying real estate in Russia's western provinces.   Mostly Germans were hit by this move.   Germany retaliated a few months later, this time in the field of finance and commerce.   In March 1887 Germany had already considerably increased its agrarian tariffs made in 1879, with the result that Russia's export of surplus grain to western Europe was hit.   In November 1887, after an inspired and intensive press campaign in Germany, Bismarck ordered that Russian loans from the capital market in Berlin should be stopped.   This second economic blow within a year finally drove Russia into the French camp, although only for financial reasons.   From 1888 onwards Russia began to satisfy her demand for loans in Paris, where enough capital was available for investment.   The financial partnership was therefore the beginning of the political alliance between Russia and France. (17)

THE SPECTRE OF WAR ON TWO FRONTS

Tension between Germany and Russia had, in spite of the Reinsurance Treaty, risen to the point that towards the end of 1887, the German general staff once more advocated a preventive war, this time against Russia.   Moltke even pleaded for a winter campaign against Russia using the element of surprise.   Bismarck succeeded in calming the general staff, (18) as he had done in 1875, in the case of France, but in times of crisis the general staff would demand preventive war again, the last time a few weeks before the outrage of Sarajevo. (19)

The new crisis between Germany and Russia again brought up the question of relations with Britain.   With the help of the Mediterranean 'Entente', England had - at least where problems with Turkey and the Balkans were concerned - been indirectly linked with the Triple Alliance via Italy and Austria-Hungary.   The Italian and Austrian wish for a more precise formulation of British commitments in autumn 1887 came to nothing, because Britain did not want to act without Germany's support. (20)   Germany, at this time, was becoming increasingly paralysed by its monarchical structure.   Emperor Wilhelm I was not expected to live very much longer (he died in March 1888 at the age of nearly 91).   His successor, married to the eldest daughter of Queen Victoria, was supposed to have liberal inclinations, but was hopelessly ill.   He died in June 1888 of cancer.   His son, Prince Wilhelm, was notoriously unreliable and impetuous.   In spite of his family links with Britain he preferred a Russian reorientation to Germany's 'rapprochement' with liberal Britain.   Thus Britain's hesitation was all too understandable. (21)

When Bismarck turned to Salisbury, the Conservative Prime Minister, in a long letter on 22 November 1887, his aim was not to win Britain for an alliance with Germany, but only to persuade Britain into fulfilling the Italo-Austrian desire for more precision which had been expressed in 1887.   Bismarck was successful.   The relevance of Bismarck's move does not lie in this ephemeral diplomatic success, but can be seen from the reasons he gave to his British colleague.   Bismarck chose to expound the difficulty of the German situation with remarkable frankness.   He informed Salisbury about the Dual Alliance with Austria-Hungary and stressed the defensive character of German foreign policy, though admittedly founded on military power.   His words were in a similar vein to his speech in the Reichstag on 20 January 1887 where he spoke against France. (22) He spoke openly of his fear that a war on two fronts against France and Russia, even if Germany were to remain victorious, would always be a serious burden.   Germany, according to Bismarck, was interested in avoiding war with Russia 'as long as it is compatible with our honour and security and as long as the independence of Austria-Hungary, whose existence as a Great Power is for us a necessity of the first order, is not questioned'.   Bismarck continued in pleading for the strengthening of all powers who were capable of preventing Russia from starting war or of opposing Russia successfully in the case of war.

This is why German foreign policy will always be obliged to join a war, if the independence of Austria-Hungary were threatened by a Russian attack or if Italy were menaced with attack by French armies.   German policy, thus, is following, by sheer necessity, a course which is dictated to it by the political situation of Europe; it could be deflected from its course neither by the antipathies nor the sympathies of a Monarch or a First Minister.

Peace-loving as Bismarck's words may have been intended at the time, they contained elements of conflict for the future.   Once German statesmen had reached the conclusion that Bismarck's qualifying statements had become reality - that Austria's independence was threatened by Russia and that Germany's honour was at stake - the reservations about a war against Russia would have been removed.

This situation was reached in the summer of 1914, and German statesmen could always claim to act in accordance with the great Bismarck.

THE IMPERIAL CLAIM TO DEFEND THE CONSERVATIVE PRINCIPLE

Only a few months after Bismarck's letter to Salisbury, both Wilhelm
I and Friedrich III had died.   In June 1888 Wilhelm II succeeded to
the throne.   During 1888 foreign policy was almost suspended, as if
Europe and the cabinets of the Great Powers were watching the events
in Berlin in suspense, waiting until they could assess their political consequences.   In May 1888 Wilhelm II, then only Crown Prince,
had made it clear that he would give greater emphasis to military
considerations and to conservative principles.   Bismarck tried to
dampen the zeal of the young Emperor to use the usual round of first
visits to the Royal or Imperial Courts of Europe for spectacular
political demonstrations. (23)   His first State visit as Emperor
was to St Petersburg, and not to London, as his grandmother, Queen
Victoria had expected.   In explaining to the Queen his reasons for
giving Tsarist Russia priority over liberal Britain, Wilhelm II revealed his ideological motivations, which coincided with the general
structure of his own Empire.
    At the end of this month I shall inspect the fleet and take a
    trip in the Baltic where I shall hope to meet the Emperor of
    Russia which will be good for the peace of Europe and for the
    rest and quiet of my Allies.   I would have gone later if poss-
    ible but State interest goes before personal feelings and the
    fate which sometimes hangs over nations does not wait till the
    etiquette of court mourning has been fulfilled.   I deem it nec-
    essary to look out for dangers which threaten the monarchical
    principle from democratic and republican parties in all parts of
    the world. (24)
Wilhelm II saw himself in the role of the supreme guard to protect
conservative and monarchical principles.   The Kaiser became the
spokesman of the ruling classes in Germany, in spite of his many
personal shortcomings.
    Queen Victoria immediately grasped the political implications of
Wilhelm II's accession to the throne as she commented on his letter
by writing to her Conservative Prime Minister, Lord Salisbury: 'I
trust we shall be very cool, though civil, in our communications
with my grandson and Prince Bismarck, who are bent to the oldest
times of government.' (25)   The Queen's distate of the reactionary
turn in Germany 'to the oldest times of government' was apparently
shared by Salisbury.   In January 1889, when Bismarck offered an
alliance to Britain, which would have to be ratified by Parliament,
Salisbury reacted in such a restrained manner that his answer was
equivalent to a refusal.   Salisbury had little confidence in
Bismarck's policy, even though he may have complained to Herbert
von Bismarck, Bismarck's son and then Secretary of State in the
Auswärtiges Amt, that unfortunately, aristocracy was no longer
ruling, as in Pitt's times, but democracy. (26)   While the dreaded
alliance between Russia and France was looming on the horizon,
Bismarck clung to his hope of compensating it by an alliance with
Britain.   After his rebuff from Salisbury he had not the time or

occasion to try again.   When his successors in office did try, they did so only half-heartedly.   As a result, an alliance with Britain was out of the question within a few years after Bismarck's death. (27)

At the end of his superficially brilliant career Bismarck was on the brink of failure, although this became clear only a generation later.   The German Empire was nearing its climax of outward power and prestige, the 'Iron Chancellor' had not succeeded in overcoming the basic discrepancies of its structure at home or abroad.   In the long run, the hierarchical structure of a feudal-bourgeois monarchy could not be conserved against the rising forces of democracy and socialism.   France could not be kept in isolation forever.   In Russia the forces of democracy and revolution, whether in the guise of Pan-Slavism or Socialism, together with the forces of national emancipation in the Balkans could not be suppressed indefinitely. By stressing the conservative or even reactionary principles of the German Empire, Wilhelm II alienated the Reich from the liberal western Powers, who had no sympathy at all with the turbulent elements in Russia in the Balkans.   This was shown by Queen Victoria's sensitive reaction to her grandson Wilhelm II's policy.   Bismarck had neither been successful in preserving Germany's free hand on the Continent, nor in winning a first-rate ally in East or West. Instead, Germany had to be content with second-rate allies of doubtful value, i.e. Austria-Hungary and Italy.   Austria-Hungary in particular turned out to be more of a liability than an asset, as developments were to show before the outbreak of the First World War.   The inherent deficiences in the structure of the Reich left no other choice for foreign policy than to ally with a political corpse, and no diplomatic refinement could, in the long run, spirit away the basic weakness of German foreign policy, however powerful Germany may have seemed to be at the time.

The 'Grand Old Man' of German foreign policy was to fall over a question of his special domain. (28)   The decisive break between the Kaiser and the Chancellor occurred in March 1890 over the fear that a Russian attack was imminent.   This time the war scare had been provoked by alarmist reports from the German counsul in Kiev on extensive army manoeuvres in Russia, scheduled for summer 1890. When the Kaiser learned of the reports via the Auswärtiges Amt, he dramatized their relevance, coinciding with his intention formulated two years earlier as Crown Prince of putting more weight on military considerations.   Wilhelm II accused Bismarck of informing him insufficiently.   Bismarck's calming reassurances, made the same day, were in vain.   The last official exchange of correspondence between Kaiser and Chancellor was dated 17 March 1890.   One day later Bismarck offered his resignation, which the Kaiser accepted two days later.   The pilot was chased out of office before it became apparent that he had steered the German Empire into troubled waters.

Chapter 7

THE 'NEW COURSE'-
YEARS OF INDECISION, 1890-5

GERMANY AFTER BISMARCK

Bismarck's fall made a deep impression in Germany and Europe. For Europe Bismarck had become a kind of symbol for stability in Germany. The regret of seeing him fall was correspondingly great; as illustrated by the famous cartoon in 'Punch', 'Dropping the Pilot'. In Germany, however, the reaction was more or less characterized by a sigh of relief. The feeling had become widespread that Bismarck was blocking more and more the normal process of decision-making by trying to absorb even more ministerial responsibilities without being able to cope with new developments which were becoming increasingly complex. (1) The result was largely government by postponement, and the feeling of brooding stagnation, strengthened by the uncertainty of the death of two German Emperors - Wilhelm I and his son Friedrich III - and the arrival of young Kaiser Wilhelm II in 1888. The Bismarck cult emerged only a few months after his dismissal. It was a reaction of right-wing elements against Bismarck's successor as Chancellor, Caprivi, who was comparatively liberal in spite of being a Prussian general. (2)

The period between Bismarck's downfall and the inauguration of German 'Weltpolitik' in 1897-8 is one of transition and full of discrepancies. On the one hand, Bismarck's departure resulted in a more liberal policy, as suggested in the 'New Course' towards the Socialists and the working class. On the other hand, it liberated forces which, reacting to Caprivi's relative moderation, pressed for more reactionary and chauvinist policies at home and abroad. Caprivi's relative liberalism expressed itself in his refusal to prolong the discriminatory laws against the Socialists or to provoke a showdown with them that might have led to civil war with Germany's working class. He further introduced limited concessions for the Poles in Prussia, whose parliamentary representatives he needed, paradoxically enough, for the expansion of the Prussian army. Caprivi also tried to decentralize what Bismarck had overcentralized; he gave wider scope to the Secretaries of State, directly placed under the Chancellor, and in general to the Prussian Ministry. Finally, Caprivi tried to break the paralysing deadlock, resulting from the approximate balance of agrarian and

industrial forces within Germany's ruling class, (3) in favour of
the more modern section - industry and the population in the industrial centres.   To achieve this he reduced the agrarian tariffs,
introduced by Bismarck in 1879, (4) to attract cheaper grain from
abroad.   Prices for foodstuffs in the cities were thus lowered,
while the structural crisis of German agriculture was inevitably
sharpened, and Caprivi earned himself the hatred of German agriculture.   At the same time, Caprivi concluded long-term commercial
treaties with several European states.   He thus gave a vigorous
push to the German export industry and helped to overcome the relative stagnation or period of slow economic growth, known as the
'Great Depression'.
     Caprivi's foreign policy reflected to some extent the character
of his liberal domestic policies.   It may be summed up as an
attempt, although perhaps not a conscious one, to try to concentrate
Germany's forces in Central Europe and to forgo adventurous ambitions outside Europe.   The first visible expression of his increased caution abroad was the exchange of shadowy German claims to
Zanzibar in the Indian Ocean and to parts of Uganda in East Africa
for the material possession of the small, but strategically valuable
island of Heligoland in the North Sea, facing the mouths of the
Rivers Elbe and Weser. (5)   Although Bismarck had initiated the
transaction as early as 1884 and had been responsible for most of
the negotiations, while his successor only concluded them by reaching the Heligoland-Zanzibar Agreement on 1 July 1890, the wrath of
all colonialist, expansionist and imperialist-minded chauvinists in
Germany fell upon Caprivi.   The outcry of those elements against
the Heligoland-Zanzibar Agreement crystallized into the formation
of the Pan-German League, on a provisional basis in 1891, to be
made more permanent in 1894. (6)   The Pan-Germans became the most
influential political pressure groups in Imperial Germany and never
ceased to call for a more 'energetic' foreign policy of the German
Empire.
     Similarly, in reaction to Caprivi's favouring German industry,
the 'Bund der Landwirte' was organized in 1893 to represent agrarian interests.   It was organized mainly by and in the interest of
the Prussian Junkers east of the River Elbe.   They tried to give
their reactionary group an air of democratic mass support by also
appealing to the peasants and farmers all over Germany, who were,
indeed, the real victims of the structural crisis in German agriculture. (7)   The 'Bund der Landwirte' provided a kind of organized
basis for the Conservative Party, mostly in Prussia, while the Pan-
Germans tried to do the same with the educated middle class.   The
Pan-Germans had links with both industrial and agrarian interests,
with Ministries and the Court, but also with university circles.
They helped to create a favourable climate for 'Weltpolitik', and
once it had been inaugurated they constantly tried to egg on the
German government into even riskier policies.   During and after
the First World War, the Pan-Germans represented the respectable
wing of the proto-Fascist element in Germany.   They formed the
hard core of the 'Deutsche Vaterlandspartei', founded in 1917,
which became the most important forerunner of the Nazi Party in
1919.
     Another political pressure group, though only of regional impact,

was the 'Ostmarkenverein zur Förderung des Deutschtums', also founded
in 1894, as a pressure group against the Poles in the eastern provinces of Prussia. (8)   It had close contacts with the Pan-Germans.
One of the key leaders of Pan-Germans, Alfred Hugenberg, started his
political career in the Prussian 'Ansiedlungskommission für Posen
und Westpreussen', the official agency in Posen and West Prussia to
combat the extension of Polish land-holdings, set up by Bismarck in
1886 with a grant of 100 million marks.   During the First World War,
Hugenberg was a director with Krupp, and during the Weimar Republic
he became the leader of the conservative 'Deutschnationale Volks-
partei' in 1928, the greatest press lord in Germany and an ally of
Hitler in 1929, ending up as Minister of Economy in Hitler's first
Cabinet in 1933.   Pan-Germans were strongly represented in the
'Ostmarkenverein', which was one of the chief forerunners of Nazi
anti-Slav propaganda and policies.

THE NEW CONTINUITY: THE KAISER AND HOLSTEIN

It was into this ferment of social stress and political ideas,
expressed by new organizations of conservative-chauvinist character,
that young Kaiser Wilhelm II came into his own after Bismarck had
left the political scene.   He himself was the product of the new
German society.   Apart from his personal deficiencies, he represented the German Empire almost perfectly, in particular the aristo-
cratic-bourgeois amalgamation of Germany's ruling class. (9)   He
always saw himself as the highest feudal lord in the German Empire,
but he also acted occasionally as the highest-placed representative
of German industry abroad, in particular regarding underdeveloped
countries, such as Russia and Turkey.   In spite of his feudal background and ideals, he took an active interest in modernization,
e.g. industry, shipbuilding and varied technical innovations.   His
open mind for modern technical developments clashed with his
basically reactionary ideas in politics, which amounted to re-
establishing a kind of Divine Right of kings in the modern world of
rising democracy and socialism.   He was, indeed, 'bent on a return
to the oldest times of government', as his grandmother, Queen
Victoria, quickly discovered at the beginning of his political
career in 1888. (10)
     The Kaiser's personal unreliability, his unwillingness to square
alternatives and to choose between them, his combination of recklessness and touchiness, of arrogance and selfpity were representative of political thinking in Germany in the late nineteenth and
well into the twentieth century.   The British Ambassador to Berlin,
Sir Frank Lascelles, gave an apt description of the mind of Imperial
Germany, mirrored through its Emperor at the height of his power,
in 1908.
     In one respect the Emperor may perhaps be considered as a typical
     German.   Very shortly after my arrival in Berlin, M. Herbette,
     who was then the French Ambassador, described the Germans as
     being 'inconscients', a word for which I am unable to find an
     exact equivalent in English.   They were the most sensitive
     people in the world, and at the same time it would never enter
     into their heads that they could by any possibility be offensive

themselves, although in reality they often were.   It was not
long before I realized that the Emperor himself shared to a very
large extent the sensitiveness which M. Herbette considered a
characteristic of the German people generally. (11)
Despite his laziness in the most industrious and industrialized
nation of the Continent, Wilhelm II embodied the German Empire in
his own inimitable manner.   His physical deficiency was also symbolic: the left arm withered from birth was a handicap not to be
overcome.   The discrepancy between the modern material basis of
the Empire with its social and political structure, consisting of
both modern and antiquated elements, combined with hopelessly out-
dated political ideas and ambitions.   It was adequately embodied
and crowned by the Kaiser, 'the most brilliant failure', as his
uncle, the Prince of Wales, later King Edward VII, called him.
     The symbolic value of the Kaiser alone would suffice to justify
a rather detailed analysis of his complex personality and of his
position within a complicated social and political structure such
as the German Empire.   But the Kaiser also exerted a considerable
amount of influence on the formulation and execution of German
foreign policy, due to his personal will to rule and owing to the
cringing subservience of many German ministers, ambassadors,
generals and politicians in response to the demands of their
Imperial master.   In principle, Wilhelm II was for German 'Weltpolitik', and he took his part in key decisions before and during
the First World War.   His chief instruments were comments or instructions written as marginal notes on documents submitted to him.
At critical moments the Kaiser used to summon 'ad hoc' political
meetings with his political and/or military advisers.   Such meetings had not been envisaged by the Constitution; they were irregu-
lar and occasionally chaotic, also in a formal sense - as a rule,
no records were kept, thus making it difficult for the historian to
know what actually happened. (12)
     The Kaiser's individual weaknesses further aggravated the prob-
lems created by Germany's complex and contradictory structure.   His
brilliant but irritating rhetoric proved to be yet another millstone around Germany's neck.   It is doubtful whether a more
cautious and rational Emperor could have avoided the collision with
practically the whole world in the First World War, once Germany's
ruling class had decided on a course of imperialist 'Weltpolitik'.
The restraint from any Kaiser would probably only have angered the
ruling class and driven the Emperor into resignation or even abdication.   This would have resulted in the Kaiser's oldest son,
Crown Prince Wilhelm, a Pan-German, pursuing German imperialist
ambitions even more recklessly than his father actually did.   The
Kaiser alone was not responsible for German foreign policy between
Bismarck's dismissal and the First World War.   But German foreign
policy during this time bore the personal stamp of the Kaiser.
He found it more or less congenial and in keeping with his personal
ambitions and his style of behaviour, as he himself was the product
of Germany's ruling classes, whose upstart aspirations he articulated and tried to realize in his own way.
     During most of the Kaiser's reign in times of peace, there was
another element of personal continuity in German foreign policy.
Between 1890 and 1906, German foreign policy was greatly influenced

by the Director of the Political Department in the Auswärtiges Amt,
Friedrich von Holstein.   In contrast to his flamboyant Imperial
master, Holstein preferred to remain in the background, giving him
the air of an 'éminence grise'.   (13)   His importance was increased
by the fact that between 1890 and 1897 he was the only one in the
inner circle of the Wilhelmstrasse who had been in diplomatic service under Bismarck; Caprivi and his Foreign Secretary, Marschall
von Bieberstein, had no experience at all in foreign policy.   In
the past Holstein was made the great scapegoat of the failures of
German foreign policy under the Kaiser.   Modern research has done
him full justice.   Holstein was a complex figure, an odd mixture
of errors and penetrating insights.   A staunch conservative and
loyal monarchist, he saw some of the weaknesses of the German system
and of the Kaiser.   He often tried to warn and to correct mistakes,
but his criticism never transcended the system of the German Empire.
His errors of judgment, in particular when agreeing with the
Kaiser, contributed to the catastrophe of German 'Weltpolitik'
ending up in the First World War.

CAPRIVI: 'MITTELEUROPA' AS AN ALTERNATIVE TO 'WELTPOLITIK'

These preliminary remarks on the Kaiser and Holstein should make it
clear that Bismarck's departure from office in 1890 was not the
decisive turning-point in the history of German foreign policy as
has often been thought in the past, both by contemporary observers
and by historians.   Young Kaiser Wilhelm II may have introduced
new trends due to his personal flamboyance, but he always kept
within the general frame of the German Empire.   The Kaiser cheerfully tried to overcome apprehensions at home and abroad by proclaiming that 'the course remains unaltered.   Full steam ahead!'.
But was the course really the same?   In his domestic policy the
Kaiser had already inaugurated what he himself called the 'new
course'. (14)   In spite of the usual promises to follow former
policies, the four years of Caprivi's chancellorship and the first
two years under his successor Hohenlohe were a transitional period
in many ways.   Bismarck's policy of concentrating on Europe was
carried on by Caprivi, even if with different methods, but was
abandoned under Hohenlohe.   The result was a policy of open imperialism, known as 'Weltpolitik'.
     It is not surprising that this period of transition showed
different forces at work.   On one hand, there were those elements
that stood for imperialist expansion, i.e. for 'Weltpolitik' - the
Kaiser and his Court, the navy and heavy industry, the National
Liberals and the Pan-Germans.   On the other hand, Caprivi's policy
of restraint was supported by most of his government colleagues, by
the Catholic Centre Party, the left-wing Liberals, and the Socialists.   Although it was hardly articulated as a coherent programme
at the time, it could have opened up the chance for a workable
alternative to 'Weltpolitik' by abstaining from imperialist ambitions and concentrating Germany's energies on Europe.   Two possible
results would have been: (i) Germany would have kept the policy of
hegemony in Europe within bounds, avoiding a collision with other
World Powers; (ii) peaceful methods abroad and at home might have

effected the gradual transformation of the German Empire into a
truly peaceful Power.
   It is well known that the forces of militarism and imperialism
won the day in Germany, as their opponents were too weak to overcome the structure of the Empire from within.   The fact that only
the historian can detect the potential chances for a policy different from that actually followed, explains why the short span of
six years between 1890 and 1896 is so important and can easily be
misunderstood.   It was the only period between the wars of 1870-1
and 1914-18 that the German Empire was able to choose between two
alternatives with radically different effects.   An analysis of this
very complex situation is made even more difficult, because no open
and clear-cut debate on the two alternatives took place in German
society at the time.   Absurd as it may sound, the momentous
decision between 'Weltpolitik' and continental moderation, between
potential war and potential peace, was never discussed coherently,
either in public or behind closed doors.   At best exchanges of
statements on particular points took place, but even they still
need systematic treatment by future research in journals, books and
private papers.   So far, most of the attempt to reconstruct the
two political alternatives facing the German Empire between 1890
and 1895, has had to consist of theoretical deductions.
   Bismarck, as Chancellor of the German Empire, had largely succeeded in retaining his original policy of continental restraint,
apart from the short aberration of limited colonial expansion in
1884-5. (15)   Even in 1887, during the Boulanger crisis, he warned
against any policy based on pure power and prestige, in particular
against preventive war. (16)   Bismarck's words were more quoted
than heeded by Germans in years to come, perhaps because Bismarck
had also said words of contrary meaning on the problem of preventive
war, (17) and because his foreign policy had already pulled together
some of the explosive matter that was to erupt in the First World
War.   But as long as Bismarck remained in office, he managed to
withstand he pressure of the then unorganized forces which no longer
felt 'satiated'.   After his dismissal, however, these forces became
his allies against his successor Caprivi, who tried to keep to the
more rational ideas of Bismarck's policy after 1871, i.e. continental moderation.   In his resentment over his fall, Bismarck allowed
the incipient Pan-German movement to use him as their patron in
their struggle against the comparatively moderate Caprivi and his
successors, when they were reluctant to execute their wild variety
of German 'Weltpolitik'.
   Caprivi emerges as a potential alternative to 'Weltpolitik' by
following Bismarck's line as Chancellor.   One of the rare documents
of the time which analysed the situation, if only in the sketchiest
terms, laid down the alternatives, but at a time when Caprivi had
already been overthrown as Chancellor and when his policy was about
to be replaced by the new 'Weltpolitik'.   In 1896 Captain von
Müller, later Admiral and Chief of the Imperial Naval Cabinet for
many years, wrote in a private memorandum to Admiral Prince
Heinrich, the Kaiser's brother:
   General von Caprivi believed that Germany had no chance at all of
   becoming a world power, and consequently his policy was designed
   only to maintain [Germany's] position on the European continent.

He was therefore acting quite logically in working at home for
the strengthening of the army, limiting the navy to the role of
defending the coastline ... and seeking good relations with England as the natural ally against Russia, the country which
threatened Germany's position in Europe.

Caprivi's policy, now so widely ridiculed, would have been
brilliantly vindicated by history if the German people were not
coming to accept an entirely different opinion of their ability
and duty to expand than that expressed in our naval and colonial
development so far.... Now, the Caprivi policy has been officially abandoned, and the new Reich government will hesitantly put to
the nation the question - in the form of the new Navy Bill -
whether the other policy, 'Weltpolitik', really can be
adopted. (18)

Caprivi's position was too weak for his alternative to become the
long-term and clear-cut policy of the German Empire. 'Weltpolitik'
had to fail disastrously twice - in the First World War and in the
Second World War - resulting in fatal consequences for the German
Empire, before Caprivi's policy, then 'so widely ridiculed', began
to be 'brilliantly vindicated by history', because it now emerges
as the only real alternative to the policy of German self-destruc-
tion through 'Weltpolitik'.

THE KAISER'S NAPOLEONIC DREAMS AND REALITY - THE FRANCO-PRUSSIAN
DUAL ALLIANCE, 1892-4

Wilhelm II provoked considerable modification in Bismarck's policy
through his personal ambition and preoccupation with the military
factor. He was also caught between two conflicting aims, because
he wanted to be remembered in history as the Kaiser of Peace
('Friedenskaiser') and for strengthening his Empire ('Mehrer des
Reichs') at one and the same time. The result was that he failed
on both counts. After he had publicly professed his peaceful
intentions on the inauguration of the Reichstag after his accession
on 24 June 1888, he could confide his conflicting ambition only to
his most intimate friend and adviser, Prince Eulenburg. In the
summer of 1892, on one of his first cruises to Norway, he told
Eulenburg that he dreamed of establishing 'a sort of Napoleonic
supremacy', albeit 'in the peaceful sense'. (19) His dream of
'peaceful' German hegemony, however, squared with war against
Russia, which he had thought inevitable since the crisis of 1887
and Bismarck's downfall in 1890. In the summer of 1892 Wilhelm II
had the extraordinary illusion that the Poles were craving to be
'liberated from the Russian yoke' and annexed by Germany.

The Kaiser's anti-Russian feelings showed that he was in general
agreement with the leaders in the Wilhelmstrasse after Bismarck
had left. Holstein in particular had pleaded for a policy of confrontation with Russia during Bismarck's last years, thus running
the risk of provoking the Franco-Russian alliance, which Bismarck
had tried so laboriously to avoid. After 1894, when the Franco-
Russian alliance had materialized, (20) many high-placed Germans
believed they could continue Bismarck's policy of preserving a free
hand even on the higher level of 'Weltpolitik' and above all against

Britain.   Bülow, Holstein and others thought that the basic differences between Russia and Britain would remain too great ever to be
solved peacefully.   The two Powers would never be allies, so that
Germany need not commit herself vis-à-vis Britain.   Such was the
'dogma of the impossibility of a Russo-British understanding'.   (21)
It was only in 1907 that the Anglo-Russian Agreement shattered
German illusions.   But until 1907 Germany blew hot and cold in its
relationship with both Britain and Russia, always in the hope of
obtaining fleeting and short-term advantages in power politics.   It
is obvious that such alternating treatment was not likely to produce
any sound results.

Holstein's anti-Russian policy was also decisive for Germany's
refusal to prolong the Reinsurance Treaty with Russia after
Bismarck's dismissal.   Count Shuvalov, the Russian Ambassador to
Berlin, joined in the climax of the crisis over Bismarck with his
government's demand to open negotiations to prolong the Treaty.
Hearing of Bismarck's impending fall, the Russians seemed to hesitate to deal with anybody else.   The Kaiser assured them of his
willingness to renew the Treaty, and Caprivi, Bismarck's successor,
was on the verge of following the Kaiser's view.   Caprivi, being a
new arrival to the Wilhelmstrasse, suddenly saw himself confronted
with such a serious problem.   Holstein made him consult the leading experts of the Auswärtiges Amt about a week later.   All of
them pleaded against prolonging the Reinsurance Treaty.   Their
main argument was that the Treaty, with its secret protocol in
particular, was incompatible with the Triple Alliance and could
therefore entangle Germany in a conflict, provoked by Russia,
without German interests being involved.   Furthermore, Germany
would remain in the hands of Russia who could any time, through
deliberate leakage of the secret protocol, engender mistrust
towards Germany with her allies, in particular Austria-Hungary.
Placed in this predicament, Caprivi could not but follow the well-
founded advice of his most competent experts;   they changed his
mind, and the Kaiser followed suit. (22)   The Russians then were
even prepared to leave out the secret protocol and Article II of
the Treaty, which supported Russian aims in Bulgaria.   The German
government, however, did not react to the last Russian offer at
all.   Caprivi, with his straightforward honesty, did not want to
continue Bismarck's policy of juggling with five balls at the same
time.   Both Caprivi and Holstein wanted to make Germany's position
in Europe less ambiguous by dropping a treaty that was conflicting
with other obligations.

The Russian government quickly grasped the inner logic of the
German rebuff, without knowing Holstein's anti-Russian views in
detail.   Russia reacted promptly: one obstacle to the 'rapprochement' between Russia and France had been removed by Bismarck's
successors in 1890.   The last obstacle was the renewal of the
Triple Alliance in 1891 and official information of the Mediterranean Entente of 1887. (23)   Russia now felt as isolated as France
had been since 1871.   By now an alliance between the two isolated
powers became doubly plausible.   In August 1892 they concluded
the Franco-Russian Military Convention, ratified by the Tsar in
January 1894. (24)   The Franco-Russian Dual Alliance was directed
against Russia or France by Powers of the Triple Alliance, in par-

ticular by Germany (against France) or Austria-Hungary (against Russia).

GERMANY BETWEEN BRITAIN AND RUSSIA - BLOWING HOT AND COLD

The Wilhelmstrasse took the completion of the new Dual Alliance comparatively calmly, considering that Germany had endeavoured to prevent such an alliance for the last twenty years.   The Aus- wärtiges Amt, however, found comfort in Holstein's strategical con- cept, mentioned above, that Germany should avoid committing itself vis-à-vis Britain, once France and Russia had formed an alliance. (25)   Such a course was illogical according to the rules of power politics in Europe at the time.   Once German policy had developed away from Russia after 1887 and 1890, a corresponding 'rapproche- ment' with Britain would have been the normal answer to the Franco- Russian Dual Alliance instead of holding it in abeyance.

Britain was to become - until 1914, and even in the First World War itself - a pivot for German foreign policy, as Britain was the only Great Power in Europe to remain uncommitted.   Even after the Anglo-French 'Entente Cordiale' of 1904 and the Anglo-Russian Agreement of 1907, Britain remained free from any formal treaty obligation towards a European power.   Under Bismarck the new phase of Anglo-German relations, after the irreparable estrangement between Germany and Russia had become evident in 1887, was inaugu- rated by Bismarck's famous offer of an alliance to the Conservative Prime Minister Salisbury in 1889. (26)   The only tangible result, however, was the Heligoland-Zanzibar Agreement, concluded after Bismarck's fall. (27)   With Heligoland, Germany acquired, a few years before beginning her phase of active 'Weltpolitik', a strat- egically important base for her navy, soon to be dramatically ex- panded.   The Agreement helped to speed up the imminent Franco- Russian alliance, which in its turn spurred Germany to intensify its relationship with Britain for a while.   With Gladstone's return to office in 1892 and as long as the Liberals were in power, Germany's efforts came to nothing, (28) but they were resumed after the Conservatives took over again in 1895.

The worsening of Anglo-German relations under the Liberals was demonstrated by several events.   Late in 1892 a group of Anglo- French businessmen tried to prevent the completion of the projected railway line to Bagdhad, planned and financed by a consortium under the leadership of the Deutsche Bank.   This move caused serious anger in Berlin.   In the autumn of 1893 Germany complained about Britain's obstruction of German economic expansion in the Far East and in the Pacific, in Central and South Africa. (29)   At about the same time, Germany tried to exploit British difficulties with France over Siam (Thailand) and the Mekong Valley by bringing Britain into the Triple Alliance.   When Gladstone persistently dodged this idea, Germany, inspired by Holstein, began to show Britain the dangers of potential isolation by a policy of needle- pricks against Britain.   Berlin thus hoped to make Britain aware of the value of German friendship and to bring her into closer con- tact with the Triple Alliance. (30)   Several fields were open to Germany for a policy of calculated but limited provocations.

After Caprivi's dismissal late in October 1894 and the almost
simultaneous change in Russia with the accession of Nicholas II as
the last Russian Tsar, Germany might pursue a course of reorientation
towards Russia to impress Britain.   Germany could also demonstrate
its nuisance value in the vast field of colonial expansion.
Finally, it could build a powerful battle fleet of its own. (31)
     Under Caprivi, all diplomatic manoeuvres were aimed at the Conti-
nent and 'Mitteleuropa', which for the first time emerged as a factor in German foreign policy, after the protective tariffs and the
Dual Alliance with Austria-Hungary had created a provisional basis
in 1879.   After Caprivi's downfall in 1894, the same tactics began
to serve the more ambitious 'Weltpolitik' in true Wilhelmian style.
Nevertheless, Caprivi's more solid policy of restraint had also
helped to expand and consolidate the basis for 'Weltpolitik',
because the way to German industrial expansion into neighbouring
countries was now open, thanks to Caprivi's policy of commercial
treaties. (32)   The pressure of German industry on neighbouring
markets was perfectly compatible with the aim of giving a more
solid economic foundation to the Triple Alliance through economic
expansion and the integration of Germany, Austria-Hungary and
Italy.   Smaller neighbouring states could therefore be bound to
Germany by economic links.
     Between 1891 and 1894 Germany concluded a whole series of com-
mercial treaties over a twelve-year period, based on low tariffs
which could only be modified by an agreement with the partner concerned.   Germany concluded such treaties with Austria-Hungary,
Italy, Switzerland, three Balkan countries - Roumania, Bulgaria and
Serbia.   A similar commercial treaty with Russia, then Germany's
most important potential market, was concluded in 1894, but only
after a brief and violent tariff war against Russia, thus forcing
her to accept German conditions.   The Commercial Treaty with
Germany left bitter memories in Russia, which were strengthened
when Germany forced the renewal of the Commercial Treaty with even
harsher conditions upon a Russia weakened by war and revolution ten
years later.   Germany's policy of economic humiliation thus helped
to cement the Franco-Russian Dual Alliance, which Germany, on the
other hand, hoped to weaken by diplomatic means, time and again.
     Nevertheless, autumn 1894 saw the beginning of a new phase of
limited cooperation between Germany and Russia on the basis of
common interests as conservative Powers, due to a new Chancellor in
Germany and a new Tsar in Russia.   Caprivi had been overthrown by
his Conservative enemies for domestic reasons, because he refused to
pursue a policy of renewing repression against the Socialists or
staging a 'coup d'état' from above in the Bismarck tradition.
Caprivi's successor, Prince Hohenlohe-Schillingsfürst, also had a
liberal record as Bavarian Prime Minister around 1870.   But his
wife owned large estates in Russia, which meant links with that
country.   Furthermore, the German Kaiser had secretly doubled his
income as Chancellor, thus making Hohenlohe more dependent on the
whims of his Imperial master.   Finally, Hohenlohe was 75 years old
when he became Chancellor.   His old age and ill health made him an
even more pliant instrument in the hands of the Kaiser whose ambition was to establish his own 'personal rule'. (33)
     After the death of his comparatively liberal father Tsar

Alexander III, Nicholas II represented a new turn to conservative
autocracy in Russia.   He had strong sentimental links to monarchical Germany, through his German wife, daughter of the Grand-Duke of
Hessen-Darmstadt, and his slightly older, but more dynamic and
brilliant cousin - Emperor Wilhelm II.   Nicholas II returned to
the traditional autocracy of the Romanovs with deadly consequences.
He was open to conservative and reactionary influences not only
from his court and army, but also from the Baltic barons of German
origin.   This structure enabled Germany to find points of ideological affinity and common interest with Tsarist Russia against
republicanism, democracy and socialism. (34)   Whenever the German
Empire appealed to Tsarist Russia, it was in the spirit of reactionary class solidarity, symbolized by dynastic links and aristocratic interests. (35)

The new phase of limited partnership between Russia and Germany
soon found a field of cooperation in the Far East.   Both Powers
protested against the Peace Treaty of Shimonoseki, imposed by
victorious Japan on China at the end of the Sino-Japanese War of
1894-5. (36)   The Kaiser's versatile mind indulged in fantasies of
Europe being threatened by the 'Yellow Peril' under the leadership
of Japan. (37)   The Kaiser also wanted to distract Russia's attention from the Near East and the Balkans to the Far East.   The
intervention of Germany and Russia forced Japan to drop plans for
territorial expansion in China.   Because the German protest was
particularly strong, it provoked bitter resentment in Japan not
only against Russia, but also against Germany, culminating in the
conquest of Tsingtau in November 1914 by Japanese troops.

Russia's intervention had more direct consequences for both
countries.   Russo-Japanese rivalry brought Japan on to the side of
Russia's main rival in the world - Britain, who, with the conclusion
of the Anglo-Japanese Alliance of 1902 was leaving her state of
voluntary isolation in   world politics. (38)   Russia became involved with Japan in the Far East, leading to the Russo-Japanese
War of 1904-5.   It had serious repercussions on Russia, culminating
in the first Russian Revolution of 1905-6, but also had an impact
on German foreign policy. (39)

Intervention in Shimonoseki in 1895 started Germany on its short-
lived career of active imperialist policy in the Far East.   The
loss of Japan as a potential ally was contrasted by Germany's active
engagement in China. (40)   The commander of the German Far East
Squadron, Admiral von Tirpitz, was sent to the Far East not only to
demonstrate German sea power in Chinese waters; he also took the
opportunity to find a suitable port for a German naval base against
Britain.   He decided on Tsingtau Bay, which was seized by Germany
in a well-planned action only two years later. (41)   It is only
logical that Tirpitz became the driving force within German government circles for building a powerful battle fleet as an instrument
of German 'Weltpolitik'. (42)

The period of limited cooperation between Germany and Russia provoked new friction with Britain, especially when Germany was entering its phase of 'Weltpolitik'.   While Germany had not given up the
hope of pressuring Britain into the Triple Alliance, even the Conservative Cabinet under Salisbury was far from being enthusiastic.
The Germans, it is true, were not particularly helpful either.

Salisbury was irritated by the way in which the Kaiser rejected his idea of forming an ȧgreement on the Near East question, once the Ottoman Empire disintegrated, as Salisbury envisaged. (43)   On the other hand, two moves taken by the Kaiser in the autumn of 1895 to induce Britain to join the Triple Alliance found no echo in London.

The tense situation in 1895 was aggravated by the Jameson Raid and its failure in January 1896.   The Kaiser was carried away by the general enthusiasm for the Boers in Germany and wanted to humiliate Britain publicly.   In one of his typical councils with his closest military and political advisers, who were hastily summoned to the Chancellor's Office on 3 February 1896, the Kaiser suggested fantastic projects, such as proclaiming the Transvaal a German protectorate or sending German troops to the Transvaal, even at the risk of war with Britain.   To neutralize the Kaiser's wildest ideas, his political advisers found a compromise, which in itself was wild enough, i.e. the Kaiser should send President Krüger of the Republic of Transvaal a telegram of congratulation. (44)

The effect on public opinion was shattering on both sides of the Channel: German public opinion was enthusiastic, Britain was exasperated.   For the Kaiser the Jameson Raid was a welcome excuse to fulfil his fondest dream of building a German battle fleet. Anti-British reactions to the Krüger telegram in Germany encouraged him to go ahead with his plans. (45)   Elevated by his new popularity over questions of foreign policy and the feeling that Germany was crossing the threshold to a new phase, he exclaimed a fortnight later, on the occasion of the twentyfifth anniversary of the founding of the Second German Empire: 'The German Empire has become a World Empire.' (46)   In his impatience, however, the Kaiser tried to anticipate the results of the period of German 'Weltpolitik' in an unknown future.   The Imperial announcement was doubly rash - Germany was not yet a 'World Empire' ('Weltreich');   on the contrary, it was never to become one.

'WELTPOLITIK' AND NO WAR-
1896-1912

Chapter 8

THE EMERGENCE OF 'WELTPOLITIK', FROM DOMESTIC POLICY, 1896-8

By 18 January 1896 Germany had not yet become a world Empire, but it was crossing the threshold to 'Weltpolitik'. Although some German leaders immediately saw and accepted the risk of war as a conse- quence of 'Weltpolitik', (1) others fostered the illusion that war could be avoided. Just before the First World War it was a group of liberals around Chancellor Bethmann Hollweg who believed in the chances of 'Weltpolitik' and no war. (2) In 1913 historical events appeared to justify their optimism, because in spite of the many crises and war scares, peace between the Great Powers of Europe had not been shattered - yet. In 1913, however, basic decisions on war or peace had already been taken behind the scenes in Germany, (3) and important factors that made for war outside Germany were in action. (4) The years between the emergence of 'Weltpolitik' and the basic decision in Germany to go to war - for without war 'Welt- politik' would have been a failure - may be seen as another period in the history of German foreign policy between the wars of 1870-1 to 1914-18.

ECONOMIC AND DOMESTIC REASONS FOR 'WELTPOLITIK'

In 1896-7 one important precondition of German 'Weltpolitik' had become reality: the Great Depression had been overcome and had given way to a long-term period of prosperity which lasted until 1914. German export industry, favoured by Caprivi's policy of com- mercial treaties, entered a period of breathtaking expansion. Within less than two decades German industry succeeded in overtaking Britain in key sectors of modern economy - mining and steel produc- tion - and took the lead in new sectors - chemical and electrical industries. (5) The rapid rise in production and population crea- ted a new sense of power in Germany, and Germany's ruling class was tempted to follow up economic growth by a corresponding growth of military power. When Germany entered the period of Imperialism in earnest, one of the most far-reaching decisions was to seek additional military power not on land - Prussia's and Germany's traditional domain - but at sea.

By building a powerful battle fleet Germany would sooner or

later come into collision with Britain, the traditional sea Power.
Modern research has proved beyond doubt two important points: the
German battle fleet was conceived for domestic and foreign political
reasons.   At home it was intended to rally the ruling and the
middle classes around the throne of the Hohenzollern and to weaken
Parliament by giving the Crown a powerful instrument outside the
control of the Reichstag. (6)   On the other hand the battle fleet
was designed to challenge Britain, once it was completed.   The new
fleet was to give Germany a better chance of winning a full-scale
sea battle.   The political and military calculation of Germany's
leaders failed because they did not sufficiently take into account
what would happen if the world's strongest Power on land wanted to
become the second strongest Power at sea as well.   But their
reasoning dominated Germany's foreign policy leading up to the
First World War and political thinking in Germany until recently.

In order to understand the reasons behind the basic decisions
taken in the crucial years of 1896-7, one has to recall the structure of the German Empire. (7)   Powerful economic and political
interests of the ruling classes were at work when the German Empire
began to develop as an Imperialist Power.   A spectacular, dazzling
and successful policy abroad would hopefully offer a distraction
from tensions at home.   This escape mechanism had been seen by
German historians at work in France under Napoleon III and in Russia
under Nicholas II;   but they refused to see that this method was
being used at home under Wilhelm II as well.   The 'Weltpolitik' of
Imperial Germany had many of the characteristics commonly ascribed
to Bonapartism.   Recent research has discovered this trend in
Bismarck's colonial policy, and his method of unifying Germany was
criticized by many of his opponents in similar terms. (8)

The dynamics of German 'Weltpolitik' can also be understood
against the background of German history in the nineteenth century.
United Germany was to expand into the world, as Prussia had expanded
within Germany. (9)   Twenty-five years after the founding of the
German Empire, conditions for an imperialist policy seemed favourable: Germany's unification in 1871 had created the territorial
basis for future imperialist expansion.   The Triple Alliance, the
acquisition of Heligoland and the system of commercial treaties
under Caprivi had expanded and consolidated both the economic and
political basis of Germany's position in Europe. (10)   The spell
of colonial activities under Bismarck pointed to the direction of
further expansion in a period of active 'Weltpolitik'.   The rise
of German industry and commerce made further expansion and the
building of a strong German fleet plausible and possible, to protect German commerce and colonies overseas, as the argument ran.
This, in its turn, created the demand for naval bases all over the
world, which would have to be protected by an even stronger fleet.

By 1896 another factor at home had matured sufficiently to prepare the way for the beginning of 'Weltpolitik':   the Kaiser's
'personal rule' had become reality.   His personal ambitions therefore could influence German foreign policy even more directly than
before.   In a great ministerial 'clean-up' all Prussian Ministers
who had dared to contradict the Kaiser under Caprivi, even if only
in the field of domestic policy, especially the problem of social
reform, had been dismissed by 1896 and replaced by more reliable

servants of the Crown. (11)   The Kaiser returned to a more reactionary domestic policy and took up ideas of a 'coup d'état' against
the Socialists, which he had rejected in 1890 in his struggle with
Bismarck.

The formal strengthening of the Kaiser's position was contrasted
by the fact that the structural weakness of the German Empire was
again becoming apparent.   Caprivi's commercial treaties and the end
of the Great Depression was destroying the precarious balance
between agrarian and industrial interests in favour of the latter.
While agriculture continued to decline, prospering industries brought
handsome profits for German industrialists.   But rapid industrialization and urbanization made it all the more urgent to appease the
growing urban population and working class by a minimum of concessions, if only to keep them away from the SPD.   But the steady
growth of the Socialists also provoked serious dissensions among the
ruling classes.   How were they to combat the 'threat' of emerging
Socialism, or even of social revolt?   By repression or concessions?

Economic and political factors were corroding Bismarck's coalition, formed in 1878-9 to protect agrarian and industrial interests,
(12) less than twenty years later.   An atmosphere of protracted
crisis prevailed in the mid-1890s, jealousy and mistrust between
the agrarian and industrial sectors of Germany's ruling class on
the one hand, fear of social revolt from below and 'coups d'état'
from above, aggravated by the Kaiser's ambition for 'personal rule'.
It was in this tense situation that the Prussian Minister of
Finance, Johannes von Miquel, the 'strong man' in Germany at the
time, returned to Bismarck's principle of class solidarity at home
and spectacular policy abroad.   In the summer of 1897 Miquel was
made Vice-President of the Prussian Ministry and Tirpitz was appoin-
ted Secretary of State for the Navy.   In the autumn Bernhard von
Bülow formally became Secretary of State in the Auswärtiges Amt,
after being acting Foreign Secretary some months earlier.   With
Bülow's arrival at the Wilhelmstrasse the Kaiser had completed his
ministerial crew to launch the new 'Weltpolitik'.   Miquel was to
prepare the domestic basis, Tirpitz to plan the modernization and
expansion of the German navy as an important instrument of 'Weltpolitik', while Bülow was to carry out 'Weltpolitik' first as
Secretary of State, then, between 1900 and 1909, as Chancellor.
He was in basic agreement with his Kaiser, but sometimes he had to
make the best of the Kaiser's more irrational brain waves.

Miquel, who had been a friend and follower of Karl Marx in 1848-
9, had become the leading spokesman of the Conservative faction in
the National Liberal Party, representing mainly industrial interests.
But he pleaded for the protection also of agrarians, because he saw
in them the strongest pillar of the monarchy and conservative structure.   Industry was, however, indispensable for modern power politics.   This is why, in view of the coming General Elections of
1898, he wished to renew the former alliance of agriculture and
industry of 1878-9 and Bismarck's 'Kartell' of 1887, thus forming a
common front of all Conservative forces against Social Democracy and
left-wing Liberalism.   Miquel found an arousing battle-cry in
'rallying all productive classes' ('Sammlung der produktiven
Stände') around the Imperial throne and in 'Weltpolitik'.   To unite
the possessing classes in their common economic and political

interest, it was necessary, however, to act in strict conformity
with the Constitution.   The Liberal elements of the middle classes
might react strongly when confronted with a return to playing with
open repression, 'coups d'état', etc.

As compensation for forgoing political adventures at home, Miquel
stressed possibilities abroad.   He was not only for strengthening
'national sentiments by treating the Poles harshly, and this even
against the Centre party', but also for bringing questions of
foreign policy before the Reichstag to a greater extent than before.

He [Miquel] had entertained the hope that colonial policy would
turn our attention outwards, but this had happened only to a
limited extent.   We would therefore have to introduce questions
of foreign policy into the Reichstag, for in foreign affairs the
sentiments of the nation would usually be united.   Our undeniable successes in foreign policy would make a good impression in
the Reichstag debates, and political divisions would thus be
moderated. (13)

A breathtaking foreign policy was intended to unite the nation
and, through 'mobilization of the masses' would increase her power.
Miquel's reasoning agreed on this point with an observation made by
Holstein in late 1894.   While criticizing the Kaiser's tendency to
personal rule in a letter to Wilhelm's close friend Eulenburg, he
agreed with Eulenburg that 'a successful war would have a very salu-
tary effect'.   But Holstein added: 'there is little prospect now
of a defensive war, because no one wants to do anything to us.' (14)
Holstein saw dismal consequences arising from a German war of aggression.   Bülow, the future Secretary of State and Chancellor, who
had been drawn into the discussion by Eulenburg, put the issue even
more sharply:

The way to win popular support for the monarchy was to revive
the 'national idea'.   A victorious war would of course solve
many problems, just as the wars of 1866 and 1870 had rescued the
dynasty from the steady decline which had begun in 1848.   On
the other hand, an unsuccessful war would mean the end of the
dynasty because, after Bismarck's attacks, 'our Kaiser cannot
afford to have any major setbacks'. (15)

THE IMPORTANCE OF HAVING A BATTLE FLEET

'Weltpolitik' therefore came into existence as a red herring of the
ruling classes to distract the middle and working classes from
social and political problems at home, at the risk of war and of
losing war, monarchy and all.   But short-term economic and political advantages were more attractive than warnings of possible
defeat.   'Weltpolitik', basically an enterprise of national dema-
gogy, also became a vested economic interest: the building of a
large battle fleet brought quick and long-term profits for the
steel industry in general and the Krupps in particular.   The building programme of the fleet gave work to the steel industry, the
capacity of which had been inflated far beyond the needs of the
German market. (16)   Krupp, therefore, was mainly responsible for
founding and financing the 'Flottenverein' (Naval League) in 1898,
which, hand in glove with Tirpitz at the Naval Office, organized

powerful agitation for the building of a modern battle fleet. (17)
German university professors were amongst the most persuasive agi-
tators.   At the same time, the German middle classes were favoured
by economic measures, while political and administrative pressure
on the Poles was again taken up, in contrast to Caprivi's policy
and in conformity with Miquel's programme. (18)

The battle fleet was an instrument of the German middle class
'par excellence'.   It was both a symbol and vehicle of collective
and individual power and prestige, for the Empire and for individual
members of the German middle class as naval officers.   Thus, the
fleet was not just a whim of an eccentric Kaiser, but represented
the massive economic interests and social aspirations of the most
prosperous and dynamic elements of German society.   Politically,
the building of the battle fleet now resulted in the same conflict
that Bismarck had had with parliament over the modernization and
expansion of the Prussiam army in the early 1860s.   Then, the army
had been Bismarck's most spectacular instrument for the creation of
the German Empire.   Now, Tirpitz wanted to repeat Bismarck's coup
by forging his Kaiser an instrument for the Empire's 'Weltpolitik'.

But Tirpitz had to be careful and tried to veil his twofold aim
by a series of devices.   He wanted a powerful battle fleet against
Britain, independent of changing majorities in Parliament, i.e. of
a Liberal-Socialist majority in the future.   Through his system of
Naval Laws and Amendments ('Novellen') he tried to keep the true
dimensions of the future battle fleet dark as much as he could.
By 1920, when the rate of building was to be levelled off, Germany
would have the most modern and efficient battle fleet in Europe,
giving it more than a sporting chance against the British navy.
Britain must not feel challenged before the German fleet was at
least strong enough to fight a defensive battle within reach of
German waters - this was the true meaning of the famous word
'Risikoflotte'.   The Reichstag, on the other hand, should not discover too soon that, according to Tirpitz's reckoning, the fleet
would be independent of the Reichstag's budgetary powers after
1920, when the fleet was to renew and modernize itself automatically
on the same quantitative level. (19)

Tirpitz succeeded in quietening suspicions at home.   He failed
abroad, however.   Britain reacted to the German building programme
by always remaining ahead of the German navy in numbers, deplacement
and calibre of her capital ships.   In spite of German superiority
in some technical aspects, i.e. gunnery and handling of ships in
battle, its battle fleet was a strategical failure and a political
liability.   It drove Britain into the camp opposing Germany.
When Britain joined the war in August 1914, the German fleet was
not able to beat the Royal Navy, as the Battle of Jutland showed in
1916. (20)   In the hour of defeat, the Germany Empire first broke
down through a revolt of the battle fleet in the autumn of 1918.

Even before the war, the battle fleet had disastrous results for
the German Empire in other respects.   The sums invested for building and modernizing it were so high that the expansion of the army,
which should have formed the basis for a purely defensive policy,
practically stagnated up to 1912.   Then it was too late to increase
it sufficiently to wage a victorious offensive war. (21)   The per-
manently unprepared state of the fleet created another dilemma for

German leaders whenever they had to decide the question of war or
peace.   At the insistence of the navy, Germany was forced to adopt
a policy of restraint, even when an opportunity for a lightning war
on land presented itself, i.e. in 1904-5 during the Russo-Japanese
War and the first revolution in Tsarist Russia. (22)

THE CLAIM FOR GERMAN 'WELTPOLITIK'

All the economic, demographic, political, military and naval factors
mentioned above converged in the last few years of the nineteenth
century.   They resulted in the irresistible claim that Germany
should also enter a period of imperialist expansion.   The chief
exponents in public opinion were once again German university professors, just as before 1870: from the Pan-German historian,
Heinrich von Treitschke to the originally Pan-German, later liberal
sociologist Max Weber. (23)   They drew on German history in order
to give their arguments added plausibility.   Just as little
Brandenburg had expanded to become Prussia in the eighteenth century, and Prussia had created the German Empire in the nineteenth
century, the German Empire as a World Power appeared possible in
the twentieth century.
    The first voices, pleading for Germany's expansion overseas, were
heard in 1875.   One of their arguments was that colonial expansion
would help to overcome economic depression and Socialism at
home. (24)   After public opinion had been successful in bringing
about colonial expansion in the 1880s, (25) the argument was taken
up by even more influential sections of society, now in the service
of future 'Weltpolitik'.   The Kaiser's secret dream of German hegemony on the Continent in 1892 (26) pointed in that direction.
After the founding of the Pan-German movement in 1891, Max Weber
began a phase of imperialist agitation in public with his famous
Inaugural Lecture at Freiburg University in 1895.   In it he pleaded
for a new policy of striving for the status of a World Power:
    We have to grasp that the unification of Germany was a youthful
    prank which the nation committed in its olden days and which
    would have been better dispensed with because of its cost, if it
    were the end and not the beginning of a German 'Weltmacht-
    politik'. (27)
    Max Weber's words spread through Germany like a bushfire.   Poli-
tical intellectuals, such as the Liberal Friedrich Naumann and the
mildly Conservative historian Hans Delbrück, were enthusiastic,
even if Delbrück was regretful: 'Where is it, this German 'Welt-
machtpolitik'?   We have not even entered into such 'Weltmacht-
politik'.' (28)
    When Delbrück felt that 'Weltpolitik' had begun in earnest, he
became one of its ardent heralds. (29)   At about the same time,
Admiral Tirpitz wrote to the Chief of the Admiralty, Admiral Stosch,
in the same vein as the early imperialist propagandists in the
1870s about the need of furthering the 'new great national aim',
because, together with 'the economic profit that goes with it', it
would act as medicine 'against educated and uneducated Social
Democrats'. (30)
    With a pathos reminiscent of Max Weber and his own proclamation

of Germany as a World Power on 18 January 1896, (31) the Kaiser,
in December 1897, described Germany's interests overseas as the
'logical consequences' of what his grandfather and Bismarck had
achieved in the field of politics, his father as a soldier 'with
the sword on the battlefield'.   The Kaiser himself linked economic growth with imperialist expansion, for he declared that commercial interests in Germany had developed to such an extent that
he felt obliged to protect them.   In contrast to the 'old Hanse' of
the Middle Ages, the 'new Hanse' had Imperial protection.   'The
German Empire is created, ... German commerce flourishes and grows',
because 'it can feel secure under the power of the Reich.   Imperial
power means naval power.   Both depend on each other, so that one
cannot exist without the other.' (32)

The economic drive behind German 'Weltpolitik' was also well described by Kurt Riezler, the influential adviser to Chancellor
Bethmann Hollweg and probably the most brilliant intellecutal mind
in Germany's political Establishment just before and during the
First World War.   In a book written for a wider, educated public
just before the outbreak of the war, Riezler wrote under a pseudo-
nym:

The young German Empire pushed out into the world.   Its population grows annually by 8-900,000 people, and for these new
masses food must be found, or, what amounts to the same, work
.... The economic interest had to be followed by the political.
The enormous potential and achievement of the rising nation
pushed the young Empire into its 'Weltpolitik'.... Germany's
unification was, on the one hand, a culmination of the national
development, a fulfilment of national aspirations.   On the
other hand, it was the beginning of a new development, the germ
for new, more far-reaching aspirations.... Parallel to the increasing interest in 'Weltpolitik', German nationalism orientated itself towards 'Weltpolitik'.   The demands of the German
nation for power and prestige, not only in Europe, but throughout the world, have increased rapidly. (33)

Another motive was voiced by Treitschke and Hans Delbrück - the
fear of coming too late when the non-European world was carved up,
if only because Powers without a sufficient share in the world
would be relegated to secondary importance. (34)   But what was a
fair share for Germany in the world?   There was no answer to that
crucial question.   German aspirations remained undefined and bound
to provoke suspicion everywhere, more so because this vague claim
to becoming a World Power might just be another step to an even
more ambitious aim - world domination.   The suspicion was articulated by the Entente Powers in the First World War, but angrily
rejected by Germans as malicious propaganda.   Riezler, however,
felt before the war that all nations were preoccupied with limit-
less expansion until the highest goal - world domination - had been
reached. (35)   His war diary, published only recently, makes it
clear that he saw the First World War, as long as Germany appeared
to be militarily successful, as another step to German world
domination. (36)

THE CONSEQUENCES OF 'WELTPOLITIK' - WORLD WAR

But even if German ambitions were limited to achieving the status
of a World Power, those ambitions, undefined as they were, would
only provoke all the other imperialist powers to turn against this
upstart who was a threat to them all.   This was a normal reaction
and has nothing to do with anti-German resentment.
      The dilemma of 'Weltpolitik' was indeed insoluble.   When
Bismarck's system of isolating defeated France collapsed with the
Franco-Russian Dual Alliance of 1892-4, 'Weltpolitik' might have
succeeded if Germany had joined one of the existing World Powers
as a kind of junior partner, or if it had succeeded in keeping the
World Powers isolated.   Germany refused to join another World
Power, because it was unable to lay down priorities as a result of
divergent economic interests within the Empire itself. (37)
Germany failed to keep its rivals isolated, because it was unable
or unwilling to define or limit its imperialist ambitions.
      By deciding to go it alone, German 'Weltpolitik' ran the risk of
uniting the other imperialist powers against it, because Germany's
claim to a 'place in the sun' could be satisfied only at their
expense.   The logical conclusion of 'Weltpolitik' - world war - was
realized by members of Germany's ruling class, but it was unflinch-
ingly accepted in the tradition of Prussian militarism.   Eulenburg,
Hohenlohe and Bülow had discussed the welcome domestic consequences
of victorious war as early as 1894. (38)   Admiral von Müller, in
his memorandum of 1896, took war as a result of economic tensions
for granted.
      The war which could - and many say must - result from this situa-
      tion of conflict would, according to the generally accepted
      opinion in our country, have the aim of breaking England's world
      domination in order to lay free the necessary colonial posses-
      sions for the central European states who need to expand. (39)
      In his warning against a future struggle between the British and
the German Empire over the question of world domination, Müller
pleaded for the use of 'any surplus political power to further the
struggle for the predomination of the Germanic race' (including the
British).   He was single-minded in his advocacy of the new
'Weltpolitik':
      Here, too, our motto must be all or nothing.   Either we harness
      the total strength of the nation, ruthlessly, even if it means
      accepting the risk of a major war, or we limit ourselves to con-
      tinental power alone. (40)
Müller's advice of 'all-or-nothing' became the basis of German
'Weltpolitik' resulting in two world wars.   Germany, it is true,
tried to appease Britain on the one hand and bully Russia on the
other into neutrality or passivity in the case of war.   But there
was no fundamental change in German foreign policy until 1914 for
all the desperate changes in tactics towards Britain and Russia.
      The consequences of 'Weltpolitik' could be seen immediately in
German military planning.   Belgium, neutralized by international
law since 1839, suddenly acquired a new strategic value in the
coming war with France and Britain.   As early as 1897, the Kaiser
ordered his naval staff to work out a plan of operations against
Britain.   It consisted of a lightning stroke against Antwerp from

the sea.   The city would then be held   until the German army had
raced through Belgium.   The operation was to be the beginning of a
German invasion of Britain.   The plan came to nothing and was
quietly buried, not because Germany's leaders had moral scruples
about invading a neutral country without declaration of war, but
because of military and naval problems. (41)   After 1905, when
General von Schlieffen drew up his famous plan during a period of
Russian weakness, the planned attack on Antwerp from the sea was
replaced by the immediate invasion of Belgium and Holland on
land. (42)

   The episode of the Schröder plan (called after its author,
Korvettenkapitän Schröder), strange as it may appear today, demonstrates that Germany's ruling class was about to accept a strategy
of daring coups or gambling to overcome obstacles to 'Weltpolitik'.
Even at a time when there was no 'encirclement' in sight, the German
Empire was staking everything on the speed and efficiency of military action, first laid down in the Schröder plan, later in the
Schlieffen plan.   Diplomacy was relegated to second place, serving
to create the most favourable conditions for   going to war, once it
became necessary in the struggle for becoming a World Power.

Chapter 9

THE DIPLOMACY OF 'WELTPOLITIK', 1897-1902

The translation of 'Weltpolitik' into practice was the main task of German diplomacy until 1907, when the Triple 'Entente' between France, Russia and Britain was formed.   In that decade, the German Empire tried to expand its territorial possessions overseas and its liberty of action through a kind of sustained political offensive, even though contemporary observers may have been more impressed by the apparent dispersion of German activities almost all over the globe.   After ten years, positive results were meagre, even negative: Germany's liberty of action was restricted by the Triple Entente.   The acquisition of various scattered bases and territories was minimal and gained only at the price of hostility from all sides.   Germany's strategic position was not in any way improved, because the German colonies and territories were almost impossible to defend in case of war.   They were 'sitting ducks', were objects of prestige and more of a liability than an asset for Germany.

   This rather unsettled impression of German foreign policy at this time is increased by the now familiar phenomenon of Germany's inability to opt either for Britain or Russia.   The many details of German diplomatic activity are interesting today only for the light they shed on how Germany saw and moulded its new role in world politics.   This is also true of Germany's attitude to the two Hague Peace Conferences in 1899 and 1907, because it revealed the official German opinion in reaction to suggestions for international arbitration and disarmament.

THE OPENING BANG OF 'WELTPOLITIK' - EXPANSION IN CHINA, 1898

The first German coup, or the inauguration of 'Weltpolitik', was the seizure of Kiaochow (Tsingtau) in 1897.   This had only been possible through German cooperation with Russia in the Far East, which grew out of the common intervention against Japan at Shimonoseki. (1)   By establishing a regular steamer line to China in 1886, Germany had demonstrated its interest in China, the 'sick man' of the Far East.   China presented an interesting potential market for German goods and was apparently the last great country

to be divided amongst the imperialist powers.   This time, Germany
did not want to come too late, and a naval base seemed to be an
appropriate beginning.   As early as November 1894, the Kaiser had
ordered his new Chancellor, Prince Hohenlohe, to annex Formosa (and
Mozambique). (2)   After Tirpitz had returned from the naval demonstrations in the Far East in 1895, preparations were made for the
occupation of territory in the Kiaochow Bay, which was considered
by Tirpitz to be a suitable naval base. (3)   A fitting pretext for
taking action was presented by the murder of two German missionaries
during riots in the Shantung province in November 1897. (4)   In a
hastily improvised meeting on 15 November 1897, it was decided to
execute the prepared plan of intervention in China.   To avoid war
with China, her sovereignty was to be formally respected by leasing
territory.   It was further laid down that German demands were to be
so high that China could not fulfil them. (5)   A demonstration of
German naval power together with a landing by naval infantry, forced
China's Imperial government to 'lease' the German Empire the Bay of
Kiaochow for ninety-nine years.   As soon as the 'lease' had been
agreed upon, Germany treated the territory as though it was now
under permanent German sovereignty.

   The seizure of Kiaochow by Germany made Russia and Britain press
for compensation.   Russia received Port Arthur to the south, and
Britain Wei-hai-wei between Kiaochow and Port Arthur.   The partition of China appeared to be imminent.   Another consequence of
Germany's territorial conquest on the Chinese continent was closer
cooperation between Japan and Britain against the Russo-German cooperation in the Far East, leading to the Anglo-Japanese Alliance
in 1902.   It marked the end of Britain's 'splendid isolation' and
preceded the Triple Entente of 1904-7. (6)   The very first attempt
by Germany to implement its new 'Weltpolitik' thus provoked other
powers into a policy of containing Germany, even if only in the Far
East.   Gaining territory plus apparent prestige in China really
weakened Germany's position in the world.

BRITAIN'S KEY ROLE

Once Germany had embarked on a course of expansion abroad, conflict
with Britain was inevitable.   Ever since, Britain loomed almost
obsessively in German political thinking.   The objective situation
between the two countries was complicated and tense enough.   It
was further aggravated by mixed subjective feelings in Germany
towards Britain. (7)   On the one hand, there was the traditional
admiration for Britain, the mother country of the industrial revolution, and for the British Empire.   On the other hand, public
opinion in Germany became increasingly governed by resentment and
an inferiority complex.   By the end of the nineteenth century,
public opinion in Germany was decidedly more anti-British than
British public opinion was anti-German.   Bülow, then Secretary of
State, admitted this state of affairs in a memorandum to the Kaiser
in November 1899, adding with a sigh of relief: 'How good that nobody in Britain really knows how anti-British German public opinion
is.' (8)   The Kaiser, however, if only for family and dynastic
reasons, was never wholly anti-British and adopted a pro-British

feeling in fits and starts, so representing his Empire also in that respect far better than he realized.   Because German leaders could not be violently and openly anti-British for tactical reasons, they pursued a policy of formal restraint.   But they were under the pressure of an overwhelmingly anti-British public opinion, with the Kaiser moving unsteadily between the two.

Britain's irritation over Kiaochow in the Far East was even more aggravated by the new German battle fleet.   The quicker Germany built its fleet, the more Britain felt challenged in her traditional element and the more British opposition to the expansion of German power increased.   In contrast, it became even more important for Germany to maintain at least tolerable relations with Britain, if only to prevent Britain and the Empire joining in a possible continental war against the Reich.   Any 'rapprochement' was bound to founder on developing Anglo-German antagonism through the German battle fleet, unless an agreement could be made as to the strength of the two navies.   German diplomats tried to find solutions to geographically and politically marginal problems, such as the Baghdad Railway and the future of the Portuguese colonies.   But without tackling the most important problem, Germany could only achieve an improvement of atmosphere in the relations between the two countries.   Germany never managed to make up its mind to draw clear-cut political conclusions from the German naval building programme.   All attempts to establish closer links failed because of this, regardless of from which side the initiative came.

After this general analysis, it is easier to understand the complex and often confusing details of Anglo-German relations during the various phases of German 'Weltpolitik'.   The basic problem remained the same, but in the different political constellations the form and the subject of the negotiations changed.   Three attempts to reach an understanding between Germany and Britain can be distinguished: from 1898 to 1902;   in 1912 with the Haldane mission;   and in early 1914 with negotiations which took place immediately before the outbreak of the First World War.   In this chapter only the first will be dealt with.

THE FIRST ROUND OF ANGLO-GERMAN TALKS AND THE FUTURE OF PORTUGAL IN AFRICA, 1898

In early 1898,the initiative for the first round of diplomatic activity came from the British.   Britain then was in an awkward position.   The costly reconquest of the Sudan was imminent, and with it the risk of a subsequent confrontation with France;   Fashoda was looming over the political horizon.   So was the coming of war in South Africa.   The idea of a Continental League under German leadership, put forward by the Kaiser in 1896, (9) had not materialized.   But Russo-German cooperation in the Far East seemed to make new and more permanent groupings plausible.   Russia, Japan and the USA then refused to help Britain out from further isolation. On 24 March 1898 London learned that Russia insisted on staying in Port Arthur.   The following day, the Sino-German Treaty over Kiaochow was concluded.   On 28 March the Reichstag passed the first Navy Law to build a German battle fleet.

Since Bismarck's move in 1889, (10) Anglo-German relations had
deteriorated, especially after the Krüger telegram of January
1896. (11)   On 29 March 1898, one day after the Navy Law had been
passed in Berlin, the British Colonial Secretary, Joseph Chamberlain, acting on behalf of the Prime Minister Salisbury, who was ill,
had a long interview with the German Ambassador, Count Hatzfeldt.
Chamberlain explained that Britain, faced with many difficulties
throughout the world, would revise her present policy of non-
alliance.   He would prefer an alliance with Germany above any
other, because frictions between Germany and Britain were only
secondary.   Such an alliance would be ratified by parliament, and
would 'amount to' Britain joining the Triple Alliance.   Hatzfeldt,
however, reported to Berlin that Britain would be prepared to join
the Triple Alliance; he thus missed the subtle meaning behind
Chamberlain's words. (12)

The chance presented itself for Germany to come to an agreement
with Britain although 'Weltpolitik' and the naval building programme were still in 'statu nascendi'.   In reality, however,
Anglo-German talks had a narrow political basis - on both sides;
Chamberlain and the Chancellor of the Exchequer, Arthur Balfour,
were practically the only persons in the cabinet and in British
public opinion who believed a move towards Germany was necessary.
The truth was that Whitehall had tried other ways to overcome
tensions over China.   But again Russia, Japan and the USA had re-
buffed Britain for various reasons.   Only then had Chamberlain's
argument a chance in Britain.   He had warned the Germans, however,
that Britain would have to look for an alliance with Russia and
France, if an Anglo-German alliance failed.

Berlin's reaction to Chamberlain's initiative was one of
caution.   Hatzfeldt received no explicit instructions to continue
negotiations or to clarify British proposals.   Instead, Bülow
treated the whole matter as a clever tactical move in view of an
imminent Anglo-French war over the Sudan.   He advised Britain
indirectly to clarify her position with France as soon as possible,
as long as Germany could neutralize Russia more easily before the
Trans-Siberian Railway was completed.   Such advice was bound to
arouse Salisbury's suspicion that the Germans wanted to goad
Britain into a war with France for their own political ends. (13)
Bülow's assurance that Germany was interested in the preservation of
British power was of little comfort to London.   Two reasons for
German restraint are apparent.   Berlin feared that Britain wanted
to use Germany to fight Russia, while the Germans hoped that the
British would have to face even greater difficulties in their
foreign policy, especially when faced by a powerful German navy -
and would therefore be forced to offer even better conditions.   The
Germans thought that they were in a position of strength and could
afford to wait for new and better British proposals.

The last serious meeting during the first phase of Anglo-German
talks took place between Hatzfeldt and Balfour on 5 April 1898.
Balfour rather modified Chamberlain's ideas by admitting that ratification of an Anglo-German Treaty in parliament would not be so
easy.   He also believed in a 'rapprochement' with Germany, but
acted with greater restraint.   This was paralleled in Berlin by the
Kaiser's reaction when he was told about the talks for the first

time.   He was for a friendly relationship with Britain, but also wanted to put off the conclusion of a formal alliance by subtle diplomacy.

It was now clear that neither Britain nor Germany was seriously interested in a fully-fledged alliance, and but for the intervention of Hermann von Eckardtstein, Councillor at the German Embassy in London, all further negotiations would have ended then.   But Eckardtstein thought he could further his social and political ambitions by bringing about the alliance between Germany and Britain. He used Hatzfeldt's illness artificially to revive negotiations. Without any authorization from Berlin, he tried to make Chamberlain believe that the Kaiser wanted to conclude an alliance with Britain, and he reported to Berlin that Chamberlain wanted to conclude an alliance with Germany.   It took some time for both sides to see through the web of false information, and the new round of talks was consequently a farce. (14)

Hatzfeldt continued talks with Chamberlain on 25 April and Salisbury on 2 May, having no knowledge of Eckardtstein's unauthorized initiatives.   The British, however, did not realize that Hatzfeldt was completely ignorant of the Kaiser's alleged views reported to them by Eckardtstein.   Both sides were, of course, at cross purposes.   The inevitable result was disappointment and suspicion on both sides when they found out the truth.   Chamberlain's great speech, given in his Birmingham constituency, informed the British public of the talks, but did not help to save the situation. Nevertheless, Salisbury accepted Balfour's suggestion of replacing the idea of a general alliance by bilateral agreements for special problems.   As Berlin agreed, the two powers were able to reach at least piecemeal agreements on problems such as the Baghdad Railway, Samoa and the Portuguese colonies.

In 1898 Britain's most critical point in her relationship with Germany was not yet the naval building programme, but Delagoa Bay in the Portuguese colony of Mozambique.   The more war with the Boer Republics was approaching, the greater became the strategic value of Lourenço Marques, the end of a railway line built with the help of German capital to the Transvaal.   The problem was further complicated by Portugal, Britain's oldest ally since the Middle Ages.   Germany, however, wished to round off its colonial possessions in Africa by the acquisition of colonial territory from Portugal.   The failure of negotiations over an Anglo-German Alliance resulted in the Treaty of 30 August 1898, between Britain and Germany.   The very complicated stipulations were that if Portugal wanted to have an international loan to solve its chronic financial problems and offered the custom revenues of Angola and Mozambique as securities, Germany and Britain would unite to grant the loan and share the revenues.   If Portugal decided to sell its colonies, they would be divided between both powers.   Britain would receive northern Angola and southern Mozambique, and Germany southern Angola and northern Mozambique. (15)   Both territories were adjacent to German colonies, South-West Africa and German East Africa (Tanganyika) respectively.   Germany would then be nearing its long-term aim of possessing a colonial block in Africa, i.e. 'Mittelafrika' as a counter-part to 'Mitteleuropa'. (16)

Britain took the agreement with Germany to be purely hypothetical

and felt free to grant Portugal a loan without the securities envisaged by Germany.   Britain even offered a territorial guarantee
to Portugal for its colonies in the secret Windsor Treaty of 1899.
Germany, however, believed that the Anglo-German agreement would
make a division of Portuguese colonies certain in the near future.
Germany felt double-crossed by the British loan, where none of the
clauses mentioned above had been fulfilled.

GERMANY'S THRUST INTO THE MIDDLE EAST AND THE PACIFIC, 1898-9

After the Anglo-German talks, 'successes' in the Near East and in
the Pacific became even more problematic.   In the autumn of 1898
the Kaiser visited the Ottoman Empire from Constantinople to
Jerusalem.   In Damascus, on 8 November, he proclaimed himself as
protector and a friend not only of the Sultan, but also of the 300
million Muslims. (17)   The Kaiser's spectacular coup saw the
beginning of a new phase of German economic penetration in Turkey,
resulting in Turkey's joining the First World War as Germany's ally
in November 1914.   The Baghdad Railway, formally started by a concession to build the Konia-Baghdad-Basra line, opened up dazzling
prospects for Germany.   The Ottoman Empire then reached to the
Persian Gulf and almost to the Suez Canal; Egypt and Libya were
also formally under Ottoman suzerainty.   The vast Turkish Empire
offered undreamt-of economic and military possibilities for German
enterprise, e.g. by training and equipping the Turkish army along
German lines.   In contrast to China and Africa, Turkey had the
advantage of being nearer to Germany.   'Mitteleuropa' was, in
fact, separated from Turkey only by little Serbia.   The Turkish
Empire was centralized but also weak and therefore open to outside
influences.   Germany succeeded in replacing older sympathies
towards Britain and France by giving Turkey a kind of 'development
aid' in various fields for political ends. (18)
     The offensive of German imperialism in the Near East, however,
weakened Germany's precarious position as a potential World Power.
Germany entered a strategically sensitive region where Russian and
British interests met.   Secondary fronts against Russia (in the
Caucasus) and Britain (against the Suez Canal) of the future First
World War began to emerge.   The expansion of Germany into 'territories beyond those allotted to it by Destiny' (Bismarck, 1887)
alarmed the two world powers already established in the region -
Russia and Britain.   It is no coincidence that they met to arrange
the protection of their interests in Persia only a decade later.
(19)
     Furthermore, the German Empire had encumbered itself with the
internal problems of another decaying empire.   Older and even more
reactionary than Austria-Hungary and the German Empire, Turkey
became a millstone around Germany's neck, militarily in the First
World War, but also politically and morally even before, e.g. by
Germany's acquiescence in the Turkish massacres in Armenia towards
the end of the nineteenth century and again during the First World
War.   Defeats suffered by Turkey in coming years were also indirect
defeats for Germany who had equipped and trained the Turkish army.
German relations with Italy became complicated when the latter con-

quered Libya from Turkey in 1911, estranging Italy from the Triple
Alliance.   In the First World War, Turkey was a great burden for
Germany. (20)   It is almost logical that the military and political
collapse of the Central Powers started in autumn 1918 with the
collapse of Turkey in the Middle East, followed by that of Bulgaria
in the Balkans.   Germany's drive into the Middle East became an
expensive adventure, a 'fata morgana', contributing to the failure
of 'Weltpolitik'.
      Even more illusory than the Middle and Far East were German
dreams of expansion in the Pacific.   Germany had occupied Eastern
New Guinea ('Kaiser-Wilhelm-Land') and some groups of Pacific
islands in 1885-6.   In 1898 Germany took the opportunity to use
Spain's defeat by the USA to buy most of the Marian and Caroline
islands as 'compensation' for the Philippines, which were annexed
by the USA. (21)   The following year, Germany exploited the Boer
War and riots in Samoa to push Britain out of the tripartite con-
dominium with the USA and divided Samoa with America.   On that
occasion, Germany was even prepared to push Britain to the point of
breaking diplomatic relations. (22)   The discrepancy between a
particular aim and the methods applied become painfully clear in
the dispute over Samoa: Germany's risking a war with an established
World Power for the control of a few additional islands on the
other side of the globe is absurd to the point of making a farce of
diplomacy.

GENERAL DISARMAMENT AND COMPULSORY ARBITRATION AS A THREAT TO
'WELTPOLITIK' - GERMANY ON THE FIRST HAGUE PEACE CONFERENCE, 1899

Russia's invitation on 24 August 1898 to a disarmament conference
added to the tensions of the time.   Tsar Nicholas II's initiative
was enthusiastically received by public opinion of most countries
(with the exception of Germany), but most governments were suspicious of Russian motives.   The idea of the conference was icily
rejected in Berlin, by the Kaiser down to the Auswärtiges Amt. (23)
The Tsar's realistic view that increasing armament was too heavy a
burden·for the peoples of the world, was an object of special
derision - any kind of pacifism was distasteful for the German
Empire, and the Russian project was applauded in particular by pacifist and international socialists.   The Russian suggestion with
its 'socialist' tinge, thus became doubly unacceptable in Germany.
Disarmament and compulsory arbitration, suggested by the Russians,
were completely out of the question: Germany had just begun her
career as a potential world power, and her leaders knew that they
would need military power to achieve their aim through 'Weltpolitik'.   Germany's ruling class was unwilling to liquidate 'Weltpolitik' in a peace conference.   German policy in both Hague Peace
Conferences was governed by the social and political structure of
the Reich, by the tradition and power of German militarism and,
most of all, by 'Weltpolitik'.
      When confronted with the question of war and peace on a more
abstract level by the Russian initiative, again no public or government debate took place on the basic issues.   Behind closed doors,
official opinion was expressed by Holstein and the Kaiser.

Holstein, the conservative intellectual in German diplomacy, clothed his rejection of compulsory arbitration in a dogma of the nature of the state and of the principle of permanent international antagonism: The highest aim of the State must be to preserve its own interests. With a Great Power the latter are not necessarily identical with the preservation of peace; they are much more likely to imply the violation of an enemy and rival by a stronger combination formed for that purpose. (24) Holstein's memorandum for Bülow was incorporated into the official instructions of Germany's first delegate to the Peace Conference in order to 'guide' him 'in dealing with the question of arbitration'. (25)

Such an attitude made it impossible to tackle any suggestions for disarmament or at least for limiting armament. Other Great Powers were also sceptical or hostile, but it is possible that the plan was definitely dropped as a result of Germany's massive opposition. On the other hand, Germany could have allied with Britain to overcome the reluctance of other governments by a more positive attitude.

The German position with regard to arbitration was more complicated. Originally, the Russians had suggested facultative arbitration. Soon after the opening of the Conference, the British delegate, Sir Julian Pauncefote, moved the establishment of a permanent Court of Arbitration. After some hesitation, all the powers save Germany accepted the new principle of compulsory arbitration. Germany was visibly isolated for the first time. The Wilhelmstrasse tried to modify the bad impression created by introducing more flexible tactics in the sub-committee stage of the Conference. But German hostility to the 'generally dangerous project' ('gemeingefährliches Projekt') (26) remained unchanged. The German representative in the sub-committee, Professor Zorn, was instructed by Ambassador Münster 'to add so many safety valves into that artificial apparatus that everything will turn into dust that can be thrown into the eyes of public opinion'. (27) An important motive was formulated in a memorandum of the Auswärtiges Amt, saying that Germany must 'reserve and secure complete freedom of action for all time'. This would ensure that a future government in Germany that might become 'disorientated under the pressure of public opinion', would not be compelled to accept the ruling of a Permanent Court of (compulsory) Arbitration, once it had been established. (28)

Again, just as in the case of the Tirpitz plan to make the battle fleet independent of a future Liberal-Socialist majority in the Reichstag, behind such an argument lurked the fear of Germany turning democratic one day. When 'Weltpolitik' began, the German Empire refused to be bound by any international treaty that might have limited or even have obstructed its capability to go to war. Five days later Bülow sent an instruction to the German delegate in The Hague on the same lines as the memorandum. Münster thought it could have wrecked the sub-committee, or 'perhaps even the whole Conference'. (29) It was only for tactical reasons that the German delegation did not act on the instructions from Berlin. Instead, they tried to destroy the scheme for a Permanent Court of (compulsory) Arbitration by less spectacular methods. Germany was successful again. Mainly as a result of German opposition, the Conference was forced to agree to the original Russian suggestion

of voluntary arbitration.   It was, of course, ineffective in times
of serious crisis, such as in July 1914.
    Nevertheless, the Kaiser claimed that he had helped the Tsar to
save his face as a monarch.   The implications are clear enough:
for Imperial Germany, anything more than the meagre results would
have been a blow to the monarchical cause.   The Kaiser added in
conclusion to Bülow's report on the Conference: 'But I will rely
in practice later only on God and my sharp sword.   And damn all
those decisions.' (30)

GERMANY AND BRITAIN, 1899-1901

Germany's isolation in the Peace Conference over compulsory arbitration was soon forgotten by the Boer War.   Apart from the limited
gain on Samoa, (31) German diplomacy was unable to exploit British
embarrassment further, owing to the divergence between the vehemently anti-British public opinion in Germany and the necessity of
outward restraint for the Imperial government.   Any possibility of
German mediation to avoid war in southern Africa had to be ruled
out, because the German government was in no position to satisfy
either Britain or public opinion at home. (32)   In contrast to the
Jameson Raid, Germany this time remained strictly neutral.   In
spite of bitterness and friction after the Royal Navy had confiscated German ships, Germany warded off a Russian project of mediation
between Britain and the two Boer Republics in March 1900, after war
had broken out.   Berlin demanded that before any mediation could
be attempted by Russia, France and Germany, the three powers 'should
guarantee each other their territorial possessions in Europe for
many years ahead'. (33)   The Wilhelmstrasse had cleverly thrown
into the problem of mediation in South Africa the question of
Alsace-Lorraine, which meant that France and Russia were unable to
move.   Britain was relieved, and the Prince of Wales expressed
Britain's gratitude for the service rendered by Germany. (34)   The
Kaiser's official visit to Britain in November 1899 - with violent
opposition from public opinion in Germany - even amounted, in retro-
spect, to Germany's support of Britain.
    Nevertheless, Anglo-German relations remained ambivalent.
During the Kaiser's visit to Britain, Bülow and Chamberlain agreed
to use the improvement of relations during the Boer War to effect
a more substantial 'rapprochement'.   Both statesmen were to influence public opinion by public speeches.   Chamberlain fulfilled
his part of the bargain by his great speech at Leicester, on 30
November 1899, in which he pleaded for an alliance between Germany
and Britain, 'the great Germanic Empires', and the USA.   German
public opinion, however, angrily rejected Chamberlain's suggestion
and was furious about the British stopping and searching a German
ship, the 'Bundesrath'.   Bülow, frightened by this new outburst
of anti-British resentment in Germany, held back his promised
counterpart.   In his speech in the Reichstag, on 11 December 1899,
he spoke of Anglo-German relations in a rather detached manner and
even stressed the necessity for Germany to build a strong fleet of
its own. (35)   The atmosphere of growing excitement and suspicion
on both sides of the Channel became tense, almost to breaking

point, when the Royal Navy confiscated three German mail boats in
December 1899.   Just as over the Samoa dispute, Berlin seriously
considered severing diplomatic relations with Britain.   The German
government did not take the plunge, but feelings were running high
in Germany.   It was in such an atmosphere of anti-British hysteria
that the second Navy Law was passed in the Reichstag, bringing the
projected battle fleet to the strength of thirty-six capital ships.
The naval race between Germany and Britain had begun.

The diplomatic interlude over mediation in the Boer War in March
1900 (36) seemed to ease the tension.   It was further relaxed in
the summer of 1900, when the imperialist powers undertook a joint
expedition against China to quell the so-called 'Boxer Rising', the
last serious revolt to shake Imperial China before the Revolution
in 1911.   The Kaiser used the expedition to relieve the Western
diplomatic missions besieged in Peking, as a spectacular demonstration of German power and 'Weltpolitik'.   Wilhelm II insisted on
the appointment of his old friend, Field-Marshall Waldersee, as
Commander-in-Chief for the international forces taking part in the
campaign against Peking.   The Kaiser made his notorious 'Hun'
speech at the departure of 'Weltmarschall' Waldersee, as he was
nicknamed, and the German contingent in Bremerhaven on 27 July
1900.

You are well aware that you have to face a brave, well-armed and
savage foe.   When you make contact with him, you know that no
pardon will be given, and prisoners will not be made.   Anyone
who falls into your hands falls to your sword!   Just as the
Huns under their King Etzel created for themselves a thousand
years ago a name which men still respect, you should give the
name of German such cause to be remembered in China for a thousand years that no Chinaman, no matter if his eyes be slit or
not, will dare to look a German in the face. (37)

The impression of this bloodthirsty speech was so appalling that
its publication was allowed only in an abridged form.   The Kaiser
had thus provided Allied propaganda with one of the most effective
slogans to use against the German Empire during the First World
War.   'Weltmarschall' Waldersee and his German troops arrived at
Peking when the revolt had already been suppressed by an expeditionary corps of Western (plus Japanese) troops.   But once on
Chinese soil, the German troops made bloody raids on the Chinese
population, in accordance with the motto of their Imperial master.

The question of China's future had been raised again, and her
fate of partition along African lines seemed to be sealed in the
summer of 1900.   Only the mutual suspicion of the imperialist
Powers saved China: she was too large to be controlled or conquered
by one imperialist Power, and rivalry between the different Powers
paralysed any further common action against China.   France and
Russia tried to prevent a further spread of British influence in
China;   Britain tried to limit Russian pressure on China from the
north, through Manchuria and Korea;   while the USA tried to protect
her interests by proclaiming the principle of 'open door' in China
for all imperialist Powers in July 1900.   In Kiaochow, Germany was
caught between two stools.   It was bent on making further gains in
China, but wanted to avoid a conflict with either Russia or
Britain.   Germany, therefore, tried to neutralize the Yangtse

Valley by cooperation with Britain.   The Yangtse Treaty of 16
October 1900 upheld the American 'open door' policy.   Only if other
imperialist Powers were to achieve territorial gains in China, would
Britain and Germany seek an understanding about further action to be
taken. (38)
     Now, once again, Germany hoped to be able to bind Britain to the
Triple Alliance.   The Wilhelmstrasse had realized during the German
State visit in November 1899, that Balfour and Chamberlain were
still hoping for future allies.   If Germany was not to be Britain's
partner, France and Russia would make it. (39)   Holstein, who was
sceptical about Germany's naval ambitions, as they were incompatible
with good relations with Britain, (40) wanted to continue the policy
of closer ties with London, without letting it appear that the initiative came from Germany.   At this stage, in January 1901,
Eckardtstein again intervened using his same method of making both
sides believe that the other was actively interested in an alliance.
As a result, each side was waiting for an advance from the other,
both trying to avoid the impression that they were eager for an
alliance. (41)
     The main reason why nothing came of the diplomatic hide-and-seek
between Germany and Britain was that whilst Germany only wanted
closer ties with Britain in the form of a regular treaty binding
Britain to the Triple Alliance as a whole, Britain would have
agreed only to a looser arrangement with Germany, similar to that
made with France in 1904 and Russia in 1907.   Britain joining the
Triple Alliance would have meant enormous advantages for Germany,
while Britain would have been obliged to guarantee the territorial
integrity of Austria-Hungary.   British statesmen, however, saw
that after the dissolution of the Ottoman Empire the dissolution
of Austria-Hungary would be next on the agenda, and they were
reluctant to be enmeshed in the maze of Balkan problems and the
disintegration of two dying Empires. (42)   On the other hand,
Germany feared not so much an attack from Russia and France, but
having to cope one day with the problems in the Balkans resulting
from the alliance with Austria-Hungary.   Germany wanted to
strengthen its position by winning Britain over to its side, without any intention of making concessions in the one field Britain
became more and more interested in - the German battle fleet.
     Negotiations between Britain and Germany between 1898 and 1901
were fruitless because both Powers had incompatible aims.   Neither
Britain nor Germany was seriously interested in a positive outcome
in 1901:   Britain no longer needed Germany after military victory
in South Africa;   Germany clung to the illusion that an understanding between Britain on the one hand, and Russia and France on the
other, would never be possible in the near future.   By May 1901
the chances for aggeneral arrangement with Britain had disappeared,
and by December 1901, the chances for at least a partial arrangement.   Landsdowne later put it in a nutshell when he told Lascelles
that the Germans had wanted 'all or nothing'. (43)   A treaty of
alliance, ratified by parliament in London, was out of the question, and Germany was not interested in the kind of loose, but
effective arrangement concluded by Britain with France and Russia
a few years later.   In December 1901 Anglo-German talks had come
to an end.   One month later, on 30 January 1902, Britain entered

into an alliance with Japan, the emerging Great Power in the Far East.   Britain was leaving her phase of 'splendid isolation', a move which was to have serious repercussions on German foreign policy.

Chapter 10

THE BEGINNING OF GERMANY'S CONTAINMENT, 1902-6

THE COMING OF THE RUSSO-JAPANESE WAR, 1902-4

The Anglo-Japanese Alliance opened a new phase of international diplomacy. It amounted to the beginning of a policy of containing
Germany in reaction to German 'Weltpolitik'. A few months before
the Anglo-Russian Agreement of 1907, Sir Eyre Crowe defined British
foreign policy along such lines, although he did not use the word
'containment'. (1) At the end of the period under review, on 1
August 1914, the Austrian Foreign Minister, Count Berchtold, did
use the word when characterizing British policy. According to
Berchtold, Britain aimed at the 'diplomatic containment ('Eindämm-
ung') of German influence'. (2) Although it may not have been
the original intention behind the Anglo-Japanese Treaty, its overall effect was to start a process of realignment which ended in the
formation of the Triple Entente in 1907. Thus, the period between
1902 and 1906 may be taken to be the formative years of a policy of
containment.

The treaty with Japan demonstrated that it was possible to make
the British parliament ratify a formal treaty covering British
interests as far away as East Asia. The treaty provided for neutrality in a war with one Power, but active military assistance, if
one partner was involved in war with two or more Powers at the same
time. A common interest was the containment of Russian pressure
on Manchuria and Korea. This new grouping was a logical sequence
of the assistance Britain had given Japan in 1895 during the
German-French-Russian intervention at Shimonoseki. According to
the rules of international power politics, the alliance between
Britain and Japan would resurrect the Shimonoseki confrontation -
the Continental Powers, especially Germany and Russia, against the
Naval Powers, Britain and Japan. Indeed, as a reaction to the
Anglo-Japanese Treaty, the Russians cautiously suggested in Berlin
a joint French-Russian-German declaration to the effect that the
three Powers also wanted to uphold the 'status quo' in China.
Bülow, Chancellor of the Empire since 1900, rejected the suggestion, pretending that he thought such a declaration could be the
beginning of a return to the idea of a Continental bloc against
Britain. The reason put forward was the pretended fear that such

an alliance would encourage Russia into starting a policy of conquest in Manchuria which could also be embarrassing to Germany. (3)
   In reality, Germany was trying, as early as 1901, to get Russia
and Japan embroiled in a war over Manchuria and Korea. (4)   The
first aim was to prevent an agreement between the two Powers, suggested by Japan, on the partitioning of spheres of influence:
Russia was to be given a free hand for expansion in Manchuria,
Japan in Korea.   Germany at that time was interested in closer
ties with Russia on the basis of a common fight against 'anarchism
and revolution'. (5)   Berlin quietly gave indirect encouragement
to the enemies of Lamsdorff and Witte, the Russian Foreign Minister
and Minister of Finance respectively, who stood for a policy of
peaceful understanding with Japan in the Far East.   In the meeting
between the Kaiser and the Tsar at Reval, in the summer of 1902,
Bülow and the Kaiser apparently tried to persuade the Russians that
German neutrality in the case of war with Japan would also keep
Britain neutral, according to the Anglo-Japanese Treaty.   Wilhelm
II's parting telegram to the Tsar - 'From the Admiral of the Atlantic to the Admiral of the Pacific' - suggests that the Kaiser, in
his fraternization with the Tsar, may perhaps have promised more
than just neutrality. (6)   When the Russians bluntly asked the
Germans in the summer of 1903 whether Germany would support Russia
in a war against Japan, they dodged the question, protesting their
friendship for Russia.   Bülow approvingly commented that it was
important not to get the Russians frightened to the point 'that
they seek agreement with Japan [= Britain] '"à tout prix"'. (7)
   In spite of mounting tension between Russia and Japan, no war
had broken out by the autumn of 1903, to the great disappointment
of both Bülow and the Kaiser.   When the showdown approached, Berlin,
behind the façade of neutrality, was eagerly waiting for the outbreak of the war between Russia and Japan, because it was hoped
that it would block any 'rapprochement' between Russian and Britain.
Formal restraint was judged as the best method to make war certain.
Once war had broken out in February 1904, Germany tried to use
Russia's difficulties in the Far East to break up the Franco-
Russian Dual Alliance in Europe.   The Dual Alliance had been formed
to avert a military attack from the Triple Alliance against Russia
or France, and France was not obliged to assist Russia against
Japan.   Nevertheless, French neutrality was a serious strain on
the French alliance with Russia.

ITALY AND THE RENEWAL OF THE TRIPLE ALLIANCE, 1902

The situation was complicated, however, by the divergence of
interests between Austria-Hungary and Italy, making the renewal of
the Triple Alliance difficult.   It had been possible to gloss over
differences between Austria-Hungary and Italy as long as France was
still isolated and Italy had not developed imperialist ambitions of
her own coming into conflict with Germany's aims.   After France
had left her enforced isolation her foreign policy towards Italy
became more active. (8)   Italy and France reached a secret agreement on 30 June 1902 (officially on 1 and 2 November 1902), to
remain neutral if the other Power were attacked 'by one or more

Powers'.   Italy would also remain neutral 'if France, in consequence of direct provocation, should find herself compelled in
defence of her honour and her security to take the initiative in
the declaration of war'. (9)
        The Triple Alliance was partially paralysed.   Italy's plans to
expand into Northern Africa, realized in 1911 by the Italo-Turkish
War, further corroded the Triple Alliance, because it came into
conflict with Germany's policy of preserving the integrity of the
Ottoman Empire as long as possible.   It also raised the question
of the true nature of the Triple Alliance.   Was it primarily an
instrument for defence ('Versicherungsgesellschaft') or for making
gains ('Erwerbsgenossenschaft')? (10)   The Triple Alliance was in
fact both.   Ostensibly a defensive pact, (11) it was used not only
by Italy, but also by Austria-Hungary and Germany as a basis for an
active, or rather expansive policy - Austria-Hungary in the Balkans,
Germany in the world at large with her 'Weltpolitik'.
        The Triple Alliance was renewed again on 28 June 1902, but only
two days before the Franco-Italian Agreement. (12)   From then on,
differences between Italy and Austria-Hungary could no longer be
bridged, not because of Italy's 'infidelity', but because of the
divergence oᶜ Italy's social and political structure from that of
the German Emᴗire and Austria-Hungary.   Although attempting to
become an imperialist power, Italy's more liberal and parliamentary
system, and her sympathies for the national movement in the Balkans,
opened up a gulf with the more conservative empires in Central
Europe.   Italy began to drift away from the Triple Alliance from
1902 onwards and left it completely in 1914-15.

THE 'ENTENTE CORDIALE', 1904

While Germany still clung to the illusion of being able to keep its
options open even in the period of 'Weltpolitik', the very basis
of the latter started to crumble.
        Even before Italy began to move away from the Triple Alliance,
negotiations opened between Britain and France which were to lead
to the 'Entente Cordiale'. (13)   On 30 January 1902, the same day
as the Anglo-Japanese Treaty was signed, the German Ambassador to
London, Metternich, reported talks between Chamberlain and the
French Ambassador to London, Paul Cambon, for the first time.   The
end of the Boer War in May 1902 removed an important psychological
obstacle in French public opinion, and talks on colonial matters
were resumed thereafter.   In May 1903 Eckardtstein, who had left
the diplomatic service, emphatically warned the Auswärtiges Amt
that an agreement between Britain, France and Russia was imminent.
Holstein and Bülow, however, derided Eckardtstein's views, which
were, for once, realistic and well-founded.   The Wilhelmstrasse
still thought an agreement was impossible, due to tension between
Britain and Russia. (14)   However, even the Tsar had suggested in
1902 that France should try to reach an agreement with Britain.
        Egypt and Morocco were the two main points of compromise in
colonial matters.   France recognized Britain's position in Egypt,
while Britain supported France in her claim on Morocco.   The
pledge of mutual diplomatic support over Egypt and Morocco, given

in the 'Entente Cordiale' of 8 April 1904, was by no means a formal
alliance.   But it initiated political cooperation between France
and Britain that soon spread to military and naval spheres.   France
agreed to limit further naval expansion and concentrate on the army.
France's navy was eventually concentrated in the Mediterranean,
while Britain could concentrate the Royal Navy in the North Sea.
Britain had thus partly destroyed one central premise of Tirpitz's
plan - the dispersion of the British fleet throughout the world.
The first Moroccan crisis of 1905 led to talks between the British
and the French general staffs, once the possibility of a German
attack against France had been envisaged.   Without being a formal
treaty, the 'Entente Cordiale' amounted to an Anglo-French Alliance.
It represented the first visible major blow to German 'Weltpolitik'.
    The German leaders were quick to see the point.   The Kaiser,
on one of his cruises in the Mediterranean, made sarcastic remarks
about his political advisers when he learned of the 'Entente
Cordiale'. (15)   Outwardly, the German leaders tried to remain
calm, but behind the scenes, an atmosphere of despondency was
taking over. (16)

A SALLY TO THE EAST - DETACHING RUSSIA FROM FRANCE, 1904-5

The German government hoped to make up for their setback by a
short-term diplomatic success to divert attention from the long-
term failure of 'Weltpolitik' that loomed behind the 'Entente
Cordiale'.   Morocco was an interesting object to bind the wounds
of the German Empire.   But before Germany was able to act, other
world events brought temporary relief.
    Russia was weakened by her military defeat against Japan in the
Russo-Japanese War, followed by the first Russian Revolution, but
also by a crisis for the Franco-Russian Dual Alliance over French
neutrality.   The new situation tempted Germany into trying to re-
isolate France on the Continent and thus neutralize the newly
formed 'Entente Cordiale' with Britain by destroying the Franco-
Russian Dual Alliance at the same time.   Germany made it clear
that its official neutrality was in Russia's favour, e.g. by
supplying coal to the Russian Baltic fleet on its way to the Far
East.   On the other hand, Germany imposed a harsh commercial
treaty on Russia to make her dependent on Germany's export industry.   The Russians at first offered resistance to German pressure,
but they were in a weak position.   They gave way only when
Chancellor Bülow took up the matter himself and pressed the German
advantage ruthlessly.   In July 1904 the new commercial treaty was
concluded. (17)   Germany's rude exploiting of Russia's weakness
only increased resentment against the German Empire.   When Russia
was further weakened by the revolutionary unrest which began in
January 1905, the German government resorted to the former idea of
coming to an agreement with Russia.   If the Germans had been
successful, Russia and Germany might have been able to win France
over and Britain would have had most of Europe united against her.
The 'Entente Cordiale', the cohesion of which was not yet known,
would have been suffocated soon after its birth, and German hegemony in Europe would have been established by diplomatic methods.

The Wilhelmstrasse struck twice, in November 1904 and July 1905. The first opportunity presented itself in the Dogger Bank incident, at the end of October 1904.   Russian ships, belonging to the Baltic fleet bound for the Far East, fired on British fishing boats near the Dogger Bank in the middle of the night, because the Russians in their excitement thought they were Japanese torpedo boats.   Anti-Russian feeling in Britain ran high.   The Kaiser quickly saw his chance to detach Russia from France and thus destroy the emerging Triple Entente.   On 27 October he suggested an alliance of the Continental Powers against Britain and Japan to the Tsar.   The Kaiser even went so far as to ask if the Russians were willing to order some capital ships to be built by German shipyards. (18)   In November 1904 negotiations between the Germans and the Russians progressed as far as the exchange of the first drafts for a treaty of alliance between the two countries. (19)   The crucial point, however, was France.   The Germans wanted to conclude a bilateral treaty of alliance and defence with Russia alone, compelling France, if necessary through the Franco-Russian Dual Alliance, to follow suit.   The Russians were only ready to conclude a treaty if France had been informed and asked to join.   Germany's position would thus have been weakened and because the Russians insisted on their 'modus procedendi', the Germans lost all interest in the deal and let the matter drop. (20)

Another German initiative, this time on the part of Bülow in St Petersburg in February 1905, did not get so far.   There was not even a discussion with the Russians on the subject.   But the Chancellor's suggestion in a memorandum to the Kaiser sheds further light on the ideological basis of German foreign policy.   Bülow discussed the permanent crisis in Austria-Hungary and the forecasts from revolutionary groups, that Germany and Russia would soon find themselves in conflict, upon Austria-Hungary's disintegration. To avert a conflict, the German Chancellor thought that a treaty between Russia and Germany could help, which bound both Powers to a policy of territorial disinterestedness towards Austria-Hungary. Neither Russia nor Germany was to exploit Austria-Hungary's internal difficulties for territorial gains.   Bülow's argument for such a deal once more demonstrates the conservative character of the German Empire:

> I make this suggestion, although I know the loyalty of my
> Imperial master. On the other hand, I, am convinced that the
> government of Tsar Nicholas abhors the idea of annexing any
> Austrian territory and incorporating further subversive ele-
> ments, which would be the result. To my mind, such a Germano-
> Russian treaty of 'désinteressement' would not only remove the
> only cause of possible mistrust between Russia and Germany in
> the future, but would also confirm in practice the universally
> recognized principle of monarchical solidarity against the sub-
> versive forces of revolution. (21)

Nothing came of Bülow's idea this time.   But it illustrates that the Kaiser's next spectacular move, during his meeting with the Tsar at Björkoe in July 1905, was generally in line with the attempt of official German foreign policy to bring Russia into closer relationship with Germany, but without risking an attack by Britain on Germany as a result of an alliance with Russia. (22)

It was then that Germany's leader began to conjure up the spectre of 'Germany's encirclement'. (23)

A SALLY TO THE WEST - THE SCHLIEFFEN PLAN AND THE FIRST MOROCCAN CRISIS, 1905

Germany's 'second offer of an alliance to Russia',(24) however, was preceded by a sally against France. If Russia could not be detached from France, perhaps France could be detached from Britain, or at least the rather delicate ties existing between the two countries might be loosened. Theoretically, there were two different approaches, diplomatic and military. Germany could attempt to put mere political pressure upon France to enter the orbit of the German Empire on one form or another. Germany could also resort to war against France, while Russia was still paralysed in the Far East and at home. The German general staff under Count Schlieffen was eager for a 'preventive war' against France, apparently in agreement with Bülow and Holstein. France would have been the only 'pawn' on the Continent, accessible to a German attack by land, Britain being beyond German striking power. (25)
   It is only logical that the famous Schlieffen plan, which was to influence German foreign policy until 1914, took shape in 1905, at a time when Russia was no military factor to be considered by Germany. (26)   The plan was carried out in 1914 in a slightly modified form at a time when Russia was again a first-rate military power in Europe. Schlieffen and his successors believed they could throw the bulk of the German army against France in a lightning campaign, while they were relying on weak German forces in the East, together with the Austro-Hungarian army, to contain the Russians. The Schlieffen plan could not be adapted to the changing political situation in the years before 1914 because Germany's political leaders were only hazily informed about the intentions of the general staff and had no influence at all on strategic planning. By 1914, when Russia had to be counted again as a military factor, the absurdity of the Schlieffen plan was probably clear to any political observer of medium intelligence. But political leadership in a military monarchy like the German Empire lacked the degree of self-confidence and independence necessary to oppose the military structure that was one of the mainstays of the Empire.
   Further faults should have provoked criticism of the plan from the politicians: the violation of Belgian (also originally Dutch) neutrality and the arrogant belittling of Britain's power in Europe. Schlieffen was confident that any British Expeditionary Force that dared to support France would be 'arrested' by the victorious German armies. German political leaders willingly bowed to the wisdom of German generals and field-marshals, as long as everything seemed to be running smoothly. But the Schlieffen plan also demonstrates the adventurous character of German 'Weltpolitik'. When its failure became visible a few years after it had been launched with such high hopes, the German Empire desperately staked everything on a lightning war with France, lasting six weeks; afterwards the German armies would be sent to the east where Russia would be defeated in about the same length of time.

In spite of Russia's helplessness, Germany did not strike against France in 1905, as the general staff had wished.   The Kaiser took fright at starting a war over Morocco, and the commanding generals of the Prussian army were disappointed when he told them so on New Year's Day 1906. (27)   Large parts of public opinion, the Liberals and the Socialists, strongly opposed any war against France because of Morocco.   The navy under Tirpitz took the same line, because the admirals feared a war against Britain resulting from a German attack on France, and the subsequent destruction of the German battle fleet.   The chronic dilemma of German 'Weltpolitik' between the permanent readiness of the army in contrast to the permanent unreadiness of the battle fleet made itself felt for the first time.   Its effect was to paralyse Germany's action by conflicting advice coming from the army and the navy.

If France could not be eliminated by war, because the German battle fleet was not yet ready for war against Britain, Germany could try to exploit France's relatively weak position by political pressure.   A major diplomatic defeat of the French might weaken the Franco-Russian Dual Alliance and disrupt it altogether. Germany, in 1905, started a political offensive against France to humiliate her by a direct or indirect threat of war - a repetition of German strategy in 1875. (28)   This time, however, France was no longer alone, although the Franco-Russian Dual Alliance existed only on paper as long as Russia was engaged in the Far East and was in turmoil at home.

The 'Entente Cordiale' was only a colonial arrangement, and its real value still had to be tested in Europe.   The first test was Germany's political offensive against France, culminating in the first Moroccan crisis of 1905-6.   The field chosen for attack was favourable for German diplomacy, because French expansion into Morocco conflicted with the Treaty of Madrid of 1880.   Germany, on the other hand, originally did not have territorial ambitions in Morocco as a protectorate without the agreement of the powers who had signed the Treaty of Madrid was tantamount to excluding the other powers.

Germany, believing itself to be in a strong position, suggested an international conference on Morocco.   Because it would be impossible to block French expansion in Morocco completely, the idea was at least to impose conditions with the help of the international community.   Holstein now also hoped to obtain some territorial gain in Morocco as compensation for German concessions to France. (29)   After a major diplomatic defeat, France would join the combination led by Germany, and the 'Entente Cordiale' would be strangled right at the beginning.

German speculations turned out to be diplomatic disaster because of the clumsy way in which Germany pressed for the Conference on Morocco.   German initiative had closely followed the Kaiser's spectacular landing at Tangiers on 31 March 1905 to support the Sultan's position against the French.   The Kaiser was most unwilling to land at Tangiers, but the Wilhelmstrasse insisted on it as a demonstration of German interest in Morocco.   They gave rise, however, to suspicions as to Germany's true aims and motives for convening an international conference, because Germany had rejected any French initiative for bilateral negotiations between France

and Germany.   Germany stood pat on its conference proposal with
the clear aim of isolating and humiliating France before the
world. (30)
Even before the Conference could begin the Germans had managed
to bring about the downfall of Delcassé, the French Foreign Minister.   As the chief initiator of the 'Entente Cordiale' from the
French side, he was heartily detested in Germany.   The Wilhelmstrasse let the French know that Delcassé was the only obstacle
preventing a reasonable arrangement between the two powers.
Germany thus encouraged Delcassé's enemies at home, and particularly
the groups who feared that France was too weak to stand up against
Germany.   To avert the possibility of Germany making war against
France at this time, the French Premier Rouvier urged Delcassé to
resign in order to appease the Germans.   When Delcassé did resign,
on 6 June 1905, a few days after the destruction of Russia's Baltic
fleet in the Battle of Tsushima, the Germans did not drop the conference project, but on the contrary vigorously pushed it ahead.
However, at the Conference of Algeciras, Rouvier, who had taken
over the Foreign Ministry as well, defended French interests so
energetically that it came as a surprise to the Germans.

GERMANY'S 'SECOND OFFER OF ALLIANCE TO RUSSIA' AT BJÖRKOE, 1905

Flushed with their diplomatic victory over France after Delcassé's
downfall under German pressure, the Germans turned to the East
again.   In the summer of 1905 Germany's 'second offer of alliance
to Russia' culminated in the abortive treaty of Björkoe.   During
a meeting between the Kaiser and the Tsar at Björkoe, the Kaiser
tried to talk the Tsar into an alliance with Germany.   The next
day, the Kaiser was successful, and the Tsar signed the draft of a
treaty, based on the German draft of November 1904. (31)   The
Kaiser, in his report to the Auswärtiges Amt, boasted about his
'historic' success. (32)   Although Bülow and Holstein were
generally pleased with the Kaiser's success, they were unhappy
about two modifications, introduced by the Kaiser on the spot.
The alliance covered only an attack from a European power within
Europe, and the treaty would only be valid after the Russo-Japanese
War. (33)   The first point relieved Russia of any obligation to
march against India in a common war with Britain.   The second
point made it necessary to revise German policy during the Russo-
Japanese War.   Just as Germany had studiously (and apparently
successfully) tried to bring Russia and Japan to loggerheads in the
Far East to obstruct any mediation between the two powers before
and after the outbreak of war, the Kaiser and Bülow had done
everything to prop up Russia's will to continue war as long as
possible. (34)   Now, Germany would be interested in a speedy end
of the war, because only then would the treaty of alliance with
Russia become valid.   Apart from these particular points, Holstein
criticized the Kaiser for not exploiting the Tsar's weak position
enough.   The Kaiser was only impressed by the Chancellor's criticism after Bülow offered his resignation, which was, however, not
accepted. (35)   ·
The internal wrangle dampened German enthusiasm over the

Kaiser's diplomatic success.   They found comfort in the belief
that the Tsar's signature was sufficient to make it binding for
Russia.   But to the consternation of the Germans, the Russian
government refused to endorse the signature of their monarch,
because they did not want to take action behind France's back and
realized that Russia would have given herself into Germany's hands.
It took some months for the Germans to realize that Björkoe was a
diplomatic 'fata morgana'.

The situation was complicated by several factors.   For tactical
reasons, the Germans thought it opportune to advise the Tsar,
during the first Russian Revolution, to grant a constitution.   But
such a constitution would have favoured the Liberals and Socialists
in Russia who became increasingly hostile to Germany because she
sought to support the hated Tsarist regime wherever possible. (36)
The second problem was of a financial nature.   As long as the
Germans clung to their hope that the Russians would come around to
the idea of an alliance with Germany after all, they once more
employed the weapon of banning German capital from participating
in an international loan for Russia, until Russia had declared
herself for Germany.   The effect was similar to that in 1887. (37)
The Russians did not give in to German pressure and obtained the
loan mainly from France in 1906.   The Franco-Russian alliance,
which had been shaken during the Russo-Japanese War, was strengthened again.

GERMAN FAILURE AT ALGECIRAS, 1906

The third factor had the same effect - the development of the
Algeciras Conference.   After Delaassé's fall in June 1905, negotiations about the conference and its agenda took the rest of the
year 1905.   At the end of September 1905, Germany, under Russian
pressure, gave way to French wishes for the agenda, because the
chance seemed to present itself for setting up a Continental bloc
against Britain after all.   By the end of November 1905, however,
it was clear that Russia would not easily be separated from France,
and the German concession had been all in vain.

When the Morocco Conference opened at Algeciras, a small Spanish
town, on 16 January 1906, Germany had dragged the Powers against
their wishes to the conference table.   Soon it became obvious
that Germany's calculations had been wrong.   However justified
Germany's stand may have been legally, Germany was nearly isolated
in its opposition to French expansion in Morocco.   The suspicion
was widespread that Germany was merely looking for an excuse to
provoke war against France.   Apart from Austria-Hungary, no other
power supported Germany, not even Italy, the third partner in the
Triple Alliance.   Suddenly confronted with international isolation, Holstein, who had been the first to suggest the project of
the conference, wanted to abandon it at once.   But Bülow, in
agreement with the Kaiser, saved the conference by giving in to
France on the principle of French control in Morocco, while France
made concessions on details of procedure to ease Germany's retreat.
Morocco was practically handed over to France, veiled only by an
international agreement in which Germany was allowed to take part.

After weary further negotiations, the Algeciras Act was signed on 7 June 1906, a year after Delcassé's fall. (38)

It was a resounding defeat for Germany, which attained none of its aims, short-term or long-term, because it had overreached itself.   Neither its powerful position on the Continent nor its strong legal position over the Moroccan question helped to save it. The 'Entente Cordiale' had been put to the test by Germany's political offensive against France and developed into an informal political alliance.   It was soon followed by military talks between the British and the French general staffs and by the Anglo-Russian Agreement in 1907, which formally concluded Germany's containment.   Personal consequences were considerable.   The French Foreign Minister had fallen at the beginning of the first Moroccan crisis, and Holstein fell after its inglorious end.   Holstein died only three years later, but Delcassé moved to St Petersburg as French Ambassador and was triumphantly recalled to the French Cabinet in August 1914.

The historical significance of Germany's first sally in the West was the creation of an ambiguous situation in Morocco which tempted Germany to open a second round with similar methods five years later, again with similar results. (39)   During the first Moroccan crisis three more factors came into existence that influenced German foreign policy on its road to war in 1914:   the encirclement complex, the Schlieffen plan and the abhorrence of German leaders of any kind of international conference which could decide on German aspirations.   The experience of international isolation at Algeciras in 1906 had been too painful.

Chapter 11

TRIPLE ENTENTE AND THE BOSNIAN CRISIS, 1907-9

Within a few years, 'Weltpolitik' had resulted in the loss of
Germany's political initiative in the world. Since Algeciras, the
German Empire had increasingly to react to the policy of the other
Great Powers, who, in their turn, largely reacted to German policy.
The situation began to worsen for Germany with the formation of the
'Entente Cordiale' in 1904: Britain was apparently returning to
her traditional policy of trying to check the political ascendancy
of any power on the Continent. But even two years before,
'British naval and military leaders made up their minds that the
most likely foe in a future war was Germany'. (1)   The Committee
of Imperial Defence, established in May 1904, one month after the
'Entente Cordiale', started its work under such premises. Britain
acted with restraint, however, as long as doubts existed as to
Germany's true ambitions.

CROWE'S ASSESSMENT OF 'WELTPOLITIK' AND THE TRIPLE ENTENTE, 1907

Two and a half years after the conclusion of the 'Entente Cordiale',
and more than half a year before the Anglo-Russian Agreement of
1907, Sir Eyre Crowe, the Permanent Under-Secretary of State in
the Foreign Office, tried to assess the character of German 'Weltpolitik' and its implications for the future, in his famous memorandum of 1 January 1907. (2)   Crowe was very well informed about
Germany through family connections. His memorandum, decried for
a long time by German historians as anti-German, was the most
realistic analysis of German 'Weltpolitik' at the time. It amounted to accepting German expansion in the world, as long as it was
essentially peaceful and in accordance with the interest of the
other imperialist Powers, but he warned of a policy of appeasing
Germany by making unjustified concessions. (3)
    Crowe's memorandum became the basis of British foreign policy
until 1914.   The next logical step was the Anglo-Russian Agreement
of 31 August 1907.   Like the 'Entente Cordiale', it covered
matters outside Europe - Persia, in the first place, Afghanistan
and Tibet in the second - but it served to remove or lessen frictions between Britain and Russia on problems of quasi-colonial

character.   Again like the 'Entente Cordiale', the Anglo-Russian
Agreement was no formal treaty of alliance.   But, although the
term is not really correct, the relationship between Britain, France
and Russia between 1907 and 1917 came to be known as the Triple
Entente, in contrast to the Triple Alliance, led by Germany.   There
was no formal instrument of alliance, but only a system of a bilateral treaty (Dual Alliance between France and Russia) combined with
bilateral agreements between Britain on the one hand, and France
and Russia on the other.   The Triple Entente was not so much
directed against the Triple Alliance, but rather against Germany
and its 'Weltpolitik'.   From now on, Germany's 'containment' was
complete.
     Germany had been given a warning.   The Triple Entente was not
an aggressive alliance, and Britain was in a position to veto any
aggression of France or Russia against Germany of the Triple Alliance.   But it had become obvious that the Powers of the Triple
Entente would stand up against Germany, as soon as it were to
'overstep the line of legitimate protection of existing rights' (4)
and were thus to violate the rules that existed even within the
anarchy of imperialism.   In other words, Germany's further expansion was possible only by taking into account the interests of the
other imperialist Powers.   German foreign policy up to the First
World War, however, almost completely disregarded that element of
international power politics of the day.

THE NAVAL RACE FOR BATTLESHIPS AND BRITISH BIDS FOR A NAVAL
AGREEMENT WITH GERMANY, 1907-8

One of the key arrangements Germany could have found with at least
one of the Great Powers, was a naval agreement with Britain.   In
1902 Britain was so alarmed at the rate at which the German fleet
was expanding, that the new capital ship of the 'dreadnought' type
was introduced in 1905 to conserve the superiority of British sea-
power. (5)   The naval arms race had begun in earnest, because
Germany tried to follow Britain only one year later.   In May 1906
the Reichstag passed a bill for the extension of the Kiel Canal
and of the docks and harbour facilities at Wilhelmshaven, so that
they could also accommodate German capital ships of the dreadnought
type.   However, the German battle fleet continued to lag behind
the Royal Navy in one important respect - heavy artillery.   In
1916 British capital ships carried guns measuring up to 38.1cm,
whereas German guns only reached 30.5cm.   The dreadnought had only
apparently destroyed Britain's superiority in her pre-dreadnought
fleet.   In reality, Germany's financial and naval potential was
overstrained by the self-imposed obligation to follow the pace of
British naval armament. (6)
     The consequences for German foreign policy were no less serious.
After the dreadnought, Germany's naval preparations for war at sea
had practically to start again from scratch.   The instant preparedness of the Reich for war on land and sea was thus drastically reduced and made for a chronic dilemma, which made itself felt for
the first time in 1905 over Morocco and Russia: the army was ready
for war, the navy was not. (7)

The prospects of a costly arms race at sea against Germany made
Britain even more anxious to come to an agreement. The new Liberal
government, coming into power in 1906, wanted to give first priority to problems of domestic and social reforms and would have preferred to avoid the financial burden of the naval arms race. On
the other hand, even the Liberals insisted on preserving the superiority of the British navy, and they were prepared, if necessary, to
impose financial sacrifices on the British taxpayer for that end.
It was in line with such reasoning, that in 1907 the Liberal government, this time backed by many of the other powers, suggested that
Europe should try to pick up the scattered pieces of the 1899 Hague
Peace Conference to limit armament by an international understanding.

Germany, followed by Austria-Hungary, was again mainly responsible for the failure of this initiative. (8)   At German insistence,
the deadly arms race had to go on, because the German Empire refused
to limit its armaments, the final weapon for achieving the aims of
'Weltpolitik'.   The short-term result of Germany's stand on the
Second Hague Peace Conference in 1907 was to repeat the spectacle
of Algeciras, this time in a field in which the wrongs were clearly
on Germany's side - the all but complete isolation of the German
Empire in the world, this time not only politically, but also
morally.

After the multilateral approach to limit armament had failed in
1907, Britain tried again one year later, now on a bilateral basis,
directly with Germany. Prospects were not too bright.   In November 1907, one day after the otherwise successful visit of the
Kaiser's to Windsor, the German government had announced their
decision to reduce the period of service of capital ships from
twenty-five to twenty years. The net result was further expansion
and modernization of Germany's battle fleet.   Undaunted, in the
summer of 1908 the British presented their suggestions for a bilateral agreement on limitations of armaments, in three different
ways: (i) through the influential banker of German extraction,
Sir Ernest Cassel, and Albert Ballin, Director of HAPAG, who was
influential with the Kaiser; (ii) through the Permanent Under-
Secretary at the Foreign Office, Sir Charles Hardinge, during
Edward VII's visit to Kronberg near Frankfurt/Main; and (iii) in
talks between the new Secretary of State at the Foreign Office,
Sir Edward Grey, and the Chancellor of the Exchequer, Lloyd George,
with the German Ambassador to London, Count Wolff-Metternich. (9)
On each occasion, official or unofficial, the British tried to
make clear their point of view to the Germans - Hardinge at Kron-
berg even directly to the Kaiser. (10)   They won the support of
Metternich, who, from 1908, warned in several reports that the
German battle fleet was the one concrete obstacle standing between
Britain and Germany and that it would have serious consequences.
(11)

All warnings were in vain. Berlin arrogantly rejected any
British initiatives for an agreement of mutual limitations of
British and German armaments. The two individuals most responsible for the German attitude were without doubt the Kaiser, who had
no wish to lose his favourite toy and Tirpitz, who could not bear
to see his life's work restricted or even destroyed. But they

were also under pressure from chauvinist elements in public
opinion, whose emergence they themselves had encouraged ever since
the beginning of 'Weltpolitik'.   Given the social and political
structure of the Reich, the chauvinist elements in public opinion
would have vetoed any major concession, such as was implied in an
agreement sought by Britain, because it would have been against
the tradition of German militarism and the material interests of
heavy industry in Germany.

Chancellor Bülow let himself be carried along by the political
currents in public opinion and at the Imperial Court.   In an
instruction to the German Ambassador to London, of 5 August 1908,
Bülow even justified his refusal of any agreement on limitation of
armaments by the imputation that unilateral limitation of armaments
was requested only from Germany, and that the German nation would
rather prefer 'war on several fronts' to 'such a violation of its
honour and dignity'. (12)   A few weeks before Bülow, in a circu-
lar instruction to German missions, had defined the German position
in even stronger terms: 'We will not consider discussing arrangements made with the intention of limiting our armed forces.   A
country who makes such a request, must be aware that such a request
will mean war with us.' (13)

The basic issues can also be seen in Wolff-Metternich's report
of 1 August 1908, on conversations with Grey and Lloyd George.
Lloyd George had suggested a ratio of British and German naval
forces of 3:2.   The German ambassador contended that Germany could
easily cope with increased armament expenditure, because its capacity for taxation had not been exploited to the full.   When Lloyd
George hinted at the possibility that Britain, in the face of a
growing German battle fleet, could not rely on her navy only but
would have to build up a strong army as well, on the basis of
national conscription, even the moderate Wolff-Metternich retorted:
'If we see Britain introducing national conscription with a view
to Germany and to become worthy of an alliance with France, I do
not believe that we would quietly wait for the conclusion of the
development.' (14)

Germany thus obliquely threatened a preventive war, which at
that time could only be directed against France.   The question of
war or peace came also to the fore in the Kronberg conversation
between Hardinge and the Kaiser.   According to the Kaiser,
Hardinge pressed for an agreed limitation of the German building
programme, and Wilhelm II is claimed to have answered: 'Then we
shall fight, for it is a question of national honour and dignity.'
(15)

The Germans had shattered all British hopes for an agreement on
the limitation of naval armaments.   But there was a subtle nuance
in the positions of the Kaiser and his Chancellor.   Bülow was a
little more elastic and wanted to make the British believe that an
agreement could possibly be considered in the future.   The Kaiser,
however, was adamant and refused to hear of any agreement.   Bülow
was only pursuing cleverer tactics, because he proceeded even more
strongly from the conviction that war with Britain was approaching.
For that contingency, he reckoned with Germany's involvement
against France, Russia and Britain - the very constellation of
1914.   But even that perspective did not deflect the German

Chancellor from his collision course.   On the contrary, the growing element of irrational recklessness in German foreign policy
was well illustrated by Bülow's final remark in his report to the
Kaiser, assuring him that in the case of war, he would see to it
that 'we, however the chances may be, will throw many corpses at
the feet of our enemies'. (16)   German 'Weltpolitik' had lost much
of its self-confidence only one decade earlier.   Bülow's remark
betrays a kind of 'Götterdämmerung' atmosphere, which reached its
first height in the Kaiser's outburst at the end of July 1914. (17)

THE BOSNIAN CRISIS, 1908-9

The excitement over the failure of the British initiatives to reach
some agreement on the limitation of naval armament had barely
passed, when a new crisis burst upon the European scene, which,
this time, demanded the attention of all governments.   After the
first crisis in the West, the Moroccan crisis of 1905-6, the annexation of Bosnia and Herzegovina by Austria-Hungary provoked the
first major crisis in the East in the new century.   The Bosnian
crisis leads into the heart again of the eastern question, caused
by the simultaneous decline of both the Ottoman and the Habsburg
Empire and the emergence of the south Slav national movement on the
Balkans.   It was now that the German Empire was irrevocably drawn
into those problems. (18)   Austria-Hungary's foreign policy had
remained relatively passive ever since the occupation of Bosnia
and Herzegovina in 1878 and since the Triple Alliance of 1882. (19)
The turmoil of domestic affairs in Austria-Hungary had left no
energies for a policy of expansion abroad, i.e. in the Balkans.
Austria-Hungary was just strong enough to control areas directly
adjacent to her territory, above the small but dynamic kingdom of
Serbia.   Ideas of Austria-Hungarian expansion as far as Saloniki   •
remained the empty dreams of a few chauvinists, because it would
have been impossible to rally the forces necessary for such an
adventurous policy. (20)
     Under Bismarck, the alliance with Austria-Hungary had the func-
tion of neutralizing, as much as possible through good relations
with Russia, the tensions arising from the Balkans, which could
spark off a European conflagration.   Germany's main interest was
to prevent an alliance between the imperial ambitions of Tsarism
in Russia with the revolutionary and democratic national movement
of the south Slavs under the banner of Pan-Slavism with its powerful backing in Russia. (21)   In the phase of 'Weltpolitik',
Austria-Hungary gradually acquired a different place in the concept of German foreign policy.   Germany's main interest now was
one of broadening its territorial basis on the Continent.   Austria-
Hungary began to play the role both of an extension of the German
Empire through the concept of 'Mitteleuropa' (which remained, however, below the political surface until the outbreak of the war in
1914) and of a strategically vital transit to reach Turkey, the
vast field of German expansion before and after 1914. (22)   Germany
was now interested in the preservation of the Danube Monarchy not
only for domestic reasons of its own, (23) but also for reasons of
power politics.

Austria-Hungary's position within the Triple Alliance also changed. At the conclusion of the Dual Alliance in 1879, she had still been a partner on the footing of equality, even although she owed her existence and independence to Prussia's relative restraint after Sadowa in 1866. By the early twentieth century, Austria-Hungary had become almost a German satellite. To strengthen its position Germany had forced its partners in the Triple Alliance to attend the Algeciras Conference in 1906, and after it, the Kaiser condescendingly described Austria-Hungary, much to her embarrassment, as having played the part of a 'brilliant second' at Algeciras. (24)

The period of 'muddling on' ('Fortwursteln') at home and relative passiveness abroad came to a certain conclusion in 1906. The suspension of the Hungarian constitution in 1906 led to a compromise between the Crown and the Magyar gentry at the expense of the south Slav nationalities. This did not improve the situation. On the contrary. The south Slav nationalities, organized in the Croatian-Serbian Coalition, had set great hopes on the former Hungarian opposition. When their leaders, Franz Kossuth and Albert Apponyi, joined the government camp in Budapest, they supported harsh measures of further Magyarization, with the result of bitterly disappointing the south Slavs. Since the Magyars could maintain their domineering position only by the backing of the German Empire, it was inevitable that the south Slav opposition in the Habsburg Monarchy became increasingly hostile to Germany as well. The leaders of the south Slav nationalities, although originally loyal for a very long time indeed, saw no chance any more of obtaining equality within the existing power structure, the Habsburg Monarchy. It became inevitable that sooner or later they would have to look elsewhere for support -- beyond Austria-Hungary.

The Archimedean point was Serbia, from which Austria-Hungary was to be destroyed only one decade later, in 1918. The political leadership of Austria-Hungary did everything to drive their south Slav nationalities towards Serbia with self-defeating energy: in domestic policy by stepping up the policy of Magyarization in Hungary after 1906 with the support of the former Hungarian opposition; in foreign policy, only two years later, by the annexation of Bosnia-Herzegovina and increasing hostility against Serbia. Until 1903 Serbia had, approximately, the position of a protégé or satellite state of Austria-Hungary. The overthrow of the corrupt Obrenovic dynasty by a group of young patriotic officers in 1903 initiated a dramtic change: Serbia broke away from Austrian tutelage and took up the ideal of national unification of all south Slavs. The dynamism of the south Slav programme was bound to hurt Austria-Hungary most, because most of the southern Slavs lived there. Austria-Hungary herself increased the dynamism of the south Slav national movement when launching a political offensive against Serbia with two aims: curbing Serbia, which had become unruly ever since 1903, and thus dampening down the nationalist movement amongst the south Slavs at home. (25)

In October 1906 Goluchowski, the exponent of a passive foreign policy, was replaced by Baron von Aehrenthal as Foreign Minister. His personal ambition of going down in history as a kind of Austrian Bismarck, fitted exactly into what Austria-Hungary's

ruling class had been looking for - some political success abroad
to improve the situation at home. (26)   After Aehrenthal's arrival
at the Ballhausplatz, his first move was a logical result from the
social and political structure of the Habsburg Monarchy.   In April
1906 part of the compromise, enforced by the Hungarian nationalists,
had been higher tariffs on agrarian products from Serbia, especially
pigs, to protect their own agrarian interests on the domestic market
of the Danube Monarchy as a whole.   This had been the price for
keeping German as the comman language of command within the Austro-
Hungarian army.   Vienna abrogated the commercial treaty with Serbia
and increased agrarian tariffs on Serbian products as a reprisal for
Serbia's refusal to buy arms from the Austrian firm Skoda.   Serbia,
however, contrary to expectation and to her policy before 1903, did
not submit to Austrian pressure, but found other outlets for her
products in Europe.   And Germany's industry did not resist the
temptation to replace Austria-Hungary as the main supplier of industrial goods to the Serbian market.   German industrialists were
apparently slow to grasp the connection between German 'Weltpolitik'
and Serbian pigs.

Furthermore, Serbia obtained loans and weapons from France,
instead of Austria-Hungary, and exported her cattle via Salonika
which was Turkish at the time. (27)   The trade war of 1906-11,
which Austria-Hungary had provoked to subdue Serbia, backfired,
however, because it mobilized south Slav nationalism among
Serbia's peasants who had been hit directly by the increased
Austrian tariffs to the advantage of their Magyar competitors.
From 1907 onwards, intellectuals of the Serbo-Croat coalition
inside Austria-Hungary, formed in 1905, even began to talk of
Serbia as the 'Piedmont of the south Slavs', to the utmost horror
of Austria-Hungary's ruling class who were well aware of the
threatening political implications of that historical allusion. (28)

After the weapon of commercial sanctions had failed, Aehrenthal
hoped to solve the 'south Slav question' by uniting the south Slavs
within the Danube Monarchy in order to forestal their unification
without or outside Austria-Hungary, as happened in 1918 after the
dissolution of the Habsburg Monarchy.   Aehrenthal's concept would
have led to a kind of trialism, i.e. to the equality of Germans,
Hungarians and south Slavs, and from there to a full-fledged system
of federation.   But Aehrenthal's grand design would have necessi-
tated the destruction of Serbia.   Indeed, Aehrenthal dreamed of
dividing Serbia between Austria-Hungary and Bulgaria, who from now
on became Vienna's favourite Balkan country. (29)

Another condition had to be fulfilled first, the annexation of
Bosnia and Herzegovina, occupied in 1878, (30) with possible repercussions both at home and abroad.   Annexation would have removed
a thirty years' old interim solution and paved the way for an
effective integration of the two south Slav provinces into the
Habsburg Monarchy.   The annexation was intended to strengthen
Austria-Hungary's position abroad.   Since Bosnia was for historical reasons a province close to the heart of all Serbian nationalists, Serbia might allow herself to be provoked to some rash
action, which could provide a perfect excuse for war against Serbia.
The annexation of Bosnia and Herzegovina as the first step towards
the destruction of Serbia, was also intended to inaugurate a new

phase of an active and dynamic foreign policy, independent of
Germany.

In reality, however, all conditions for the success of such an
ambitious offensive for strengthening the decaying system of the
Habsburg Monarchy, any attempts at transforming the existing dual-
ism into trialism, were bound to fail, because the ruling Magyar
aristocracy would see their privileged position in Hungary threatened by the rise of the south Slavs to equality.   Conditions of
success were also lacking abroad.   Serbian resistance was not
easily subdued, nor did Serbia rush into the trap laid by
Aehrenthal.   Furthermore, Russia, after her defeat in the Far
East, returned to the Near East and the Balkans, and backed up
Serbia.   But Russia was militarily still so weak that she dis-
couraged Serbia from any rash policy.   Aehrenthal's adventurous
policy also had to rely on German support for its success, thus increasing Austria-Hungary's dependence on Germany even more, in
spite of all Austrian endeavours to achieve more independence.

Since the end of 1907, Aehrenthal had been preparing for his
great coup. (31)   He was, for his part, under pressure from the
Austro-Hungarian army.   In particular the Chief of the Austro-
Hungarian General Staff, Baron Conrad von Hätzendorff, had made it
his 'idée fixe' that Austria-Hungary could be saved only with the
help of some military success.   For geographical and historical
reasons there were only two countries eligible for the role of a
lightning-rod to deflect Austria-Hungary's internal tensions abroad
- little Serbia and medium-sized Italy.   Italy - unfortunately for
Conrad a partner to the Triple Alliance - represented the painful
memory of a humiliating defeat at the hands of a national movement
in 1859 and 1866.   Serbia conjured up thoughts of defeat at the
hands of another national movement in the near future.

Since Serbia was in the weaker position, Austro-Hungarian leadership concentrated on presenting the developing conflict between the
south Slav national movement and the older principle of the dynastic monarchy as the necessity to destroy the 'nest of anarchism'
at Belgrade in the name of European peace and security.   Vienna
attempted to obtain a mandate from the European Powers to finish
troublesome Serbia.   The destruction of the 'south Slav conspir-
acy' became an obsession for Austro-Hungary.   Victorious war
against Serbia was thought to be the panacea against all evils of
the Danube Monarchy. (32)

The obsessions of Austria-Hungary's ruling class in open decline
would become a menace to peace in Europe, if they succeeded in selling their anti-Serbian line to Germany, their more powerful ally.
Once German leaders became convinced that little Serbia was blocking the advance of German 'Weltpolitik', because she threatened, in
the final analysis, the very existence of Austria-Hungary and of
the monarchical principle, the German Empire would identify its
imperialist interests with the interests of the ruling class in
Austria-Hungary.   From then onwards, any serious conflict between
Austria-Hungary and Serbia would be escalated by Germany's involvement into a continental war, or even into world war.   On the
other hand, Germany's backing would enhance Austria-Hungary's
weight, because Germany was in a position to deter Russia from
active military intervention on behalf of Serbia, as long as Russia

herself was still suffering from her defeat in the Far East and at home. Such was the mechanism of the first major crisis started in the East by the annexation of Bosnia and Herzegovina.

Apart from finding a convenient excuse and date for action, Aehrenthal's greatest problem was to obtain the agreement of Turkey and of the other signatory Powers of the Treaty of Berlin to change Article 25 of the Treaty, i.e. to annex the two provinces occupied in 1878. Aehrenthal thought that the evacuation of the Sanjak (roughly equivalent to a county) of Novibazar would be a suffi- cient concession to win over Turkey and the Powers. Furthermore, he took up the idea of the new Russian Foreign Minister, Izvolsky, on 2 July 1908, to strike a political bargain. Russia would con- sent to the annexation of the two provinces, while Austria-Hungary would support Russia in changing the rules governing the Straits, in favour of Russia.

Only four days later, the Young Turk revolution, which started at Saloniki and quickly spread throughout the Turkish Empire re- opened the question of annexation. The Young Turks reintroduced the Turkish constitution of 1876, suspended by Sultam Hamid V, and issued writs for holding general elections in all parts of the Turkish Empire, including also Bosnia and Herzegovina, which were only nominally under Turkish rule. To forestall Turkish claims for a return to effective Turkish rule over Bosnia and Herzegovina, Austria-Hungary, in early October 1908, announced the annexation of the two provinces. Thus began one of the most complicated crises before 1914. Details are interesting here only in so far as they help to understand German policy during the crisis.

Vienna had not informed any other government, including Germany, of her intentions, with the exception of Russia, during Izvolsky's visit to Buchlau. But Aehrenthal had left Izvolsky in the dark as to how imminent the annexation would be, while he pocketed the Russian agreement to it in principle. When the annexation was proclaimed as early as 5 October, Izvolsky felt deceived and humil- iated. The annexation of Bosnia and Herzegovina provoked violent protests in Serbia and the demand for territorial compensation at the expense of Austria-Hungary. Russia, still feeling too weak to support Serbia, if necessary by going to war, insisted on an international conference to settle the crisis, and was supported by Britain, France and Italy on this point. (33)

Berlin was placed in an awkward position. On the one hand, Germany saw its relation to Turkey complicated by the Austrian move; on the other hand German leaders, from now on, expressed their fear of losing their last major ally, if they let down Austria-Hungary. (34) Germany, therefore, backed Austria-Hungary in her rejection of an international conference on Bosnia and Herzegovina. Chancellor Bülow did not even pretend to act as a mediator between Vienna and St Petersburg, but encouraged Aehren- thal to remain firm against Russia. In January 1909 he even advised Aehrenthal to make use of the documents that showed that Izvolsky, originally, had approved to the annexation. (35)   After months of diplomatic haggling, Austria and Germany succeeded in preventing the conference - the trauma of Algeciras made itself felt for the first time.

During that period, the mechanism of escalation leading to

continental war over Serbia was frankly discussed between Vienna
and Berlin, apparently for the first time.   In January 1909, Conrad
informed his German colleague, General Moltke, of Austrian anxiety
that Russia might turn against Austria-Hungary in the event of an
Austrian attack against Serbia.   If a war between Austria-Hungary
and Germany on the one hand, Russia and France on the other, were
to result, which Power would be tackled by Germany first - France
or Russia?   In the middle of the Bosnian crisis, the political
groupings and the strategic problems of the outbreak of the First
World War had already emerged.   Even the mechanism which would
start the conflagration was already to be seen.   Moltke answered,
on 21 January 1909, that Serbia was heading towards a showdown with
Austria.   'The moment can come, when the Monarchy's patience will
come to an end in the face of Serbian provocations.   The Monarchy
will have no other choice but to invade Serbia.'   Russia's intervention would constitute the 'casus foederis' for Germany: 'At the
same time Russia mobilizes, Germany will also mobilize all of its
army.' (36)

Moltke and Conrad in the   end agreed that Germany would throw
its armies mainly against France first, leaving only thirteen divisions in East Prussia.   What is even more important, Moltke's
first reply shows   that he was fully aware of the   mechanism that
governed the crisis of July 1914 and the outbreak of the First
World War, as far as the East was concerned: Serbian 'provocations'
would lead to an Austrian attack against Serbia, to Russia's mobilization and to Germany's immediate counter-mobilization.   This is
exactly what happened in July 1914 - on Moltke's insistence.   The
Moltke-Conrad Agreement of 1909 prepared the practical application
of the potentially aggressive turn in the Triple Alliance. (37)
Only one month later, in February 1909, the Kaiser calculated the
consequences for the western part of the escalation that led to
World War in summer 1914.   In his minutes on a telegram from
Tschirschky, the German Ambassador in Vienna, to Bülow, he envisaged
exactly what was done at the end of July 1914.   In the event of
the 'casus foederis' for Germany against Russia, Germany was to
enquire of France as to her attitude if there were a war between
Germany and Russia.   Germany would want France to declare 'that
in that case she would make no war at all against us.   Neither at
the beginning of the war nor later.'   The refusal of such a positive answer was to be taken as a cause for war against France and
to be used by German propaganda. (38)

The Kaiser had reacted to Aehrenthal's letter to Bülow of 20
February 1909, in which he intimated for the first time his intention to break the Serbian refusal to recognize the annexation of
Bosnia and Herzegovina by an ultimatum and even by war.   His strong
line tallied with the pledge given to Conrad by Moltke with the
knowledge and approval of the German Chancellor. (39)   Meanwhile,
however, Aehrenthal had dropped his earlier plan to divide Serbia
between Austria-Hungary and Bulgaria, because the incorporation of
additional south Slav territory into the Monarchy would have aggravated the domestic problem of the south Slavs.   Instead, he now
aimed at a war indemnity of 500 million crowns to be paid by Serbia
and the occupation of the Serbian capital Belgrade as a pawn, (40)
again an idea that came up in late July 1914. (41)

As early as mid-February 1909, the Russians had got wind of
Austria's intention to put an ultimatum to Serbia, to be followed
possibly by a 'punitive expedition'.   Sir Edward Grey suggested
a common intervention of the other Powers in Vienna to restrain
Austria-Hungary from such strong action.   France, Russia and
Italy approved; but Germany refused, and suggested instead a
common intervention at Belgrade, because it was the source of all
provocation. (42)   At French insistence, Russia urgently advised
Belgrade to drop the demand for territorial compensation from
Austria-Hungary, as the other powers would not agree to it; Serbia
was then to appeal to the other Powers for help against Austria-
Hungary.   Vienna, however, remained adamant and wanted to deal
with Belgrade only, and on the basis of Serbian submission. (43)
On 10 March 1909 Serbia gave in and notified that she renounced
any territorial compensation from Austria-Hungary.   But this declaration did not satisfy Austria-Hungary.   War with Serbia seemed
inevitable, after all, when the Austro-Hungarian Council of
Ministers decided to confront Serbia with a three-day ultimatum.
On 31 March Belgrade accepted the conditions dictated by Vienna -
unconditional recognition of the annexation of Bosnia and Herzegovina and renunciation of any south Slav agitation against the
Habsburg Monarchy. (44)   This was the very declaration to which
the Austrian ultimatum to Serbia referred in July 1914. (45)
     Serbia had given way because of Russia's military weakness,
which had been underscored by Germany's massive intervention in St
Petersburg of 21 March 1909.   Bülow had lost his relative patience
over the Bosnian Crisis, after it had dragged on for more than half
a year.   He was prepared to cut through the Gordian knot, at the
risk of a European war.   He turned directly to Russia.   Against
the idea of a European Conference, aired again by Russia, he outlined his alternative on 14 March: the Powers would sanction the
annexation by an exchange of diplomatic notes; Russia would have
to give her consent and put pressure upon Serbia to give in.
Otherwise, Bülow threatened, Germany would allow 'developments to
take their course', (46) an indirect threat with Austria making
war against Serbia.   When Izvolsky gave an ambiguous answer, Bülow
followed up his move by his famous instruction of 21 March 1909 to
the German ambassador to St Petersburg.   Bülow insisted on obtaining from Russia 'an unequivocal answer - yes or no'.   He repeated
his threat that any unclear answer would make Germany retire and
let 'developments take their course'. (47)
     The German 'démarche' was considered by the Entente as an ulti-
matum, while German historians always denied this.   The truth
seems, this time, to lie between both views.   The instruction of
the Chancellor to St Petersburg was not formally an ultimatum, as
no time limit was set and there was no open mention of the consequences for Russia, if she rejected the German demands.   But its
content and effect amounted to a full-dress ultimatum.   Russia,
whose government had already decided a week earlier, on 13 March,
that Russia was in no state to wage war at the time, immediately
gave in after the German 'démarche' and exerted pressure on Serbia
to give in as well.   Even German public opinion at the time did
not conceal the truth.   It claimed that the German Empire, in its
'shining armour', had solved the crisis by an act of German
'Nibelungentreue'.

However, Bülow himself, was apparently not quite happy about his own high-handed conduct.   After his fall as Chancellor he claimed to have told the Kaiser, as a warning to his successor Bethmann Hollweg: 'Don't repeat the Bosnian coup!' (48)   Bülow was right, for the conditions for Russia's backing down before Germany would never be as favourable as they were in the winter of 1908-9.   The more Russia were to recover as a military Power, the less likely it would be that she would yield once more to German bullying.

The outcome of the Bosnian crisis appeared as a resounding victory for Austria-Hungary, indirectly also for Germany.   But Bülow's warning not to stage another coup showed how questionable its value was.   Russia and Izvolsky had been publicly hurt and humiliated.   After the Bosnian crisis any return to a conservative collaboration of the kind of the Three Emperors' League was definitely ruled out.

Even more serious was that Austria-Hungary had condemned herself to certain death by the annexation of the two south Slav provinces. With its tariff war over Serbian pigs, Austria-Hungary had aroused nationalism amongst the Serbian peasants in Serbia.   The Bosnian Crisis mobilized south Slavs inside and outside Serbia and gave their new political consciousness a clear south Slav orientation. In the days immediately following the annexation of Bosnia and Herzegovina, Serbia felt threatened by an Austrian invasion.   It was then that 'Narodna Odbrana' emerged as a powerful nationalist movement, a cross between an organization for south Slav propaganda and one for waging guerrilla warfare in the event of an Austrian invasion.   It was planned that in that event guerrilla warfare would be expanded to Bosnia and Herzegovina.   Secret and illegal contacts were established with Serbs in both provinces.   They received weapons and were trained for sabotage and guerrilla warfare. Such was the nature of the 'subversive' contacts between Belgrade and the emerging 'Young Bosnian' opposition groups amongst the small intelligentsia - students and young teachers.   They were driven to political despair and underground by the annexation of Bosnia and Herzegovina and by Austria-Hungary's incapability of offering any constructive political perspectives within the Habsburg Monarchy.   The result was the spread of south Slav nationalism in both provinces.   Gavrilo Princip and his friends, the plotters of Sarajevo, came from the 'Young Bosnian' opposition which had contacts with Belgrade, (49) and the Serbian 'Narodna Odbrana' was to figure prominently in the Austrian accusations against Serbia - contained in the Austrian ultimatum of July 1914 - although by that time, the 'Narodna Odbrana' had stopped any activities for preparing sabotage and guerrilla warfare, and had restricted itself to purely propaganda work.

By the annexation of Bosnia and Herzegovina, Austria-Hungary herself accumulated much of the dangerous matter which was to explode in the summer of 1914.   What is perhaps even more interesting here is that those responsible in Austria-Hungary and Germany were fully aware of the mechanism that could bring about the deadly explosion.   Just like the first Moroccan crisis in the West, the Bosnian crisis in the East was a kind of dress rehearsal for the First World War.   Political and military leaders in Germany had seen during the crisis that an attack by Austria-

Hungary on Serbia would provoke Russia's intervention, once Russia had returned to the scene as a military Power.   Germany was willing to answer Russian intervention for Serbia by going to war with Russia, which would drag in France, in one form or another.   The mechanism which made for war in July 1914 became visible during the Bosnian crisis and was grasped at least by Germany's leader in its full implications.   Later on, German leaders repeated their calculation again and again, (50) so that they must have known by heart in the summer of 1914 the chain of events, once the 'punitive expedition' against Serbia was started by Austria-Hungary. Germany's political leaders from early 1909 onwards were fully aware of the consequences which any German support for Austria-Hungary acting against Serbia in such manner must have.   On the other hand, Germany now had an instrument at its disposal to provoke a continental war almost any time it chose by giving a free hand to Austria-Hungary against Serbia.   But before that stage was reached, Germany's leaders had to take the general resolve to resort to war for achieving their overall aim of 'Weltpolitik' - making Germany a first-rate World Power.   That stage was not yet reached in early 1909.   It took one more major crisis in the West and in the East before Germany's leaders had made up their minds. (51)

THE COMING OF WAR, 1909-14

'ENCIRCLEMENT' AND GERMANY'S SELF-ISOLATION

Germany had tried to use the two great diplomatic crises for testing the strength of the new Entente - 1905-6 with the first Moroccan crisis provoked by Germany, 1908-9 with the Bosnian crisis, provoked by Austria-Hungary in 1908, but escalated by Germany to the brink of war in March 1909.   In both cases Germany suffered setbacks. After the first Moroccan crisis the 'Entente Cordiale' was extended to the Triple Entente, while the Bosnian crisis only strengthened the Triple Entente, in spite of all secondary tensions between Russia and France on the one hand, and Russia and Britain on the other. (1)

MYTH AND REALITY OF 'ENCIRCLEMENT'

The ring of containment around Germany held and was even strengthened.   Embarrassment in Germany was correspondingly great.   The Bosnian crisis made a new slogan popular that described the scene as seen from the German side - 'encirclement' ('Einkreisung'). The idea behind the slogan was that Germany was encircled by mischievous enemies only waiting to attack the Empire and its few allies whenever it might suit best.   The word was probably coined by Holstein, (2) but first used by Bülow in public in his speech in the Reichstag on 14 November 1906.   On that occasion he even sketched the consequences of German reaction to 'encirclement' violent conflict.

A policy aiming at the encirclement of Germany and seeking to form a ring of Powers in order to isolate and paralyse it would be disastrous to the peace of Europe.   The forming of such a ring would not be possible without exerting some pressure. Pressure provokes counter-pressure.   And out of pressure and counter-pressure finally explosions may arise. (3)

More than two years later, the German 'Encirclement' psychosis was well expressed by Field-Marshal Count Schlieffen, who remained the most influential general in Wilhelmine Germany even after his retirement in 1906.   In January 1909 he published an article in the 'Deutsche Revue'.   It contains all the popular ideas about 'encirclement', repeated again and again by German propaganda in

the following years, before and after the First World War:
Britain's envy of Germany's rapid progress in industry and commerce,
French desire for revenge for the defeat of 1870-1; Pan-Slav
Russia's hostility to Germans; insidious Italy, turning against
Austria-Hungary. Being a famous general, it is not surprising
that Schlieffen described the situation in military terms:
    Germany and Austria stand defenceless in the centre; around
    them, behind their fortifications, the other Powers.   The poli-
    tical position is analogous to the military.... An endeavour is
    afoot to unite all these Powers for a concentrated attack on the
    Central Powers. When the moment comes the gates will be flung
    open, the drawbridges will be lowered, and hordes of enemies
    will pour into Germany over the Vosges, the Maas, the Königsau,
    the Niemen, the Bug and even over the Isonzo and the Tyrolean
    Alps, destroying and annihilating all in their path.   The
    danger is gigantic. (4)
If the situation really was as alarming as Schlieffen suggested,
it was only logical to rely on Germany's 'sharp, good sword', as
the Kaiser liked to put it.   An attack across the 'drawbridges'
was also possible in the opposite direction, to forestall the
threat of attack against Germany.   A German 'preventive war'
against the imminent invasion from 'encircling' powers would have
become plausible - if Schlieffen was right.   In fact though, however widespread the cliché of 'encirclement' may have been in
Germany during most of our century, the objective substance behind
it is very slight indeed.   The simplicist 'fairy-tale of encirclement' (H. Kantorowicz) was, in reality, the reflex of a very complex situation - objectively it reflected Germany's situation of
self-provoked isolation in the world as a reaction to her 'Weltpolitik'; subjectively it was made up of a whole bundle of German
fears or complexes, which in itself gave a distorted picture of the
political realities.
    Of the various complexes, making up the German 'encirclement
complex', only the 'Copenhagen' complex has been analysed in some
detail, (5) while the others have only been sketched, so far, in
the most cursory manner. (6)   British envy of Germany's economy
and trade ('Handelsneid'), Russian Pan-Slavism, French thirst for
'revenge', Italian infidelity - they all converged into the obsession of Germany being persecuted everywhere in the world, full of
vicious enemies ('Feinde ringsum!'), which ended up in the heroic
posture of 'many enemies, much glory' (viel Feinde, viel Ehr').
It was a remarkable case of self-fulfilling prophesies, because in
two world wars Germany's isolation in a 'world of enemies' became
reality, yet mainly as a result of German foreign policy.   Behind
the various complexes, historical analysis can detect objective
factors, which Germany's policy had partly created itself.   In
any case, Germany was unable to cope with them in a constructive
and peaceful manner.
    Of all complexes, historically the oldest and directly connected
with the emergence of the Second German Empire, was that of French
'revenge'.   The historical substance behind it is easiest to
demonstrate, because after 1871 there was indeed a French chauvinism, which had as its supreme aim the regaining of Alsace-Lorraine.
It was strongest in the 1880s under Déroulède and Boulanger. (7)

But time was healing old wounds also in France after the beginning
of the twentieth century. The Third Republic having consolidated
itself after the Boulanger crisis in 1887, the importance of French
chauvinism declined in the following decades, so much so that in
the last pre-war elections in France, in May 1914, Socialists and
Radical-Socialists won a majority of near pacifist complexion. But
the painful memory of Alsace-Lorraine was kept alive in France by
Germany itself. Germany was unable to assimilate and integrate the
'Reichslande' into the Empire on an equal footing and to provide
them with that minimum of political rights which the two provinces
had been used to ever since the French Revolution of 1789. (8)
France's humiliation during the first Moroccan crisis, culminating
in Delcassé's fall under German pressure in 1905, (9) and Germany's
increasing bragging about its military power provoked in France a
new sentiment of national determination, the 'nouvel esprit'. It
was a reaction to the new German threat since 1905, but was not
aggressive as such. Limited autonomy for Alsace-Lorraine in 1911
could have blunted the 'nouvel esprit', but the Zabern incident
rudely tore open old wounds in 1913, when the predominance of
Prussian militarism and the inferior status of the French population
of Alsace-Lorraine in the German Empire was demonstrated so
blatantly. (10)

Yet all the resentment in France against Germany did not make
for an active policy of liberating Alsace-Lorraine by a French war
of aggression. The reports of the German Ambassador to Paris
during the last pre-war years again and again stressed the predominantly peaceful disposition of the French and the practical isolation of the few chauvinists. (11) In addition, the French
middle class became increasingly hostile to the burden of armaments
and national conscription. (12)

Similarly, German propaganda worked up the spectre of Russian
Pan-Slavism for domestic consumption. The political substance
behind it and Germany's reaction to it again point to the essentially reactionary character of the German Empire. Its ruling
class could not or would not realize that 'Pan-Slavism' was one
expression of the new principle of national self-determination, in
that case of the Slav nationalities. Even if Russian imperialism
had not allied with Pan-Slavism, Imperial Germany appeared incapable of reacting rationally to the movement of national self-
determination. (13) Some reports to the German Auswärtiges Amt
immediately before the outbreak of war in 1914 suggest that
Russian Pan-Slavism was far from being as powerful as represented
by German propaganda and historical writing since 1914. This,
perhaps, also explains why those documents were not published in
the great collections of German documents on pre-war foreign
policy. (14) According to the German experts on the spot, above
all the German Ambassador to St Petersburg, there did exist in
Russia a widespread feeling of Pan-Slav solidarity for the south
Slavs on the Balkans and in Austria-Hungary. But it could become
virulent only during times of crisis, e.g. in 1875-7 or in 1908-9,
and the exponents of aggressive Pan-Slavism were isolated and of
little influence on Russian foreign policy.

A really modern and peaceful foreign policy of the German Empire
would have made sure that the key condition for the Pan-Slav

sentiment becoming a driving force of Russian foreign policy did
not become a reality - an aggression or threat against the south
Slavs, in particular against Serbia, by the 'Teutonic' Central
Powers, Austria-Hungary with the backing of Germany.   In the
critical situation of summer 1914, Germany refused to prevent an
Austrian aggression against Serbia, for reasons well known by
now. (15)

Even if France and Russia pursued a policy of aggression against
Germany and the Triple Alliance, Britain's joining them in the
informal way of the 'Entente Cordiale' and the Anglo-Russian
Agreement of 1907 could have been an effective protection for
Germany against any aggression.   Britain was not willing to
support any aggression of her new partners in Europe, as the
German diplomats in London reported again and again. (16)   The
Triple Entente was in effect of a defensive nature, trying to
preserve the 'status quo' in the world, which, of course, was of
great advantage to them.   The Triple Entente, which has been so
vigorously denounced in Germany for so long as an instrument of
strangling Germany, in fact could serve to block any aggressive
intentions of Russia or France.   Britain could and certainly
would simply remain neutral in a war of aggression started by
Russia and/or France against Germany and/or Austria-Hungary.
Even the threat of British neutrality in such a conflict could
have calmed down any aggressive elements in Paris or St Petersburg,
because they knew that without Britain, they stood no chance of
winning a war against Germany.

This function of preserving peace with the help of Britain's
neutrality in a war of aggression against the Triple Alliance was
no empty claim or the invention 'post festum' of the historian.
That it really worked in that way is proved by the fact that not
only Germany, but also Russia and France eagerly sought to avoid
any impression of appearing to be aggressors in periods of crisis,
always with an eye to Britain whose position would be decisive.
(17) A truly peaceful and constructive foreign policy of the
German Empire should have turned these factors to German advantage and to preserving peace, instead of pursuing German 'Weltpolitik', which only led to the 'cul de sac' of self-isolation,
called 'encirclement' in Germany, and to the desperate will some-
how to break out of the impasse.

Even in the distorted picture they gave of reality, the various
German complexes allow an instructive insight into the German
official mind before 1914.   German fears of an alleged 'encirclement' can now be understood as a reflex of Germany's will to power
through expansion, going as far as German world domination, as the
Pan-Germans implied with their war aims after the outbreak of war,
and as Kurt Riezler explicitly envisaged from August 1914
onwards. (18)   German insistence on the alleged threat of French
'revenge' reflected both a guilty conscience over the annexation
of Alsace-Lorraine in 1871 and the intention to recover the two
provinces by war, once Germany actually lost them (as happened
during the Second World War in 1940).   The complex of 'aggressive
Russian Pan-Slavism' points to the strength of Pan-Germanism in
the German Empire, which, however, lacked the potentially progressive element of the support for the national movement of the

south Slavs.   Pan-Germanism turned out to be the most important
proto-Fascist element in Germany.
    The alleged British 'envy' of Germany's economic progress rather
reflects German envy of Britain, which was already fully established
as an industrial and imperialist Power.   The result was Germany's
curious love-hate, in its imperialist phase, of Britain, which was
best embodied by both the Kaiser and the Führer.   The 'Copenhagen'
complex with the German fear of an imputed sudden attack by Britain
on the German fleet was similarly a reflex of the most hidden desire
to invade Britain some day, (19) and of the German technique practised in two world wars to attack other countries without even
declaring war, even if 'only' smaller countries, such as Belgium
and Poland, became victims of undeclared German aggression in 1914
and 1939.   German fear of an allegedly threatening attack from
Russia was a psychological compensation for German ideas of a
'preventive' war against Russia. (20)   Russia's recovering as a
military power from 1910 onwards was one of the excuses for increased German rearmament on land, just as Britain's refusal to
give Germany a free hand on the Continent by binding herself in
advance to remain neutral in case of a continental war, supplied an
excuse for increased German armament at sea. (21)

'ENCIRCLEMENT' AND WAR

However hysterical German public opinion and German political
leaders may have been in their public reaction to Germany's isolation, there are suggestions that at least the political leaders
of the German Empire themselves did not believe in the 'fairy-tale
of encirclement'.   There are several confidential statements on
record which make one point clear: Germany's leaders knew that
the other Powers did not want to attack Germany, and that a major
war could be caused only by Germany itself.   The first pertinent
quotation aptly illustrates the connection between a reactionary
domestic policy and an expansive foreign policy of the German
Empire.   In late 1894, even before the inauguration of German
'Weltpolitik', Philipp Eulenburg, then for about a decade the
Kaiser's most intimate adviser and friend, pleaded with Holstein
for the establishment of the Kaiser's personal rule as a return
to absolutism.   He rightly foresaw, however, that such an attempt
would lead to a constitutional conflict within Germany.   His
remedy was simple: 'I fear that only a successful war will give
the Kaiser the prestige he needs to win this battle.' (22)
Holstein's reply is no less revealing:
    In one point I share your opinion, namely that a successful war
    would have a salutary effect.   But as a precondition for this
    a righteous cause, as in 1870, would be necessary.   You will
    agree that if we undertook a war of aggression we would have to
    be prepared for strange surprises ... at any rate outside the
    old Prussian provinces.   There is little prospect now of a
    defensive war, however, because no one wants to do anything to
    us.
Bülow, the coming Secretary of State and Chancellor, was informed
by Eulenburg of Holstein's ominously liberal ideas on the domestic

side of the problem.   Bülow, answering with a 30-page essay, saw
as a way to win popular support for the Kaiser's personal rule and
for the monarchy some spectacular success and the revival of the
'national idea'.   The historian who was first to discover and
quote the document, rendered Bülow's views as follows:

A victorious war would of course solve many problems, just as
the wars of 1866 and 1870 had rescued the dynasty from the steady
decline which had begun in 1848.   On the other hand, an unsuccessful war would mean the end of the dynasty because, after
Bismarck's attacks, 'our Kaiser cannot afford to have any major
setbacks'. (23)

Here we see the man who, only three years later, was to conduct
German foreign policy for twelve years, looking out for some successful war to pave the way for monarchical reaction, or,as Queen
Victoria had put it shrewdly in 1888, for the 'return to the
oldest times of government'. (24)   Since Eulenburg and Holstein
shared his view that such war would help to ease domestic problems, we may assume that other political leaders in Germany did as
well.   If this was so, they cannot have been serious with their
later complaint about 'encirclement', because they must have known
that they had provoked Germany's isolation themselves.

About twenty years later, in the middle of the first Moroccan
crisis, the German Ambassador to London, Count Wolff-Metternich
used almost the same words as Holstein had done in 1894 when
explaining why there was no prospect for a defensive war, providing
a 'righteous' cause for Germany's next war: 'But if we eliminate
the Moroccan question, our position will be very peaceful indeed,
for no one has it in mind to do anything against us.   Neither
England nor France, nor anybody else has any intention of attacking us.' (25)   In 1910 Kiderlen-Wächter, Secretary of State in
the Auswärtiges Amt from 1910 to 1912, was very emphatic on the
same point: 'If we do not conjure a war into being, no one else
certainly will do so.'   And he added in a talk with his Roumanian
friend Take Jonescu:

The Republican government of France is certainly peace-minded.
The British do not want war.   They will never give cause for
it, whatever the press may write on the subject.   Russia knows
that she stands no chance in a war against us. (26)

With so many eloquent witnesses whose testimonials contradict
the public hysteria about 'encirclement', it becomes impossible to
believe that Germany's leaders could have been intellectually
honest.   Just as they knew from the start that 'Weltpolitik'
would land Germany into world war, so they knew that only Germany
could provoke a major war after the other powers had seen the
dangers of 'Weltpolitik' and tried to contain and warn Germany by
forming the Triple Entente.   But Germany did not heed the warnings.   Its leaders became even more determined in their will to
see German 'Weltpolitik' through.   In his 'encirclement' speech
of November 1906, Chancellor Bülow also pointed to the 'ultima
ratio' of Imperial Germany.

Germany need not be afraid of isolation.... A nation of 60
millions, with an army such as the German army, will never be
isolated as long as it remains true to itself.... As long as we
keep our sword sharp, we will be in the position to make our-

selves useful to our friends and to become a nuisance to our
enemies. (27)

Just as Bülow had hinted in 1906 at the possibilities of 'explosions', if German expansion were to be checked even by political
means, Riezler, who had started his career as an occasional ghost-
writer for Bülow in December 1906 (28) (i.e. after the Chancellor's
'encirclement' speech), hinted at sinister consequences of any
attempt to contain Germany in the summer of 1914, just before the
outbreak of war.

> Hemmed in by unfavourable frontiers it [the German nation] needs
> to display in defence considerable power, because it is obstruc-
> ted in many ways from freely pursuing its 'Weltpolitik'.   For
> the sake of its liberty of action in its world policy, it must
> be guarded against any eventuality.   It cannot allow those
> spheres of activity to be blocked which are still open for its
> 'Weltpolitik'.   The attempt to contain such activities might
> be temporarily successful, but in the long run it will fail
> because of the nation's effective power and its tremendous
> 'élan vital' (Lebensdrang'). (29)

With Bülow's and Riezler's definitions of German foreign policy,
any rational differentiation between aggression and defence must
blur.   To anybody who accepted the 'encirclement' version any
sally of Germany against the 'strangulating' ring must have
appeared as an act of legitimate defence.   Such was the German
propaganda line and such was the argument of German historians,
when they claimed in all seriousness that Germany's foreign policy
before 1914 had been defensive, because it did not care about
Germany becoming a World Power.   It 'only' wanted to preserve for
Germany the chance to obtain a full share in the domination of the
world. (30)   The truth is, however, that Germany reacted aggres-
sively to the policy of containment and produced, as Bülow had
predicted correctly in 1906, 'explosions' - the two world wars.
In contrast to Riezler's optimism, the policy of containing Germany
was successful in the long run, even if at the price of two world
wars.

The admission that Germany had been isolated as a result of its
'Weltpolitik' was, by implication, a declaration of bankruptcy.
But if the 'sharp German sword' was the last resort to ensure its
success, then it was only logical that Germany pressed in the last
pre-war years to increase its armaments, in particular on land.
(31)   And if Germany's situation was really as bad as Schlieffen
had maintained in early 1909, fully approved by the Kaiser in a
speech to his commanding generals, (32) there were only two ways
out of the impasse.   Either giving up 'Weltpolitik' altogether
and returning to a more prudent course; or going ahead with increased vigour to remove the obstacles to German expansion in the
world by war, if necessary by a 'preventive war', before the other
powers - in particular Russia - became too strong even for Germany.
There was no drastic revision of Germany's political course, either
at home or abroad.   While tensions in the world and in Europe,
which were, however, only partly caused by Germany directly, were
further building up, the desperate determination grew in Germany
to stake everything on a successful war.   This is the main content of political development in Imperial Germany during the last
few years before the First World War.

Chapter 13

GERMANY'S POLITICAL OFFENSIVE AGAINST 'ENCIRCLEMENT', 1909-12

The German attempts to prevent the formation of the Triple Entente
in 1905-6 and its consolidation in 1909 had failed.   Germany's
position had been weakened, because the Triple Entente had strengthened.   But the two German sallies had been rather improvised.
There was no strategical concept behind them.   During the lull of
the following years a new kind of strategy developed;   it consisted
of probing the ring of the Triple Entente in search of weak
points - France, Russia, Britain.

FROM BÜLOW TO BETHMANN HOLLWEG, 1909

Parallel to the preceding phase of German 'Weltpolitik' there had
been some developments inside Germany that make the more cautious
and elastic phase of German foreign policy more plausible, in
particular the 'Daily Telegraph' affair in 1908 and the failure of
Bülow's project of a reform of German finances in 1909.
    The 'Daily Telegraph' affair was directly connected with
Germany's foreign policy towards Britain. (1)   The Kaiser had
boasted of his friendly disposition towards Britain, as shown by
his strategic advice given freely for the conduct of the Boer War,
and in contrast to anglophobe public opinion in Germany.   British
anger over the Kaiser's condescending tactlessness was even surpassed by anger in Germany over the Kaiser's clumsiness and bending
over backward towards Britain.   The result was a domestic crisis
which could have led to the Kaiser's abdication and the introduction of the parliamentary system but for the fact that the German
Crown Prince Wilhelm was a notorious Pan-German and that the
adherents of a parliamentary system were not strong enough.   But
the Kaiser had been cowed for a time, while the explosion of anti-
British feelings in Germany did not help to improve relations
between the two countries.
    More serious was the conflict over the reform of taxes and
finance in Germany, although, at first sight, it had nothing to do
with foreign policy or 'Weltpolitik'. (2)   In fact, however, the
need for such a reform had arisen because of the domestic repercussions of Germany's ambitious 'Weltpolitik', which had been

launched to divert attention from domestic troubles.   Just at the
same time, when the Kaiser's personal rule, which was to be established by 'Weltpolitik' (3) was going down in the outcry over the
'Daily Telegraph' interview, 'Weltpolitik' had run into an impasse,
and domestic problems were returning more urgently than ever before.
The basis of 'Weltpolitik' was also crumbling at home, because now
the question was arising of how Germany's costly expansion was to
be financed.
    Traditionally, the German Empire had been short of liquid
capital and, owing to its federal structure, it had been financially
dependent on the various member states making up the German Empire.
They, and not the central government in Berlin, received all the
income from the lucrative direct taxes, while the central government received only the indirect taxes, together with additional
sums from the federal states, fixed by quotas based on the number
of inhabitants.   Chancellor Bülow proposed that the landed aristocracy should also contribute to meet the rising financial
demands of the central government by the introduction of an income
tax and hereditary tax.   The aristocracy, however, refused and
the Conservatives rejected Bülow's reform bill in the Reichstag in
1909.   Bülow, whose personal relationship with the Kaiser had been
undermined since the 'Daily Telegraph' affair, offered his resignation, and the Kaiser was glad to get rid of him on that occasion.
    With Bülow's fall and the failure of his reform bill, the Con-
servatives could celebrate their last political victory in Imperial
Germany.   They had succeeded in leaving the financial burden for
building the fleet with the urban masses by clinging to indirect
taxes.   They thus increased discontent in the industrial centres
of Germany and played into the hands of the SPD.   In January 1912
the Socialists won a resounding victory at the last pre-war general
elections in Germany.   For the first time, they obtained 34 per
cent of all votes and rose to the position of the strongest parliamentary party in the German Reichstag.   The very basis of the
German Empire seemed to be threatened from within.   'Weltpolitik'
as an instrument for preserving the 'status quo' was on the brink
of failure within Germany itself less than three years after
Bülow's fall.
    Bülow's successor was Bethmann Hollweg.   He embodied the alli-
ance between the two wings of Germany's ruling class.   His family
originated from a banking family at Frankfurt/Main; but his particular branch had bought themselves into the landed gentry of East
Elbia near Berlin, only two generations earlier.   Yet his social
background was not typical of Germany's ruling class.   He was
rather modest and lacked all the arrogance of the Prussian Junker
and the chauvinist German bourgeois of the time.   He carried on a
certain liberal tradition and sympathy for the West, in particular
for Britain and France without, however, disagreeing on the
principles of German 'Weltpolitik'.   In contrast to Bülow, Bethmann
Hollweg had risen in the Prussian bureaucracy, first to the Prussian
Ministry of the Interior, and to Secretary of State of the Interior
under Bülow in 1906. (4)   His main field of activities as Chancellor was intended to be domestic affairs, because he was reputed to
have good contacts with the Socialists.   His chief task was to
integrate the working class and the SPD into the monarchical state

of Imperial Germany without making substantial concessions to
Social Democracy.   In the hardware of domestic affairs - finances
and taxes - he was closer to the Conservatives, however, but he
was prepared to neutralize the opposition of the SPD by a few
minor concessions in the field of social reform and civil liberties
for political associations.
     The Kaiser, on the other hand, had recovered sufficient self-
confidence by 1909 to think that he himself could direct foreign
policy, using his new Chancellor more or less as a figure-head.
Bethmann Hollweg, however, also had ideas of his own on foreign
policy, even if they fitted harmoniously into the demands of German
'Weltpolitik' in its critical phase.   His more liberal attitude
towards the SPD corresponded with his readiness to come to agreement with Britain at least on more peripheral matters.

THE IMPORTANCE OF KEEPING BRITAIN NEUTRAL

Bethmann Hollweg, perhaps more than his predecessor, seemed to be
fully aware of the crucial role Britain would play in any major
conflict on the Continent, simply by staying or refusing to stay
neutral.   After all, Germany's leaders must have realized by 1909
that their options in foreign policy had been reduced to either
giving up 'Weltpolitik' altogether in order to preserve peace, or
to going ahead with it with the certain risk of world war.   The
important modification introduced by Bethmann Hollweg was to try a
course between the two extremes.   By a display of more flexibility
Britain might be won over to promise her neutrality in advance, if
war broke out on the Continent.   Germany would have stood an
excellent chance of winning such a war against Russia and France
or of bullying both Powers into accepting any change of the balance
of power demanded by Germany in its favour.
     Such was the concept of German foreign policy under Bethmann
Hollweg, from 1909 until the first months of the First World War.
This concept makes the many, sometimes bewildering moves of German
foreign policy before the war more plausible.   But as a counter-
part to any commitment by Britain to remain neutral, as Germany
wished, Germany would have to accept a limitation of her battle
fleet, as Britain wished.   Bülow in his last months as Chancellor
had seen this. (5)   In his first major report on foreign policy
for the Kaiser, the new Chancellor, in mid-August 1909, again
linked both complexes.   He even implied that he would use a naval
agreement only as an instrument to obtain Britain's promise of
neutrality in case of war on the Continent. (6)   The kind of conflict assumed by the Chancellor, which would lead to continental
war, allows glimpses into the official mind of the German Empire.
Britain was to be expected to stay neutral, 'if we [i.e. Germany]
are attacked by France and/or Russia, or if we have to assist
Austria-Hungary on the strength of our alliance with her, if she is
attacked by Russia'. (7)   The probability of an attack by France
and/or Russia was low, as German leaders knew themselves (8) while
they took an intervention to save Austria against Russian attack
as constituting the 'casus foederis' for Germany. (9)   In other
words, the German Empire aimed at achieving British neutrality for
the very grouping which in fact did occur in July 1914. (10)

This was the main point Germany wanted to make in all negotiations with Britain until 1914, in spite of all tactical modifications of the subject matter under discussion. (11)   This was what Bethmann Hollweg meant by an 'understanding' with Britain.   But he was bound to fail even with his more flexible methods, because of the incompatibility of aims and methods.   The promise of British neutrality would have fulfilled the wish of the new Chancellor, who, according to Kurt Riezler's evidence, wanted to throw the Triple Entente into confusion. (12)   If such an aim was 'natural' as Bethmann Hollweg's first biographer innocently claimed, (13) then it was also 'natural' that the Triple Entente should try to prevent such a development.

Later negotiations with Britain show that Germany was mainly interested in a free hand on the Continent, even in the event of German aggression, or of an aggressive act manipulated through Austria-Hungary against Serbia.   Bethmann Hollweg apparently was bound by Tirpitz who told the Kaiser of his 'political demand' on 8 February 1912:   'Britain must not intervene in any war between Germany and France, whoever may be the "aggressor".' (14)   Since Britain did not want to tolerate any aggression amongst the great powers or encourage it by remaining neutral, all German attempts to persuade Britain to the commitment of neutrality had to fail. Britain remained firm in her resolve to preserve the balance of power in Europe, if necessary also against Germany.   Neither Bethmann Hollweg's appeals nor Tirpitz's hinted threats with the German battle fleet in the future could deflect Britain from her course.   Thus, Bethmann Hollweg's more flexible policy of finding a middle course between scrapping 'Weltpolitik' and war turned out as another illusion.

The main reason was that Germany, under pressure from Tirpitz and all the vested interests in a strong battle fleet, rejected any compromise on the limitation of naval armaments that could have been acceptable to Britain.   As with the Schlieffen plan on land, German foreign policy was paralysed at sea through the Tirpitz plan. (15)   Finding an agreement with Britain along German lines without a substantial naval agreement thus amounted to squaring the circle.   It is not surprising that the Chancellor failed in his hopeless task.   Instead of the hardware - substantial concessions on the reduction of the building programme for the German battle fleet - the Chancellor tried his luck with selling his political software - agreements on colonies and the Baghdad Railway Line, diplomatic cooperation over the Balkans in 1912-13, (16) or a visit of the Royal Navy to Kiel in June 1914.   Even cumulatively, such improvements could not deceive Britain into granting a free hand to Germany on the Continent, because it would have destroyed the balance of power and opened the way for German domination in Europe.

Germany's diplomatic search for weak points in the Triple Alliance and wooing its members varied in intensity.   It was almost negligent towards France, Germany's 'arch-enemy', even more distasteful for being a republic.   It was of medium intensity towards Russia, once the traditional conservative ally from the days of the Holy Alliance and the Three Emperors' League. (17)   Its intensity was greatest towards Britain, who had preserved herself the greatest amount of liberty of action.

TRYING TO TALK FRANCE OR RUSSIA OUT OF THE TRIPLE ENTENTE

Germany's only attempt to find some accommodation with France at the
time developed out of the aftermath of the first Moroccan crisis.
Still under Bülow, Germany used as a lever negotiations on a bilateral agreement to follow up the decisions of the Algeciras Conference.   Talks from 1907 onwards had bogged down in continuing
differences over Morocco and over various incidents between the two
countries.   Only in January 1909, under pressure of the Bosnian
crisis, did Bülow insist upon reaching some agreement.   The French
rejected the German desire for a special position in Morocco as a
price for Germany's recognizing French preponderance in Morocco.
After some more haggling, Bülow was satisfied with an agreement
that only confirmed the results of Algeciras: equal rights for
Germany in the economic sphere, but special political rights for
France. (18)   The political gain for Germany out of the Franco-
German Agreement on Morocco of 9 February 1909 has to be seen in
the improvement of the political atmosphere between France and
Germany in the following months.   It may have contributed to
France's withholding her full support from Russia during the final
stage of the Bosnian crisis in March 1909, (19) much to the anger
of the Russians.   Whatever points Germany may have scored with
France in early 1909, they were more than offset by Germany's provoking the second crisis over Morocco in 1911. (20)
      Of greater weight were the talks with Britain, which took place
in fits and starts from 1909 to 1912.   The first round opened in
August 1909, just after Bethmann Hollweg's arrival at the Wilhelmstrasse.   The new Chancellor operated on the basis of the package
deal, analysed above (21) - (limited) naval agreement without substantial reduction of the German building programme only in
exchange for British unconditional neutrality laid down beforehand
in a bilateral treaty. (22)   The British, however, wanted to
negotiate a naval agreement first, to be followed by a political
understanding. (23)   The priorities of both partners, therefore,
conflicted with each other, and the British suggestion to negotiate
both problems at the same time came to nothing.   The Chancellor's
insistence on British neutrality, even 'if Germany were to be
forced into war by provocations of a third power', (24) and
Tirpitz's attempt to bind Britain to a naval agreement fixing the
ratio of British to German strength in capital ships as 3:2 must
have sounded ominous to the British. (25)   In November 1909 talks
came to a halt when the Kaiser was angry over British opposition
to the completion of the Baghdad Railway Line. (26)
      Almost a year later Germany turned to the eastern front, probing
Russia.   Izvolsky's successor as Russian foreign minister from
the end of October 1910 was S.D. Sazonov.   He was thought of in
Germany as a prudent exponent of Russian foreign policy.   Immediately after his appointment, he had to accompany the Tsar to a
meeting with the Kaiser at Potsdam in early November 1910.   The
Germans hoped they could make a fresh start with the new man in
charge of the Russian Foreign Ministry.   They aimed at the sore
point where British and Russian interests met - Persia. (27)   They
offered German recognition of Russian influence in Persia, while
Russia should refrain from obstructing the completion of the

Baghdad Railway Line and its connection with the future system of
railways in northern Persia, where Russian influence was preponderant.   The idea was to lure Russia away from the Triple Entente
by engaging Russia in a secret agreement not to take part in any
British action against Germany.   The Germans prepared another trap
for Russia.   They protested that any strengthening of Turkey would
also be in the interest of preserving the 'status quo' in the
Balkans, although Russian interest was, of course, not to see Turkey
strengthened.   The Germans, furthermore, assured the Russians that
Austria-Hungary was not pursuing any policy of expansion in the
Balkans. (28)   Germany could not for long sustain towards Vienna
such an indirect disavowal of its Austrian ally.   Germany appeared
to be willing to plunge back into the maze of the Reinsurance
Treaty. (29)
   The Russians, however, were cool in their reaction to German
advances and refused to treat anything but the Persian question.
They fully informed their partners of the Triple Entente.   Germany
had vainly tried to lure Russia into giving a written statement
that she would not support any anti-German line on the part of
Britain, (30) which could have become the thin edge of a wedge
between Russia and Britain, as the Chancellor apparently hoped. (31)
The Russo-German Agreement, concluded on 19 August 1911, in the
middle of the second Moroccan crisis, was limited strictly to questions of infrastructure, mainly railways, in Persia. (32)   It was
to be the last friendly exchange between Russia and Germany before
the war.

GERMANY'S MOVE TO THE BRINK OVER MOROCCO, 1911

By late 1910, her probing of the Triple Entente having come to
nothing on all fronts, Germany started her second round on a much
more massive scale - against France with the second Moroccan crisis
in 1911.   During the second Moroccan crisis, German willingness to
go to war was highest - in public opinion, in the Reichstag and
in court and government.   Again the initiative lay with Germany,
when it protested against French violation of the Algeciras Agreement.   Continuous revolts against the Sultan of Morocco were
taken by France as an excuse to occupy Rabat and Fez in April and
May 1911.   Germany reacted by dispatching the gunboat 'Panther' to
Agadir, a port in southern Morocco, thus opening the new crisis
with a bang. (33)
   There was, however, a serious divergence of tactics in Germany,
which affected the course of German foreign policy during the
crisis.   Kiderlen-Wächter, Foreign Secretary since October 1910,
wanted to use Morocco mainly as a lever to extort colonial 'com-
pensations' for Germany somewhere else;   while the Pan-Germans,
who emerged for the first time as a powerful factor in the times of
crisis, pleaded for permanent German colonization in Morocco.   In
his second talk with the French Ambassador to Berlin, Jules Cambon,
after the crisis had opened on 15 July 1911, Kiderlen-Wächter
demanded the cession of the French Congo (Brazzaville) as a price
for Germany's recognition of France's going beyond the line drawn
at Algeciras. (34)   Two days later the French government under

Caillaux rejected the German demand.   The same day the Kaiser
suddenly changed his mind and warned not to provoke France, as she
might be supported by Britain. (35)   Kiderlen-Wächter interpreted
the Kaiser's move as a disavowal of his policy and offered his
resignation.   The reasons he gave make it clear that this time the
readiness to go to war if necessary was so great that most of the
responsibility would have fallen on Germany, if war had broken out
in August 1911.   For Kiderlen-Wächter was prepared to push German
demands for the French Congo so forcefully, that the French 'are
firmly convinced that otherwise we are resolved to go to the
extreme', (36) i.e. to war.   There was not yet a definite decision
to go to war, but Berlin then practised what has subsequently been
called the policy of 'brinkmanship'.   Germany was prepared to see
through its policy of bluffing, even at the risk of the bluff being
called, i.e. going to war.   Even if France continued to refuse the
cession of the French Congo, Kiderlen-Wächter did not think of
reacting by a declaration of war on France, because of Britain.
But he intended to drive France to the wall by diplomatic means,
taking his stand on the Algeciras Agreement, in order to force
France's withdrawal from Morocco altogether.   If France were to
remain intransigent, Kiderlen-Wächter was not explicit as to the
alternative.   But it can be implied from the historical context
and from the evidence - war.   This view is strengthened by a new
source, even if only an indirect one: Riezler's diary.   According
to Riezler, Kiderlen-Wächter, who emerges as the real driving force
of German foreign policy then, did not want to provoke war at any
cost, but both he and the Chancellor used the threat of war as an
instrument to achieve their aims.   They were convinced that the
German people needed a war, and this was why they consciously faced
the risk of it. (37)
    Germany, however, could not go to the lengths of war.   Britain
saw immediately the consequences of French submission to Germany -
the breaking up of the Triple Entente.   British suspicions were
increased by the fact that Germany had not consulted Britain before
launching its action, although Britain, after all, had signed the
Algeciras Agreement just as much as Germany.   Germany had to face
strong criticism from Britain, and this is why Berlin preferred
bilateral negotiations with France.   Kiderlen-Wächter, however,
made the mistake of overplaying his hand, because he provoked a
clarifying statement from Britain.   It came on 21 July, on the
evening of the same day when the British Foreign Office definitely
saw the potentially aggressive motives of Germany's action against
France.   In his famous Mansion House speech, Lloyd George, without
mentioning Germany, made it unmistakably clear that Britain would
not let France down in the face of the German threat. (38)   Germany
withdrew gradually from her exposed position, starting with the
Kaiser's order on 19 July, after his return from his Nordic voyage
ten days later. (39)   From that point he earned himself among the
Pan-Germans the contemptuous nickname of 'Guillaume le timide'
(timid William).
    At the end of August 1911, nevertheless, the threat of war seemed
to return when agitation for war in the German press flared up
again. (40)   But just as Britain's intervention on 21 July had
cooled down most hotheads in Germany's leading circles, a panic at

the Berlin Exchange on 9 September had a similar effect.   The
hectic run on banks in Germany was a massive vote of no confidence
of the German public against the financial strength of the German
Empire.   It also made the limitations of German power, which resulted from the notorious lack of liquid capital in Germany, painfully clear. (41)
     After laborious negotiations the Franco-German agreements on
Morocco and Equatorial Africa were concluded on 4 November 1911,
which formally ended the second Moroccan crisis.   Compared with
Germany's ambitious aims at the beginning of the crisis, the result
was nothing but a thinly disguised defeat for the Empire: Germany
recognized definitely French domination in Morocco and obtained, as
a concession, some territories of the French Congo, among them two
'feelers' ('Fühlhörner') to the river Congo, which pointed to the
direction of further German colonial aims. (42)
     The overall result of the second Moroccan crisis was, on the
one hand, growing frustration and anger in Germany, (43) on the
other, further consolidation of the Triple Entente.   At the height
of the crisis, in July 1911, Anglo-French talks between the respective general staffs laid down the plan for military cooperation in
the event of war with Germany.   It provided for the immediate
dispatch of a British Expeditionary Force to the left wing of the
French army, just as in August 1914.   A year later, in November
1912, a secret exchange of letters between Sir Edward Grey and
Paul Cambon, the French Ambassador to London, laid down close political cooperation in the event of a threatening attack from a third
Power (i.e. Germany), as a substitute for a full-fledged alliance,
which could hardly be ratified in the British parliament. (44)

GROWING READINESS FOR WAR IN GERMANY

The most important repercussion of the second Moroccan crisis on
Germany was to increase even more the willingness to face the risk
of war.   The crisis had produced an ominous change in the relationship between government and public opinion in Germany.   Before and
at the start of 'Weltpolitik', the Imperial government had thought
it necessary to work up German public opinion into adopting more
nationalist positions.   By 1911, except for the left-wing Liberals
and Social Democrats, most of the press and political parties had
overtaken the government in pursuing chauvinist and imperialist
aims, and they were now pushing the government forward.   Just
before the crisis, Kiderlen-Wächter had secretly encouraged the
Pan-Germans to attack the government for alleged weakness so that
he could extort more concessions abroad by pointing to the pressure
at home. (45)
     When the government beat a retreat after the Mansion House
speech of Lloyd George, the Pan-Germans and their allies, now with
all the inner conviction at their disposal, denounced the retreat
as 'treason'.   The government, from now on, was under real pressure from the chauvinist section of public opinion, which for the
first time openly pleaded for going to war, even over Morocco so
that the government now had to play it cool. (46)   In the
Reichstag debate on the agreements on Morocco, 9 November 1911,

the leader of the National Liberals, Ernst Bassermann, could accuse
the Chancellor of having let down the German nation, which, according to Bassermann, never had been so ready to go to war to that
extent as in the summer of 1911.   German public opinion had been
misled by the government.   Its failure, violently denounced by
Bassermann, was apparently in having avoided war, contrary to conservative and nationalist expectations. (47)   The warlike sentiments of the summer and autumn of 1911 were the logical preparation
for the explosion of chauvinism and enthusiasm immediately before
and after the outbreak of war in the summer of 1914.   From then on,
the press and publicists spoke openly, the government secretly,
about preparing for the great war, which was thought to be unavoidable.   It was then that German war aims were discussed in public
for the first time. (48)

General Bernhardi's book, 'Germany and the Next War', published
in 1912, (49) was eagerly received in Germany.   It was only the
best-known tip of an iceberg, to which the Imperial government also
belonged.   In August and early September 1911, when Germany, egged
on by its chauvinist wing of public opinion, seemed about to go to
war after all, the permanent dilemma became painfully clear behind
closed doors.   When the Kaiser, for a change, pressed for immediate
war, he was coolly reminded by his admirals that the German fleet
was in no state to wage war with Britain.   Just as in a conference
with Chancellor Bülow in June 1909, (50) the key factors were the
extension of the Kiel Canal and the finishing of a harbour on
Heligoland for submarines. (51)   At the same time Bethmann
Hollweg must have warned against starting a war, for the Kaiser, a
year later, was pleased to see that the Chancellor had changed his
mind. (52)

Two months after the formal conclusion of the second Moroccan
crisis, in January 1912, Germany's 'Weltpolitik' suffered another
resounding defeat, this time at home.   The dramatic increase of
the SPD in the last pre-war general elections seemed to threaten
the very basis of this policy at home.   'Weltpolitik' had also
been started in order to neutralize the Socialist opposition by a
spectacular foreign policy. (53)   Now the dreaded social revolution
seemed to raise its ugly head after all.   The Socialist victory at
the polls produced a deep shock in the Conservative camp of all
shades and provoked two reactions.   The Pan-Germans, as the spear-
head of all conservative and chauvinist forces in the Empire,
violently agitated for a drastic increase of the army, as the most
trusted safeguard of German victory in the coming war;   secretly
they pleaded for staging a 'coup d'état' against the Socialists,
just as in the 1890s.   In October 1913 the Pan-German leaders sent
a confidential memorandum to the Crown Prince who forwarded it to
the Kaiser, in order to put pressure upon the Chancellor.   Their
programme was a logical consequence of their reactionary views:
'coup d'état' by abolishing the general suffrage to the German
Reichstag, elimination of Socialists by force, of the Jews by dis-
criminating laws, as preparation for the next step - war of aggression and conquest. (54)   But even the Pan-Germans did not believe
that the other Powers would attack Germany.   Therefore, the
Empire would have to take the initiative.   If Germany showed her
'mailed fist', there would be 'no one on the Continent (and

probably not even Britain) who would not give in'. (55)   If the
other Powers did not give way to German threats, the result would
be obvious - war.

LAST TALKS WITH BRITAIN OVER NAVY AND NEUTRALITY - THE HALDANE
MISSION TO BERLIN, FEBRUARY 1912

Britain's being singled out by the Pan-Germans in 1913 pointed to
another repercussion of the second Moroccan crisis upon Germany.
British intervention in July 1911 to save France had mobilized all
the hatred and hostility in Germany against 'perfidious Albion'
for daring to block German expansion by preserving the 'status
quo' against the German Empire.   The government, however, faced
the necessity to try again, after all that had happened, to secure
British neutrality in advance for a continental war that had to be
fought for the extension of German power on the Continent.   After
the experience of 1911, the government's task had not become
easier.   In the second round of Anglo-German talks the same two
problems cropped up - naval agreement (limitation of German naval
rearmament) and political agreement (British neutrality).   During
the second Moroccan crisis, the Kaiser had become angry when he
was reminded of the permanent unpreparedness of his navy for war.
(56)   It was obvious that the navy lobby would use the crisis for a
further strengthening of the German battle fleet.   Indeed, they
scored a success of doubtful value with the announcement of another
Naval Amendment on 6 February 1912, one day before Lord Haldane,
the British Minister of War, arrived at Berlin for talks with the
German government.   This deliberate provocation, of course, condemned the talks to immediate failure, because the Germans were
not prepared to revise their position.   Nevertheless, the Chancellor argued in talks within the ruling circles that the building of
the German battle fleet should be somewhat reduced in speed and
extent, so that Britain might yield to the German desire for a
political agreement after all.   But the Chancellor was unable to
carry his point with the Kaiser and Admiral Tirpitz.
     Undaunted, the Chancellor concentrated in his talks with Haldane
on persuading his British partner to accept the German formula of
a political agreement on British neutrality, although he came away
empty-handed as far as the naval problem was concerned.   Thus
they moved in the same circle as in 1909, which Bethmann Hollweg
was unable to square: Haldane rejected any promise of absolute
neutrality and was only prepared for a statement of general character that both powers would not participate in an aggressive combination against the other partner and would not pursue an aggressive policy themselves. (57)   The Kaiser and Tirpitz had separate
talks with Haldane and definitely refused once more to reduce the
building programme for the German battle fleet.   With that, also,
the Kaiser's hopelessly unrealistic wish for a political entente
with Britain came to nothing, not only because it would have destroyed the Triple Entente.   The basis for the last serious talks
on the crucial issues standing between Britain and Germany had been
destroyed by German intransigence.   After Haldane's departure,
a final exchange of drafts for a political agreement could not

yield any results.   But the final formulae illustrate once more
the divergence between the two countries.   The last German offer
contained in a draft for a treaty in March 1912, fitted perfectly
into the strategy of the Schlieffen plan:

> If either of the high contracting parties becomes entangled in
> a war with one or more powers in which it cannot be said to be
> the aggressor, the other of the high contracting parties will
> at least observe towards the power so entangled a benevolent
> neutrality and use its utmost endeavour for the localization
> of the conflict.   If either of the high contracting parties
> is forced to go to war by obvious provocation from a third
> party they bind themselves to enter into an exchange of views
> concerning their attitude in such a conflict. (58)

Grey's last formula was shorter and more sincere: 'England declares
that she will neither make nor join in any unprovoked attack upon
Germany and pursue no aggressive policy towards it.' (59)

After March 1912 no more talks took place between Germany and
Britain on a political agreement, although the Chancellor still
cherished the hope of obtaining some kind of agreement after all.
In July and early August 1914 he so modelled his policy (as if the
agreement with Britain did exist) that he tried to make Russia and
France look guilty of aggression, so that Britain could remain
neutral.   Germany's insistence on being provoked by Russia and
France to declare war can best be accounted for by the need to keep
Britain neutral, while the Socialists were to be dragged into the
united front for defending the Fatherland.

Chapter 14

THE DECISION TO GO TO WAR, JANUARY to 8 DECEMBER 1912

GERMANY'S POSITION IN 1912

In late 1912 the balance of 'Weltpolitik' after fifteen years must have been depressing for Germany's leaders. The German Empire, it is true, had a more powerful position in Europe than ever before, based on its ever-increasing economic potential, its army and its rapidly expanding fleet. But for the fleet, these factors had, however, been in existence before 'Weltpolitik', while the fleet turned out to be more and more a liability for Germany, because it was bound to provoke Britain's hostility. Germany's colonial empire overseas had scarcely grown, apart from the acquisition of Kiaochow, a few isles in the Pacific and territorial gains in the Cameroons, obtained by Germany in 1911 - at a costly political price. (1)
  Germany had two allies who hated each other - Austria-Hungary and Italy. Austria-Hungary was rapidly becoming Europe's 'sick man' number two, unable to modernize its petrified social and political structures, and moving into headlong collision with the south Slav national movement. (2) The only other ally, Roumania, was unreliable, because her social and political structures were closer to those of Serbia, and the ties with the Triple Alliance consisted of a secret treaty, known only to the Roumanian king, the Hohenzollern dynasty and a few chosen ministers. With Turkey, Germany had another potential or informal ally whose structure as the 'sick man' number one in Europe was even more anachronistic and hopeless than Austria's. (3)
  In the preceding years, moreover, the German interest of conserving Turkey as a whole and the Italian ambition to see Turkey carved up clashed more openly than ever before during the Tripoli War in 1911-12. The Italian war against Germany's protégé in the Middle East also created internal divergences in Germany. The Kaiser had put his personal prestige into the preservation of the Ottoman Empire ever since his first spectacular visit to Turkey in 1898. (4) Thus in the autumn of 1911 he pleaded for Turkey, while his politi-cal advisers, the Chancellor and the Auswärtiges Amt, were more inclined to support Italy, if only to keep the Triple Alliance together. (5) Austria-Hungary, on the other hand, did not mind

Italy's attention being turned away from the Balkans, where Italian
and Austrian expansionist interests clashed, to North Africa.   But
her chief of staff, Baron Conrad von Hötzendorf, pleaded for a preventive war against Italy so persistently that he was dismissed from
his post in December 1911. (6)
    When, in the spring of 1912, Italy wanted to extend military
operations from North Africa to the islands off the Turkish coast,
Vienna objected because the Austrians feared Italy's return to the
Balkans.   Germany, in contrast, was prepared to accept the provisional occupation of the Dodecanes by Italy, because the renewal of
the Triple Alliance was just due and Germany did not want to lose
Italy as an ally.   The (last) renewal of the Triple Alliance thus
took place without further difficulties in December 1912, after
Italy's Libyan War had ended and the First Balkan War had broken
out in October 1912. (7)   But the Triple Alliance was clearly in
disarray.   Moreover, it stood under the shadow of the First Balkan
War, which changed the balance of power on the Balkans so dramatically that only two years later tensions there provided the famous
spark to set Europe in flames.

AUSTRIA'S PREDICAMENT ON THE BALKANS

The First Balkan War again embarrassed Germany's leaders.   The
rapid collapse of the last Turkish positions on the European Con-
tinent and Serbia's doubling in size and number of inhabitants by
the annexation of parts of Macedonia, indirectly also weakened
Germany's and Austria's position in the Balkans.   The Serbian
'Piedmont' was greatly strengthened, which was bound to increase
Austria's internal difficulties with her own south Slav minorities.
For the Germans Serbia's function as a roadblock to Germany's drive
to Constantinople became more irritating than ever before.   Little
Serbia as an Austrian satellite before 1903 had been no serious
obstacle to German expansion into the Middle East.   But a self-
confident, dynamic and ever-growing Greater Serbia with the tendency
to disrupt Austria-Hungary by uniting most or all south Slavs, all
that in tacit alliance with Russia, would be able to deal a deadly
blow to Germany's drive to the Middle East, to its position on the
Continent, and thus indirectly also to German 'Weltpolitik'.
    The more direct consequences of the First Balkan War can be seen
in Austria-Hungary.   Conrad von Hötzendorf returned to his post of
chief of general staff in December 1912, now with a firm mind to
finish Serbia as soon as possible by a 'preventive war'.   This
time, the Austrian government was unable to resist his warlike
pressure.   Before the First Balkan War, Austria-Hungary had tried
to prevent a war against Turkey by diplomatic means.   She demanded
reforms for the Turkish Balkan provinces from the Turkish government, while she demanded that the Balkan countries should not resort
to war against Turkey.   But the other Powers, including Germany,
refused to support Austria-Hungary, and nothing came of the
initiative. (8)   The First Balkan War did break out and wrought
disaster on Turkey's position in Europe.   During the war, Germany
warded off all attempts by Austria-Hungary to intervene against
Serbia, because the German Empire was not yet prepared to go to war

over Balkan problems.   But Germany was again prepared to come to
Austria's assistance, if Russia were to intervene in the Balkans
in such a way that war with Austria-Hungary would result.   (9)
   Germany's policy of relative restraint, therefore, had little
room for manoeuvring, because on the one hand Berlin had, for
tactical reasons, to keep back Austria at least for a while, without refusing or appearing to refuse support in the event of full-
scale war with Russia for strategical reasons.   The dilemma of
German foreign policy during the Balkan Wars seemed to be overcome
by cultivating Germany's role of a peace-keeping power in ostentatious collaboration with Britain.   This had the double advantage
of keeping back Austria without giving her the feeling of being
let down by Germany and of gaining points with Britain in the hour
of need, when British neutrality would become vital for Germany.
Diplomatic cooperation on the Balkans in 1912-13 appeared to become
the most effective instrument to create that degree of British confidence in Germany's peaceful intentions that would help to obtain
British neutrality after all.   In fact, Bethmann Hollweg did point
to that collaboration, when in July 1914 he tried to neutralize
Britain in the First World War. (10)

THE REPERCUSSIONS OF THE FIRST BALKAN WAR ON GERMAN FOREIGN POLICY

But in fact, Germany's dilemma could not be resolved.   Because the
Chancellor did not want to lose Austria-Hungary as an ally, he put
public announcements of his new concept of diplomatic collaboration
with Britain on the Balkans in such warlike terms that Britain took
fright;   which, in its turn, had serious repercussions on German
foreign policy.   In his speech in the Reichstag, on 2 December
1912, the Chancellor confirmed the principle that Germany would
come to Austria's assistance, if the latter were to be attacked
'by a third partner' (in other words, by Russia), 'and if her
existence were thus threatened'.   Then Germany 'would also fight,
in order to preserve our position in Europe and to defend our future
and security'. (11)
   The Foreign Office in London was alarmed and immediately calculated the consequences of Germany's militant stand on Austria's side
in the Balkans.   As early as 4 December, pointing expressly to
the Chancellor's speech in the Reichstag, Sir Edward Grey warned
the German ambassador to London, Prince Lichnowsky, of the illusion
that Russia would give way once more to German pressure, as had
happened in 1909.   Grey and his closest collaborators in the
Foreign Office pointed out to Lichnowsky the same kind of chain of
reactions that the Germans had seen themselves before and that was
to lead to the explosion of August 1914:   Austrian war against
Serbia, Russia's intervention and war against Austria, Germany's
war against Russia and France.   The British made it clear that it
was Britain's vital interest to prevent another defeat of France
at the hands of Germany and that Britain would come to the assistance of France.   At about the same time Russia warned Austria-
Hungary not to attack Serbia, and the Germans knew it. (12)   The
day before Lichnowsky had discussed the same problem with Haldane,
the British Minister of War, Haldane had told Lichnowsky that

Britain intended to preserve the balance of power and could, for
that reason, 'not tolerate under any circumstances the defeat of
the French', even less so, if Britain 'were to face afterwards one
block of continental powers under the leadership of one single
power', i.e. Germany. (13)

Although Haldane (and Grey one day later) had repeated only
well-known positions of British foreign policy, which were firmly
rooted in centuries of British tradition, the Kaiser's reaction
this time was one of uncontrolled rage, with serious consequences
for the course of world history.   Immediately after reading
Lichnowsky's report on Haldane's warning, he fulminated against the
British, the 'nation of shopkeepers' ('Krämervolk'), against the
'balance of power', and British 'envy and fear of our expansion'
('Neidhammelei, Angst unseres zu Grosswerdens').   He even saw the
Anglo-Saxons joining the Slavs in the coming showdown between the
Germanic peoples on the one hand, the Slavs and the Latins on the
other. (14)   Just as in July 1914, Wilhelm II escalated his anger
into a 'Götterdämmerung' psychosis: 'Germany's existence is at
stake' ('Es geht um Sein oder Nichtsein Deutschlands').   This is
why he wanted to scrape together a motley of allies: Turkey,
Roumania, and even Bulgaria and Japan, both despised and hated by
the Kaiser for a long time - now they were all to be enlisted for
the 'defence' of the Fatherland.

The Kaiser's fit of rage very well demonstrated the underlying
assumptions or hopes of German foreign policy in those years:
Britain would remain neutral in a major war, giving Germany a free
hand on the Continent, above all against Russia and France.   The
very moment the Kaiser saw that his hope had become an illusion,
he denounced Britain violently, because she was about to upset all
German plans or hopes.   The Kaiser's reactions to Lichnowksky's
transmission of British warnings did not remain the Kaiser's personal affair.   He provoked the decision of German top leaders to
wage war once certain conditions were to be fulfilled.

THE 'WAR COUNCIL' OF 8 DECEMBER 1912

In an atmosphere of hectic activity, the Kaiser gathered his top
military and naval advisers to one of the informal meetings so
typical of the Kaiser's style.   It took place on 8 December 1912
and was unknown until a few years ago.   A detailed entry in the
diary of Admiral von Müller and the reports of the Bavarian and
Saxon Military Plenipotentiaries who were informed of the proceedings provide adequate sources to piece together the discussions in
outline.

The Kaiser opened the conference, which was attended by Tirpitz,
Moltke, Admiral von Heeringen, Chief of Naval Staff, and Admiral
von Müller, Chief of the Kaiser's Naval Cabinet.   The Kaiser reported what Haldane had told Lichnowsky five days before and drew
the same conclusion as Haldane and Grey: an Austrian attack
against Serbia would draw Germany into the war.   Bulgaria,
Roumania and Turkey as allies would help Germany to 'fight the war
with fury against France', while 'the fleet must naturally prepare
itself for the war against England.' (15)   Submarines to torpedo

British troop transports, and laying mines in the river Thames, were
possibilities envisaged by the Kaiser.   Since the German submarine
arm then consisted only of one flotilla, the Kaiser demanded a rapid
increase of the numbers of submarines.

The Kaiser's conclusions only revealed once more the chronic
German dilemma - the different stage of preparedness for war of the
army and the navy.   General Moltke pressed for war at an early
date, because he believed war to be 'unavoidable' in any case, and
he even went as far as to state: 'War the sooner the better.'
Admiral Tirpitz, on the other hand, preferred 'to see the postponement of the great fight for one and a half years'.   Moltke's re-
joinder was unanswerable and apparently remained unanswered: 'The
navy would not be ready even then and the army would get into an
increasingly unfavourable position, for the enemies were arming
more strongly than we were, as we were very short of money.'

Moltke, then, was for war as soon as possible.   One of his
reasons was that Germany, for financial reasons, was falling behind
the Entente in arming.   The net result of the conference was a compromise between the views of the army and the navy: war was postponed for eighteen months, until the extension of the Kiel Canal
had been completed, as had been suggested as early as 1909 and
again in 1911 in the aftermath of the second Moroccan crisis. (16)
Meanwhile the political leadership executed the Imperial instruction, submitted to the Chancellor after the conference, 'to enlighten
the people through the press of the great national interests at
stake also for Germany, if war were to break out over the Austro-
Serbian conflict'. (17)   This was in line with Moltke's advice
during the conference to 'prepare the popularity of a war against
Russia, as suggested in the Kaiser's discussion'.   While Moltke
clearly had named one enemy - Russia - the instruction to the
Chancellor spoke of war in general terms, and was unmistakably
clear:

> The people must not be in the position of asking themselves only
> at the outbreak of a great war, what are the interests that
> Germany would be fighting for.   The people ought rather to be
> accustomed to the idea of such a war beforehand. (18)

One of the first who may have become 'accustomed to the idea of
such a war beforehand' was presumably the Chancellor himself.   The
Kaiser, then, thought it remarkable 'that even the Chancellor now
appears to be accustomed to the idea of a war, although he had said
only a year ago that he would never be capable of advising war'.
(19)   Perhaps the Kaiser did not know that a year earlier, during
the second Moroccan crisis, Bethmann Hollweg had not been princi-
pally against war. (20)   Nevertheless, it emerges that the Chancellor was also more and more inclined to war.   He was probably
not just for war.   As a liberal Conservative he was not so agres-
sive against the West - France and Britain.   But he increasingly
turned against the East - Russia and Serbia - more energetically
than is compatible with the image of the 'philosopher of
Hohenfinow'.   There was no opposition from the political leadership against the Imperial instruction of 8 December 1912, according
to the record, unless one prefers to interpret as such his slightly
ironical reference to the conference as a 'war council'. (21)
With the knowledge of the conference of 8 December, German foreign

policy from then onwards until July 1914 readily becomes plausible as the execution of the programme laid down on that occasion.

Bethmann Hollweg's remark about the 'war council' was thus not so far from the mark, although he may then not have meant it so literally. The character of the secret meeting is also borne out by the report made by the Saxon and Bavarian Military Plenipotentiaries at the Court of Berlin. They corroborate and complement both each other and Admiral Müller's version. Both reports, obviously based on second-hand accounts, substantially agree with each other. (22)   Leuckart, the Saxon, reported to Dresden 'Moltke wants war.'   Wenninger, the Bavarian, had learned 'Moltke was for immediate action' ('Losschlagen'). The two reports, however, vary in the reasons given for Moltke's position, although they neatly fit with each other. France would be embarrassed by war now, 'as could be gathered from France's plea for a peaceful solution of current problems' (Leuckart). On the other hand, 'since the existence of the Triple Alliance the moment was never as favourable as now' (Wenninger). Both reports knew of Tirpitz's demand for delay, until the Kiel Canal and the submarine base on Heligoland were completed; but they reduced the time from eighteen months (Müller) to only a year.

Wenninger put some more interesting details on paper: 'The Kaiser was reluctant to accept the delay.' Apparently all participants of the conference knew that the basic decision for war had been taken, that its implementation had only been postponed for practical reasons. Above all, the military preparation of the German Empire had to be pushed ahead. Indeed, the Prussian Minister of War was instructed by the Kaiser the following day 'to prepare immediately a big army bill. Tirpitz was ordered to do the same for the fleet.' Also in the following item the Kaiser emerges as Germany's 'Supreme Warlord' in full action: he ordered both the general staff and the naval staff 'to prepare plans for a full-scale invasion of England. Meanwhile, his [i.e. the Kaiser's] diplomatic service is to win allies everywhere' (Wenninger).

The Kaiser's instructions define the substance of German foreign policy until July 1914: increased armament on land and sea; diplomatic activities to secure or win allies; psychological preparation of the German people for war. All this had to happen in an atmosphere of outward peace, as much as possible. Obviously, nothing was known to the public of what had happened behind the scenes as top secret decisions of the German Empire. No wonder that the Bavarian Military Plenipotentiary could close his confidential report on the Conference of 8 December 1912, and its immediate consequences, in a satisfied mood: 'Your Excellency will see that behind the scenes the picture is essentially different from that on the official stage.'

Indeed, as long as the Kaiser's secret instructions were not yet translated by his ministers into openly visible policy, Germany's policy must have appeared to be peaceful. But the picture changed in the following year when the bills for increasing the army and the navy were discussed and passed by the Reichstag. Once psychological and military rearmament as a consequence of the decisions of 8 December 1912 were starting in earnest, this could not be kept secret. The German war machine's gathering momentum in the last year of peace had to happen in public.

This look into the most intimate secrets of the German Empire,
brought to light only a few years ago, makes sense of a number of
otherwise apparently incoherent events.   With the decision of 8
December 1912, the German Empire had entered a course which was to
lead straight to war.   All relevant measures after it can be interpreted as an attempt to manoeuvre the Empire into a favourable
position in view of the coming war and to complete German armament
as far as possible.   The decision to go to war was not explicitly
formulated, as far as the new sources go, but at least implicitly
it can be seen as the net result of the conference on 8 December
1912, in conjunction with the measures taken immediately after it.
War had only been postponed for the moment.   The overall task
assigned by the Kaiser to his military and political advisers,
was, from now on, to create the best conditions for war.   They
had to prepare the German Empire for war in all respects, and they
had to choose the moment most favourable, or rather least disadvantageous, to go to war.   No definite date was given.   But as one
of the minimum conditions of military preparations the completion
of the Kiel Canal and of the submarine base on Heligoland had been
mentioned ever since the last Moroccan crisis. (23)   In December
1912, eighteen months had been computed for doing the job, which
would carry us to June 1914.   Both projects were, in fact, completed in June 1914.   The Kaiser, indeed, received the news of
the murder of Sarajevo during the ceremony for the reopening of the
widened Kiel Canal on 28 June 1914.

Chapter 15

PREPARING FOR WAR, DECEMBER 1912 - JUNE 1914

MILITARY PREPARATIONS

After the 'war council' of 8 December 1912, the logical measures
taken in execution of its decision followed each other rapidly.
On the same afternoon Admiral von Müller passed on the Kaiser's
instruction for the Chancellor to launch the psychological preparation of the coming war.   The following day, the Kaiser ordered his
military and naval staffs to work out a plan for a combined
invasion of Britain. (1)   The strategic value of that move may
have been low, but it sheds some light on the consequences of the
'war council', as seen by German leaders themselves - war against
Britain.   At the same time the Naval Office and the Prussian
Ministry of War were ordered to prepare bills for the expansion of
the German navy and the army. (2)
     The Army Bill had first been discussed at a meeting between the
Kaiser and Chancellor Bethmann Hollweg, his Foreign Secretary,
Kiderlen-Wächter, and representatives of the army, among them the
Chief of the General Staff, Moltke, and General Heeringen, the
Prussian Minister of War on 13 October 1912 at the Imperial hunting
lodge at Hubertusstock.   Details of it are so far not known, but
the idea of drastically expanding the army had been rejected by
successive Prussian Ministers of War.   They feared that the influx
of middle-class officers and social-democratic non-commissioned
officers would change the composition of the army and would make
it less reliable as an instrument in the hands of the Crown and of
the conservative interests it stood for.   The Prussian general
staff, however, was against thinking in terms of such narrow, class
arguments.   Officers, such as Ludendorff, Max Bauer and Wilhelm
Groener, who had risen from middle-class families to the centre of
the Prussian-German Empire, only saw the increase of military
power for the German Empire.   From the spring of 1912 onwards,
they had pleaded for an increase of the army by three more Army
Corps, so far without success.   The sudden military defeat of the
Turks in October 1912 changed the situation.   In mid-November the
Chancellor backed up the demand of the general staff and indirectly
also asked the Prussian Ministry of War to accept the three new
Army Corps.   Heeringen still dragged his feet, but the Imperial

order of 9 December removed the last resistance of the Prussian
Ministry of War against a massive expansion of the army.   The
very day the Kaiser's instruction reached the Ministry, it promptly
asked the general staff to specify its demands.   As early as 21
December Moltke answered with a detailed memorandum.   After
further discussions in January 1913, the new Army Bill was completed on 5 March.   The army was to be increased by 4,000 officers,
14,900 non-commissioned officers and 117,000 men - the biggest
increase of the German army in peacetime during the second German
Empire.
    The sudden and massive expansion of the German army - after
years of stagnation - drove the German Empire into another dilemma.
As the Prussian Minister of War had correctly seen, the increase of
the army in 1913 was reaching the limits within the given class
structure of the German Empire.   Further steps in the same direction would introduce an element of democracy into the German army
and would make it necessary to cover the additional costs by
introducing direct taxes.   This course was favoured by the unofficial coalition left of centre, consisting of the Catholic
Centre Party, the left-wing Liberals and the Social-democrats, at
the expense of the ruling traditional classes in Prussia.   The
very political basis of the German Empire would change towards a
direction abhorred by Germany's rulers, who, on the other hand, did
not believe they could go without a more powerful army in order to
overcome the diplomatic impasse of their 'Weltpolitik'.
    But, in the conditions of 1913, the German Empire was unable
either to reduce its military establishment by way of a general and
multilateral disarmament (for ideological reasons discussed in
connection with the two Peace Conferences of the Hague) (3) or to
carry the financial burden of intensified armament for any long-term
period.   Even the short-term financial resources could only be
mobilized by adding new financial burdens on the working class by
increased indirect taxation, which could only give another boost to
the SPD, which had become the strongest party of the Reichstag in
January 1912.   Further financial burdens would only work even more
in their favour.   Domestic reforms would have the same effect as
the expansion of the army - the German Empire moving in the direction of parliamentary government and democracy - the very last
thing Germany's ruling class wanted to see as a consequence of
their imperialist 'Weltpolitik'.   The only alternative to escape
all those inner tensions and conflicts - the discrepancies between
the need to reform and the unwillingness and inability to introduce
major reforms of structure - was the traditional way, to externa-
lize domestic tensions.   Since the instrument of 'Weltpolitik' had
been spent already for that purpose, there was only one way out -
war.
    It is against that background that one has to understand the
jubilant reaction in Germany when war approached and had broken
out, the wonderful feeling, described so often in enthusiastic
terms by contemporaries, of all internal differences and tensions
having disappeared in the common front against the enemy outside.
The almost orgiastic 'Augusterlebnis' has its real background in
the hopeless impasse Germany had got into at home and abroad by
1914.   In such a situation, war came as a heroic relief, as the
saviour from all internal troubles. (4)

A kind of rehearsal for August 1914 was provided in 1913, first by the passing of the Army Bill in the Reichstag in June 1913 and the Special Financial Bill voted by the Reichstag to cover the additional expenses. The SPD unanimously approved of the 'Deckungs- vorlage' because they included a modest share of direct taxation of the privileged wealthy. (5)   It was then that the Chancellor made a slogan popular by only indirectly taking it up - the coming war would be a 'struggle between Teutons and Slavs'.   France's recent change from two years' to three years' national service was taken as an excuse for the expansion of the German army, although the general staff had demanded the increase from the spring of 1912 onwards, the Kaiser since October, and the Chancellor since November 1912, and although.the French had introduced their exten- sion of national service only after the new Army Bill had been announced by Germany.   The general staff, from 1912 onwards the most powerful element of Germany's policy, had won with the help of the Kaiser's intervention; again a precedent for July 1914.

In the spring of 1913 the general staff also made war inevitable by another decision.   In April 1913 it stopped keeping up to date an alternative to the Schlieffen plan, which would have enabled Germany to begin a war on two fronts by attacking Russia in the East, while remaining on the defensive against France in the West. Apparently this was only a technical detail of little political importance.   In fact, however, it pushed Germany further along the road to offensive war in the West, as a Swiss scholar has recently demonstrated in detail. (6)   It also brought up again the problem of a 'preventive war', which pretended to forestall a threatening aggression from abroad, while it merely masked an offensive war of one's own.   Admirers of Bismarck in Germany have again and again praised his diplomatic skill in engineering war in such a way as to let the opponent appear as the 'aggressor'. After the founding of the German Empire, the concept of 'preven- tive war' had played an important part in major diplomatic crises, from 1875 to 1911. (7)   During the first Moroccan crisis at least junior officers in the general staff and the Prussian Minister of War had been for a 'preventive war' against Russia.   After the second Moroccan crisis Moltke had been bitterly disappointed that the chances for a welcome war had not been used. (8)   Moltke was in agreement with large sections of the German public, but in con- trast to journalists and party politicians he had real power to influence the course of events, e.g. by scrapping the plan for deploying the German army mainly in the East.

This decision has also to be seen in the light of the decision of 8 December 1912, and the subsequent events. (9)   If Germany was heading towards a continental war, it was no longer worthwhile to invest energies in a plan which would probably never become reality, that is, offensive war against Russia alone while France remained neutral or passive.   Instead, the general staff could concentrate on the more probable scenario - war against both Russia and France - and on the Schlieffen plan which was designed to lead Germany to swift victory both in the west and in the east. (10) By the turn of the year 1912-13 Russia had sufficiently recovered from her defeat of 1904-5 to be reckoned with again as a first- rate military power, if only for sheer numbers.   The building of

railways in western Russia and in Poland with French credits   would
shorten the time of deployment for the Russian army.   The Germans
computed that the strategical railways would be completed by 1916.
By 1917 the extremely favourable conditions of the time when the
Schlieffen plan had been conceived - the military vacuum east of
Germany - would no longer exist.   The Schlieffen plan would have
become a reckless gamble, because only one army, one eighth of
Germany's field troops, would be too weak against the whole Russian
army, even if the latter had also to fight Austria-Hungary.
The scrapping of the plan to march, if possible or necessary,
mainly to the East could make strategic sense only if Germany had
its war before 1916 or 1917, before the full weight of Russia's
military power would weigh on the eastern front of the Central
Powers, checking Germany's ability to fight France.   Indeed, the
magic date 1916-17 did appear in the pleas of the German generals
for an early 'preventive war' against Russia. (11)   On 12 May 1914
Moltke told his Austrian counterpart, Conrad von Hötzendorf, that
the Central Powers would worsen their chances if they waited any
longer: 'We [i.e. the German Army] are ready, the sooner the better
for us.' (12)   A few weeks later, Moltke pressed the Foreign
Secretary Jagow to open a 'preventive war' as soon as possible:
'In two or three years Russia will have completed her armaments'.
(13)   This brings us to 1916-17.   Immediately before the outbreak
of the war in 1914 the same dates are mentioned in the reasoning
for Germany's decision. (14)
But the general staff could commit themselves in their strategic
planning in the spring of 1913 only after the basic decision had
been taken on 8 December 1912 to seek war at a later, more favourable date.   This was essentially a political decision, even if in
the German Empire the political leaders were not present and had
only to execute what the Kaiser and his military advisers had
decided for them.

PSYCHOLOGICAL PREPARATIONS: THE JUBILEES OF 1913

But in the spring of 1913 the moment had not yet come.   The favourable conditions had not yet been created, either at home or abroad.
The massive increase of the army could make itself felt only from
1914 onwards.   For diplomatic reasons, Austria-Hungary had to be
held back during the Second Balkan War. (15)   But the last year of
peace for the German Empire - 1913 - was also the last year of
national jubilation.   The centenary of the War of Liberation in
1813 was celebrated and also the twenty-fifth anniversary of the
Kaiser's accession to the throne. (16)   Also the Kaiser's only
daughter was married in that year, which provided the occasion for
a dazzling last meeting of Europe's crowned families in Berlin.
A host of official and academic functions with enthusiastic speeches
provided many occasions for whipping up Germans into a patriotic
fever. (17)   The climax was the inauguration of the monument near
Leipzig in commemoration of the Battle of Leipzig on 18 October
1813, exactly one hundred years after the event.
In addition to this, the agitation for the Army Bill and the
increase of the army and the navy worked in the same direction.

The German nation was being 'accustomed to the idea of ... war beforehand', as the Kaiser had ordered on 8 December 1912.   Most of the press took an active part, in particular by harping on Bethmann Hollweg's suggestion in the Reichstag on 7 April 1913, that the next conflagration might be a conflict between 'Slavs and Teutons'. (18)   Since the German middle class hardly needed any more brainwashing for being prepared to go to war, the propaganda effort of 1913 must have been directed towards the one section in German society that was least integrated and reliable in the view of Germany's ruling classes - the working class and the SPD. Bethmann Hollweg and his Secretary of the Interior, Clemens von . Delbrück, intensified their policy of integrating the working class into the Empire by flimsy verbiage without introducing any substantial reforms.   Their overall aim was to create the conditions for a united patriotic front beforehand for the hour of need; culminating in Delbrück's order, on 24 July 1914, not to arrest automatically all key Socialist leaders the day war began, because he felt the majority of the SPD would behave loyally in the case of war. (19)

The propaganda effort of 1913 also reflected the uneasiness of Germany's leaders.   The Moltke-Ludendorff memorandum of 21 December 1912 was involuntarily revealing in that respect.   It saw certain victory only if the leaders of the Empire 'succeeded in formulating the 'casus belli' in such a way that the nation will take up arms unanimously and enthusiastically'. (20)   That was the rub.   The attempt to paint Russia as the potential aggressor in advance for supporting Pan-Slavism and Serbia against Austria-Hungary is sufficiently accounted for by the reasoning of Moltke and Ludendorff, as far as the home front was concerned.

DIPLOMATIC PREPARATIONS: HOLDING BACK AUSTRIA-HUNGARY IN EARLY 1913

But for Germany's relations abroad it became imperative that Germany and her ally Austria-Hungary act, from now on, with a maximum of restraint until the moment came for military action. Until then, it was Russia that was to appear as the eternal trouble-maker for peaceful Europe.   The Empire's diplomacy faced a difficult task, because Austria-Hungary had to be held back from a premature attack on Serbia without becoming frustrated to the point of being driven into the arms of the Entente, or at least of France and Britain.   At the same time, Germany's ostentatious peace-loving attitude on the Balkans might endear Germany to Britain so that the latter might, after all, remain neutral if war broke out over unruly Serbia.

The weeks after the conference of 8 December 1912 offered ample opportunities for becoming active in the directions outlined.   The Kaiser informed Franz Ferdinand, the Austrian heir apparent, of the warnings from London, which had provoked him into the decisions discussed above.   Franz Ferdinand understood, or rather misunderstood, the Kaiser's motives as indicating a German desire for early war, and the Archduke himself now pressed for war against Serbia with the new Foreign Minister, Count Berchtold.   But the Chancellor

once more stopped the Austrians from rushing into action too
early. (21)

The Kaiser also sounded out the situation in one vital section
of the future Western front at this time.   It so happened that he
met the Belgian King Albert on 19 December 1912.   The Belgians
were worried about German intentions in the event of war.   But
the Kaiser calmed them, by telling King Albert - perhaps in all
subjective innocence because he did not know of the secret plann-
ings of the general staff, or because he had just forgotten them -
that Germany did not plan to violate Belgian neutrality in a war
against France.   Germany was only interested in a 'secure right
flank', as the Kaiser tactfully put it.   Two days later, the
Kaiser reported his conversation with Albert to Moltke and Bethmann
Hollweg.   By then, at the latest, the Kaiser and his Chancellor
must have learned of the intention to violate Belgian neutrality,
because Moltke answered the Kaiser:

> He [Moltke] must reconsider the situation.   Our deployment
> against France is, as is well known ('bekanntlich') based on
> our marching through Belgium.   Nothing could be changed for
> the time being until 1 April 1913.   The strengthening of the
> Belgian Army must first take place.   Before that Belgium is
> probably too weak to defend her neutrality by arms. (22)

Moltke, as we have seen, did not change his plans for Belgium as
from 1 April 1913.   On the contrary, by scrapping the alternative
plan for the East, he made the violation of Belgian neutrality
even more certain.

Finally, the Conference of Ambassadors in London on the Balkans,
which opened on 18 December 1912, seemed to offer the chance for
the German Empire to collect points as the champion of peace in
that region at least, (23) although Lichnowsky warned the Auswärtiges Amt against their illusion that Britain would let France
down in the event of a continental war. (24)   In spite of all
efforts in London, tensions increased between Austria-Hungary and
Russia in early 1913.   The bone of contention was the frontiers
of the new buffer state Albania, the creation of which Austria-
Hungary had demanded to block Serbia's expansion to the Adriatic.
(25)   The war party in Vienna under Conrad and General Potiorek,
the military governor of Bosnia and Herzegovina, used the new
tensions to agitate once more for an attack against Serbia.   This
time, they also wanted to include Montenegro, because Russia wanted
to give her the disputed town Skutari, while the Austrians wanted
to give Skutari to Albania, the intended Austrian satellite state.

Feelings were running so high that, in early February 1913,
Berlin feared a war between Austria-Hungary and Russia over Skutari.   Just two months after the conference of 8 December 1912, at
a time when the complicated preparations for war had not yet even
begun in Germany, war at such an early date and over such a remote
place as Skutari would have upset all the strategic planning of
the Germans.   This is why, on 10 February 1913, both the Chancellor and the German chief of staff wrote to their respective counterparts in Vienna, Berchtold and Conrad, warning them not to start
war now.   Bethmann Hollweg told Berchtold that Austria's attack
against Serbia would provoke Russian intervention and a confrontation between the Triple Alliance and the Triple Entente.   But

Britain might reconsider her position in the Triple Entente, which
could happen only if the present crisis did not lead to conflict.
The Chancellor thought it 'a mistake of incalculable consequences'
to provoke war at a time 'when at least there is a remote chance
for us to have the conflict under conditions much more favourable
to us'. (26)   What Bethmann Hollweg alluded to was, of course,
his hope for British neutrality in exchange for Germany's peaceful
behaviour during the Ambassador's Conference in London.

Moltke was more open and direct.   His concern to find a suitable
formulation for the 'casus belli', as expressed in his memorandum
of 21 December 1912, was echoed when he wrote to his colleague
Conrad that a war which was fought for the existence of a state
needed the 'enthusiasm of the people'.   If Russia attacked Austria-
Hungary, Germany would support her ally enthusiastically.   But
it would be very difficult to find an effective slogan if Austria
were to provoke a war now, for which the German population could
not see any reason.   Moltke remained convinced 'that a European
war is bound to come sooner or.later, in which the issue will be
one of a struggle between Germandom and Slavdom.   To prepare themselves for that contingency is the duty of all states which are
the champions of Germanic ideas and culture ('Geisteskultur'). (27)
Although Austria-Hungary contained more Slavs than Germans, the
German Empire wanted to fight the world on the flimsy ideological
basis of a 'struggle between Slavs and Teutons'.   And Moltke told
the Austrian military attaché in Berlin in early February 1913:
'When starting a world war one has to think very carefully.' (28)
The logic is clear: Germany had decided on war, but in February
1913 had come to the conclusion that she was not yet fully prepared
for world war and that it was inopportune to begin over such a
trifling matter as Skutari.   But in April Germany had to repeat
her pressure on Vienna, before, in May 1913, the Skutari crisis
could be solved as Austria-Hungary had wished; Montenegro had to
give up Skutari and hand it over to Albania. (29)

With the coming of the Second Balkan War, however, new
differences of opinion appeared between Vienna and Berlin.   While
Austria-Hungary remained adamant in her hostility towards Serbia,
Germany was for building up an alliance of Balkan countries against
Bulgaria under the patronage of Austria-Hungary, including
Roumania, Greece and Serbia.   When Bulgaria collapsed so quickly
in July 1913 during the Second Balkan War, Berlin took that turn
of events fairly calmly, while Vienna took it as another blow at
their prestige and seriously considered military intervention in
favour of Bulgaria.   Thus, in the summer of 1913 Germany had
again to hold back Austria-Hungary from untimely war.   Vienna, by
now, was becoming angered and frustrated.   The alliance between
Germany and Austria-Hungary became strained, the more so, when the
Peace Treaty of Bucharest in August 1913 almost doubled the territory and population of Greece, Montenegro and Serbia.   Austria-
Hungary felt humiliated, only a few years after Aehrenthal had
launched his campaign of building up the power and prestige of the
Danube Monarchy in the Balkans.

ENCOURAGING AUSTRIA-HUNGARY IN LATE 1913

Austria-Hungary's alienation, however, had not been the intention
of Germany's leaders when pleading for a contemporary course of
restraint.   From the autumn of 1913 onwards, Germany tried to
regain the confidence and sympathy of Austria's statesmen by
systematically cultivating her relations with Vienna.   When, in
September 1913, the Serbs refused to withdraw their troops from
northern Albania, Berlin, on this occasion, felt obliged to support
Vienna in taking a strong stand against Serbia;   otherwise Austria
might have been completely lost for Germany.   Vienna, with German
support, confronted Serbia with an ultimatum to withdraw within ten
days, at the risk of war, as the Austrians had already told the
Germans.   Serbia gave in and peace was patched up once more.
     As in other instances, it was the Kaiser who first articulated
the change of position in Germany.   On 18 October, the very day
that the Austrians sent their ultimatum to Serbia, Berchtold
expressed his appreciation for Germany's support, adding his hope
that the Serbs now would give way.   When the Kaiser saw the
report of the German chargé d'affaires in Vienna on his talk with
Berchtold, he minuted it with one of his notorious remarks: 'That
would be regrettable!   Now or never!   Order must be restored down
there one day.' (30)   'Now or never!'   That was, of course, the
language of July 1914, in fact exactly the same words. (31)
     The day of the ultimatum to Serbia also saw the ceremonies for
the inauguration of the great monument near Leipzig as the climax
of the centenary of the war against Napoleon of 1813.   During the
ceremonies, the Kaiser gave the most direct and massive encouragement to General Conrad von Hötzendorf, the Austrian Chief of Staff.
The Kaiser incited the Austrian to make war against Serbia and to
take Belgrade in a few days.   Although, as he claimed, an adherent
of peace, he thought that a situation might arise in which a Great
Power could not passively tolerate provocations but had to draw the
sword. (32)   The Kaiser's words, communicated to Vienna the next
day by Conrad, made a deep and favourable impression on Emperor
Franz Joseph and his Foreign Minister Count Berchtold.   'This
time he acted very loyally,' Franz Joseph commented full of satisfaction. (33)   A few days later, Kaiser Wilhelm II toured Austria-
Hungary, evidently with a mission to soothe the wounded pride of
his Austrian ally.   Again he talked of drawing the sword, and this
time Berchtold was able to hear it himself from the Kaiser.   On
26 October he told Berchtold in Vienna what he thought was the
only conceivable solution - the complete dependence of the south
Slavs and the 'hegemony of the Monarchy' in the Balkans.   The
Serbs were to place their army under the command of Austria-Hungary
and if they refused, violence would have to be applied.

     For if His Majesty the Emperor Franz Joseph demands something
     the Serbian government has to accept it, otherwise Belgrade
     will be shelled and occupied until the demands of His Majesty
     are fulfilled.   And you can be certain that I support you and
     am ready to draw the sword whenever your action may make it
     necessary. (34)

Less than a year later the situation had arisen in which the Kaiser
acted and made the Austrians act in the very way he had bragged
about in October 1913.

The reason for Germany's new hostility against Serbia was also given by the Kaiser in his talk with Berchtold.   The Kaiser rejected Franz Ferdinand's suggestion to renew the Three Emperor's League with Russia with an argument which had been traditional since the fall of Bismarck.   Wilhelm II explained that 'since Alexander III one has to reckon with a different Russia, with a power hostile to us and bent on our destruction, being governed by elements totally different from the Tsar'. (35)   This was in line with Bismarck's plea for an alliance with Austria-Hungary in 1879 as a protection against Tsarist Russia, infected by and supporting revolutionary Pan-Slavism. (36)   The Kaiser only articulated a wide-spread feeling of resentment and fear of Russia, which was shared by Moltke, Bethmann Hollweg and Jagow about the same time and expressed in parallel pronouncements. (37)

THE STRATEGIC VALUE OF THE BALKANS, TURKEY AND 'MITTELAFRIKA' FOR GERMAN 'WELTPOLITIK'

In order to strengthen its own position 'vis-à-vis' Russia, Germany wanted to reconsolidate Turkey after its defeats of 1911-12, mainly by increased German military aid and help in fortifying Constantinople and the Straits.   This was the purpose of the mission of General Liman von Sanders, announced by the Kaiser in his talk with Berchtold.   But the Germans apparently did not see that in bottling up Russia in the Black Sea by such a startling move the dreaded eruption in Russia was to be provoked even more certainly.

The new German military mission under Liman von Sanders at that time was a provocation to Russia; even more so was Liman von Sanders's taking over the command of the First Turkish Army Corps stationed in and about Constantinople.   When the Russians began to realize the extent of the German military mission in Turkey in early November 1913, they protested in Berlin so vehemently that they provoked the last great crisis between Germany and Russia before 1914.   War with Russia at that time would still be too soon, but Germany's position was so strong that she succeeded in solving the crisis on 15 January 1914 without giving way in substance to Russian opposition.   Liman von Sanders gave up the command of the First Army Corps in Constantinople but he remained Inspector-General of the Turkish Army and Director of the Turkish War Academy, which meant that he kept key positions in his hands. Even after the patching up of differences between Russia and Germany, resentment lingered in both countries.   The Russians saw themselves provoked, while the Germans resented the Russian protest as an unjustified intervention into Turkish domestic affairs and into Turko-German relations. (38)

The Liman von Sanders affair was only the most spectacular symptom of increased German interest in the Balkans, linking the Central Powers with Turkey.   At the same time, however, Germany also reached the limits of its 'Weltpolitik' in the Balkans, both financially and politically.   An active German policy in the Balkans required additional investment in the form of loans and subsidies of one kind or another that the German Empire, already staggering under the burden of intensified armament both on land

and sea, was unable to provide, owing to a general lack of capital and the beginnings of an economic crisis. (39)

By unreservedly identifying with Austria-Hungary against Serbia and the south Slav movement from autumn 1913 onwards, the German Empire also got into the maelstrom of tensions and problems in the Balkans.   The old-fashioned policy of repression, as recommended by the Kaiser to Conrad on 18 October on the battlefield of Leipzig and on 26 October to Berchtold in Vienna, (40) began to emerge as the safest and easiest way out of the Balkans maze and the mess inside the Habsburg Monarchy.   Repression of the south Slavs, however, also meant aggression against Serbia.   And Germany's leaders themselves had calculated the consequences of such a move, had heard it from others, mainly Britain, and had themselves warned their Austrian ally when they thought it necessary for tactical reasons - war against Serbia would provoke war with Russia, would entail continental war, probably even Britain's intervention, i.e. world war. (41)

Germany's increased involvement in the Balkans was perhaps covered by increased cooperation with Britain, for reasons dis-cussed earlier. (42)   Germany's policy in the Balkans and towards Britain in the last months before the war, thus centred on increas-ing tensions in the Balkans by giving strong support to Austria-Hungary.   The hope was that this would reduce tensions in coopera-tion with Britain with an eye to securing British neutrality in a war provoked by conflict in the Balkans with Germany's help.   In the effort to neutralize Britain beforehand, other more traditional problems apart from the Balkans seemed to be open for cultivating better relations with Britain - the Baghdad Railway and African colonies.   German foreign policy concentrated upon them in the last months before the outbreak of the First World War.   Negotia-tions took place even in July 1914, and a first agreement was initialled.   But events overtook all provisional agreements and exploded the illusions about Britain's position in connection with them.

The material objectives of Germany were to carve up the Portu-guese colonies in Southern Africa, and if possible also the Belgian Congo.   The overall aim in that region was the creation of 'Mittel-afrika', as it had emerged since the second Moroccan crisis in 1911 and was to assert itself as Germany's main colonial war aim after the outbreak of war. (43)   German foreign policy in that respect is best illustrated by a memorandum drawn up by the Chan-cellor on 12 February 1912, i.e. at the time of the Haldane mission to Berlin.   Bethmann Hollweg explicitly mentioned Angola and parts of the Belgian Congo as German colonial aspirations.   One month earlier, he had even dreamed of the Dutch colonies, and all taken together these would 'form a great colonial empire'. (44)

Germany's colonial ambitions were, however, linked to the Baghdad Railway, as the Germans saw it themselves.   Intensified rivalry between Britain and Germany at sea, because of Germany's refusal to regulate and limit naval armament by mutual agreement, had forced Britain to seek qualitative improvement of her battle fleet by changing from coal to oil for fuelling the Royal Navy. Since then, southern Persia, where most of British oil came from, acquired additional strategic value and, as a consequence, the

projected section of a railway line, linking Baghdad to Basra and
to the Persian Gulf.

In mid-1912 Anglo-German talks had been broken off, but were resumed in February 1913. (45)   But because Germany also began to
be interested in oil from the Middle East, in this case from Mesopotamia, British and German oil interests in neighbouring regions
blocked each other also regarding the Baghdad Railway.   Only when
the American Standard Oil Company tried to implant itself in the
Middle East were Britain and Germany spurred into speedy agreement
in March 1914.   A joint Anglo-German company was formed to exploit
oil resources in Mesopotamia - the Deutsche Bank, representing
German oil interests, holding only 25 per cent of the capital.
The reason given by the Deutsche Bank for German concessions sheds
some light on the weaknesses of German 'Weltpolitik' in general:
Germany was unable to raise on her own the funds necessary for
exploiting the Turkish oil fields in Mesopotamia.

For the same reason Germany was unable to raise a loan for the
Turkish government in the spring of 1914;   in fact most of the
capital for the 500-million gold francs' loan had to come from
France, which was notoriously more liquid than Germany.   As a
consequence, the Chancellor saw Germany's position in Turkey
undermined.   In a report to the Kaiser he made it clear that
Germany was interested in Turkey only as long as it believed the
Ottoman Empire to be open to German influence.   Bethmann Hollweg
even feared that Turkey might change sides and pass over to the
camp of the Entente.   Germany could not keep Turkey, 'because we
are short of funds'. (46)   The financial bankruptcy of German
policy in the Near and Middle East was also revealed by the fact
that the capital market in Germany could only at best raise one
loan at a time for satisfying German economic interests - either
Krupp's in supplying arms to Turkey, or those of the Deutsche Bank
in exploiting the oil fields of Mesopotamia.   German 'Weltpolitik'
in that region seemed threatened for sheer lack of money, and its
failure could best be veiled by a war that might secure German
interests by other means.   This was certainly not a primary motive
for German leaders in July 1914, but one more obstacle for any war
policy thereby seemed to have been removed.

PROPPING UP DECAYING AUSTRIA-HUNGARY BY WAR

The decision that led immediately to war, however, was connected
with Austria-Hungary.   In the first months of 1914 doubts as to the
stability of Austria-Hungary reached leading circles in Germany, as
testified by a private letter of the German Ambassador to Vienna,
Tschirschky, to Jagow of 22 May 1914.   Tschirschky asked himself
and the German Foreign Secretary, whether it was really worth
while to preserve the Danube Monarchy, and he recommended that
thought be given to what could happen after the 'decomposition' of
Austria-Hungary. (47)   During the crisis of July 1914, we find
an echo of Tschirschky's sceptical remarks in a private letter of
Jagow to Lichnowsky, the German Ambassador to London, of 18 July.
Jagow conceded that it was an open question 'whether we get all
our money's worth from an alliance with that increasingly disinte-

grating political structure on the Danube'. (48)   But both
Tschirschky and Jagow saw, for the near future, no alternative to
clinging to Austria-Hungary as long as possible.   The best way of
preserving it was seen in an offensive 'defensive', as underlying
the concept of 'preventive war' against the rising south Slav
movement.

In both Central Powers pressure for 'preventive war' increased,
in Austria-Hungary against Serbia, in Germany against Russia - the
more so, after Russia had answered the Liman von Sanders mission
with an intensified armaments drive.   The obvious result would be
that in the near future Russia would no longer give in so easily
to German demands as in 1909 and even in January 1913.   The
German press began a campaign against Russia to build her up as
Germany's immediate enemy. (49)   To win over Liberals and Socialists to the idea of war against Russia great play was made of the
reactionary character of Tsarism, although the government had seen
through the formal façade of Tsarism ever since Bismarck in 1879.
The anti-Tsarist propaganda battle-cry proved effective, as events
were to show in August 1914.

Nevertheless Tschirschky, in a talk with Conrad on 16 March
1914, identified two obstacles to the war party at most unexpected
places - in Austria-Hungary it was Arch-duke Franz Ferdinand, in
Germany the Kaiser himself.   The explanation Tschirschky offered
is instructive.   Both Franz Ferdinand and Wilhelm II would go to
war only on the basis of a 'fait accompli'. (50)   Franz Ferdinand,
it must be concluded, apparently feared the revolutionary consequences of a great war for the Monarchy, as did occur in 1918.
Wilhelm II was widely suspected in German chauvinist circles of
not seeing a major conflict through.   'Guillaume le timide', as
he was surreptitiously called after the second Morrocan crisis,
might get cold feet again at the height of an international crisis.
This assessment also became justified by the Kaiser's accommodating
view on 28 July 1914. (51)   Only fourteen weeks later, one of the
high-placed 'obstacles' to war had been removed - Franz Ferdinand
through the outrage of Sarajevo - while the other was swept by the
same event into advocating a policy of a 'fait accompli' which was
to lead straight to general war.

GERMANY AND THE ANGLO-RUSSIAN NAVAL TALKS, JUNE 1914

But war could be sparked off by the shots of Sarajevo only because
Germany also saw her position in the world threatened vis-à-vis the
other World Powers.   The last months of peace were overshadowed in
Germany by the almost obsessive fear of Russia's military recovery
and of the Entente consolidating to the point of becoming a formal
alliance between Britain, France and Russia.   Berlin had been
worried when most of the British fleet in the Mediterranean was
moved to the North Sea in 1912, because an intimate Anglo-French
collaboration in case of war was thus indicated.   In October 1912
France and Russia had concluded a naval convention.   Since the
turn of the year 1913-14, i.e. as a consequence of the Liman von
Sanders mission to Constantinople, Russia also asked for a corresponding naval convention with Britain, which could have helped to

relieve the Straits blocked by the Germans, as was attempted with
the Gallipoli expedition in 1915.   But Britain, fearing adverse
repercussions on Germany, remained cool.   It was only on 7 June
that talks began in London, and the British envisaged a rather
leisurely pace for them.

The German government, informed by their permanent spy in the
Russian Embassy, (von Siebert, of Baltic German origin) became
nervous. (52)   Through Ballin and Theodor Wolff, one of the leading German journalists of the time, editor of the liberal 'Berliner
Tageblatt' and owner of the 'Wolff'schen Telegraphenbüro', the
German government initiated a press campaign with the aim of
frightening Britain from concluding a naval convention with Russia.
In his last great instruction before Sarajevo to Lichnowsky, on 16
June 1914, the Chancellor conjured up the spectre of chauvinist
pressure on the 'moderate' government in Berlin.   Not only they,
but also more level-headed politicians became more and more convinced that Russia was planning to attack Germany in the near
future.   A further increase of the army and of the navy would be
demanded;   in the summer or autumn of 1914 a new 'armament fever'
would sweep through Germany.   Bethmann Hollweg conceded that he
did not believe in Russia's aggressive intentions, that she only
wanted to prepare herself for the next Balkan crisis.   But he
answered Russian aspirations with the oblique threat that during
the next crisis a 'European conflagration' could only be prevented
by Britain and Germany transcending their respective obligations
to the Triple Entente and the Triple Alliance.   Otherwise any
minor incident could spark off war between Russia and Austria-
Hungary. (53)

What may have sounded plausible in mid-June 1914 acquired a
different ring after July 1914.   Bethmann Hollweg tried to lure
Britain into the trap of cooperating with Germany without regard
to the Triple Entente, i.e. Russia and France, while Germany did
not even dream of doing the same.   In fact, in July 1914 Germany
took a rigid stand on its alliance obligations towards Austria-
Hungary and gave them an excessive interpretation. (54)   The
Chancellor stressed the importance of the projected Anglo-Russian
naval convention by a further passage which contained the oblique
threat that even a formal commitment for naval cooperation between
Russia and Britain in the event of war against Germany would be a
provocation for the German public. (55)

Traditional and apologetic historians tried only a decade ago
to find an excuse for Germany's war policy in the project of an
Anglo-Russian naval convention. (56)   Sir Edward Grey, it was
suggested, had lied when denying the existence of such a convention in the house of Commons, and had thus undermined Bethmann
Hollweg's confidence in his honesty.   But the means by which the
German Chancellor had obtained his information were far from honest
(a spy in the Russian Embassy), nor did the naval convention exist
at the time of Grey's denial.   The truth was that the Chancellor
tried to blackmail Britain into neutrality by using the projected
naval convention for conjuring up the well-known Pan-German threat
against peace and security.   The German Chancellor very well knew
that the German Empire and Austria-Hungary between them had it in
their hands to escalate tensions, even any minor incident in the

Balkans to the dimension of war, both continental and world wide.
The incident which allowed Germany to push the button for starting
the deadly mechanism of crisis and conflict occurred only twelve
days later - the murder of Archduke Franz Ferdinand and his wife
at Sarajevo, on 28 June 1914.   Germany allowed the Balkans to
provide the spark that touched off the First World War because
Germany's leaders saw no other way out from the mounting difficulties, contradictions and tensions inside and outside Germany,
which had been aggravated by almost two decades of 'Weltpolitik'
and rapidly progressing industrialization.

Part five

GERMANY'S WAR OF AGGRESSION AND CONQUEST

GERMANY'S WAR OF AGGRESSION: THE CRISIS AND THE OUTBREAK OF WAR, 28 JUNE – 4 AUGUST 1914

The shots that killed Archduke Franz Ferdinand and his wife at
Sarajevo on 28 June 1914 did not automatically unleash the First
World War.   But they did mobilize all the tensions that had been
building up during half a century of imperial and imperialist
policies – the conflict between the rising national movement in
the Balkans against Austria-Hungary, incapable of reforming herself
sufficiently to give scope to the legitimate aspirations of south
Slav nationalism; Russia's indirect support of south Slav nationalism by backing up Serbia, in contrast to her own autocratic and
conservative structure; finally, all the tensions that had been
accumulated by German 'Weltpolitik' during the last two decades
throughout the world, in particular with France, Russia and Britain.
      Yet, given the will of all the powers concerned to find a peace-
ful solution in July 1914, peace could have been preserved any
time until 29 July 1914.   On that day, Austria-Hungary, under
pressure from Berlin, prematurely opened hostilities against Serbia
by shelling Belgrade, thus provoking Russian general mobilization
one day later. (1)   From then on, all efforts to save peace were
bound to fail.   It was the bombardment of Belgrade – mild compared
with what the world has seen since – that started the famous
mechanism of mobilizations and railway tables.   But even before
29 July, German decisions proved decisive in all stages of the
developing crisis, above all in Vienna.

THE GERMAN DECISION, 4-6 JULY 1914

After the many oscillations of German policy towards Serbia and
Austria-Hungary since the Bosnian crisis of 1908-9 and the two
Balkan Wars 1912-13, (2) the government in Vienna was at first
divided in its counsels between a party of war and one of circumspection.   Most outspoken of the war party in Vienna was Conrad
von Hötzendorf, the Austro-Hungarian Chief of General Staff.   His
sympathies were with the German aristocracy, the middle classes in
Austria and the Magyar aristocracy in Hungary, who felt threatened
by the rising tide of Slav nationalism and democracy.   He represented a section of circles in Austria-Hungary who chose to stake

everything on a preventive war - Germany against Russia, Austria
against Serbia - to solve all their domestic troubles.

The golden opportunity seemed to present itself in June 1914
with the outrage at Sarajevo.   Yet, the immediate reaction in
Austria and Germany was confusion. (3)   It took some days before
a clear political decision crystallized.   In Vienna, Conrad at
once wanted to seize the chance and make war against Serbia as soon
as possible, and he was supported by the clamour of the German press
in Austria and by leading members of the Austro-Hungarian Ministry
of Foreign Affairs.   Foreign Minister Count Berchtold, however,
hesitated to go as far as that.   The Austrian Prime Minister,
Count Stürgkh, preferred to wait for the results of the official
investigation at Sarajevo.   Emperor Franz Joseph took the same
view and was not sure whether Germany would support Austria-Hungary
against Russia in case of war.   Count Tisza, the Hungarian Prime
Minister, was even more outspoken on that point and actually feared
Russian intervention and German neutrality.   Even bellicose Conrad
admitted the force of the argument and was prepared to make the
Austrian decision dependent on the position that Germany, the more
powerful ally, would adopt.   To clear this point, the Austrians
despatched Count Hoyos, Berchtold's principal aide in the Foreign
Ministry, in all haste to Berlin, where he arrived on 5 July, armed
with a memorandum on the Balkan problem and a covering letter from
Franz Joseph to the German Kaiser. (4)   Hoyos was to find out
what the Germans would do after Sarajevo.   Thus the ultimate
decision was squarely placed in Berlin.

It also took some time before the ruling group in Germany made
up their minds after Sarajevo.   Now, when the chances for an early
showdown seemed to be as good as at any time before, the political
leaders seemed to hesitate because they saw clearly the likely
outcome - world war.   From the start the Auswärtiges Amt counselled
moderation to both Austria and Serbia, perhaps without clear instructions from the Chancellor.   German diplomacy was thus in
accordance with the reaction in the capitals of the other Great
Powers: Sarajevo was seen as a grave incident, but not one which
could or should lead to war if Austria-Hungary and Serbia acted
reasonably. (5)   The German general staff, on the other hand,
immediately resumed its pressure for a preventive war against
Russia. (6)   General von Moltke, drinking the waters of Karlsbad,
did not even trouble to return to Berlin.   His deputy, General von
Waldersee, gave the impression to at least one competent observer,
the Saxon Military Plenipotentiary in Berlin on 3 July, 'that they
would regard it with favour if war were to come about now',
because 'conditions and prospects would never become better' for
Germany. (7)   On 3 July, the prevailing impression in Berlin was
still that the Kaiser was in favour of maintaining peace.

The views of his political and military advisers conflicted, and
the final decision thus lay with the Kaiser.   In the last few years
he had oscillated between encouraging and restraining Austria-
Hungary towards Serbia.   After Sarajevo, however, he was incensed
and thought that Austria had to act now if she still wanted to be
taken seriously as a great power.   When he read the report of the
German ambassador in Vienna, Tschirschky, which reflected the prevailing mood of moderation and restraint of the German Foreign

Ministry, the Kaiser angrily minuted, 'Now or never!' and 'The
Serbs must be idsposed of, and that right soon!' (7)   This
happened on 4 July. (8)   One day later Hoyos arrived from Vienna
on his special mission to Berlin and handed over his documents to
the 73-year old Austro-Hungarian ambassador, Count Szögyény.   The
The documents as such did not plead for war, at least not directly
and openly.   But Hoyos, who belonged to the war party in Vienna,
may have given them a warlike twist in conversation.   Szögyény, a
Magyar aristocrat like Hoyos, apparently seized upon the more bellicose interpretation.   During the special audience accorded to him
by the Kaiser on 5 July, Szögyény seems to have pressed for a warlike solution, perhaps by stressing the seriousness of the situation.   Before lunch, the Kaiser hesitated to commit himself.
After lunch, Szögyény pressed his point again.   This time the
Kaiser gave the assurances desired by the war party in Vienna:
Austria should act as quickly and energetically as possible and she
could fully count on Germany's support if Russia were to intervene. (9)
  The Kaiser's only reservation was that his Chancellor had to
approve the Imperial commitment.   In the afternoon, the Kaiser's
chief political and military advisers, who were at hand on that
sunny summer Sunday afternoon, were hastily summoned to the New
Palace at Potsdam.   The Chancellor nodded approval when his
Imperial master told him what he had told the Austrian ambassador
a few hours before.   Germany's top leaders then thought, as
General von Plessen, the Kaiser's principal 'aide-de-camp', noted
in his diary, that 'the sooner the Austrians make their move
against Serbia the better, and that the Russians - though friends
of Serbia - will not join in.' (10)
  The following day, the Chancellor repeated the German commitment
in a conversation with Szögyény.   Bethmann Hollweg also considered
'immediate action' by Austria 'as the best solution' of Austrian
difficulties in the Balkans.   The German 'carte blanche', issued
by the Kaiser, was duly endorsed by the proper constitutional
authority, the Chancellor.   In fact, the alleged 'carte blanche'
was more than the name suggests, because the Germans did not
merely give complete freedom of action to the Austrians, but they
prescribed to their ally the course of action to be taken - speedy
war against Serbia at any cost.   Berlin thus threw its weight in
favour of the war party in Vienna.
  Germany's leaders were fully aware of the probable consequences
of their action.   They cannot have forgotten earlier calculations
that an Austrian war against Serbia would mean war against Russia,
even world war. (11)   The last time they had said so themselves
was only a few days before, immediately after Sarajevo.   A more
recent source, Kurt Riezler's diaries, allows us a glimpse into
the reasoning of the German Chancellor.   Bethmann Hollweg did not
take the decision lightly and was apparently worried by Russia's
rearmament and by the fact that Britain and Russia seemed to be on
the verge of concluding some naval agreement.
  On 7 July, the Chancellor told Riezler: 'An action against
Serbia can lead to world war.'   The following day he outlined the
objectives sought by such 'action': 'If there is no war, if the
Tsar does not want war or if France, frightened by the prospect,

pleads for peace, we have at least the chance to divide the Entente by our action.' (12)   In other words, when taking his 'leap into the dark', as he himself called it, Bethmann Hollweg seems to have aimed at a continental war against Russia and France in the first place, and a local war against Serbia with the breaking up of the Entente only in the second place.

PREPARING THE ULTIMATUM

The German decision of 5 and 6 July had an immediate and telling effect on the Austrians.   Berchtold swung round to Conrad's belli- cose line.   His colleagues in the Cabinet followed suit, so did Emperor Franz Joseph.   For a week, Count Tisza, the Hungarian Prime Minister, held out in opposition against the idea of war against Serbia, not out of love for the Serbs, but because he felt that even without a victory over Serbia, Austria-Hungary already had enough south Slavs in her territories.   On 7 July, a great debate took place between Berchtold and Tisza in the Council of Ministers in Vienna.   Tisza warned against war without declara- tion, which apparently Hoyos had pressed for in Berlin.   Instead, Tisza suggested confronting Serbia with harsh but acceptable condi- tions.   Only if they were refused, should Austria mobilize and declare war.   Against Tisza's opposition Berchtold's views pre- vailed: war against Serbia, but diplomatically prepared by an ultimatum which was to be made unacceptable beforehand.
    Berlin was informed of Austria's decision through the normal diplomatic channels, which also ensured the necessary coordination of German and Austrian diplomacy. (13)   The decision for war and Austrian preparations for the ultimatum were veiled behind osten- tatious indulgence in summer vacations.   The Chancellor urged the Kaiser not to forgo his traditional summer cruise to Norwegian waters.   The Kaiser took the advice, but not without having made sure that his army and fleet were ready for any contingency. Moltke stayed at Karlsbad, only to return to Berlin on 25 July. After representations from Jagow, Moltke's deputy General Waldersee, went on leave, while keeping a careful eye on the military prepara- tions of the German army and on political events.   Bethmann Hollweg scuttled between his country estate Hohenfinow and the capital but always within easy reach of Berlin.   His deputy, Vice- Chancellor Delbrück, was allowed to stay on his summer vacation, but was.recalled to Berlin on 23 July.   Secretary of State for the Navy, Admiral Tirpitz, stayed on summer leave during the whole crisis.   The Prussian Minister of War, General von Falkenhayn, who had taken part in the momentous talks of 5 and 6 July at Potsdam, went on leave on 7 July, only to return on 25 July.
    The Austrians adopted the same technique.   Berchtold asked his top generals to go on leave on 8 July - Conrad, Chief-of-Staff, and General Krobatin, the Minister of War.   Both returned to their posts in Vienna on 22 July.   The Austrian Emperor enjoyed his customary summer vacation in Tyrol.   On the other hand, all those who counted in the days of diplomatic crisis, ministers of Foreign Affairs and ambassadors, remained at their posts. (14)
    The European powers were indeed misled by this camouflage.

The British and Russian ambassadors in Berlin took their summer
vacations.   The Russian ambassador even left Vienna on 21 July,
after the Austrians had assured him that they would not make any
demands that could lead to international complications. (15)   The
French President Poincaré and his Prime Minister and Foreign
Minister, Viviani, did not cancel their State visit to Russia and
the Scandinavian countries in the second half of July.   Thus,
France was partly paralysed in the decisive days of the crisis.
This only underlines one important observation: the Entente Powers
had to wait, in any case, to see what the Central Powers would do
after Sarajevo.   They could only react to whatever action the
Central Powers were to take.
      Obviously, Austrian preparations would take some time.   The
necessary delay gave rise to doubts in Berlin, as to whether the
Austrians seriously intended to go to war.   Privately, the Germans
aired their misgivings at the lack of energy Austria displayed,
while they took every opportunity to urge upon the Austrians the
need for the greatest speed.   From one German document the true
motive of German haste is clear.   The Germans feared the Austrians
might give Serbia the chance to meet Austrian demands on their
own initiative, thus making an attack on Serbia superfluous. (16)
      Germany wanted at least a local war between Austria-Hungary and
Serbia in order to crush Serbia, humiliate Russia, irritate France
and disrupt the Triple Entente.   This is the meaning of what
Bethmann Hollweg had told Riezler on 7 July, (17) but also of
Germany's diplomatic actions.   On the same day, the Auswärtiges
Amt drafted its first instruction to this effect: Lichnowsky in
London was given the difficult task of influencing the British press
against Serbia in advance, 'but to avoid everything that could
create the impression, that we incited the Austrians to go to
war'. (18)   The task was impossible because this was exactly what
German policy was doing in the following weeks.
      On the other hand, Berlin was happy about any sign of firm
resolve on the part of the Austrians.   Berlin raised no objections
to the Austrian decision, to put an unacceptable ultimatum to
Serbia; nor to some of the harsher terms of the ultimatum.
Neither did they object to the first military preparations against
Serbia, among them the shelling of Belgrade by Austrian
artillery. (19)
      German fears about Austrian weakness were only too well founded:
the Austrians had waited to make their decisions until the German
declaration of 5 July.   Even then they were not confident and
they moved very slowly.   On 14 July they fixed 25 July as the
date for delivering the ultimatum in order to await the end of the
French State visit to Russia and the conclusion of harvesting.
Only three days later, on 17 July, they decided to deliver the
ultimatum on 23 July, apparently to please the Germans. (20)   But
even then the Germans feared their reluctant ally might still find
a chance to back out.   According to Austrian plans, mobilization
would begin only after the rupture of diplomatic relations with
Serbia, while the declaration of war and opening of hostilities
were to take place after the deployment of troops was finished.
Since Austrian mobilization would take sixteen days war against
Serbia would have begun only by about 10 August.   The Wilhelm-

strasse deemed such a delay absolutely intolerable because it might
have given the other powers a chance to intervene diplomatically.
It reacted accordingly as soon as it learned of the Austrian intentions on 24 July. (21)

BERLIN MAKES WAR INEVITABLE

Meanwhile, the Austrians had given the last touch to their ultima-
tum. When Szögyény showed it to Jagow on the evening of 22 July,
the German Secretary of State assured Szögyény 'that the German
Government is naturally in agreement with the contents of the
Note'.   The other powers, however, were taken back.   Sir Edward
Grey described the ultimatum to Serbia as 'the most formidable
document that was ever addressed from one State to another'. (22)
He immediately launched a series of proposals of mediation between
Vienna and Belgrade. (23)   They all came to nothing because Berlin
insisted that any mediation had to be between Vienna and St Petersburg. (24)   Grey was supported by the French and the Russians.
The acting French Foreign Minister, Bienvenu-Martin, put the whole
issue very clearly on 27 July, when he remarked to the German
Ambassador in Paris, Baron Schoen, that the best way to avoid a
major war was to prevent the local war against Serbia.   This
formula neatly sums up the position of the Entente Powers, and it
was only when they saw that the local war could no longer be
avoided that they lost all hope of mediation.
     At the same time, Russia made it clear that she would not be
indifferent to the fate of Serbia.   While they did not object to
Austrian demands within the limits of international law, the
Russians were not prepared to have Serbia unduly humiliated.
They advised the Serbs to be accommodating and suggested that in
the case of an Austrian attack the Serbs should withdraw their
troops and appeal to the Powers for redress.   On the other hand,
Russia decided to prepare mobilization beforehand and to mobilize
if the Austrians were to invade Serbia. (25)   On 25 July Austria
broke off diplomatic relations with Serbia.   At the same time,
partial mobilization against Serbia was ordered in Austria-Hungary.
War, according to the Austrian plan, could thus begin on 10 August.
     On 24 July the German Foreign Ministry had learned of the
leisurely Austrian schedule, much to their dismay.   The following
day, Jagow told Szögyény that the German government expected 'that
if Serbia gives an unsatisfactory answer, our declaration of war,
and war operations, will follow immediately.   Here every delay in
the beginning of war operations is regarded as signifying the
danger that foreign powers might interfere.   We are urgently
advised to proceed without delay and to place before the world a
"fait accompli".' (26)
     While the German government thus urged their Austrian ally to
open actual warfare as soon as possible, Jagow justified his
stubborn refusal to pass on British proposals of mediation by pretending to fear the Austrians might rush things and confront the
world with a 'fait accompli' in response to German pressure to
consider mediation. (27)
     German pressure on Vienna to declare war on Serbia at once, was

immediately successful.   The following day, Berchtold, vigorously
supported by the German Ambassador, Tschirschky, adopted the German
idea.   Conrad, however, was far from happy.   He would have preferred to keep to the original time-table but he gave in reluc-
tantly. (28)   On 27 July the Austrian government took the final
decision to declare war on Serbia the following day, twelve days
earlier than planned.   After Jagow had achieved one of his short-
term aims, he told the British Ambassador, Sir Edward Goschen, on
29 July, half reproachingly, half ruefully, that now the very
thing had happened that he had always warned against - Austria had
reacted violently to suggestions of mediation and had confronted
the world with a 'fait accompli'.

On the same day, 29 July, the Austrians, again in agreement
with Berlin, continued to escalate the crisis into open war by
shelling Belgrade - with devastating effect in St Petersburg.
Meanwhile Berlin had aggravated the crisis by two more steps.   On
27 July Jagow had assured the British and French that Germany
would not mobilize so long as Russia mobilized only against
Austria.   Two days later, the German Foreign Ministry received a
lengthy memorandum from Moltke which amounted to a demand for
immediate German mobilization even as an answer to Russian partial
mobilization. (29)

The second point was just as serious because the German government defeated the only initiative coming from Germany which might
have had a beneficial effect.   This time the initiative had come
from the Kaiser himself.   He had arrived at Potsdam on 27 July,
having broken off his sailing holiday in Norway on 25 July.   He
was horrified by the threat of war now it was drawing nearer.   In
particular, he was impressed by the first intimation that Britain
might join her allies.   Yet he took the compliant answer from
Serbia to the Austrian ultimatum as the face-saving plank for
beating a diplomatic retreat.   On the morning of 28 July, all his
warlike sentiments had gone for a while and he minuted the Serbian
answer: 'A brilliant achievement in a time-limit of only forty-
eight hours!   It is more than one could have expected!   A great
moral success for Vienna;   but with it all reason for war is gone
and Giesl ought to have quietly stayed on in Belgrade!   After
that I should never have ordered mobilization.' (30)

The Kaiser immediately ordered his government to tell the
Austrians they should accept the Serbian answer in principle, while
negotiating on the points not fully conceded by Belgrade.   Somewhat in contradiction to this premise, he suggested Austria should
content herself with occupying Belgrade as a safeguard for the
implementation of Serbian concessions.   The Chancellor and the
Foreign Ministry did not obey their sovereign this time.   The
Chancellor did not despatch the relevant instructions to
Tschirschky until the evening of 28 July when he knew that Austria
had already declared war on Serbia.   To make matters worse,
Bethmann Hollweg falsified the Kaiser's argument by omitting the
crucial sentence that war was no longer necessary and by distort-
ing the Kaiser's other points to fit his own policy of intransigence. (31)

On 29 July the Kaiser held another kind of unofficial Crown
Council at Potsdam.   From very meagre sources we know the discus-

sion seems to have centred around the question whether Germany
should mobilize before Russian general mobilization or not.   By
26 July the Chancellor had mapped out his strategy for the next
week which was to put the whole blame for world war on Russia in
order to keep Britain out if possible, and to bring the German
Socialists into the war.   This is why he resisted the pressure of
his generals to bring about immediate German mobilization.
Bethmann Hollweg wanted Russia to mobilize first against Germany
because, as he put it, he could not pursue military and political
actions at the same time.   On 29 July the German generals appre-
ciated Bethmann Hollweg's point and agreed, although chafing at
the delay. (32)

GERMANY DECLARES ITSELF

It was in this situation that Bethmann Hollweg risked his most
daring move - the bid for British neutrality, because in explaining
himself he had to give away his next plans.   Now Belgium entered
the scene.   On 26 July Moltke had drafted a German ultimatum to
Belgium which the Auswärtiges Amt sent to Brussels on 29 July, with
minor modifications, and with instructions to the German minister
to hand it to the Belgian government only after new instructions.
The violation of Belgian neutrality made necessary by the Schlieffen
plan, made it vital for Germany to secure at least British acquiescence.   In the evening of 29 July, after his return from the
Potsdam talks, the Chancellor summoned the British ambassador and
asked for British neutrality in return for the promise that Germany
would not annex French or Belgian territory on the Continent, re-
serving a free hand for colonies. (33)
     The reaction of the British Foreign Office was scathing, but an
official answer was no longer needed because after Sir Edward
Goschen had left the Chancellor, a telegram arrived from London.
In it Lichnowsky, the German Ambassador, reported Grey's warning
that Britain would not remain neutral in a war between Germany and
France.   Bethmann Hollweg, badly shaken, now desperately sought
to save the situation by urging Vienna to come to some terms with
St Petersburg, hoping to secure British neutrality after all, by
shifting the blame for a continental war more energetically than
ever on to Russia.   At the same time he wanted to persuade the
German public to support his policy by demonstrating his peaceful
intentions.   Yet the Chancellor did not want to put an end to the
local war against Serbia but only to improve Germany's position in
a major conflict. (34)
     Russian mobilization now became the Chancellor's obsession.
Russia's partial mobilization of 28 July had already alarmed the
German general staff.   The news of the shelling of Belgrade convinced the Russian generals that war with Austria and Germany was
imminent.   They successfully pressed the Tsar for Russian general
mobilization on 29 July, as Russian mobilization was notoriously
slower than German or Austrian.   After receiving a telegram from
Wilhelm II appealing to Nicholas II not to mobilize against Germany,
the Tsar ordered a halt to general mobilization and a return to
partial mobilization.   The next afternoon the generals and Foreign

Minister Sazonov renewed their pressure on the Tsar.   Nicholas
gave way.   Russian general mobilization was ordered for a second
time on 30 July at 6 p.m. (35)
    While the Russian generals definitely carried their point on 30
July, their German counterparts became impatient as well.   In the
evening of 30 July they told the Chancellor that he had to make up
his mind on declaring German mobilization immediately.   The Chancellor, still hoping for news that Russia would mobilize against
Germany first, won a last delay until noon next day.   But his
options were clearly spent. (36)   During the morning of 31 July
the Germans waited for the news of Russian general mobilization.
At 11.55 a.m., just before the self-imposed dead-line, the long-
awaited telegram from St Petersburg arrived.   At 1 p.m. the state
of imminent war was proclaimed in Germany, the phase of military
preparations which automatically preceded German mobilization
(which was always a general one).   While an ultimatum was sent to
Paris and St Petersburg, the Foreign Ministry prepared the respective declarations of war the same afternoon. (37)   War had
become inevitable because German mobilization alone meant immediate hostilities against Luxembourg and Belgium.   From now on
the famous mechanism of mobilizations and counter-mobilizations
set in.
    On 1 August, at 5 p.m., Germany ordered formal general mobili-
zation, five minutes before France did the same.   Last-minute
illusions, such that Britain might stay neutral if Germany were to
refrain from attacking France, came to nothing. (38)   France,
while not willing to forsake her Russian ally under German pressure,
tried desperately to secure British assistance which seemed far
from being certain at the moment.   The Russians, the French and
Sir Eyre Crowe in the Foreign Office, urged Grey to make Britain's
position clear. (39)   It was only under the pressure of events -
the German declaration of war on Russia on 1 August, and on France
two days later - that Grey gradually committed himself, because he
knew that the country and the Liberal Party were not united on the
issue of war.   The German invasion of Belgium on 4 August removed
his last hesitations.   The same day Britain sent an ultimatum to
Berlin demanding the immediate withdrawal of German troops from
Belgium.   When Germany refused, Britain entered the war against
Germany automatically, after the time-limit of the ultimatum had
expired at 11 p.m. Greenwich time or midnight German time. (40)

THE GERMAN DECISION IN PERSPECTIVE

Two points in German arguments for war are of particular interest
here, because they once more illustrate the essentially conservative character of the German Empire.   First, war against Serbia
was justified because in the name of order and stability in Europe
Austria-Hungary had a kind of mandate to take military action
against the 'nest of anarchism', etc. (41)   Second, whenever the
Germans urged Russia not to support Serbia, they did so on Conservative grounds.   The Tsar would betray the monarchical
principle if he protected revolutionary regicides, in the company
of Liberal Britain and Republican France. (42)   Both aspects

were combined with a third in the German White Book, published on
3 August 1914 - the victory of national revolt in the Balkans
would also affect the German Empire.   Austria's gradual collapse
and the 'subjection of all the Slavs under Russian sceptre' would
render the 'position of the Teutonic race in Central Europe untenable'. (43)   Later events show that, indeed, the position of
the German Empire became untenable after the dissolution of Austria-
Hungary.

The perennial question of whether the First World War was a
defensive war or not on the part of Germany, can be answered against
wider historical perspectives. (44)   Certainly, the German Empire,
the bulwark of conservative forces in the world then, wanted to
preserve its position and its social and political order against
democratic forces of one kind or another.   But being unable to
solve its internal problems of modernization peacefully by political means, Germany turned its energies outside and chose military
aggression in 'self-defence', if one prefers.   But such a subtle
understanding of 'defence' becomes absurd in the face of actual
warfare.

Chapter 17

GERMANY'S WAR OF CONQUEST: GERMAN WAR AIMS, 1914

War in 1914 was a further escalation in the political practice of the German Empire to preserve its social order and political structure by a combination of pressure at home and abroad. Soon after the outbreak of war, German war aims were formulated that had been prepared by official pre-war 'Weltpolitik' and at least partly foreshadowed by German writers in the last few years before the war. (1) These aims, both official and private, amounted to achieving Germany's hegemony on the European continent as a basis for an even more expansive 'Weltpolitik'. At the same time, they also carried on the chronic dilemma of pre-war 'Weltpolitik': Germany's incapacity to lay down priorities in East or West, (2) which also affected German strategic planning and military actions during the war. Again, Germany sought to expand in all directions at the same time. Throughout the whole war, Germany never succeeded in concentrating its military and diplomatic forces on one front or the other, either by making concessions in the East and throwing its full military weight against the West, or the other way round, seeking military decision in the East by a political solution to the West.

FORMULATION OF GERMAN AIMS BEFORE THE WAR

Our knowledge of official war aims in Germany is recent, but extremely thorough thanks to the research of Professor Fritz Fischer. (3) But it is still very difficult indeed to pin down definite aims on the continent for the time before war had started, at least at government level. Documentary material is largely missing, and it is unlikely that new material will be found by future research. The main reason for this is so elementary that it needs little explanation. Crowe had put it shrewdly in his famous memorandum of 1 January 1907: 'Ambitious designs against one's neighbours are not as a rule openly proclaimed.' (4) One could add that they are even less openly proclaimed beforehand. Pre-war Germany was no exception to that rule. Furthermore, if basic problems of foreign policy were rarely discussed in Imperial Germany by properly constitutional bodies, which could leave

adequate documentary sources for the historian, it is also not to
be expected that the delicate question of future expansion on the
Continent was discussed before the war.   Germany's political and
military leaders may have given thought to what they should do, if
they were to win the coming war, but they were careful not to
commit themselves on paper concerning future war aims in times of
peace.   If any talks did take place before the war, they were
hushed up and treated as top secret.   Had such ideas become known
in peace-time, they would have been even more damaging to the Reich
than they were in war.   And even in war all discussions and plan-
nings of war aims at government level were kept strictly secret,
only to be found out by the historian almost fifty years later.
     Yet it is inconceivable and would run counter to all historical
and political experience that leading Germans should not have
given thought, at least privately, to the consequences of their
persistent demand to make Germany a world Power.   The widespread
idea that Germany's frontiers were too disadvantageous (5) implied
that something had to be done about them, once the opportunity
presented itself - in war.   At least the Pan-Germans and their
allies accepted this as a consequence of the second Moroccan crisis
- territorial aggrandizement on the Continent was a necessary precondition of any successful 'Weltpolitik'.   They either only
hinted at the need to annex territories after 'the next war'
(Bernhardi), or they openly said that annexations would be necessary, but that it would be inopportune to go into details now.
A few writers even ventured into the open before the war. (6)
Their suggestions are strikingly similar to plans formulated in
government circles after war had broken out. (7)
     As for the German government and the Kaiser, we have only frag-
mentary evidence for the time before the war, but masses of evidence
for the war period itself.   But even the meagre sources from the
pre-war period suggest that the Kaiser and his government were
affected by expansionist ideas prevalent in German society - and
how could it have been otherwise?   The little we know fits into
both the pattern of pre-war publications and that of actual plans
during the war.   The Kaiser's early dream of Germany's 'Napoleonic
supremacy', albeit 'in the peaceful sense', while the Poles,
'liberated from the Russian yoke', would ask the Kaiser to annex
them to Germany, (8) points to that direction as early as 1892.
Some fourteen years later, Bethmann Hollweg, then Secretary of
State of the Interior, seems to have supported similar ideas of
the Kaiser's, to the utmost horror of Chancellor Bülow, as the
latter claims at least in his post-war memoirs. (9)   The same
illusions about Poland, however, reappeared shortly before the
actual outbreak of war. (10)
     All remained quiet on the western front until late July 1914.
It is only then that indirect evidence of German desires to annex
neighbouring territories in the west became evident.   In the
German ultimatum, drafted by Moltke on 26 July, passed on to the
Auswärtiges Amt on 29 July and delivered to Belgium on 2 August,
Germany 'offered' to respect Belgium's territorial integrity after
the war only if German troops were allowed to march through Belgium
without meeting any resistance. (11)   This meant, on the other
hand, that Germany obliquely announced her intention to feel free

to annex Belgian territory, if Belgium were to defend her neutrality, as guaranteed by international law, by arms against German
invasion.   Similarly, Chancellor Bethmann Hollweg in his momentous
bid for British neutrality on 29 July, promised to refrain from
annexations of French and Belgian territory on the European continent if Britain were to remain neutral in the coming war.   The
Chancellor, when pressed by the British ambassador, refused to
include Belgian and French colonies in Africa in his promise. (12)
Three important points can be deduced from the German move: the
Chancellor revealed Germany's definite intention to go to war
against France and to violate Belgian neutrality.   The annexation
of French and Belgian colonies in Africa, even if Britain had
remained neutral, would have completed the drive of pre-war 'Weltpolitik' for 'Mittelafrika'.   Germany claimed a free hand for
annexations in Western Europe if Britain were to join the war
against Germany.
    One might dismiss such indirect evidence as irrelevant if the
German government had not followed up the threats implied in their
'offer' to Belgium and Britain by devising, in addition, plans for
direct annexations and more subtle forms of indirect rule in the
West.

WAR AIMS IN THE HOUR OF APPARENT VICTORY: PAN-GERMANS AND THE
CHANCELLOR'S SEPTEMBER PROGRAMME

Once war had broken out, the Kaiser and his Chancellor protested
the innocence of German intentions by proclaiming that Germany was
'not driven by the lust of conquest', just as Crowe had predicted
seven years earlier. (13)   Such protestations seemed roughly
plausible only as long as the official war aims of Imperial
Germany were not too well known.   Of course the Reich and its
ruling class were not literally 'driven by the lust of conquest'.
Conquest was not an end in itself, but it had a pretty important
place in their political thinking.   Since the new turn in research
on German war aims in the First World War we can dismiss the
official German protestations, echoed by generations of German
historians and politicians, as sheer propaganda.   They are wholly
inconsistent with the fantastic outburst of annexationist sentiment in Germany after the war had started.   It is not enough to
play down that phenomenon as a regrettable but psychologically
understandable reaction to the stress of war, (14) because the
climate for the 'annexationist fever' had been prepared well before
the war.   The only rational explanation can be found in the strong
will for expansion and more power, which propelled German society
on its disastrous course.   This strong will was restrained in
times of peace only be the fear of giving away secret ambitions
too early.   Once that tactical inhibition had been removed by war
and by the prospect of early victory, the dam burst and let loose
a flood of annexationist plans, which increased with the likelihood
of German victory.   'In victoria veritas'.
    On 11 August 1914 the Kaiser, now in a different mood, swore to
his Imperial Guards, when they left Berlin for the front, that he
would not sheathe his sword until he could dictate peace. (15)   In a

similar vein the Bavarian King made the same promise.   Their most
devoted political servants in the Reichstag, the Conservatives,
did their best to prevent the only element in Germany that was at
least theoretically anti-annexations from stating their case in
public.   When, in the first days of August, the Social Democrats
wanted to include in their formal endorsement of the government's
policy the warning that they would resist any attempt to convert
the defensive war into a German war of conquest, the spokesman for
the Conservative Party, Count Westarp, forced them to withdraw this
clause.   Otherwise, Westarp threatened, the Conservatives would
reject the Social Democrats' statement in the plenary session of
the Reichstag at the risk of provoking an open debate on one of
the most delicate points of German policy on the very day when the
need for national unity was to be proclaimed.   The Social Democrats, as usual, gave in.   The government, in particular, was
very interested in preventing a public debate on German war aims
when war had barely started, again for tactical reasons.   They
apparently knew German sentiments too well, and had no illusions
about the demands that would come to the fore.

Furthermore, they feared that public demands for far-reaching
war aims would commit the government one way or another, in either
case with dire consequences.   If they came out against expansionist war aims, they would not only act against their inner wishes,
but would also alienate the traditional supporters of an expansionist policy at home and abroad.   If they came out in favour of
expansionist war aims in public, they also feared a bad impression
at home and abroad.   The German working class, essential for
waging any modern war, might rebel.   On the other hand, the
peoples of the Entente Powers would be even more determined in
their resistance, and the neutral states would be unfavourably
impressed.

Since the German government had not sufficient trust in the
intellectual and political self-discipline of the German public,
they imposed, in August 1914, a formal ban on any publications
discussing peace terms and war aims in other than vague and general
terms.   This is why the pent-up expansionist energies in German
society could only emerge rather furtively and in semi-public
memoranda and meetings.   Nevertheless, some of the memoranda,
printed 'privately' and spread amongst national groups and government circles, might have a considerable circulation.

After the outbreak of war the Pan-Germans, a comparatively
small, but closely-knit and influential group, were the first to
fill the vacuum created by the government's ban on public discussion of war aims.   On 28 August their Executive Committee held
its first wartime session to lay down their plans for the period
after victory, which, a week before the Battle of the Marne,
seemed to be just around the corner.   A few days later the Pan-
German League circulated their views in a 'privately printed'
memorandum to the limited audience of people in the know that was
so typical of politics in Germany during the first half of the
war.   The Pan-German overall aim was the creation of 'Mitteleuropa'
comprising at that time no more than Germany and Austria-Hungary,
but 'inclusive of those areas to be acquired by the German Reich
and Austria-Hungary'.   Heinrich Class, the leader of the Pan-

Germans, added cheerfully: 'The Netherlands and Switzerland, the
three Scandinavian states and Finland, Italy, Roumania and Bulgaria
will attach themselves to this nucleus gradually and of compulsive
necessity, without need of the least pressure from the nucleus
states. If one includes the dependencies and colonies of these
states, the result will be a vast economic unit capable of assert-
ing and maintaining its independence against any other in the
world.'

The Pan-Germans also explained what they understood by 'areas
to be acquired' by Germany: Belgium in some kind of indirect rule;
the area of Longwy-Briey in northern Lorraine, rich in iron-ore,
plus the French Channel coast as far as the Somme and French border
areas from Belfort to Verdun, including those two fortresses. In
the East the Pan-Germans demanded the annexation of a broad belt
of Polish territory along the German border, Lithuania and the
Baltic provinces. Russia was to be reduced to her territorial
status of the late seventeenth century before Peter the Great.
The Pan-Germans claimed that their demand for 'Mitteleuropa' was
not only 'absolutely imperative' but also 'widely accepted as
such', presumably by the German public. And how right they were,
because 'Mitteleuropa' struck a note with the Germans comparable
only to the mystical idea of the Reich, and in fact 'Mitteleuropa'
served as a kind of substitute for the old medieval Roman Empire,
which had been run by Germans.

With their desire for annexations, the Pan-Germans found themselves more and more in the mainstream of German political thought.
Representatives of heavy industry, a potent political factor
indeed, took up Pan-German ideas, and some went even further, such
as Hugo Stinnes and August Thyssen. Since many heavy industry
owners were notoriously close to the Pan-Germans, they served to
increase the power of the extreme right in the debate on war aims.

Yet industrialists also found allies in more respectable
political groups. The Catholic steel magnate, Thyssen, had secured
the assistance of Matthias Erzberger, a member of the Catholic
Centre Party and one of the most active members of the Reichstag.
Erzberger, a political busybody at that point in his career, set
out his dreams for German expansion in a memorandum to the Chancellor. These were even more startling than those of the Pan-
Germans, perhaps because he added to the list of desiderata the
creation of a 'liberated' Polish kingdom under German hegemony,
while Austria-Hungary was to be given the Ukraine, Roumania and
Bessarabia. Erzberger modestly called his sweeping scheme 'the
minimum which all sections of the German people should demand on
the conclusion of peace'. That Erzberger's wild ideas were not
the maximum is revealed by Thyssen's own war aims. He admitted
himself that the main targets of his claims were the iron ore
deposits in northern France and southern Russia. In the East he
attained Alexandrian dimensions (which even Ludendorff caught up
with only in May 1918), pleading for a land-bridge, dominated by
Germany, across Russia and the Ukraine to the Caucasus.

Outside and, indeed, inside German government circles the annexationist fever seemed to run so high in the first weeks of the war
that one Minister, the Secretary of State for Colonies, Solf,
thought it wise and necessary to divert general attention from the

European continent to Africa.   When asked by the Secretary of
State at the Foreign Ministry, Jagow, to submit a memorandum on
desirable colonial war aims, Solf proceeded from the assumption
that, although victory over France was imminent, there would be no
substantial annexations in Western Europe.   As a kind of 'ersatz'
(substitute) Solf painted the emergence of 'Mittelafrika' in the
most glowing colours.   'Mittelafrika' would be set up in three
successive stages: annexation of Angola and northern Mozambique
(although Portugal at that time was still neutral); of the French
and Belgian Congo, plus Dahomey and parts of the Western Sudan as
far as Timbuktu; and once Britain was conquered, the whole of
Nigeria would be added to round off 'Mittelafrika'.   Chancellor
Bethmann Hollweg accepted the gist of the scheme yet continued to
hope for annexations in Europe as well.   For him 'Mittelafrika'
was apparently nothing more than the colonial complement to
'Mitteleuropa'.

The government's war aims on the European continent developed
with such ominous speed once war had broken out that it seems most
unlikely that all those ideas should have arisen just from the
excitement of war.   Two days after the Chancellor's oblique hints
to the British government about possible German annexations in
France and Belgium, the Kaiser told the Prusso-Polish magnate and
courtier Count Hutten-Czapski that he thought of restoring a
liberated Polish kingdom with close relations to Germany once
Russia was defeated.   In early August, in fact, German troops in
Poland did spread proclamations of the liberation of Poland, and
this object remained one of the favourite slogans of German propaganda during the war.

On 6 August the Chancellor first formulated the programme of
reducing Russia to its pre-Petrine territorial status when laying
down instructions for fostering open revolt in Finland against
Russian rule.   On 11 August the idea of setting up the Ukraine as
a buffer state was formulated by the Chancellor in an instruction
to the German ambassador in Vienna.

Germany's military advance in the West from mid-August 1914 onwards and the hope for quick military victory over France brought
forth the first concrete crystallization of German official war
aims in East and West.   On the evening of 19 August a 'long discussion' took place in the German Headquarters at Koblenz, apparently between Kurt Riezler and at least the Chancellor, 'on Poland
and the possibility of loosely attaching other states to the
Reich'.   The idea was to combine a 'mid-European system of
differentiated customs' with 'Greater Germany' ('Gross Deutschland')
and Belgium, Holland, Poland as protected states ('Schutzstaaten')
in a narrow sense, Austria in a wider sense'. (16)   Three days
later, it emerges from the Riezler diaries, pressure had risen in
Germany's leading circles to annex Belgium.   The Chancellor, to
encounter such demands coming from the generals, proposed to
divide up Belgium between France and Holland.   Riezler, however,
pleaded for leaving Belgium intact as a whole (after some re-
shuffling of territory involving France, Holland, Luxemburg and
Prussia), but to subordinate her to Germany as a satellite state
('Schutzstaat').

It was then that the ideas emerged which Riezler pulled together

in the by now famous 'September programme'.   It was signed by the
Chancellor on 9 September, at the height of the Battle of the
Marne. (17)   Since it was a provisional formulation of German war
aims in the hour of expected victory over France it went into
detail only for aims in the West, but it became a key document for
understanding German war aims as such during the First World War.
According to Riezler and Bethmann Hollweg it was official German
policy in the war 'to achieve security for the German Reich in west
and east for all imaginable time' by weakening France so 'as to make
her revival as a great power impossible for all time' and by thrust-
ing Russia back 'as far as possible from Germany's eastern frontier'.
France would have to cede 'Belfort and western slopes of the Vosges'
and a 'coastal strip from Dunkirk to Boulogne', if the German military thought it necessary.   The ore field of Briey ('which is
necessary for the supply of ore for our industry') was 'to be
ceded in any case'.   A high war indemnity was to cripple France,
a commercial treaty was to bind her to Germany and open the
French market to German industry.   Belgium, mutilated by direct
annexations in favour of Germany (Liège, Verviers, possibly
'Antwerp, with a corridor to Liège'), 'must be reduced to a vassal
state'.   Luxemburg, which had become independent in 1867, but remained attached to Germany through a customs union, was to 'become
a German federal state', enlarged by 'a strip of the present
Belgian province of Luxemburg and perhaps the corner of Longwy'.
Holland was to be attached to the German Empire by subtle links.
And all this was to be crowned by the economic and political
structure of 'Mitteleuropa', at the same time to camouflage and to
'stabilize Germany's economic dominance over "Mitteleuropa"'.
This was mainly Riezler's programme as first outlined in late
August 1914.
    'Mitteleuropa' was hardly more than the basis and camouflage
for German hegemony over Europe, a kind of umbrella covering all
the specific annexations and the various forms of indirect rule by
economic and political means.   That the combination of traditional
and of modern war aims - direct annexations and indirect ties -
would have established Germany's hegemony must have been clear to
German leaders.   At least Riezler openly drew that conclusion in
his diary.   He even went one step further.   For him at least, as
the Chancellor's political adviser, 'Mitteleuropa' was the basis
for future German world domination. (18)   We may assume that the
Pan-Germans, who were criticized by Riezler mainly for being too
open about their war aims, may have cherished similar aspirations
in their hearts.   The Riezler diary also confirms what could be
gathered from the documentary material known before its publication, namely that the war aims programme of the Pan-Germans and of
Riezler, plus Bethmann Hollweg (i.e. of the openly chauvinist wing
and of the moderate government in imperial Germany) did not really
differ in substance.   There were differences of scope, of methods
and of priorities, to be sure.   But there was one common denominator in the war aims of both groups - expanding and consolidating
the basis for German 'Weltpolitik'. (19)
    Germany's strategic defeat at the Marne on the very day the
September programme was officially formulated, however, dashed all
German hopes for a lightning victory in the west.   The September

programme, therefore, could not be translated into political
reality.   Nevertheless, it may be considered as a kind of blue-
print for German war aims in the. First World War.   Not that it
was a programme rigidly adhered to all the time.   In fact it was
never referred to again after October 1914.   But a closer analysis of later war aims programmes makes it clear that they were
not too far from the September programme.   Due allowance has to
be made for the varying fortunes of Germany in the war.   The
scope of annexations and other forms of indirect domination varied
accordingly.

AFTER THE MARNE: THE SEARCH FOR SEPARATE PEACE

The war had reached a turning point in the middle of November
1914, which made a fresh look at German war aims necessary.   The
offensive against France had, after the setback at the Marne,
definitely failed, while the situation in the east remained precarious because of Austrian defeats.   The German war plan first
to crush France and then Russia had plainly gone sour.   In this
situation it was Tirpitz who suggested a new strategy of separate
peace with Russia in order to throw Germany's military weight
against France and Britain.   Falkenhayn took up the suggestion
and elaborated it in a long conversation with the Chancellor on 18
November.   Bethmann Hollweg agreed and passed on to the Foreign
Ministry in Berlin a detailed report, in which he also gave an unequivocal definition of the aims he hoped to achieve by a
separate peace with Russia:
>   Then we could, if we thought it right, even reject any peace
>   offer that might come from France, and if the fortune of arms
>   favoured us, so force France to her knees that she had to
>   accept any peace that we liked, and at the same time, if the
>   navy lives up to its promises, also impose our will on England.
>   Thus, for the price of having our relations with Russia remain
>   essentially what they were before the war, we would create what
>   conditions we liked in the west.   At the same time, this would
>   end the Triple Entente. (20)
After the failure of speedy total war on both fronts, the Chancellor was apparently willing to conclude a compromise peace in the
East in order to gain total victory in the West.   Zimmermann, the
Under Secretary of State in the Foreign Ministry, however, opposed
such a course.   He still clung to the concept of total victory on
all fronts.   Zimmermann's opposition was typical of that of party
politicians and spokesmen of vested interest who interpreted any
partial compromise as a betrayal.   Perhaps also to salvage as
much as possible from one grandiose dream in the East, the Chancellor instructed experts to work out in detail what minimum demands
should amount to in case of a separate peace treaty with Russia.
Both civilians and military experts were asked, including
Ludendorff who was Chief of Staff to Hindenburg in the East,
during the Chancellor's visit to Hindenburg's headquarters at
Posen.   The overall result of the enquiries was the advice to
annex Polish territory along the lines suggested by the Pan-
Germans.   It was only in 1915 that the answer to the enquiries
from the government crystallized into official policies. (21)

The year 1914 thus closed with all the military plans of Germany and her allies awry, while the political leadership had not sufficiently adjusted to the new situation.   The result was that a separate peace could not be achieved on either front.   At the same time 'Mitteleuropa', the supreme German war aim, began to take shape.

But the concept of 'Mitteleuropa' (22) could not conceal the true character of German war aims: a continuation of pre-war aspirations and policies, they led the German Empire from a war of aggression to a war of conquest.   More than once it was laid down by German leaders that Germany would have to continue the war until certain war aims had been reached.   The illusions of military victory in 1915 and early 1918 strengthened the illusion of a greater Germany. The length of the war and its final outcome pushed ahead polarization within Germany to the extreme right and left, which foreshadowed both the Third Reich and the victory of Fascism in Germany, as Kurt Riezler had seen in the middle of the war, (23) and the breaking up of the German Empire, once it tried to take revenge for the defeat in the First World War by provoking the Second World War in 1939. (24)

DOCUMENTS

1 ARNIM TO BISMARCK, PARIS, 3 OCTOBER 1872
(GP 90; also in G.O. Kent, 'Arnim and Bismarck')

... M. Thiers not only shares infallibility with the Pope, but also
loquacity. The end-product of all conversation with the President
can be summed up in these sentences:
The country is wise - everybody wants peace - I lead the country
where I wish - passions are reduced to silence - the army is incom-
parable - Europe admires us, and is waiting impatiently for us to
resume our role in Europe.
M. Bülow's reports give information about the state of the army.
- It is in about the same state as at the outbreak of war....
[M. Thiers'] adroitness in negotiation, which we have used to
secure for us the payment of the milliards, is now being used to
forge weapons against us - weapons which M. Gambetta will seemingly
make use of, if we do not intervene beforehand.... The least desirable course of events would be one which would bring Gambetta's
party to the helm, in an atmosphere of ostensible patriotism, after
we had evacuated France.
... I do not know whether the downfall of France will be the
salvation of mankind. But I have no doubt about the fact that the
German Reich cannot exist side by side with the present French
powers that be, any more than Rome could coexist with Carthage or
Old Prussia with Poland.
To keep France down in a political sense is therefore our first
task, and if the French want to create the trouble for themselves
by internal conflict that we have hitherto been forced to create
by warlike means, nothing could be better -
The practical result of this is that we can begin gradually to
deprive M. Thiers of the moral support that we have given him up to
now, and which he has used not without selfishness and not entirely
without gratitude - . Once it is clear in France that we can be
won over for other combinations we shall not lack offers.

2   MEMORANDUM BY BISMARCK, KISSINGEN, 15 JUNE 1877
(GP 294)

A French newspaper said recently of me that I had 'le cauchemar des
coalitions';   this kind of nightmare will be a very justified one
for a German minister to have for a long time to come, if not indeed
for ever.   Coalitions against us could be formed on the basis of
the western powers with the addition of Austria, or - perhaps more
dangerous still - on a Russian-Austrian-French basis;   a great
intimacy between any two of the three last-named powers would give
the third of them the means to exercise very effective pressure on
us at any time.   In view of these dangers - which might become
real not immediately but in the course of years - I would regard
it as desirable from our point of view if the present Near Eastern
crisis led to:
 1 The gravitation of Russian and Austrian interests, and thus of
    their mutual rivalries, towards the east;
 2 The adoption by Russia of a strongly defensive position in the
    Near East and on her coastline, so causing her to need our
    alliance;
 3 A 'status quo' satisfactory to England and Russia, which would
    give them the same interest in maintaining the present situa-
    tion as we have ourselves;
 4 The dissolution of the bonds between England and France (which
    will always remain hostile to us) because of Egypt and the Med-
    iterranean;
 5 A relationship between Russia and Austria which would make it
    difficult for both to set up the anti-German conspiracy to
    which centralistic or clerical elements in Austria might feel
    tempted.
    If the state of my health permitted it, I would complete and re-
fine the picture which I have in mind: not that of any territorial
acquisition, but that of a general political situation in which all
powers except France need us, and are prevented as far as possible
from forming coalitions against us by virtue of their relations to
one another....

3 BISMARCK TO WILHELM I, 7 SEPTEMBER 1879
(GP 461)

The Tsar's letter of 15 August and the Russian press articles do
not represent in themselves the element of danger for us;   they
are only a symptom of the Russian mood, hints of the dangers which
threaten us from there;   these dangers will not disappear simply
by the Tsar's forgetting the letter for a while or silencing the
press.   The Russian armies would still remain on our border and
the influence of our enemies upon Tsar Alexander would remain the
same.   For two years I have had the opportunity through verbal
and written reports to keep your Majesty informed of the lessening
certainty with which we can count on Russia's friendship.   I have
never concealed my regret about this and have always done what I
could diplomatically to try to prevent this growing coolness and
cautiously to counteract the influence of the Slav revolution on
Tsar Alexander....

The Congress was convened by us only at the request of Russia and totally in the interests of Russia.   I did this, although I repeatedly expressed the fear to Your Majesty that such a Congress would put us in a difficult position of having to manoeuvre between our friends, and of perhaps having to opt for one side.   I did it in the hope that we might revive the cooling friendship of Russia, and carried out those intentions of Your Majesty which were known to me, by supporting in your name every suggestion which the Russians made....

What explains the fact that the Tsar, formerly so sympathetic and tactful, offered Your Majesty never a word of thanks for the Congress and the war, whereas he was all too willing to register to his credit Your Majesty's thanks for the events of 1870 and to exploit these diplomatically.   It is to be explained by the fact that His Majesty since the time of the Serbian troubles, and thanks to the various male and female influences, has put Russian policy and his Imperial power into the service of the Slav revolution, and conducts his diplomacy in the same spirit.   It is in line with this revolution to shift the blame for its own mistakes on to Germany;   this was already begun during the Congress and Tsar Alexander was made to aid and abet it;   and indeed not in ignorance of the truth but in full knowledge of it;   that much I know from Schuwalow.   For us there can be no understanding with the unpredictable elementary force of this Slav revolution, and it is not likely that the Tsar - and perhaps far less the Crown Prince - will free himself once again sufficiently from these influences, in order to defy the hatred of Germany of his subjects which has been artificially created by his government.   The consciousness of the German origins of the dynasty may give him cause for concern at this tendency, while his courage and the need for expansion have grown pathologically because of the war;   one could almost say, to a kind of slavonic Napoleonism.   The recent apparent change in Russian policy should not deceive us: the same ambitious Slav elements, against whom the Tsar cannot stand up, will produce again the same kind of feeling, which culminated in the Imperial attempts to intimidate us in the first half of August.   Attempts of this kind will happen again, perhaps in a few months or years, as soon as the situation in France or Austria has improved for such a policy....   The chance for concluding [an alliance with Austria-Hungary] may pass, if not taken, and history proves that, as a rule, chances missed do not return.   In a European situation, which for several years has been getting more and more difficult for Germany and which will continue to become more difficult, the opportunity presents itself to meet the dangers which will arise out of these difficulties in the future, with an insurance, which could hardly be more favourable in the future than it would be today;   an insurance, by which peace not only with Russia but also with France will be strengthened for us, and the most dangerous coalition against us - France, Russia and Austria - will be made impossible.

As Your Majesty knows from Count Andrássy's letter of 1 September, Austrian policy is also only a matter of security against Russian attacks, and not actually of hostile aspirations against Russia.   War with Russia, even if successful, can never be desir-

able as such for Austria, nor for us either.   Austria aspires to no
conquests at Russia's expense, rather it is Russia which harbours
covetous intentions at Austria's expense.   Austria will whole-
heartedly embrace the Three Emperors' League, if covered by it
against the contingency of having to face a Russian attack without
an ally.

... Germany, no less, can cultivate its friendship with Russia
carefree and to the same extent as between 1815 and 1866, if it has
protected itself by a defensive alliance with Austria against the
danger of Russia breaking the peace.   We could do without such an
insurance, if we were convinced that Russian action to break peace
not only today but also a year from now or later, is so improbable
that our policy need not reckon with such an eventuality.   This,
however, is not so.   Ever since Russia has overcome the effects
of the Crimean War and, at the same time, the Pan-Slav revolutionary
party obtained influence, Russia's policy has become even more
dangerous to the peace of Europe.   Since Napoleon's fall European
peace has only been endangered by slavophile Russia.   It is as
though Russia, under the leadership of Slav propaganda, has taken
over the heritage and mission of Napoleonic Caesarism, to become
the dark clouds on the horizon of European peace.   As long as
Russian belligerency, which resulted from a long period of peace
after the ill-fated Crimean War, sought an outlet in Asia, Europe
could hope that the passing of time and the change of mood might
perhaps remedy the evil without major damage.   But two years ago
there was a great danger that Austria would be attacked by Russia,
unless the menacing thunderstorm of war were to move to the
Balkans.   The successful campaign, the tremendous sacrifices and
the great gains have, however, not been sufficient to dampen
Russia's Pan-Slav belligerency.   The hope, entertained and
expressed by me two years ago, that victories and promotions,
Crosses of St George, Te Deums and war trophies would satisfy the
demand for action in the Russian army, has not been fulfilled.
The presumptuous deceit of the Russians has only been increased,
and compels Europe to be on her guard against the dangers which
may be conjured up by the chauvinism of Slav-Caesarism for our
peace.   The menace is becoming greater by the daily increase of
the Russian army, already enormous in numbers, although Russia is
in no way threatened.   Her aggressive intentions are thus being
made clear beyond any doubt by the building up of such an army.
In my view, the only certain safeguards against these dangers are:
not to have confidence in Russia's uncertain friendship, but to
remain firmly determined to help ourselves; and the agreement of
Russia's threatened neighbours to organize their mutual defence.
Otherwise, peace would be uncertain and always dependent on
Russia's chances of finding allies for wars of aggression.... The
guarantee for peace, however, which would be given by a defensive
alliance between Austria and Germany, would not only enable us to
live in peace with Russia and to resurrect the Three Emperors'
League, but also to re-create a basis for trade and commerce by
restoring the confidence in a peaceful future for Europe.

If the warlike tendencies of the Pan-Slav revolutionary party
in Russia were to be opposed by the firm cooperation of the two
Germanic Powers, it is to be hoped that the conservative elements

in Russia would regain courage and influence.   At the moment warlike trends of a revolutionary and propagandist nature are prevalent in Russia, and the danger exists that that great empire might
fall victim to anarchist movements in its domestic and foreign
policies.   If Russia, in order to avoid isolation in Europe, were
to feel compelled to forgo her Slav chauvinism, it is to be hoped
that the centre of gravity in the Russian Empire would return to
the conservative and propertied classes, who presently have lost
control of the state.   It is urgently to be desired that this
happens, not only in the interest of the Imperial dynasty of
Russia.   All those in Russia who have something to lose would
gratefully acknowledge any firm stand by Germany which might force
the revolutionary Pan-Slav agitation to recede.   Germany, however,
will be able to take such a firm stand only in alliance with
Austria.

Finally, taking national sentiments in the whole German Empire
into account, I may point to the historical fact that 'the German
Fatherland', according to a thousand-year-old tradition, is also
to be found on the Danube, in Styria and Tyrol, but not in Moscow
and St Petersburg.   This fact will remain of essential importance
for the solidity and popularity of our foreign relations in Parliament and in the Nation....

4   BISMARCK TO MÜNSTER, 5 MAY 1884
(GP 738)

I am delighted that our friendly attitude finds approval with Lord
Granville.   In accordance with His Majesty's wishes we are ready
to win further approval, if the English, for their part, show any
signs of reciprocity.

They would have an opportunity for this first of all in considering our complaints about the use of force against German citizens
in the Pacific, and in greater regard for our commercial interests
in Africa.

We are of the opinion that foreign trade in all regions, which
are not, beyond all doubt and by general recognition, directly
annexed by a European power, should be open equally to all nations,
and that further expansion of certain powers, as for example the
one envisaged for Portugal by the Anglo-Portuguese treaty, could
only take place under the generally accepted condition that the
continuation and extension of existing trade connections should
remain unaffected.   Only if this concession were guaranteed by
treaty would we recognize new seizures of territory by other
powers.   The Anglo-Portuguese treaty differs from this proviso in
that it places under Portugal's very exclusive colonial rule
distant coastal regions hitherto not dominated by her.

A further criterion for England's intentions to foster permanent
friendly relations with us, concerns Heligoland.   As an English
possession this ancient German island is nothing more than a foot-
hold for making attacks on the Elbe estuary and the west coast of
Holstein.... Our friendship can be very useful to England.   It
cannot be a matter of indifference to her whether the power of the
German Reich stands by her ready and willing to cooperate, or

coldly holds back. The effect which our example had on the continental powers with the latest invitation to the conference, the probability of a completely opposite effect, if Germany had sought an understanding with other powers over the Egyptian question, are illuminating....

I beg Your Excellency first of all to let me know whether you think you could broach these considerations in a confidential talk with Lord Granville, without causing any ill-feeling.... If Your Excellency thinks that it is inadvisable, in view of your confidential position there, to initiate that kind of discussion, we can postpone the matter and leave it to my son, who is going to London for a short visit in a few weeks to take his leave, to use the trust and frankness with which Lord Granville has frequently honoured him to that end....

5 THE REINSURANCE TREATY, 18 JUNE 1887
(GP 253-5)

Article I. If one of the high contracting Parties should find itself at war with a third Great Power, the other would maintain a benevolent neutrality, and would try to localize the conflict. This provision would not apply to a war against Austria or France resulting from an attack on one of these two Powers by one of the high contracting Parties.

Article II. Germany recognizes the rights historically acquired by Russia in the Balkan peninsula, and particularly the legitimacy of her preponderant and decisive influence in Bulgaria and in Eastern Roumelia. The two Courts engage to admit no modification of the territorial status quo of the said peninsula without a previous agreement between them, and to oppose in due course every attempt to disturb this status quo, or to modify it without their consent.

Article III. The two Courts recognize the European and mutually obligatory character of the principle of the closing of the Straits of the Bosphorus and of the Dardanelles, founded on international law, confirmed by the treaties and summed up in the declaration of the Second Plenipotentiary of Russia at the session of 12 July of the Congress of Berlin (protocol 19).

They will ensure in common that Turkey shall make no exception to this rule in favour of the interests of any Government whatsoever, by lending to the warlike operations of a belligerent Power the portion of its Empire which forms the Straits. In case of infringement, or to prevent it if such infringement should be in prospect, the two Courts will inform Turkey that they would regard her, in this event, as putting herself in a state of war towards the injured party, and as depriving herself thenceforth of the benefits of the security assured to her territorial status quo by the Treaty of Berlin.

Article IV. The present Treaty shall remain in force for the space of three years from the day of the exchange of ratifications. [Articles V, VI - provision for secrecy and ratification.]

Additional and very secret protocol, 18 June 1887

In order to complete the stipulations of Articles II and III of the
secret treaty concluded on the same date, the two Courts are agreed
on the following points:
1   Germany, as in the past, will lend Russia a free hand in order
    to re-establish a regular and legal Government in Bulgaria. -
    It promises not to give in any case its consent to the restora-
    tion of the Prince of Battenberg.
2   If His Majesty the Emperor of Russia should find Himself under
    the necessity of assuming the task of defending the entrance of
    the Black Sea in order to safeguard the interests of Russia,
    Germany undertakes to accord its benevolent neutrality and its
    moral and diplomatic support to the measures which His Majesty
    may deem it necessary to take to guard the key of His Empire.
3   [Protocol has same validity as main treaty.]

                                        (L.S.) BISMARCK
                                    (L.S.) PAUL SCHOUVALOF

6   BISMARCK TO HATZFELDT, 11 JANUARY 1889
(GP 943)

No. 31.
[During a recent visit to Friedrichsruh, Hatzfeldt was instructed
to take the earliest opportunity to discuss with Salisbury the
possibility of a public treaty as a guarantee of peace.]
England and Germany are not threatened by attack other than from
the French.   Only in the event of Austro-Russian entanglements
could Germany be drawn into a war with Russia, and as the latter,
even in the most propitious circumstances, could offer no acceptable fruits of war, we must use all our endeavours to avoid an
Austrian war as far as possible.
    The only threat to the two friendly powers, Germany and England,
is France, the neighbour of both;   they have no other common neighbour which constitutes a threat.   England has a clash of interests
not only with France, but also with North America and Russia.   But
a war with one of these two, even a simultaneous war with both,
will only be perilous for England if France is the ally of England's enemies.   Even the attitude of America towards England
would be more cautious than it was in the Canada and Sackville
affairs, if America had to rely on carrying out a breach with
England in isolation, and without any moral or material help from
France.   There is no surer means of preventing America from relying on France in any quarrel with England than the certainty that
France would not be able to undertake an attack on England without
being herself attacked by a German army of over a million.
America will not be inclined to transmute her past ill-feeling
towards England and the chauvinistic tendencies of her future government into practical warfare, if it is not assured of eventual
French support....
    My idea is that, if His Majesty agrees, a treaty shall be con-
cluded between the English and German governments, by which each
pledges help to the other if France in the course of the next one,

two or three years, as the case may be, should attack either power,
and that this treaty, which should be binding for the German Empire
even without any parliamentary resolution, should be laid before
the English parliament for approval, and presented openly to the
German Reichstag.

I think that a bold and open step of this kind will have a calming effect and relieve tension not only in England and Germany but
in the whole of Europe, and that it will establish the position of
the English government as the protector of the peace of the world.

Owing to her predominantly maritime strength England needs now,
just as much as she did in the last century, a continental ally,
and this need, owing to the enormous increase in military armaments on the continent, is stronger now than it ever was.   Without
such an alliance there is always the possibility, with present-day
communications, of a French invasion of England, depending on the
vagaries of the weather, provocation, and the prevailing strength
of striking power in the Channel.   With an Anglo-German alliance
France will not be in a position to plan an effective attack on
England and at the same time the defence against a German attack
on her eastern frontier.

In my opinion it would be of no advantage for England to pursue
her policy of reserve so far that all the continental powers and
especially Germany have to prepare for the safeguarding of their
own future without relying on England.   If we finally became convinced that England would continue to pursue this policy, then
Germany would find it necessary to seek its own salvation in such
international relations as it could achieve without England's participation.   Such expedients, once adopted, are in politics not
easy to undo.... I do not expect any immediate answer to this, but
will wait for as long an interval as Lord Salisbury needs to determine his own view and that of his political colleagues, before
reporting to my master the Emperor on the result.

7   MEMORANDUM OF THE UNDER-SECRETARY OF THE STATE OF THE AUSWÄRTIGES
AMT, BERCHEM, 25 MARCH 1890
(GP 1368)

The Treaty, which is due to be renewed, has the aim of provoking
warlike events, the localization of which would be unlikely.   We
could thus easily bring about that general outbreak of war, which
we could perhaps otherwise avoid and ought to avoid, as is also
Fürst Bismarck's view.   Even if we could remain neutral, we would
in the end get into the thankless position of 1878.

Through the Treaty which is to be renewed, one of us two powers
would in any case be disappointed.   But probably both neighbours
to the East would be mystified by the Treaty: first of all, we
would deny the Austrians aid under our Treaty obligations in the
opening crucial phase of the Bulgarian problem.   If the latter
were to devolop further, we would, according to the view frequently
expressed by the former Chancellor, have to fight for Austria-
Hungary anyway, if they get into trouble.   But then we would violate our obligations towards Russia.   No lasting peace could come
of it, but only lasting resentment between two great nations, as

happened as a consequence of Austria's position towards Russia
during the Crimean War.

The Treaty delivers us into the hands of the Russians even in
times of peace.   They have received a document through which they
can disturb our relations with Austria, Italy, Britain and Turkey
at any time.   During the last few years we have told Britain and
Italy in particular that we support the Sultan in Constantinople.
In that document we follow a conflicting line by handing over
Bulgaria, the gates of Constantinople and the Straits to Russia by
treaty.   As soon as things became critical for Russia, Austria -
informed by St Petersburg of this agreement - would conclude a
separate peace with Russia at our expense, which - because of the
not altogether unfounded suspicion of our felony - would not be
unpopular in Austria-Hungary.

The Treaty allows no room for reciprocity.   All advantages
accrue to Russia.   France will not attack us without being certain
of Russia's collaboration.   If Russia starts war in the Near East,
which is the intent of the Treaty, and if France, as if foreseeable,
attacks us at the same time, the only result of this constellation
will be Russia's neutrality towards us.   Even without a treaty it
would in such a case be in the interests of Russia.   The Treaty
does not therefore secure us against a French attack, but grants
Russia the right to attack Austria on the lower Danube and prevents
us from taking the offensive against France.   In any case, its
general line is hardly compatible with the German-Austrian
Alliance.

The timing of a future European war has been placed in Russia's
hands by the Treaty.   Recent symptoms make it improbable that
Russia, covered by Germany, has an interest in attacking soon.   It
remains a moot point whether our military interests and those of
our allies would thus be met.   The Agreement runs contrary to the
Triple Alliance, if not in letter, at least in its spirit.   If
the Russians were to move in the South, it would probably embroil
us with friendly powers.   The Treaty is, furthermore, virtually
unfeasible....

Articles I and III of the Triple Alliance with Italy of 1882 and
1887 and our separate Treaty with Italy (African Coast) would also
be violated in spirit by the Treaty which is now to be renewed....

We will have to conduct a calm, consistent and loyal policy in
order to retain the achievements of the last twenty-six years.
Thus the preservation and advance of the German Empire may succeed,
but not with the help of dangerous diplomatic ventures....

The danger of France getting together with Russia is today less
great than it was even a few years ago.   We have no interest in
speeding up their cooperation by counselling an adventure in
Bulgaria at a time when we cannot afford a conflict with France.

Prince Bismarck has repeatedly pointed out in the Reichstag
that a major war cannot be waged today without the enthusiastic
participation of the peoples involved.   Such an enthusiasm would
be absent and our position would be incomprehensible to the German
people, if in the event of political disturbances we were to play
an incomprehensible game, especially if we give the impression that
we wanted to let down our allies and only belatedly join in the
fray.

We have all reason therefore not to let slip the chance, created by the Russian initiative, to withdraw from the agreement. It must be done in the most friendly way.

8 CONVERSATION, KAISER WILHELM II - EULENBURG, JULY 1892
(J.C.G. Rohl, A Document of 1892 on Germany, Prussia and Poland, 'The Historical Journal', VII, I, 1964; also 'From Bismarck to Hitler', p. 55f.)

THE KAISER: I hope Europe will gradually come to realize the fundamental principle of my policy: leadership in the peaceful sense -
a sort of Napoleonic supremacy - a policy which gave expression to
its ideas by force of arms - in the peaceful sense.   I am of the
opinion that it is already a success that I, having come to govern
at so early an age, stand at the head of German armed might yet
have left my sword in its scabbard and have given up Bismarck's
policy of eternally causing disruption to replace it with a peaceful foreign situation such as we have not known for many years.
Slowly people will come to realize this....
THE KAISER: I have my good reasons for being friendly to the Poles.
After I had already discovered secretly that the mood in Posen and
Russian Poland had changed completely in my favour, my old child-
hood and student friend, the American Bigelow, has made remarkable
revelations to me from Warsaw.... He discovered to his surprise,
that the whole interest, the whole hope of the Poles is now directed towards me and that every meeting begins with a toast to me.
They are completely filled with the hope of being liberated from
the Russian yoke, and in the event of a war with Russia the whole
of Poland would revolt and come over to my side with the express
intention of being annexed by me.
EULENBURG: But with the hidden thought of attaining the creation
of a Polish Empire.
THE KAISER: No. They have given that up.   The educated elements
are aware of their own weakness.   They want to come under Prussia.
... In case of need, we could make Poland into an Imperial Territory.   Alsace and Lorraine have proved the value of such an
arrangement.   I have not imparted Bigelow's information to the
Foreign Office.   There they would treat the Polish question to a
certain extent as a political one - and I regard it for the time
being purely from the military point of view.   It is of the
greatest advantage to our General Staff and the mobilization of
our army to have Poland on our side.   To ascertain whether Bigelow's information is correct, an officer of the General Staff has
been sent secretly to Poland.   Using Bigelow's contacts and with
the help of the inhabitants, this man has been able to make incre-
dible 'studies' - of the greatest importance for our mobilization.
Everything that Bigelow wrote has been confirmed to the letter.
EULENBURG: If I, in spite of all this, still maintain my belief
that the Poles continue to hope for independence and ... wish to
use Your Majesty only as a step towards independence, I by no means
wish to belittle the value of Bigelow's information.
THE KAISER: That is 'cura posterior', anway.   For the present,
I am their aim, and we ought not to forget it.

9 ADMIRAL GEORG VON MÜLLER'S MEMORANDUM FOR PRINCE HEINRICH, THE
KAISER'S BROTHER, 1896
(W. Görlitz (ed.), 'Der Kaiser', Göttingen, 1965)

World history is now dominated by the economic struggle. This
struggle has raged over the whole globe but most strongly in Europe,
where its nature is governed by the fact that central Europe
('Mitteleuropa') is getting too small and that the free expansion
of the peoples who live here is restricted as a result of the present distribution of the inhabitable parts of the earth and above
all as a result of the world domination of England. These countries are threatened with further restrictions both in trading
activity and in the opportunity of accommodating their surplus
population in their own colonies, so to make use of them in a
national way. The war which could - and many say must - result
from this situation of conflict would according to the generally
accepted opinion in our country have the aim of breaking England's
world domination in order to lay free the necessary colonial possessions for the central European states who need to expand.

These states are the German Reich, Austria-Hungary and Italy.
The Scandinavian countries and Switzerland could with some justice
also be included. But Germany stands far ahead in the need and
indeed the right to expand - a right which is surely established
by what it has already achieved in the field of world trade.

It is of course possible that its partners in the Triple Alliance, or at least Austria-Hungary, will stand at its side in this
great battle for economic survival. But they and the German Reich
would on no account be anything like strong enough to break England's world domination. France and Russia would also have to be
won over. In France we would gain a considerable increase in
naval power; and in Russia an ally who would be able to attack the
British empire on land.

Let us now suppose that this chequered coalition really did
succeed in destroying the British world empire: what would we
have gained? The larger British colonies inhabited by Europeans -
the autonomous colonies - would obviously become republics.
Canada might even join the United States of North America - to
strengthen which would hardly be in our interest.

But the worst result of the great war would be the terrifying
increase in Russia's strength. It is possible that for a short
time our generation might be delighted at the downfall ('Untergang')
of British world power, but the next generation at the latest would
have to suffer because we permitted Russia's power to grow to the
skies - because we helped this already almost overpowerful State to
free itself from its only serious rival in the struggle for world
domination. And quite apart from that it would be a world-histo-
rical sin, a crime against general cultural progress, to deliver
India into Russia's hands.

No, if that were the price then we would rather not become a
colonial power at all. But might it not be possible to become a
colonial power, and indeed one which would be economically and
militarily stronger than would ever be possible as a result of an
anti-English coalition, by allying with England?

England has at least as much if not actually more interest in keeping Russia down as we ourselves.   If we support her in this task then perhaps we could count on England's support in the acquisition of territory outside Europe.   It is a happy coincidence that this State could also be our natural ally because we are both of the same race.   With England and ourselves fighting on the same side in this way, the economic struggle would acquire an idealistic element, i.e. the preservation of the Germanic race against the Slav and Romance peoples....

Now we cannot expect a people so boundlessly common-sensical as the English to allow us to share in its world power domination simply because we are related to them.   But we have, as we have seen, very important common interests which would surely provide the foundation for an arrangement whereby England would grant us benevolent freedom of action outside Europe or even support us directly in transforming spheres of interest into possessions or in granting Germany the areas it needs for expansion whenever foreign empires collapse.   Naturally such an arrangement would have to be based on the principle of reciprocity.   This might lead to England's being able to extend her world domination more swiftly, thanks to her much more powerful armaments, than we could expand ourselves, but even such a stronger Great Britain could never become as dangerous for us as a stronger Russia would be.

Here the objection might be raised that the end product of all this would be two Germanic world empires which would sooner or later but with absolute inevitability have to go to war to decide which of the two should dominate.   And with England's great advantage as a sea power - and this is what really counts here - the odds would not be in Germany's favour.   Well, all this is still a very long way off, and we ought surely not to exclude the possibility that two so-to-speak satiated colonial powers within each of which production would be roughly balanced against consumption could co-exist peaceably and use any surplus political power to further the struggle for the predomination of the Germanic race. Besides, it is not at all certain that the British world empire would be the stronger of the two Germanic States, for the lead which Great Britain now has over us means that she will be faced correspondingly sooner with the natural tendency for colonies to break away to form independent states.

General von Caprivi believed that Germany had no chance at all of becoming a world power, and consequently his policy was designed only to maintain [Germany's] position on the European continent. He was therefore acting quite logically in working at home for the strengthening of the army, limiting the navy to the role of defending the coastline ... and seeking good relations with England as the natural ally against Russia, the country which threatened Germany's position in Europe.

Caprivi's policy, now so widely ridiculed, would have been brilliantly vindicated by history if the German people were not coming to accept an entirely different opinion of their ability and duty to expand than that expressed in our naval and colonial development so far.

Here, too, our motto must be all or nothing.   Either we harness the total strength of the nation, ruthlessly, even if it means accepting the risk of a major war, or we limit ourselves to conti-

nental power alone.   The middle way of contenting ourselves with
a few left-over pieces of East Africa and the South Sea Islands
without any or at most an extremely limited suitability for settlement by Germans; of maintaining a fleet too strong for the mere
defence of our coastline yet too weak for the pursuance of 'Weltpolitik' - all this implies a dispersal of our strength and a
squandering of personal and material wealth which Caprivi's policy
logically wished to see diverted to the army.

Will this policy turn out to have been right?   We hope not.
It would admittedly bring the present nation comfortable days
without serious conflicts and excitements, but as soon as our
exports began noticeably to decline the artificial economic edifice
would start to crumble and existence therein would become very
unpleasant indeed.

Now, the Caprivi policy has been officially abandoned, and the
new Reich Government will hesitantly put to the nation the question - in the form of the new Navy Bill - whether the other policy,
'Weltpolitik', really can be adopted.   Let us hope that this
question receives an enthusiastic 'Yes' for an answer, but also
that then a change comes over our external relations in favour of
an understanding with England, beside which there is still a lot
of room on this earth which is empty or could be made empty and
against whose goodwill even a quite different naval development
from the one that now appears to be envisaged would not be sufficient to pursue 'Weltpolitik', in spite of Russia's friendship.

10 MIQUEL IN THE PRUSSIAN MINISTRY OF STATE, 22 NOVEMBER 1897
(J.C.G. Röhl, 'Germany Without Bismarck', p. 251)

Political divisions must be relegated to the background and the
basis for agreement sought in the economic field.   At the next
elections, national questions could also be raised.   We must
strengthen national sentiments by treating the Poles harshly, and
this even against the Centre party.   It was a disadvantage that
so few questions of foreign policy were brought before the
Reichstag.   In England, seven-eighths of the parliamentary questions concerned the foreign situation, whereas we loved to wallow
in domestic problems.   He [Miquel] had entertained the hope that
colonial policy would turn our attention outwards, but this had
happened only to a limited extent.   We would therefore have to
introduce questions of foreign policy into the Reichstag, for in
foreign affairs the sentiments of the nation could usually be
united.   Our undeniable successes in foreign policy would make a
good impression in the Reichstag debates, and political divisions
would thus be moderated.

11 THE CROWE MEMORANDUM, 1 JANUARY 1907
(BD III, annex)

For purposes of foreign policy the modern German Empire may be regarded as the heir, or descendant of Prussia.   Of the history of
Prussia, perhaps the most remarkable feature, next to the succession

of talented Sovereigns and to the energy and love of honest work characteristic of their subjects, is the process by which on the narrow foundation of the modest Margraviate of Brandenburg there was erected, in the space of a comparatively short period, the solid fabric of a European Great Power.   That process was one of systematic territorial aggrandizement achieved mainly at the point of the sword, the most important and decisive conquests being deliberately embarked upon by ambitious rulers or statesmen for the avowed object of securing for Prussia the size, the cohesion, the square miles and the population necessary to elevate her to the rank and influence of a first class State.   All other countries have made their conquests, many of them much larger and more bloody.   There is no question now, or in this place, of weighing or discussing their relative merits or justification.   Present interest lies in fixing attention on the special circumstances which have given the growth of Prussia its peculiar stamp.   It has not been a case of a King's love of conquest as such, nor of the absorption of lands regarded geographically or ethnically as an integral part of the true national domain, nor of the more or less unconscious tendency of a people to expand under the influence of an exuberant vitality, for the fuller development of national life and resources.   Here was rather the case of the Sovereign of a small and weak vassal State saying: 'I want my country to be independent and powerful.   I must have a larger territory and more inhabitants, and to this end I must organize strong military forces....'

With the events of 1871 the spirit of Prussia passed into the new Germany.   In no other country is there a conviction so deeply rooted in the very body and soul of all classes of the population that the preservation of national rights and the realization of national ideals rest absolutely on the readiness of every citizen in the last resort to stake himself and his State on their asser- tion and vindication.   With 'blood and iron' Prussia had forged her position in the councils of the Great Powers of Europe.   In due course it came to pass that, with the impetus given to every branch of national activity by the newly-won unity, and more espe- cia-ly by the growing development of oversea trade flowing in ever-increasing volume through the now Imperial ports of the formerly 'independent' but politically insignificant Hanse Towns, the young empire found opened to its energy a whole world outside Europe, of which it had previously hardly had the opportunity to become more than dimly conscious.   Sailing across the ocean in German ships, German merchants began for the first time to divine the true position of countries such as England, the United States, France, and even the Netherlands, whose political influence extends to distant seas and continents.   The colonies and foreign posses- sions of England more especially were seen to give to that country a recognized and enviable status in a world where the name of Germany, if mentioned at all, excited no particular interest. The effect of this discovery upon the German mind was curious and instructive.   Here was a vast province of human activity to which the mere title and rank of a European Great Power were not in them- selves a sufficient passport.   Here in a field of portentous mag- nitude, dwarfing altogether the proportions of European countries,

others, who had been perhaps rather looked down upon as comparatively smaller folk, were at home and commanded, whilst Germany was
at best received but as an honoured guest.   Here was distinct
inequality, with a heavy bias in favour of the maritime and coloniz-
ing Powers.
Such a state of things was not welcome to German patriotic pride.
Germany had won its place as one of the leading, if not, in fact,
the foremost Power on the European continent.   But over and beyond
the European Great Powers there seemed to stand the 'World Powers'.
It was at once clear that Germany must become a 'World Power'.   The
evolution of this idea and its translation into practical politics
followed with singular consistency the line of thought that had inspired the Prussian Kings in their efforts to make Prussia great.
'If Prussia,' said Frederick the Great, 'is to count for something
in the councils of Europe, she must be made a Great Power.'   And
the echo: 'If Germany wants to have a voice in the affairs of the
larger oceanic world it must be made a "World Power".'   'I want
more territory,' said Prussia.   'Germany must have Colonies,' says
the new world-policy.   And colonies were accordingly established,
in such spots as were found to be still unappropriated, or out of
which others could be pushed by the vigorous assertion of a German
demand for 'a place in the sun': Damaraland, Cameroons, Togoland,
German East Africa, New Guinea and groups of other islands in the
Pacific.   The German example, as was only natural, found ready
followers, and the map of unclaimed territories was filled up with
surprising rapidity.   When the final reckoning was made up the
actual German gain seemed, even in German eyes, somewhat meagre.
A few fresh possessions were added by purchase or by international
agreement - the Carolines, Samoa, Heligoland.   A transaction in
the old Prussian style secured Kiao-chau.   On the whole, however,
the 'Colonies' have proved assets of somewhat doubtful value.
Meanwhile the dream of a Colonial Empire had taken deep hold on
the German imagination.   Emperor, statesmen, journalists, geogra-
phers, economists, commercial and shipping houses, and the whole
mass of educated and uneducated public opinion continue with one
voice to declare: we must have real colonies, where German emi-
grants can settle and spread the national ideals of the Fatherland,
and we must have a fleet and coaling stations to keep together the
colonies which we are bound to acquire.   To the question, 'Why
must?' the ready answer is: 'A healthy and powerful State like
Germany, with its 60,000,000 inhabitants, must expand, it cannot
stand still, it must have territories to which its overflowing
population can emigrate without giving up its nationality.'   When
it is objected that the world is now actually parcelled out among
independent states, and that territory for colonization cannot be
had except by taking it from the rightful possessor, the reply
again is: 'We cannot enter into such considerations.   Necessity
has no law.   The world belongs to the strong.   A vigorous nation
cannot allow its growth to be hampered by blind adherence to the
'status quo'.   We have no designs on other people's possessions,
but where States are too feeble to put their territory to the best
possible use, it is the manifest destiny of those who can and will
do so to take their places.'
No one who has a knowledge of German political thought, and who

enjoys the confidence of German friends speaking their minds openly
and freely, can deny that these are the ideas which are proclaimed
on the housetops, and that inability to sympathise with them is
regarded in Germany as the mark of the prejudiced foreigner who
cannot enter into the real feelings of Germans.   Nor is it amiss
to refer in this connection to the series of Imperial apothegms,
which have from time to time served to crystallize the prevailing
German sentiments, and some of which deserve quotation: 'Our
future lies on the water.'   'The trident must be in our hand.'
'Germany must re-enter into its heritage of maritime dominion
once unchallenged in the hands of the old Hansa.'   'No question
of world politics must be settled without the consent of the German
Emperor.'   'The Emperor of the Atlantic greets the Emperor of the
Pacific,' &c.

The significance of these individual utterances may easily be
exaggerated.   Taken together, their cumulative effect is to confirm the impression that Germany distinctly aims at playing on the
world's political stage a much larger and much more dominant part
than it finds allotted to itself under the present distribution of
material power....

It cannot for a moment be questioned that the mere existence and
healthy activity of a powerful Germany is an undoubted blessing to
the world.   Germany represents in a pre-eminent degree those
highest qualities and virtues of good citizenship, in the largest
sense of the word, which constitute the glory and triumph of modern
civilization.   The world would be unmeasurably the poorer if
everything that is specifically associated with German character,
German ideas, and German methods were to cease having power and
influence.   For England particularly, intellectual and moral kin-
ship creates a sympathy and appreciation of what is best in the
German mind, which has made her naturally predisposed to welcome,
in the interest of the general progress of mankind, everything
tending to strengthen that power and influence - on one condition:
there must be respect for the individualities of other nations,
equally valuable coadjutors, in their way, in the work of human
progress, equally entitled to full elbow-room in which to contribute, in freedom, to the evolution of a higher civilization....

So long, then, as Germany competes for an intellectual and
moral leadership of the world in reliance on its own national advantages and energies England can but admire, applaud, and join in the
race.   If, on the other hand, Germany believes that greater relative preponderance of material power, wider extent of territory,
inviolable frontiers, and supremacy at sea are the necessary and
preliminary possessions without which any aspirations to such
leadership must end in failure, then England must expect that
Germany will surely seek to diminish the power of any rivals, to
enhance its own by extending its dominion, to hinder the co-operation of other States, and ultimately to break up and supplant the
British Empire.

Now, it is quite possible that Germany does not, nor ever will,
consciously cherish any schemes of so subversive a nature.   Its
statesmen have openly repudiated them with indignation.   Their
denial may be perfectly honest, and their indignation justified.
If so, they will be most unlikely to come into any kind of armed

conflict with England, because, as she knows of no causes of present
dispute between the two countries, so she would have difficulty in
imagining where, on the hypothesis stated, any such should arise in
the future.

It would not be unjust to say that ambitious designs against
one's neighbours are not as a rule openly proclaimed, and that
therefore the absence of such proclamation, and even the profession
of unlimited and universal political benevolence are not in themselves conclusive evidence for or against the existence of unpub-
lished intentions. The aspect of German policy in the past, to
which attention has already been called, would warrant a belief
that a further development on the same general lines would not
constitute a break with former traditions, and must be considered
as at least possible. In the presence of such a possibility it
may well be asked whether it would be right, or even prudent, for
England to incur any sacrifices or see other, friendly, nations
sacrificed merely in order to assist Germany in building up step
by step the fabric of a universal preponderance, in the blind confidence that in the exercise of such preponderance Germany will
confer unmixed benefits on the world at large, and promote the
welfare and happiness of all other peoples without doing injury to
any one. There are, as a matter of fact, weighty reasons which
make it particularly difficult for England to entertain that
confidence....

The greatest and classic exponent in modern history of the policy
of setting out deliberately to turn a small State into a big one
was Frederick the Great. By his sudden seizure of Silesia in
times of profound peace, and by the first partition of Poland, he
practically doubled his inherited dominions. By keeping up the
most efficient and powerful army of his time, and by joining England
in her great effort to preserve the balance of power in face of the
encroachments of France, he successfully maintained the position of
his country as one of the European Great Powers. Prussian policy
remained inspired by the same principles under his successors. It
is hardly necessary to do more than mention the second and the
third partitions of Poland; the repeated attempts to annex Hanover
in complicity with Napoleon; the dismemberment of Saxony, and the
exchange of the Rhenish Provinces for the relinquishment of Polish
lands in 1815; the annexation of Schleswig-Holstein in 1864; the
definite incorporation of Hanover and Electoral Hesse and other
appropriations of territory in 1866; and, finally, the reconquest
of Alsace-Lorraine from France in 1871. It is not, of course,
pretended that all these acquisitions stand on the same footing.
They have this in common - that they were all planned for the
purpose of creating a big Prussia or Germany....

If it be considered necessary to formulate and accept a theory
that will fit all the ascertained facts of German foreign policy,
the choice must lie between the two hypotheses here presented:

Either Germany is definitely aiming at a general political hegemony and maritime ascendency, threatening the independence of its
neighbours and ultimately the existence of England;

Or Germany, free from any such clear-cut ambition, and thinking
for the present merely of using its legitimate position and influence as one of the leading Powers in the council of nations, is

seeking to promote its foreign commerce, spread the benefits of
German culture, extend the scope of its national energies, and
create fresh German interests all over the world wherever and whenever a peaceful opportunity offers, leaving it to an uncertain
future to decide whether the occurrence of great changes in the
world may not some day assign to Germany a larger share of direct
political action over regions not now a part of its dominions,
without that violation of the established rights of other countries
which would be involved in any such action under existing political
conditions.

In either case Germany would clearly be wise to build as powerful a navy as it can afford.

The above alternatives seem to exhaust the possibilities of
explaining the given facts.   The choice offered is a narrow one,
nor easy to make with any close approach to certainty.   It will,
however, be seen, on reflection, that there is no actual necessity
for a British Government to determine definitely which of the two
theories of German policy it will accept.   For it is clear that
the second scheme (of semi-independent evolution, not entirely
unaided by statecraft) may at any stage merge into the first, or
conscious-design scheme.   Moreover, if ever the evolution scheme
should come to be realized, the position thereby accruing to
Germany would obviously constitute as formidable a menace to the
rest of the world as would be presented by any deliberate conquest
of a similar position by 'malice aforethought'.

It appears, then, that the element of danger present as a visible
factor in one case, also enters, though under some disguise, into
the second; and against such danger, whether actual or contingent,
the same general line of conduct seems prescribed.   It should not
be difficult briefly to indicate that line in such a way as to
command the assent of all persons competent to form a judgment in
this matter.

So long as England remains faithful to the general principle of
the preservation of the balance of power, her interests would not
be served by Germany being reduced to the rank of a weak Power, as
this might easily lead to a France-Russian predominance equally,
if not more, formidable to the British Empire.   There are no
existing German rights, territorial or other, which this country
could wish to see diminished.   Therefore, so long as Germany's
action does not overstep the line of legitimate protection of
existing rights it can always count upon the sympathy and good-will,
and even the moral support, of England.

Further, it would be neither just nor politic to ignore the
claims to a healthy expansion which a vigorous and growing country
like Germany has a natural right to assert in the field of legitimate endeavour.   The frank recognition of this right has never
been grudged or refused by England to any foreign country.   It
may be recalled that the German Empire owes such expansion as has
already taken place in no small measure to England's co-operation
or spirit of accommodation, and to the British principle of equal
opportunity and no favour.   It cannot be good policy for England
to thwart such a process of development where it does not directly
conflict either with British interests or with those of other
nations to which England is bound by solemn treaty obligations.

If Germany, within the limits imposed by these two conditions, finds the means peacefully and honourably to increase its trade and shipping, to gain coaling stations or other harbours, to acquire landing rights for cables, or to secure concessions for the employment of German capital or industries, it should never find England in its way.

Nor is it for British Governments to oppose Germany's building as large a fleet as it may consider necessary or desirable for the defence of its national interests. It is the mark of an independent State that it decides such matters for itself, free from any outside interference, and it would ill become England with her large fleets to dictate to another State what is good for it in matters of supreme national concern. Apart from the question of right and wrong, it may also be urged that nothing would be more likely than any attempt at such dictation, to impel Germany to persevere with its ship-building programmes. And also, it may be said in paranthesis, nothing is more likely to produce in Germany the impression of the practical hopelessness of a never-ending succession of costly naval programmes than the conviction, based on ocular demonstration, that for every German ship England will inevitably lay down two, so maintaining the present relative British preponderance.

It would be of real advantage if the determination not to bar Germany's legitimate and peaceful expansion, or its schemes of naval development, were made as patent and pronounced as authoritatively as possible, provided care were taken at the same time to make it quite clear that this benevolent attitude will give way to determined opposition at the first sign of British or allied interests being adversely affected. This alone would probably do more to bring about lastingly satisfactory relations with Germany than any other course....

There is one road which, if past experience is any guide to the future, will most certainly not lead to any permanent improvement of relations with any Power, least of all Germany, and which must therefore be abandoned: that is the road paved with graceful British concessions - concessions made without any conviction either of their justice or of their being set off by equivalent counter-services. The vain hopes that in this manner Germany can be 'conciliated' and made more friendly must be definitely given up. It may be that such hopes are still honestly cherished by irresponsible people, ignorant, perhaps necessarily ignorant, of the history of Anglo-German relations during the last twenty years, which cannot be better described than as the history of a systematic policy of gratuitous concessions, a policy which has led to the highly disappointing result disclosed by the almost perpetual state of tension existing between the two countries. Men in responsible positions, whose business it is to inform themselves and to see things as they really are, cannot conscientiously retain any illusions on this subject.

12   NOTE OF CHANCELLOR BÜLOW, 17 APRIL 1909
(GP 10 297)

His Majesty the Emperor is of the opinion that naval agreement with
Britain is only possible within the framework of a general understanding with that country, either by a general obligation to remain
neutral in case of war, by a major colonial agreement or by a
mutual agreement of non-aggression.   Such a framework should include an agreement on shipbuilding.   It would have to be based on
the principle or mutuality and could be concluded, in my view, only
with the consent of the naval authorities.... (The Emperor said),
he was more than ever convinced that conflict with Britain would
be unfortunate, and that he in no way wanted an armaments race
with Britain.   On the other hand, the government and people of
Germany would be entitled to demand that the naval programme,
adopted by the Federal Council ('Bundesrat') and the Reichstag,
was to be carried out.   Furthermore, no German government could -
once the posture of the British press were to become menacing -
give in without losing face.

13   NOTE OF CHANCELLOR BETHMANN HOLLWEG, 13 AUGUST 1909
(GP 10 325)

Today I reported to the Kaiser on the following basis: For about
half a year Ballin, with the agreement of His Majesty, has been
sounding out Sir Ernest Cassel as to whether Britain is prepared
for a naval agreement.... We have got as far as suggesting a naval
agreement to Britain.   The suggestion has not been rejected by
Britain, but has on the contrary, as yesterday's telegram from
Ballin to me shows, been favourably received.   If we do not now
continue the negotiations which have just started, Britain will
with some justification accuse our policy of being uncertain and
unreliable, and will have her suspicions once more confirmed that
with our naval programme we are harbouring evil intents against
Albion.   We cannot, on the other hand, be compelled unconditionally to continue negotiations just because of such faulty views
held in Britain.   One may be of the opinion that we have already
broken the back of the building up of our fleet, that Britain will
not attack us and that we should - with steady nerves and regardless of the British navy scare - pass through our Navy Act in the
period of time envisaged, without being bound in any way by an
agreement.   I could tend to such a view.   But no one can offer
any guarantees for such a development - Metternich does not
believe in it, but rather thinks war inevitable, sooner or later,
if we implement our Navy Act.   Of course no one can know for sure,
whether or not perhaps a minor incident could excite public
opinion in Britain to such a point that even a peaceful government
would be forced to go to war or to make such demands of us that to
meet them would be incompatible with our honour.   Our interests,
which would be put at stake through a war with Britain, are too
great, not to try to eliminate the reasons for such war, if
possible.   Furthermore, our naval armaments against an attack
from Britain are to be measured - as Admiral von Tirpitz has

pointed out on several occasions - not only by the quantity and
quality of our ships, but also - quite part from coastal fortifications - by the expansion of the Kiel Canal and the harbour
facilities and fortifications on Heligoland.   In both cases,
work in the projects is still in progress.   Any breathing-space,
in which we could complete them in peace, would be a gain for our
naval strength.   I see an albeit unavowed reason for Admiral
Tirpitz's eagerness to favour the conclusion of such an agreement
now (besides, financial considerations may also be relevant for
him)....

The chances for such an agreement seem, as far as King Edward
himself and probably also the present British government is concerned, to be not unfavourable.   Admiral von Tirpitz deems them
also favourable, in that Britain is, according to him, neither
financially nor technically in a position to carry forward a naval
programme in the way they inaugurated it, by the approval of the
four dreadnoughts ('Eventual-Dreadnoughts').   Prince Bülow had
been of the opinion that an agreement with Britain should not be
confined to the navy, but should also include colonial problems,
the Baghdad Railway, our trade relations with Britain, and, above
all, some sort of neutrality agreement.   The naval question ought
not to be burdened with the many colonial details and the question
of the Baghdad Railway, which has not yet been sufficiently cleared
up.   A trade agreement would probably be confined to the granting
of a preferential clause, if Britain were to adopt the system of
protective tariffs.   For such an agreement the consent of the
Reichstag would be necessary, which, however, ought as far as
possible to be left out of the affair.   The question whether to
aim at a general political treaty of neutrality must remain open
for the moment.   But at least Britain should be told at the outset
of negotiations on the naval agreement that a peaceful and friendly
disposition of British policy towards us should be, for us, a
matter of course.   We should also demand formal confirmation that
the treaties and ententes concluded by Britain do not contain any
points against us.   The precise formula for this remains to be
found....

14   NOTE OF SECRETARY OF STATE VON SCHOEN, 1 NOVEMBER 1909
(GP 10353)

In our view negotiations could take place, on the political agreement alone, but not on the naval agreement alone.   The most we
could agree to would be to negotiate them both at the same time.
We cannot sign a naval agreement without a political agreement, the
latter being for us a condition 'sine qua non' inseperable from the
naval agreement.

The naval agreement and the basic outlines of the political
agreement would have to be published.

If the British, as they tell us, want a naval agreement, they
have to pay a price for it in the political sphere.   We have no
desire for a naval agreement.   That is why Sir Edward Goschen and
Sir Edward Grey are wrong when they maintain that Britain could not
promise us more than France and Russia.   England wants something
from us and must pay for it.

We have nothing against Britain offering France and Russia similar
promises of neutrality to those which we want and must obtain from
Britain.

Concerning the naval agreement, it must be strongly emphasized
that we cannot move away from the Naval Law.   We are ready to build
more slowly within the framework of the Act, if Britain also builds
more slowly.   We would suggest a certain ratio between German and
British naval construction for a number of years, if Britain were
to accept that basic idea.   A definite ratio would not for the
moment be set....

As far as the Baghdad Railway is concerned, Sir Edward, if he
brings us the question himself, would be told that we are ready for
talks, as we had declared earlier.   The railway had never been
intended to be an exclusively German concern, but rather an international one....

It is not yet the time to bring up the Congo question.   On
other colonial matters we could conclude specific agreements, but
only after the naval agreement and the neutrality agreement.

15   CHANCELLOR BETHMANN HOLLWEG TO THE KAISER, 18 DECEMBER 1912
(GP **15** 560)

The ambassadorial talks started in London yesterday and, according
to all the information which has arrived here, positive results may
be reasonably expected.   Thanks to the calm and objective attitude
of Austria-Hungary and Italy, war could be provoked only by the
intransigent attitude of Serbia, instigated by Russia or France.

It is certain that war with Russia means for us war with France
also.   There are in contrast many signs that it is at least doubtful (1) (see Marginal notes of the Kaiser at the end of this document) whether Britain would actively intervene if Russia and France
were to appear directly as the provoking parties. (2)   For then
the British government would have its public opinion to reckon
with.   Statements, such as that made by Haldane and others,
only (3) suggest that Britain would only afterwards intervene on
behalf of a defeated France, and then only diplomatically. (4)   In
any case we (5) have this chance, if we avoid all provocation. (6)
As we have learned in a confidential and trustworthy way, the
Russian Ambassador in London, Count Benckendorff has outlined this
factor to St Petersburg and has repeatedly warned against any
appearance of provocation, (7) something which he would like to be
able to accuse us of. (8)

In such circumstances it is urgently to be desired that during
the present talks in London no German plans for the increase of
the army and navy become public.   Such information could easily be
used against us as evidence of provocation, and would not in any
way assist us, if war were to break out now, but could lead to an
overall undermining of confidence in the strength of our present
armaments and give British chauvinists the desired chance for
immediate and active intervention in a war against us. (9)

For this reason I ask Your Imperial and Royal Majesty in all
humility to give orders to all military and naval authorities that
they should keep any preparations for later bills absolutely secret;

nor should they inform the federal states, before decisions are taken within the departments of government at Reich level. (10) Newspaper cuttings submitted to me as well as the conduct of meetings of the Army League and the Navy League, presided over by inactive army and naval officers, suggest that vigorous agitation is taking place for another Naval Amendment. (11)   In the present political context it becomes my duty to point out that a Naval Amendment would be inopportune and indeed regrettable.   This is why I ask Your Majesty's permission to advise the Naval Secretary to this effect.... (12)

Semi-official propaganda should in my humble opinion (13) only be instigated after certain plans have been laid down and after the present political crisis - the solution of which could not be influenced by new demands - has passed.   I humbly ask Your Majesty to agree to the 'modus procedendi' suggested by me, (14) and to give me an opportunity, after Your Majesty's return from Munich, to report on the whole question, on which all your future policy depends. (15)

The Kaiser's comment at the head of the memorandum:

To be passed on immediately to the 3 cabinets and for the immediate verbal attention of the Minister of War and of the Naval Office, also to Chief of General Staff and Naval Staff.   Everything personally through the chiefs today.   1 Naval Cabinet.   2 Military Cabinet.   3 Chief of General Staff.   4 Chief of Navay Staff.

Marginal notes of the Kaiser:

1 I do not doubt it for a moment.
2 They will see to it that things look like that with the help of the mutually bribed presses.
3 Haldane has expressly stated that the possibility of defeat would not be tolerated, which means that it is certain that British intervention would be immediate and not belated!
4 Not a word about it!   That is a grave error!   Is contradicted by the concentration of the fleet, which is actually ready for war and to go to sea.
5 No!   We may believe that we have avoided any provocation and yet may be made to appear as the provoking party, as soon as the enemy and their bribed press see fit!
6 Here great value is placed on provocation.   It can always be whipped up by moderately clever diplomacy and a cleverly guided press (e.g. the candidature for the Spanish Throne in 1870) and must always be ready at hand!   Views on that will always differ on both sides!
7 Is already the case with us; witness the keeping of the reserves under the colours, to stocking of armaments and purchases!
8 Best thanks!
9 Old arguments always put forward against our bills!   The same was said last winter against our Naval Amendment, and nothing happened!

10 Agreed!
11 Is very understandable and good and commendable in the present
    situation!
12 It has absolutely nothing to do with him!
13 Nothing of the kind! But our nation is deeply excited about
    the situation and expresses its feelings on the matter.
14 Yes, but that does not change anything of the demands which
    will be made later, and which I absolutely want!
15 Aha!

16 NOTE OF CHANCELLOR BETHMANN HOLLWEG, 20 DECEMBER 1912
(GP 12 496)

1 I was only able to see Archduke Franz Ferdinand very briefly
   yesterday in Munich. He said: 'Well, we meet again but now
   at a time of peace, as opposed to the last occasion. Everything is going well in London'.
2 The Prince Regent of Bavaria told me that in the last few weeks
   it was the general opinion that His Majesty was pressing for
   war. I have denied this categorically.
3 The Prince Regent further expressed a fear that His Majesty
   was planning an invasion of Britain. When I asked him in
   amazement where he had got this utterly false information, he
   answered that he knew from an absolutely trustworthy military
   source - which he, however, refused to name - that His Majesty
   had ordered the working out of a plan for the invasion of
   Britain. I have firmly assured the Prince Regent that not
   only our policy, but also the Kaiser personally, is far from
   having any aggressive intentions against Britain.

17 CHANCELLOR BETHMANN HOLLWEG TO COUNT BERCHTOLD, 10 FEBRUARY 1913
(GP 12 818)

... I would like to remind you that stronger Russian monarchs than
Nicholas II did not succeed in putting up long-term resistance to
the onrush of Pan-Slavism. But as I see the situation in Russia,
based on information which I think is reliable, we have to reckon
with those forces behind the Pan-Slav agitation; they will win
control, if Austria-Hungary provokes conflict with Serbia. Even
more or less appreciation of the reasons which would determine the
action of the Royal and Imperial government, would probably change
nothing in the situation. Also, after objective analysis, one
has to conclude that Russia, given her traditional relations with
the Balkan States, will hardly be able to observe passively any
military action by Austria-Hungary against Serbia without a tremendous loss of face. The exponents of a peaceful approach, whom we
may doubtless recognize in the figures of Messrs Kokowzow and
Sasanow, would simply be brushed aside by the storm of public
opinion, if they were to try to oppose it. The possible results
of a Russian offensive are all too clear. It would develop into
a war conflict between the 'Dreibund' - presumably supported without great enthusiasm by Italy - against the Triple Entente, whereby

Germany would have to bear the brunt of the French and English offensive. Your Excellency will understand that it is my duty in such a perspective to request you kindly for information as to which policy Your Government intends to pursue if the crisis develops further. I would like to take this opportunity to point out a symptom which ought to be seriously taken into account - the position lately taken by British policy. During the Bosnian Crisis Britain was one of the driving powers behind Russia and pursued a policy of prestige which then rendered a peaceful settlement extremely difficult. Today Britain is a moderating element with whose help we repeatedly succeeded in exerting a calming and restraining influence on Russia. I stress this against those voices, who, as I know, impute egoistic motives to our aim not to lose close contact with Britain.

18 ENTRY IN DIARY OF ADMIRAL GEORG VON MÜLLER, 8 DECEMBER 1912 (J.C.G. Röhl, Admiral von Müller and the Approach of War, 'Historical Journal', XII, 4 1969; also 'From Bismarck to Hitler', p. 68f.)

Sunday. Called to His Majesty at 11 a.m. with Tirpitz, Heeringen (Vice-Admiral) and General von Moltke. H.M. speaks to a telegraphic report of the ambassador in London, Prince Lichnowsky, concerning the political situation. Haldane, speaking for Grey, has told Lichnowsky that England, if we attacked France, would unconditionally spring to France's aid, for England could not allow the balance of power in Europe to be disturbed. H.M. greeted this information as a desirable clarification of the situation for the benefit of those who had felt sure of England as a result of the recent friendliness of the press.
    H.M. envisaged the following:
Austria must deal energetically with the foreign Slavs (the Serbs), otherwise she will lose control of the Slavs in the Austro-Hungarian monarchy. If Russia supports the Serbs, which she evidently does (Sasonoff's declaration that Russia will immediately move into Galicia if Austria moves into Serbia) then war would be unavoidable for us too. We could hope, however, to have Bulgaria and Rumania and also Albania, and perhaps also Turkey on our side. An offer of alliance by Bulgaria has already been sent to Turkey. We have exerted great pressure on the Turks. Recently H.M. has also pressed the Crown Prince of Rumania, who was passing through on his way back from Brussels, to come to an understanding with Bulgaria. If these powers join Austria then we shall be free to fight the war with full fury against France. The fleet must naturally prepare itself for the war against England. The possibility mentioned by the Chief of the Admiralty Staff in his last audience of a war with Russia alone cannot now, after Haldane's statement, be taken into account. Therefore immediate submarine warfare against English troop transports in the Scheldt or by Dunkirk, mine warfare in the Thames. To Tirpitz: speedy build-up of U-boats, etc. Recommendation of a conference of all interested naval authorities.
    General von Moltke: 'I believe a war is unavoidable. But we ought to do more through the press to prepare the popularity of a war against Russia, as suggested in the Kaiser's discussion.'

H.M. supported this and told the State Secretary (Tirpitz) to use his press contacts, too, to work in this direction.   T(irpitz) made the observation that the navy would prefer to see the postpone- ment of the great fight for one-and-a-half years.   Moltke says the navy would not be ready even then and the army would get into an increasingly unfavourable position, for the enemies were arming more strongly than we, as we were very short of money.

That was the end of the conference.   The result amounted to almost nothing.

The Chief of the Great General Staff says: War the sooner the better, but he does not draw the logical conclusion from this, which is: To present Russia or France or both with an ultimatum which would unleash the war with right on our side.

In the afternoon I wrote to the Reich Chancellor about the influ- encing of the press.

19   GOTTLIEB VON JAGOW, STATEMENT WRITTEN AFTER THE WAR (E. Zechlin, Motive und Taktik der Reichsleitung 1914, 'Der Monat', 209, February 1966;   J.C.G. Röhl, 'From Bismarck to Hitler', p. 70f.)

On 20 May and 3 June 1914 our Majesties gave lunches in the New Palace in Potsdam in honour of the birthdays of the Emperor of Russia and the King of England ... to which the respective ambas- sadors - and therefore I too as State Secretary of the F.O. - were invited.   On one of these occasions - I cannot remember whether it was the 20.5.or the 6.6. (sic) - the Chief of the General Staff, von Moltke, who was also present, said that he would like to dis- cuss some matters with me, and asked whether I could not ride with him in his automobile on the return journey to Berlin.   I accepted the invitation.

On the way Moltke described to me his opinion of our military situation.   The prospects of the future oppressed him heavily. In two-three years Russia would have completed her armaments.   The military superiority of our enemies would then be so great that he did not know how we could overcome them.   Today we would still be a match for them.   In his opinion there was no alternative to making preventive war in order to defeat the enemy while we still had a chance of victory.   The Chief of General Staff therefore proposed that I should conduct a policy with the aim of provoking a war in the near future.

Moltke was not a man who lusted after the laurels of war.   In our first conversation, at the beginning of the year 1913, I had been able to observe that he regarded the possibility of war with great gravity but without desiring a conflict.   His present opinion was therefore all the more thought-provoking.   Moltke was a man who took his responsibilities very seriously but who rather suffered from the feeling that he was not quite up to the job - he was lacking in strategical genius.   If he now pleaded for war, this must be because of his overwhelming concern about the growing superiority of our foes.

I countered that I was not prepared to cause a preventive war, and I reminded him of Bismarck's words, that one could not see what cards were held by Providence.   I was not, on the other hand,

blind to the gravity of our position.　And I have never rejected
the idea of preventive war on principle and 'a limine'.　A preventive war would become the unavoidable duty of farsighted politicans
in certain circumstances as a defensive war - and that is how
Moltke saw it now.　If war seems unavoidable, one should not allow
the enemy to dictate the moment, but to decide that oneself.　Even
the most fanatical friend of peace will accept this rule, unless he
is a completely obsessed doctrinaire.　Even Bismarck's wars
against Austria and France were basically preventive wars.　But,
quite apart from the fact that the suitable moment had perhaps
passed already (at the formation of the Triple Entente, and in
1908-9, when Russia was notoriously still unprepared for war), I
still had the hope that our relationship with England would improve
to the extent that a general war would be virtually excluded, or
at least rendered less dangerous.　For once they could no longer
reckon with England's active support, the Russians and the French
would hardly be tempted, without this backing, to provoke a military conflict with us.　Germany would automatically become ever
stronger and more difficult to defeat if the peaceful development
of its economic position continued.　Apart from defending ourselves
from our enemies　we had no 'war aims', such as conquests, etc.,
which would justify the heavy loss of life.　Finally, I was not
free from concern for internal reasons with regard to a war:
because of the character of the Supreme War Lord.　And the Kaiser,
who wanted to preserve peace, would always try to avoid war and
only agree to fight if our enemies forced war upon us.

After my rejection, Moltke did not insist further with his suggestion.　The idea of a war was, as already mentioned, not liked
by him.

When war did break out, unexpectedly and not desired by us,
Moltke was ... very nervous and obviously suffering from strong
depression.

In July 1914, too, I hoped that a general war would be avoided.
But I cannot deny that the memory of Moltke's opinion as expressed
in this conversation gave me some confidence in a victory, should
such a war prove unavoidable.

20　LICHTENAU (1) TO VITZHUM, (2), BERLIN, 2 JULY 1914
(I. Geiss, 'July 1914', p. 67f)

I have the honour of informing you that I have taken the opportunity
of making inquiries at the　Auswärtiges Amt with regard to the
European situation and the way in which it has been affected by the
death of the Archduke, Heir to the Throne.　Here, as indeed everywhere, there is a general feeling of horror at the crime, but it is
held that this would hardly give cause for any kind of harmful consequences to Europe.　It is extremely regrettable for the internal
situation in Austria-Hungary that, with the Archduke, a powerful
force should have disappeared from the scene and that there is no
one else at present capable of taking control of affairs, since
even Count Berchtold does not show any great inclination or determination to pursue the course which has been set.　On the military
side the Chief of the General Staff, Conrad von Hötzendorf, whom
the Archduke initially removed but was subsequently obliged to

recall, will resume full command and, it is believed, provide a
perfectly satisfactory leadership. This will ensure that there is
no discontinuity in relations with Europe and in the last analysis
it might perhaps even result in a clarification and easing of relations, as the Archduke was always regarded as an unknown quantity.
His attitude to the Triple Alliance was likewise problematic as he
was an outspoken enemy of Italy and his sympathies with Germany
were only occasioned by his friendship for His Majesty the Kaiser,
whereas previously he had generally been taken for a Russophile.
His efforts had been directed towards the establishment of a
Greater Austria and centralisation of the Government; however,
this would no longer have been practicable nowadays as Hungary
would no longer allow herself to be robbed of her independence.
Had he ruled, therefore, he might also have been the cause of
severe crises in the Dual Monarchy. The main difficulty for the
policy of the German Reich was caused by the alliance with Austria-
Hungary; however it would be too late to withdraw from this now
and we can only strive to prevent being placed in too difficult a
position by our Imperial ally. The death of the Archduke with his
restless and unstable plans may bring about an improvement in this
respect.
     Austria-Hungary is planning to take vigorous action against
Serbia on account of the murder. The German Government has advised the Serbian Government to afford the maximum cooperation in
this matter in which it finds all Europe against Serbia, and the
Russian Ambassador to Berlin has also been approached and has given
assurances that he will urge his Government to influence Serbia
accordingly. The Auswärtiges Amt believes that a war between
Austria-Hungary and Serbia will consequently be avoided. Should
it break out nonetheless, Bulgaria would immediately declare war
on Greece - the dispute between Greece and Turkey fortunately having
been settled - Russia would mobilise and world war could no longer
be prevented. There is renewed pressure from the military for
allowing things to drift towards war while Russia is still unprepared, but I do not think that His Majesty the Kaiser will allow
himself to be induced to do this.
     The Auswärtiges Amt believes, as before mentioned, that it will
not come to a war between Austria and Serbia. As far as our relations with our neighbours are concerned, neither Russia nor France
has any desire to start a war. France is too preoccupied with
her internal affairs and her financial troubles. Russia, it is
true, has been rattling the sabre, but the reason for this is
apparently only to ensure that she receives the 500 million promised
by France for next year, as she, too, is suffering from a lack of
money. Our relations with England have improved, even though we
should not indulge in the illusion that we are popular on the other
side of the Channel. But England does not desire a war either, as
the times are past when she could allow nations to slaughter each
other on the continent; she would be drawn in herself and moreover her trade would be destroyed; besides our Fleet is still a
factor with which England would now have to reckon. Her colonies
would also give her a great deal of trouble. If it does not come
to a war between Serbia and Austria, then my informant believes
that peace will be preserved....

NOTES

1   Saxon Minister in Berlin.
2   Saxon Minister of State for Foreign Affairs.

21 LEUCKART (1) TO CARLOWITZ, (2) BERLIN, 3 JULY 1914 (ibid., p. 69)

I have to report to Your Excellency that in competent circles here
the political situation is regarded as very serious - also for us.
The memorial service for Archduke Franz Ferdinand gave me the
chance to talk things over with Major-General Count Waldersee,
Quartermaster-General in the Grand General Staff.   What he said
seemed to be the view of the Chief of the Army General Staff.   He
gave it as his opinion that we might become involved in a war from
one day to another.   Everything, he thinks, depends on what attitude Russia takes in the Austro-Serbian business.   In any case the
course of events is being closely watched by Supreme Headquarters.
I had the impression that they would regard it with favour there
if war were to come about now.   Conditions and prospects would
never become better for us.   But on the other hand H.M. the Kaiser
is said to have pronounced in favour of maintaining peace.
    The Royal Minister has learned the same - as far as I know from
the Auswärtiges Amt.

NOTES

1   Saxon Military Plenipotentiary in Berlin.
2   Saxon Minister of War.

22 SCHOEN (1) TO HERTLING, (2), BERLIN, 18 JULY 1914
(DD, Annex IV, 2)

I have the honour most respectfully to report as follows to Your
Excellency concerning the prospective settlement between the Austro-
Hungarian Government and Serbia, on the basis of conversations I
have had with Under-Secretary of State Zimmermann, and further with
the Foreign Office reporter for the Balkans and the Triple Alliance, and with the counsellor of the Austro-Hungarian Embassy.
    The step which the Vienna Cabinet has decided to undertake at
Belgrade, and which will consist in the presentation of a note,
will take place on 25 inst.   The reason for the postponement of
the action to that date is that they wish to await the departure
of Messrs Poincaré and Viviani from St Petersburg, in order not to
facilitate an agreement between the Dual Alliance Powers on any
possible counter-action.   Until then, by the granting of leave of
absence simultaneously to the Minister of War and the Chief of
the General Staff, the Vienna authorities will have the appearance
of being peacefully inclined;   and they have not failed in their
attempts to influence the press and the exchange.   It is recog-
nised here that the Vienna Cabinet has been proceeding quite
cleverly in this matter, and it is only regretted that Count Tisza,
who at first is said to have been against any severe action, has

somewhat raised the veil of secrecy by his statement in the
Hungarian House of Deputies.   As Mr Zimmermann told me, the
note, so far as has yet been determined, will contain the following demands:

1 The issuing of a proclamation by the King of Serbia which
   shall state that the Serbian Government has nothing to do with
   the Greater-Serbia movement, and fully disapproves of it.
2 The initiation of an inquiry to discover those implicated in
   the murder of Sarajevo, and the participation of Austrian
   officials in this inquiry.
3 Proceedings against all who have participated in the Greater-
   Serbia movement.

A respite of forty-eight hours is to be granted for the acceptance of these demands.   It is perfectly plain that Serbia can not
accept any such demands, which are incompatible with her dignity as
a sovereign state.   Thus the result would be war.   Here they are
absolutely willing that Austria should take advantage of this
favourable opportunity, even at the risk of further complications.
But whether they will actually rise to the occasion in Vienna,
still seems doubtful to Mr von Jagow, as it does to Mr Zimmermann.
The Under-Secretary of State made the statement that Austria-
Hungary, thanks to her indecision and her desultoriness, had
really become the Sick Man of Europe as Turkey had once been, upon
the partition of which, the Russians, Italians, Roumanians, Ser-
bians and Montenegrins were now waiting.   A powerful and successful move against Serbia would make it possible for the Austrians
and Hungarians to feel themselves once more to be a national power,
would again revive the country's collapsed economic life, and
would set foreign aspirations back for years.   To judge from the
indignation at the bloody deed that was now dominant over the
entire Monarchy, it looked as if they could even be sure of the
Slav troops.   In a few years, with the continuance of the operation of the Slavic propaganda, this would no longer be the case,
as even General Conrad von Hötzendorf himself had admitted.
So they are of the opinion here that Austria is face to face
with an hour of fate, and for this reason they declared here without hesitation, in reply to an inquiry from Vienna, that we would
agree to any method of procedure which they might determine on
there, even at the risk of a war with Russia.
In Vienna they do not seem to have expected such an unconditional support of the Danube Monarchy by Germany, and Mr Zimmermann
has the impression that it is almost embarrassing to the always
timid and undecided authorities at Vienna not to be admonished by
Germany to caution and self-restraint.   To what extent they waver
in their decisions at Vienna is shown by the circumstance that
Count Berchtold, three days after he had had enquiries made here
concerning the alliance with Bulgaria, telegraphed that he still
had scruples about closing with Bulgaria.
So it would have been liked even better here, if they had not
waited so long with their action against Serbia, and the Serbian
Government had not been given time to make an offer of satisfaction
on its own account, perhaps acting under Russo-French pressure.

What attitude the other Powers will take toward an armed conflict between Austria and Serbia will chiefly depend, according to the opinion here, on whether Austria will content herself with a chastisement of Serbia, or will demand territorial compensation for herself.   In the first case, it might be possible to localise the war; in the other case, on the other hand, more serious complications would probably be inevitable.

The administration will, immediately upon the presentation of the Austrian note at Belgrade, initiate diplomatic action with the Powers, in the interest of the localisation of the war.   It will claim that the Austrian action has been just as much of a surprise to it as to the other Powers, pointing out the fact that the Emperor is on his northern journey and that the Prussian Minister of War, as well as the Chief of the Grand General Staff are away on leave of absence.   (As I take the liberty to insert here, not even the Italian Government has been taken into confidence.)   It will lay stress upon the fact that it is a matter of interest for all the monarchical Governments that 'the Belgrade nest of anarchists' be once and for all rooted out;   and it will make use of its influence to get all the Powers to take the view that the settlement between Austria and Serbia is a matter concerning those two nations alone. The mobilisation of the German Army is to be refrained from and they are also going to work through the military authorities to prevent Austria from mobilising her entire Army.

NOTES

1 Bavarian Chargé d'affaires to Berlin.
2 Bavarian Prime Minister.

23 BETHMANN HOLLWEG TO THE AMBASSADORS AT ST PETERSBURG, PARIS AND LONDON, BERLIN, 21 JULY 1914 (DD 100)

The public statements of the Austro-Hungarian Government relating to the circumstances under which the assassination of the heir to the Austrian throne and of his wife took place, fully disclose the aims which the Greater Serbia propaganda had set for itself, and the means of which it availed itself towards the realisation of these aims.   The facts that have been made public must also do away with the last doubt that the centre of the activities that were to result in the separation of the southern Slav provinces from the Austro-Hungarian Monarchy and in their union with the Kingdom of Serbia, is to be found at Belgrade, and were developed there at least with the connivance of members of the Government and of the army.

The Serbian mischief-making goes back over a long term of years. The Greater Serbia chauvinism appeared in particularly marked form during the Bosnian crisis.   Only the extreme moderation and self-command of the Austro-Hungarian Government and the energetic intervention of the Great Powers can be credited with the fact that the provocations to which Austria-Hungary was at that time exposed by Serbia did not lead to war.   The Serbian Government has not made

good the assurances of future good conduct which she gave at that
time.   The Greater Serbia propaganda has since been continually
increasing in extent and intensity under the very eyes of official
Serbia, and, at least, with its tacit consent.   It is to the
account of that propaganda that the latest outrage, the trail of
which leads to Belgrade, can be charged.   It has become unmistakably evident that it would no longer comport either with the
dignity or with the self-preservation of the Austro-Hungarian
Monarchy to regard inactively any longer the mischief-making on the
other side of the border - mischief-making by which the security and
integrity of its dominions are lastingly menaced.   In such a state
of affairs, neither the procedure nor the demands of the Austro-
Hungarian Government can be regarded as otherwise than moderate and
proper.   Nevertheless, the attitude adopted of late by public
opinion as well as by the Government in Serbia does not exclude the
fear that the Serbian Government may refuse to satisfy these
demands, and that it is allowing itself to be driven into a provoca-
tory attitude toward Austria-Hungary.   In such a case there would
remain for the Austro-Hungarian Government, unless it wishes to
dispense forever with its standing as a Great Power, no other
course than to enforce its demands upon the Serbian Government by
strong pressure, and if necessary, to take military measures - a
situation in which the choice of means must be left to itself.
   I have the honour of requesting Your Excellency to express the
tenor of the foregoing argument to Mr Sazonov, (1) and in so doing
to emphasise particularly the view that the problem under discussion is one which it is solely for Austria-Hungary and Serbia to
solve, and one which it should be the earnest endeavour of the
Powers to confine to the two immediate participants.   We urgently
desire the localisation of the conflict, as the intervention of
any other Power would, as a result of the various alliance obligations, bring about inestimable consequences.
   Your Excellency will furthermore call Mr Sazonov's attention (2)
to the serious consequences which might ensue for the Monarchical
idea, if, in the case suggested above, the Monarchical Powers should
not stand solidly by the side of Austria-Hungary, setting aside for
the moment any possible national prejudices or political points of
view, inasmuch as it is a question of dealing the death-blow to a
political radicalism, now reigning in Serbia, which does not hesitate at making even members of its own rulers' families the victims
of its criminal tendencies.   Russia is fully as interested in such
a task as is Germany.   I venture to hope that Mr Sazonov will not
be blind to this fact.

NOTES

1 The relevant name was substituted in the case of London and
   Paris.
2 This paragraph was only included in the instructions to St
   Petersburg.

24   MOLTKE TO BETHMANN HOLLWEG, BERLIN, 29 JULY 1914 (DD 349)

Summary of the political situation
It goes without saying that no nation of Europe would regard the
conflict between Austria and Serbia with any interest except that of
humanity, if there did not lie within it the danger of general political complications that today already threaten to unchain a world
war.   For more than five years Serbia has been the cause of a
European tension which has been pressing with simply intolerable
weight on the political and economic existence of nations.   With a
patience approaching weakness, Austria has up to the present borne
the continuous provocations and the political machinations aimed at
the disruption of her own national stability by a people which proceeded from regicide at home to the murder of princes in a neighbouring land.   It was only after the last despicable crime that
she took to extreme measures, in order to burn out with a glowing
iron a cancer that has constantly threatened to poison the body of
Europe.   One would think that all Europe would be grateful to her.
All Europe would have drawn a breath of relief if this mischief-
maker could have been properly chastised and peace and order thereby
have been restored to the Balkans; but Russia placed herself at
the side of this criminal nation.   It was only then that the Austro-
Serbian affair became the thunder-cloud which may at any moment
break over Europe.
     Austria has declared to the European Cabinets that she intends
neither to make any territorial acquisitions at Serbia's expense
nor to infringe upon her status as a nation; that she only wants
to force her unruly neighbour to accept the conditions that she
considers necessary if they are to continue to exist side by side,
and which Serbia, as experience has proved, would never live up to,
despite solemn assurances, unless compelled by force.   The Austro-
Serbian affair is a purely private quarrel in which, as has been
said, nobody in Europe would have a profound interest and which
would in no way threaten the peace of Europe but, on the contrary,
would establish it more firmly, if Russia had not interfered with
it.   This only was what gave the matter its menacing aspect.
     Austria has only mobilised a portion of her armed forces, eight
army corps, against Serbia - just enough with which to be able to
put through her punitive expedition.   As against this, Russia has
made all preparations to enable her to mobilise the army corps of
the military districts of Kiev, Odessa and Moscow, twelve army
corps in all, within the briefest period, and is providing for
similar preparatory measures in the north also, along the German
border and the Baltic Sea.   She announces that she intends to
mobilise when Austria advances into Serbia, as she cannot permit
the destruction of Serbia by Austria, though Austria has explained
that she intends nothing of the sort.
     What must and will the further consequences be?   If Austria
advances into Serbia she will have to face not only the Serbian
army but also the vastly superior strength of Russia; thus she cannot enter upon a war with Serbia without securing herself against
an attack by Russia.   That means that she will be forced to
mobilise the other half of her Army, for she cannot possible sur-
render at discretion to a Russia all prepared for war.   At the

moment, however, in which Austria mobilises her whole Army, the
collision between herself and Russia will become inevitable.   But
that, for Germany, is the 'casus foederis'.   If Germany is not to
be false to its word and permit its ally to suffer annihilation at
the hands of Russian superiority, it too, must mobilise.   And that
would bring about the mobilisation of the rest of Russia's military
districts as a result.   But then Russia will be able to say: I am
being attacked by Germany.   She will then assure herself of the
support of France, which, according to the compact of alliance, is
obliged to take part in the war, should her ally, Russia, be
attacked.   Thus the Franco-Russian alliance, so often held up to
praise as a purely defensive compact, created only in order to meet
the aggressive plans of Germany, will become active, and the mutual
butchery of the civilised nations of Europe will begin.

It cannot be denied that the affair has been cunningly contrived
by Russia.   While giving continuous assurances that she was not yet
'mobilising', but only making preparations 'for an eventuality',
that 'up to the present' she had called no reserves to the colours,
she has been getting herself so ready for war that, when she
actually issues her mobilisation orders, she will be prepared to
move her armies forward in a very few days.   Thus she puts Austria
in a desperate position and shifts the responsibility to her, inasmuch as she is forcing Austria to secure herself against a surprise
by Russia.   She will say: You, Austria, are mobilising against
us, so you want war with us.   Russia assures Germany that she
wishes to undertake nothing against it; but she knows perfectly
well that Germany could not remain inactive in the event of a
belligerent collision between its ally and Russia.   So Germany,
too, will be forced to mobilise, and again Russia will be enabled
to say to the world: I did not want war, but Germany brought it
about.   After this fashion things must and will develop, unless,
one might say, a miracle happens to prevent at the last moment a
war which will annihilate for decades the civilisation of almost all
Europe.

Germany does not want to bring about this frightful war.   But
the German Government knows that it would be violating in ominous
fashion the deep-rooted feelings of fidelity which are among the
most beautiful traits of German character and would be setting itself against all the sentiments of the nation, if it did not come
to the assistance of its ally at a moment which was to be decisive
of the latter's existence.

According to the information at hand, France, also, appears to
be taking measures preparatory to an eventual mobilisation.   It is
apparent that Russia and France are moving hand in hand as far as
regards their preparations.

Thus, when the collision between Austria and Russia becomes
inevitable, Germany, also, will mobilise, and will be prepared to
take up the fight on two fronts.

With relation to the military preparations we have in view,
should the case arise, it is of the greatest importance to ascertain
as soon as possible whether Russia and France intend to let it come
to a war with Germany.   The further the preparations of our neighbours are carried, the quicker they will be able to complete their
mobilisation.   Thus the military situation is becoming from day to

day more unfavourable for us, and can, if our prospective opponents prepare themselves further, unmolested, lead to fateful
consequences for us.

25   GOSCHEN TO GREY, BERLIN, 29 JULY 1914
(B.D. 264)

Chancellor having just returned from Potsdam sent for me again
tonight and made the following strong bid for British neutrality in
the event of war.   He said he was continuing his efforts, to maintain peace, but that in the event of a Russian attack on Austria,
Germany's obligation as Austria's ally might, to his great regret,
render a European conflagration inevitable, and in that case he
hoped Great Britain would remain neutral.   As far as he was able
to judge key-note of British policy, it was evident that Great
Britain would never allow France to be crushed.   Such a result
was not contemplated by Germany.   The Imperial Government was
ready to give every assurance to the British Government provided
that Great Britain remained neutral that, in the event of a victorious war, Germany aimed at no territorial acquisitions at the
expense of France.
     In answer to a question from me, His Excellency said that it
would not be possible for him to give such an assurance as regards
colonies.
     Continuing, his Excellency said he was, further, ready to assure
the British Government that Germany would respect neutrality and
integrity of Holland as long as they were respected by Germany's
adversaries.
     As regards Belgium, His Excellency could not tell to what opera-
tions Germany might be forced by the action of France, but he could
state that, provided that Belgium did not take sides against Germany, her integrity would be respected after the conclusion of the
war.
     Finally, His Excellency said that he trusted that these assu-
rances might form basis of a further understanding with England
which, as you well know, had been the object of his policy ever
since he had been Chancellor.
     An assurance of British neutrality in conflict which present
crisis might possibly produce would enable him to look forward to a
general neutrality agreement between the two countries, the details
of which it would, of course, be premature to discuss at the present
moment.
     His Excellency asked me how I thought you would view his
request.   I replied that I thought you would like to retain full
liberty of action, and that personally I did not consider it likely
that you would care to bind yourself to any course of action at
this stage of events.

Minute

The only comment that need be made on these astounding proposals is
that they reflect discredit on the statesman who makes them.

Incidentally it is of interest to note that Germany practically
admits the intention to violate Belgian neutrality but to endeavour
to respect that of Holland (in order to safeguard German imports
via the Rhine and Rotterdam).

It is clear that Germany is practically determined to go to war,
and that the one restraining influence so far has been the fear of
England joining in the defence of France and Belgium.   (EAC, 30 July)

26 THE SEPTEMBER PROGRAMME, 1914
(F. Fischer, 'Germany's Aims in the First World War', 1967)

Expecting as he did that peace negotiations would be opening
shortly, Bethmann Hollweg described his programme of 9 September as
'provisional notes on the direction of our policy on the conclusion
of peace'.   The 'general aim of the war' was, for him, 'security
for the German Reich in west and east for all imaginable time.
For this purpose France must be so weakened as to make her revival
as a great power impossible for all time.   Russia must be thrust
back as far as possible from Germany's eastern frontier and her
domination over the non-Russian vassal peoples broken.'

The objectives in the east epitomized in the lapidary last
sentence of this introduction were not yet set out in detail in
the programme itself, since peace with Russia was not yet regarded
as imminent, but this does not mean that they had not yet assumed
concrete form.   The detailed enumeration of 'individual war aims'
was confined to the continental west, where alone the conclusion of
peace seemed within grasp.   They ran as follows:
1 France.   The military to decide whether we should demand
   cession of Belfort and western slopes of the Vosges, razing
   fortresses and cession of coastal strip from Dunkirk to
   Boulogne.
      The ore-field of Briey, which is necessary for the supply of
   ore for our industry, to be ceded in any case.
      Further, a war indemnity, to be paid in instalments; it
   must be high enough to prevent France from spending any considerable sums on armaments in the next fifteen-twenty years.
      Furthermore a commercial treaty which makes France economi-
   cally dependent on Germany, secures the French market for our
   exports and makes it possible to exclude British commerce from
   France.   This treaty must secure for us financial and industrial freedom of movement in France in such fashion that German
   enterprises can no longer receive different treatment from
   French.
2 Belgium.   Liège and Verviers to be attached to Prussia, a
   frontier strip of the province of Luxemburg to Luxemburg.
      Question whether Antwerp, with a corridor to Liège, should
   also be annexed remains open.
      At any rate Belgium, even if allowed to continue to exist as
   a State, must be reduced to a vassal State, must allow us to
   occupy any militarily important ports, must place her coast at
   our disposal in military respects, must become economically a
   German province.   Given such a solution, which offers the advantages of annexation without its inescapable domestic political

disadvantages, French Flanders with Dunkirk, Calais and
Boulogne, where most of the population is Flemish, can without
danger be attached to this unaltered Belgium. The competent
quarters will have to judge the military value of this position
against England.

3 Luxemburg. Will become a German federal State and will receive
a strip of the present Belgian province of Luxemburg and perhaps
the corner of Longwy.

4 We must create a central European economic association through
common customs treaties, to include France, Belgium, Holland,
Denmark, Austria-Hungary, Poland ('sic'), and perhaps Italy,
Sweden and Norway. This association will not have any common
constitutional supreme authority and all its members will be
formally equal, but in practice will be under German leadership
and must stabilize Germany's economic dominance over 'Mitteleuropa'.

5 The question of colonial acquisitions, where the first aim is
the creation of a continuous Central African colonial empire,
will be considered later, as will that of the aims to be
realized 'vis-à-vis' Russia.

6 A short provisional formula suitable for a possible preliminary
peace to be found for a basis for the economic agreements to be
concluded with France and Belgium.

7 Holland. It will have to be considered by what means and
methods Holland can be brought into closer relationship with
the German Empire.

In view of the Dutch character, this closer relationship
must leave them free of any feeling of compulsion, must alter
nothing in the Dutch way of life, and must also subject them
to no new military obligations. Holland, then, must be left
independent in externals, but be made internally dependent on
us. Possibly one might consider an offensive and defensive
alliance, to cover the colonies; in any case a close customs
association, perhaps cession of Antwerp to Holland in return for
the right to keep a German garrison in the fortress of Antwerp
and at the mouth of the Scheldt.

NOTES

INTRODUCTION

1 F. Fischer, 'Germany's Aims in the First World War' (London,
   1967), chapter 2, pp. 50-92.   I. Geiss (ed.), 'July 1914.
   The Outbreak of the First World War: Selected Documents'
   (London, 1967; New York, 1968).
2 'Die Grosse Politik der Europäischen Kabinette 1871-1914'.
   Sammlung der diplomatischen Akten des Auswärtigen Amtes, eds
   J. Lepsius, A. Mendelssohn-Bartholdy, F. Thimme, 39 vols
   (Berlin, 1922-7), hereafter abbreviated to GP.   Also, 'Documents diplomatiques français (1871-1914)'.   Ministère des
   Affaires Etrangères.   Commission de Publication des Documents Relatifs aux Origines de la Guerre de 1914 (Paris, 1929-
   40).
3 'British Documents on the Origins of the War 1898-1914', eds
   G.P. Gooch and H.W.V. Temperley, 11 vols (London 1926-38),
   hereafter abbreviated to BD.
4 'Österreich-Ungarns Aussenpolitik von der Bosnischen Krise
   1908 bis zum Kriegsausbruch 1914'.   Diplomatische Aktenstücke
   des Österreichisch-Ungarischen Ministeriums des Äussern, eds
   L. Bittner, A. Pribram, H. Srbik and H. Uebersberger, 8 vols
   (Vienna, 1930), hereafter abbreviated to ÖD.
5 'Die Internationalen Beziehungen im Zeitalter des Imperialismus'. Dokumente aus den Archiven der Zarischen und der
   Provisorischen Regierung.   German edition, ed. O. Hoetzsch,
   ser. I, 5 vols (Berlin, 1931-4).
6 L. Albertini, 'The Origins of the War of 1914'. Trans. and ed.
   Isabella M. Massey, 3 vols (London, New York, Toronto, 1952-7,
   2nd imp. 1966).
7 W.L. Langer, 'European Alliances and Alignments 1871-1890' (New
   York, 1931, 2nd imp. 1951); 'The Diplomacy of Imperialism
   1890-1902' (New York 1935, 2nd imp. 1950).   For general
   accounts, see also Heinz Gollwitzer, 'The Age of European
   Imperialism, 1880-1918' (London, 1969), and Wolfgang J. Mommsen, 'Das Zeitalter des Imperialismus' (Frankfurt/Main, 1969).
   For readers with sufficient knowledge of German, see G.W.F.
   Hallgarten, 'Imperialismus vor 1914. Die soziologischen

Grundlagen der Aussenpolitik europäischer Grossmächte vor dem Ersten Weltkrieg', 2 vols, 2nd edn (Munich, 1963).

8 F. Fischer, 'Krieg der Illusionen. Die deutsche Politik von 1911 bis 1914' (Düsseldorf, 1969), English edition: 'War of Illusions. German Policies 1911-1914' (London, 1975).

9 See above, note 1.

10 'German Diplomatic Documents 1871-1914'. Selected and trans. E.T.S. Dugdale, 4 vols (London, 1928; reprinted 1969); hereafter abbreviated to GDD.

11 W.N. Medlicott and Dorothy K. Coveney (eds), 'Bismarck and Europe' (London 1971). The annex of documents at the end of this book also draws heavily on that collection of documents with brief, but helpful introductions.

12 A. Hillgruber, 'Bismarcks Aussenpolitik' (Freiburg, 1972).

CHAPTER 1 THE SECOND GERMAN EMPIRE - HISTORICAL BACKGROUND AND SOCIAL STRUCTURE

1 For a modern discussion of the character of the German Empire in the Middle Ages see G. Barraclough, 'History in a Changing World' (Oxford, 1957).

2 For a controversial analysis of modern German history see A.J.P. Taylor, 'The Course of German History. A Survey of the Development of German History since 1815' (London, 1945, reprinted 1961, 1964).

3 Ibid., p. 6f. For a spirited discussion of the contrast between Germany's economic advanced development and her politically petrified state see Thorsten Veblen, 'Imperial Germany and the Industrial Revolution' (New York, 1915), 3rd imp. 1966. See also H.-U. Wehler, 'Das deutsche Kaiserreich, 1871-1918' (Göttingen, 1973); as usual with Wehler, a large and most helpful bibliography is included.

4 For more general accounts see O. Pflanze, 'Bismarck and the Development of Germany. The Period of Unification 1815-1871' (Princeton, 1963); 'A.J.P. Taylor, 'The Struggle for Mastery in Europe 1848-1918' (Oxford, 1954).

5 This was the starting point of the massive study of H. Böhme, 'Deutschlands Weg zur Grossmacht' (Cologne, 1966): for recent studies in English see Theodore S. Hamerow, 'Restoration, Revolution, Reaction, Economics and Politics in Germany, 1815-1871' (Princeton, 1958).

6 For a discussion of this important tradition in German history since Bismarck see M. Stürmer, Staatsstreichgedanken im Bismarckreich, in 'Historische Zeitschrift', vol. 209 (1969), pp. 566-615; see also A. Hillgruber, 'Kontinuität und Diskontinuität in der deutschen Aussenpolitik von Bismarck bis Hitler' (Düsseldorf, 1969, 3rd imp. 1971), pp. 7-9; also A. Hillgruber, 'Bismarcks Aussenpolitik' (Freiburg, 1972).

7 E. Zechlin, 'Bismarck und die Grundlagung der deutschen Grossmacht' (Stuttgart and Berlin, 1930, 2nd imp. 1960).

8 For the discussion of class interest and the introduction of general suffrage for the North German Reichstag in 1867, see

T.S. Hamerow, The Origins of Mass Politics in Germany 1866-
1867, in I. Geiss and B.J. Wendt (eds), 'Deutschland in der
Weltpolitik des 19. und 20. Jahrhunderts' (Düsseldorf, 1973),
pp. 105-20.

9   See also T. Schieder and E. Deuerlein (eds), 'Reichsgründung
1870-71'. 'Tatsachen, Kontroversen, Interpretationen'
(Stuttgart, 1970); also H. Böhme (ed.), 'Die Reichsgründung'
(Munich, 1967), dtv 428.

10   For the whole complex see W.E. Mosse, 'The European Powers and
the German Question, 1848-1871' (Cambridge, 1958). See E.
Kolb's forthcoming study on Bismarck's foreign policy during
the Franco-German War.

11   Discussed in more detail by I. Geiss, Reich und Nation.
Bemerkungen zu zwei zentralen Kategorien der deutschen
Geschichte und Politik, in 'Beilage zu das Parlament',
B 14/73, in contrast to the more traditional view in German
historiography, e.g. T. Schieder, 'Das Deutsche Kaiserreich
von 1871 als Nationalstaat' (Cologne and Opladen, 1961); also
for what follows, F. Fischer, 'War of Illusions', part I.

12   See above, note 5.

13   H. Böhme, 'Deutschlands Weg zur Grossmacht', pp. 474-586.

14   For details see F. Fischer, op. cit., pp. 11-20. See also
K. Borchardt, 'The Industrial Revolution in Germany' (London,
1972).

15   H. Rosenberg, 'Grosse Depression und Bismarckzeit. Wirtschaftsablauf, Gesellschaft und Politik in Mitteleuropa'
(Berlin, 1967).

16   J.J. Ruedorffer (i.e. Kurt Riezler), 'Grundzüge der Weltpolitik' (Stuttgart and Berlin, 1914), p. 102.

17   T. Veblen, op. cit.; also B. Russell, 'German Social Democracy'
(London, 1896).

18   Important for recent research in the Federal Republic both on
Imperial Germany in general and on the German battle fleet in
particular is E. Kehr, 'Schlachtflottenbau und Parteipolitik
1894-1901. Versuch eines Querschnitts durch die innenpolitischen, sozialen und ideologischen Voraussetzungen des deutschen
Imperialismus' (Berlin, 1930, 2nd imp. Vaduz, 1965); also
E. Kehr, 'Der Primat der Innenpolitik. Gesammelte Aufsätze zur
preussisch-deutschen Sozialgeschichte im 19. und 20. Jahrhundert', edited and with an introduction by H.-U. Wehler
(Berlin, 1965, 2nd imp. 1970); see also J. Steinberg, 'Yesterday's Deterrent. Tirpitz and the Birth of the German Battle
Fleet' (London, 1965).

19   This is the chief result of V.R. Berghahn, 'Der Tirpitz-Plan,
Genesis und Verfall einer innenpolitischen Krisen-strategie
unter Wilhelm II' (Düsseldorf, 1971); also 'Rüstung und
Machtpolitik. Zur Anatomie des "Kalten Krieges" vor 1914'
(Düsseldorf, 1973), and 'Germany and the Approach of War in
1914' (London, 1973).

20   The flood of recent research on the SPD before 1914 has become
too vast to be mentioned here in detail. For an older standard monograph in English see C.E. Schorske, 'German Social
Democracy, 1905-1917' (Cambridge, Mass., 1955); for the most
recent studies in German see D. Groh, 'Negative Integration

und Revolutionärer Attentismus. Die deutsche Sozialdemokratie
am Vorabend des 1. Weltkrieges' (Berlin, 1973).

21 For a summary of recent research, which is overcoming the old
apologia, see H.-U. Wehler, Von den 'Reichsfeinden' zur
'Reichskristallnacht': Polenpolitik im Deutschen Kaiserreich
1871-1918, in his 'Krisenherde des Kaiserreichs 1871-1918'
(Göttingen, 1970), pp. 181-99; for an older, but still useful
study full of important details see R.W. Tims, 'Germanizing
Prussian Poland. The H-K-T-Society and the Struggle for Eastern
Marches in the German Empire, 1894-1919' (New York, 1941).

22 See H.-U. Wehler, Unfähig zur Verfassungsreform: Das 'Reichs-
land' Elsass-Lothringen von 1870 bis 1918, in 'Krisenherde ...'
op. cit., pp. 17-63.

23 See below, pp. 164-8.

24 See below, p. 25.

25 See H. Herzfeld, 'Die Moderne Welt 1789 bis 1945', 2 parts
(Brunswick, 3rd imp. 1961), p. 219.

26 See below, pp. 44-51

27 See below, p. 61f, 65.

28 This fundamental mechanism was first shown by E. Kehr, England-
hass und Weltpolitik. Eine Studie über die innenpolitischen
und sozialen Grundlagen der deutschen Aussenpolitik um die
Jahrhundertwende, in his 'Primat der Innenpolitik', pp. 149-
75, as early as 1928, but brought to general attention only
in 1965.

29 See below, pp. 75-80.

30 M. Stürmer (ed.), 'Bismarck und die preussisch-deutsche Politik
1871-1890' (Munich, 1970), dtv 692, p. 51.

31 'Der Leipziger Hochverratsprozess von 1872'. Newly edited by
K.H. Leidigkeit (East Berlin, 1960), p. 256f.

CHAPTER 2 THE PATTERN OF EUROPEAN DIPLOMACY, 1871-1914

1 See below, pp. 35-43.

2 See below, p. 98f, 106f.

3 GP 294.

4 See below, p. 139f.

5 See below, pp. 99-104.

6 See below, pp. 31-4.

7 See below, pp. 44-51.

8 BD, XI, 510.

9 See below, pp. 142-5.

10 For an intelligent discussion of the Dual Alliance and its
historical background, seen from an enlightened Austrian point
of view, see S. Verosta, 'Theorie und Realität von Bündnissen.
Heinrich Lammasch, Karl Renner und der Zweibund (1897-1914)'
(Vienna, 1971). Particularly impressive is the author's
analysis of the diplomatic situation and developments, because
it is always related to the domestic structures of the European
Powers, great and small.

CHAPTER 3 FROM THE FOUNDING OF THE GERMAN EMPIRE TO THE CONGRESS
OF BERLIN, 1871-8

1 See above, p. 18f. About Bismarck's motives for the annexation of Alsace-Lorraine a violent controversy raged in the
respectable 'Historische Zeitschrift' a few years ago; see
W. Lipgens, Bismarck, die öffentliche Meinung und die Annexion
von Elsass und Lothringen 1870, 'Historische Zeitschrift', 199
(1964), p. 31f; L. Gall, Zur Frage der Annexion von Elsass
und Lothringen 1870, 'HZ', 206 (1968), pp. 265-324; W. Lipgens,
Bismarck und die Frage der Annexion 1870, 'HZ', 209 (1969),
pp. 318-56. See also L. Gall, Das Problem Elsass-Lothringen,
in Schieder and Deuerlein (eds), 'Reichsgründung 1870-71',
pp. 366-85. See also A. Hillgruber, 'Bismarck's Aussenpolitik'
for a general survey.
2 Quoted in H. Böhme (ed.), 'Die Reichsgründung', p. 30f.
3 Quoted in J.C.G. Röhl, 'From Bismarck to Hitler', p. 23.
4 A. Hillgruber, 'Bismarcks Aussenpolitik', p. 137.
5 The facts are pulled together by G.O. Kent, 'Arnim and Bismarck' (Oxford, 1968), but the historical interpretation is
more concise in N. Rich, 'Friedrich von Holstein. Politics
and Diplomacy in the Era of Bismarck and Wilhelm II', 2 vols
(Cambridge, 1965), vol. I, p. 73f. This massive study plus
two volumes of documents are, of course, indispensable for
most of the period under discussion.
6 G.O. Kent, 'Arnim ...', op. cit., p. 73f.
7 For Arnim's arguments see Document 1.
8 For the most recent treatment see A. Hillgruber, Die "Krieg-in-
Sicht"-Krise 1875 - Wegscheide der europäischen Grossmächte in
der späten Bismarck-Zeit, in 'Gedenkschrift für Martin Göhring',
ed. E. Schulin (Wiesbaden, 1968), p. 239ff. For the documentation on the German side see GP, 155-93; GDP, I, p. 1f, Ch.
1, The War Scare of 1875; for the French side see 'Documents
diplomatiques français', I, 358-430. For a well-balanced
treatment in English see W.L. Langer, 'European Alliances',
pp. 43-55.
9 GP 129.
10 See above, p. 14f.
11 See below, p. 31.
12 See above, pp. 10-12.
13 GP 127.
14 For a general treatment see M.S. Anderson, 'The Eastern Question' (London, 1966); still useful is W.L. Langer, 'European
Alliances', ch. 3 (The Balkan Problem. The Insurrection in
Bosnia and Herzegovina), IV (The Balkan War and the Conference
at Constantinople) and V (The Russian-Turkish War and the
Congress of Berlin), pp. 58-170; also V. Dedijer, 'The Road
to Sarajevo' (London, New York, 1966), ch. IV (The Congress of
Berlin), pp. 42-67; also B.E. Schmitt, 'The Coming of the War
1914', 2 vols (New York, 1930, 2nd imp. 1966), vol. I, ch. II
(The Near East), pp. 77-174, dealing with developments in the
nineteenth century up to 1913. For a general treatment of
the national movements of the Balkans see also D. Djordjevic,
'Révolutions nationales des peuples balkaniques, 1804-1914'
(Belgrade, 1965).

15 For more details see W.L. Langer, op. cit., p. 92f.
16 GP 332-7; GDD, IV, VI, The Congress of Berlin, pp. 61-87, which, in fact covers only the preliminary negotiations leading to the actual Congress.
17 GP 231-51 especially nos 234 and 251; unfortunately, the complex is not covered in GDD.
18 GP 250, GDD, I, p. 32.
19 GP 241, 251.
20 GP 273 as a first indication; see also below, pp. 36-8 and Document 3. For the impact of Pan-Slavism on the Oriental Crisis of 1875-8 see M.S. Anderson, 'The Eastern Question', pp. 162-95.
21 See below, pp. 114-18.
22 V. Dedijer, 'The Road to Sarajevo', pp. 64-6.
23 Ibid., and p. 66f.
24 See A.J.P. Taylor, 'The Habsburg Monarchy 1809-1918. A History of the Austrian Empire and Austria Hungary' (London, 1948, 2nd imp. 1964). For the most recent treatment see F.R. Bridge, 'From Sadowa to Sarajevo: The Foreign Policy of Austria-Hungary, 1866-1914' (London, 1972).

CHAPTER 4 DUAL AND TRIPLE ALLIANCE 1879-82

1 GP 446.
2 GP 447, 455, 458, 461.
3 See above, p. 22.
4 GP 447.
5 GP 449, 455.
6 GP 455.
7 GP 455.
8 GP 447.
9 GP 458.
10 GP 461.
11 GP 719.
12 See below, pp. 121-7.
13 GP 485.
14 See above, pp. 37-9.
15 W.L. Langer, 'European Alliances', p. 172f.
16 GP 455.
17 GP 709, 710, 712.
18 GP 714, 715 and note to 715. See also W.L. Langer, op. cit., pp. 185-93.
19 GP 531.
20 GP 532.
21 GP ch. XVII, 573-98; for the earlier Roumanian initiative in 1880 see B. Gebhardt, 'Handbuch der deutschen Geschichte', 8th ed., vol. 3, p. 224f.
22 GP 671.
23 See below, p. 142 for the Kaiser's wish to see Turkey an ally in early December 1912.
24 See above, p. 19
25 GP 537, Bismarck on 19 May 1881.
26 GP 545.

27 GP ch. XV, 533-72; GDD, I, pp. 110-25; see also F. Fellner,
   'Der Dreibund' (Vienna, 1960). For Italian motivation, see
   Lowe and Marzari, 'Italian Foreign Policy, 1870-1939' (London,
   1975), ch. 2 passim.
28 GP 571; GDD, I, pp. 123-5.
29 H. Kantorowicz, 'Gutachten zur Kriegsschuldfrage 1914', ed.
   I. Geiss (Frankfurt, 1967), p. 235, n. 67.
30 See below, pp. 168-71.
31 See below, p. 98f, 106f.

CHAPTER 5   COLONIAL EXPANSION AS A FIRST STEP TOWARDS
            IMPERIALISM, 1882-5

1 The oldest, but still useful, general account is Mary E.
   Townsend, 'The Rise and Fall of Germany's Colonial Empire' (New
   York, 1930); see also A.J.P. Taylor, 'Germany's First Bid for
   Colonies' (London, 1938); and W.O. Henderson, 'Studies in
   German Colonial History' (London, 1962). More recently, the
   massive collection of essays in honour of Harry Rudin –
   P. Gifford and R. Louis (eds), 'Britain and Germany in Africa'
   (New Haven, 1967), in particular the contribution by H.A.
   Turner, Bismarck's Imperialist Venture, Anti-British in
   Origin?, pp. 47-82.
2 See below, pp. 75-83.
3 The various explanations are discussed in detail by H.-U.
   Wehler, 'Bismarck und der Imperialismus' (Cologne, 1969, 2nd
   imp. 1970), pp. 412-23, who also adds a wealth of valuable new
   information on the beginnings of German colonial policy. For
   a summary of his research in English see H.-U. Wehler, Bismarck's Imperialism, in 'Past and Present', no. 48, 1970,
   pp. 119-55; also H. Pogge von Strandmann, Domestic Origins of
   Germany's Colonial Expansion under Bismarck, in 'Past and
   Present', 1969, pp. 140-59.
4 This is a view held by traditional German historians; see
   H.-U. Wehler, 'Bismarck ...', op. cit., p. 413.
5 R. Schück, 'Brandenburg-Preussens Kolonialpolitik' (Leipzig,
   1889); see also G. Ritter, Geschichtliche Erfahrungen deutscher
   Kolonialpolitik, in his 'Lebendige Vergangenheit. Beiträge zur
   historisch-politischen Selbstbesinnung' (Munich, 1958), pp.
   126-52, where Ritter naïvely regretted that earlier colonial
   initiatives of German merchants and princes had come to
   nothing (pp. 129-32).
6 H.-U. Wehler, 'Bismarck ...', op. cit., pp. 201-4.
7 The fascinating connection between schnaps of the Prussian
   Junkers, exported by Hamburg merchants – respected in Germany
   but cursed on the African Coast – and philanthropic Anti-
   Liquor Campaigns still has to be explored in detail.
8 H.-U. Wehler, 'Bismarck ...', op. cit., p. 197ff.
9 For the most recent and detailed study of that process and its
   meaning for Germany see H. Böhme, 'Deutschlands Weg zur Grossmacht', pp. 474-604.
10 The following is mainly based on H.-U. Wehler, 'Bismarck ...',
   op. cit., pp. 230-407.

11   Literature on the 'Scramble for Africa' is too vast to be
     covered in a note.   See J.D. Hargreaves, 'Prelude to the Par-
     tition of West Africa (London, 1963); R. Oliver and A. Atmore,
     'Africa Since 1800' (Cambridge, 1967), ch. 9, The Partition of
     Africa on Paper, 1879-1891, pp. 103-14.   For a brief recent
     survey see J.E. Flint, Chartered Companies and the Scramble
     for Africa, in J.C. Anene and G.N. Brown (eds), 'Africa in
     the Nineteenth and Twentieth Centuries. A Handbook for teachers
     and students (Ibadan, London, 1966), pp. 110-32.
12   Ruth Slade, 'King Leopold's Congo' (London, 1962).
13   See note 1 to this chapter;   also W.O. Henderson, 'Studies in
     German Colonial History' (London, 1962);   also regional mono-
     graphs.   For a comprehensive analysis of literature on German
     colonial rule in Africa see H. Pogge-von Strandmann and Alison
     Smith, The German Empire in Africa and British Perspectives: A
     Historiographical Essay, in P. Gifford and W.R. Louis (eds), op.
     cit., pp. 709-95.
14   See H. Bley, 'South-West Africa under German Rule, 1894-1914'
     (London, 1971);   H. Drechsler, 'Südwestafrika unter deutscher
     Kolonialherrschaft' (East Berlin, 1966).
15   H.R. Rudin, 'The Germans in the Cameroons, 1884-1914' (London,
     1938);   R. Cornevin, 'Histoire du Togo' (Paris, 1963);   H.-U.
     Wehler, 'Bismarck ...', op. cit., pp. 263-92.
16   For the beginnings of German colonial rule in Tanganyika see
     F.F. Müller, 'Deutschland, Zanzibar, Ostafrika' (East Berlin,
     1959);   on Carl Peters see also H.-U. Wehler, 'Bismarck ...',
     op. cit., pp. 333-67.
17   See J.A. Moses and P.M. Kennedy (eds), 'Germany in the Pacific
     and Far East, 1870-1914' (Dublin, 1974);   also P.M. Kennedy,
     'Bismarck's Imperialism. The Case of Samoa, 1880-90, 'Histori-
     cal Journal', XV (1972), pp. 266-83.
18   H.-U. Wehler, 'Bismarck ...', op. cit.
19   Sybil E. Crowe, 'The Berlin West African Conference' (London,
     1942);   see also GP 736-61;   GDD, I, pp. 168-94.
20   For South-West Africa see H. Bley, op. cit.
21   See K. Hildebrand, 'Vom Reich zum Weltreich. Hitler, NSDAP und
     koloniale Frage 1919-1945' (Munich, 1969).
22   See below, p. 155.
23   F. Fischer, 'Germany's War Aims', p. 102f, 596.
24   See below, p. 135.
25   See Documents 12, 13.
26   See note 21 above.

CHAPTER 6   THE TANGLE OF ALLIANCES, 1885-90

1   See above, p. 25.
2   See above, p. 18.
3   See above, p. 33.
4   See below, p. 55f.
5   See below, p. 103f.
6   See A. Hillgruber, 'Bismarcks Aussenpolitik', pp. 179-81;   for
    the role of Déroulède and Boulanger and the whole crisis also
    see W.L. Langer, 'European Alliances', pp. 372-84.

7   GP 871, 806, 873, 874, 876, 877, 987, 994, 1006, 1009, 1014, 1017, 1020, 1021, 1023, 1024, 1026;   GDD, I, p. 232f.
8   In his first speech on the military budget of 11 January 1887; for a detailed summary in English see W.L. Langer, op. cit., p. 381f.
9   Ibid.
10   See below, p. 179.
11   Thus violating the Berlin Settlement of 1878, see above, p. 33.
12   GP chs XXVI-XXVIII, 879-947;   the text of the Anglo-Italian agreement no. 887;   GDD, I, pp. 385-406 (GP 887 on p. 292f); see also F.H. Hinsley, Bismarck, Salisbury and the Mediterranean Agreements, 'Cambridge Historical Journal', 1958, pp. 76-81; C.J. Lowe, 'Reluctant Imperialists', pp. 108-12.
13   See below, pp. 124, 130-3, 170f.
14   GP ch. XXXIV, 1060-1100.
15   GP 1092.
16   For Bismarck's reasoning see also GP 1087.
17   See GP 1137-43.   For a discussion of the economic and political mechanisms behind that move within the context of German foreign policy towards Russia in that period, see H. Böhme, Politik und Ökonomie in der Reichsgründungszeit und späten Bismarck-Zeit, in M. Stürmer (ed.), 'Das kaiserliche Deutschland', p. 26ff, especially pp. 40-8;   H.-U. Wehler, Bismarcks Imperialismus und späte Russlandpolitik unter dem Primat der Innenpolitik, in ibid., p. 235ff;   also S. Kumpf-Korfes, 'Bismarcks Draht nach Russland' (East Berlin, 1968);   see also Barbara Vogel, 'Deutsche Russlandpolitik. Das Scheitern der deutschen Weltpolitik unter Bülow 1900-1906' (Düsseldorf, 1973), pp. 13-16.
18   W.L. Langer, op. cit., p. 444f.
19   See below, p. 149.
20   GP 915-41;   C.J. Lowe, op. cit., pp. 116-18.
21   GP 926;   GDD, I, p. 338.
22   GP 930;   GDD, I, pp. 345-8.
23   GP 1343.
24   M. Balfour, 'The Kaiser and His Times' (London, 1964), p. 122.
25   Ibid.;   C.J. Lowe, op. cit., 153-5.
26   GP 943, 945;   GDD, I, pp. 369-75.
27   See below, pp. 86-9, 93f, 109f.
28   J.C.G. Röhl, 'Germany without Bismarck. The Crisis of Government in the Second Reich, 1890-1900' (London, 1967), ch. 1: Dropping the Pilot, 1886-1890, pp. 27-55.

CHAPTER 7   THE 'NEW COURSE' - YEARS OF INDECISION, 1890-5

1   See J.C.G. Röhl, 'Germany without Bismarck. The Crisis of Government in the Second Reich, 1890-1900' (London, 1967);   also N. Rich, 'Holstein', I, p. 162f.
2   There exists no biography yet on Caprivi or a monograph on his period as Chancellor.   The nearest to it is J.C.G. Röhl, op. cit.
3   See above, pp. 13-15.
4   See above, p. 14

5 GP 1674-89; see also GDD, II, pp. 25-43; C.J. Lowe, 'Reluctant Imperialists' (London, 1967), pp. 134-7.
6 A. Kruck, 'Geschichte des Alldeutschen Verbandes 1890-1939'
   (Wiesbaden, 1954).
7 H.J. Puhle, 'Agrarische Interessenpolitik und preussicher
   Konservatismus in wilhelminischen Reich (1893-1914). Ein
   Beitrag zur Analyse des Nationalismus in Deutschland am Beispiel des Bundes der Landwirte und der Deutsch-Konservativen
   Partei' (Hanover, 1966).
8 R.W. Tims, 'Germanizing Prussian Poland' (New York, 1941); also
   A. Galos, F.H. Gentzen and W. Jakóbczyk, 'Die Hakatisten. Der
   deutsche Ostmarkenverein (1894-1934). Ein Beitrag zur Geschichte
   der Ostpolitik des deutschen Imperialismus' (East Berlin, 1966).
9 M. Balfour, 'The Kaiser and His Times' (London, 1964). It is
   probably the best of the many biographies of Wilhelm II (of
   uneven quality). It also brings out the more fundamental
   aspects of the social and political structure of the Reich on
   the one hand, of the personality of the Kaiser on the other.
   For an older, but still valuable biography see E. Ludwig,
   'Wilhelm der Zweite' (Berlin, 1925). It was a best-seller in
   the Weimar Republic, with many impressions. It was repub-
   lished in the Federal Republic in 1964, paperback edition 1968,
   with a postscript by the present author.
10 M. Balfour, op. cit.
11 BD, III, annex.
12 See below, pp. 71, 85, 142, 146, 165, 169f.
13 N. Rich, op. cit.; and N. Rich and H.N. Fisher (eds), 'The
   Holstein Papers'.
14 J.C.G. Röhl, op. cit., pp. 56-75; also M. Balfour, op. cit.,
   ch. VII, The New Course, pp. 167-86.
15 See above, pp. 44-9.
16 See above, p. 54.
17 E.g. before the Franco-Prussian War, but also after: Bismarck
   to Arnim, 30 October 1873: 'No government, if it regards war
   as inevitable even if it does not want it, would be so foolish
   as to leave to the enemy the choice of time and occasion and to
   wait for the moment which is most convenient for the enemy.'
   Quoted from F. Fischer, 'War of Illusions', p. 461.
18 'Der Kaiser. Aufzeichnungen des Chefs des Marinekabinetts
   Admiral Georg Alexander v. Müller über die Ära Wilhelm II', ed.
   by W. Görlitz (Berlin, Frankfurt, Zürich, 1965), pp. 36-41;
   the passage quoted is on p. 40; the English version taken from
   J.C.G. Röhl, 'From Bismarck to Hitler. The Problem of Continuity in German History' (London, 1970), pp. 56-60; see also
   below, Document 9.
19 J.C.G. Röhl, A Document of 1892 on Germany, Prussia and Poland,
   'Historical Journal', VII, I, 1964, pp. 144-7; also in J.C.G.
   Röhl, 'From Bismarck to Hitler', p. 55f; here below Document 8.
20 See below, p. 67f.
21 Barbara Vogel, 'Deutsche Russlandpolitik (Düsseldorf, 1973), ch.
   III, 2 Das Dogma von der Unmöglichkeit eines russisch-
   englischen Ausgleiches, pp. 118-23. In one of the documents
   the author mentions, Bülow thanked the Kaiser for having dis-
   pelled British suspicions that Germany wanted to goad Britain

into war with Russia, and he went on: 'This war will come one
day by elementary necessity, the sooner, the less both sides
believe that we wish for such a war.' (GP 3867). B. Vogel
commented on such strategy with the words: '"Weltpolitik ohne
Krieg", wohl aber mit dem Krieg anderer!' ('"Weltpolitik" without war', but with the war of others!'), ibid., p. 118.

22 GP 1366-9; see also N. Rich, op. cit., pp. 307-24; W.L. Langer, 'European Alliances', pp. 399-404; N. Rich and H.M.
Fisher (eds), op. cit., I, pp. 127-32; also below, Document 7.
23 See above, p. 55.
24 W.L. Langer, 'The Diplomacy of Imperialism', pp. 31-66.
25 See above, p. 66f.
26 See above, p. 58.
27 See above, p. 61.
28 The change comes out very well in the abridged version of the
'Grosse Politik, Das Amtliche Deutsche Aktenmaterial zur
Auswärtigen Politik 1871-1914'. Unter Leitung von Albrecht
Mendelssohn-Bartholdy und Friedrich Thimme herausgegeben vom
Institut für Auswärtige Politik in Hamburg, 4 vols (Berlin,
1928), vol. I, part 2, ch. 14 (England unser Freund - Frank-
reich unser Gegner - Britain our Friend - France our Enemy) and
15 (Die Wandlung: Deutschland und England als Gegner in
Vorderasien und Afrika - The Change: Germany and Britain as
rivals in the Middle East and in Africa).
29 GP 1762, 2018 (24 October and 10 September 1893, respectively);
also no. 2162 (16 November 1894).
30 N. Rich, op. cit., II, pp. 347-56.
31 See below, pp. 78-80.
32 For a detailed discussion see B. Vogel, 'Deutsche Russlandpolitik', pp. 27-35.
33 See the final chapter in J.C.G. Röhl, 'Germany without Bismarck':
The Personal Rule of Kaiser Wilhelm II 1897-1900, pp. 241-70.
34 See above, pp. 37f, 58; see also B. Vogel, op. cit., ch. II,
5: Der gemeinsame Kampf gegen 'Anarchismus' und 'Revolution',
pp. 87-103 with a wealth of new material.
35 See below, p. 171f.
36 GP 2215-75; also W.L. Langer, 'The Diplomacy of Imperialism',
pp. 186-94.
37 As illustrated in the famous picture drawn to the Kaiser's instructions with the title 'Peoples of Europe, protect your most
sacred possessions'; see also M. Balfour, op. cit., p. 189f;
for the concept of 'Yellow Peril' see H. Gollwitzer, 'Die
Gelbe Gefahr' (Göttingen, 1962).
38 G. Monger, 'The End of Isolation. British Foreign Policy 1900-
1907' (London, 1963).
39 See below, pp. 99-104.
40 On Germany's policy in China in that period see GP most of vol.
14, part I, in particular 3645-753; see also J.E. Schrecker,
'Imperialism and Chinese Nationalism. Germany in Shantung'
(Cambridge, Mass., 1971).
41 For Tirpitz in the Far East see J. Steinberg, 'Yesterday's
Deterrent. Tirpitz and the Birth of the German Battle Fleet'
(London, 1965), p. 103f.
42 J. Steinberg, op. cit.; V.R. Berghahn, 'Der Tirpitz-Plan.

Genesis und Verfall einer innenpolitischen Krisenstrategie unter Wilhelm II' (Düsseldorf, 1971).

43 N. Rich, op. cit., II, pp. 452-9; see also GDD, II, ch. XXIII, Lord Salisbury and the Future of Turkey. July-October, 1895, pp. 327-47.

44 N. Rich and H.M. Fisher (eds), op. cit., I, p. 162f; N. Rich, op. cit., II, pp. 466-70; GP 2588-629; also GDD, II, chs XXV and XXVI, The Jameson Raid. January, 1896 and The 'Kruger Telegram' and its Consequences, pp. 365-409.

45 V.R. Berghahn, op. cit., pp. 89-96.

46 'Reden Kaiser Wilhelm II' ed. by J. Penzler, 4 vols (Leipzig, n.d.), II, p. 9.

CHAPTER 8 THE EMERGENCE OF 'WELTPOLITIK' FROM DOMESTIC POLICY, 1896-8

1 See below, p. 82f.

2 H. Plehn, 'Deutsche Weltpolitik und kein Krieg' (Berlin, 1913).

3 See below, pp. 142-5.

4 E.g. the growth of the national movement in the Balkans.

5 For details see F. Fischer, 'Germany's Aims', sub-ch. Economic Expansion and World Power Aspirations, pp. 11-20.

6 This is the main result of V.R. Berghahn, 'Der Tirpitz-Plan'.

7 See above, pp. 6-16.

8 H.-U. Wehler, 'Bismarck und der Imperialismus'; see also an abridged version in English, Bismarck's Imperialism, in 'Past and Present', no. 48, 1970, pp. 119-55.

9 F. Fischer, op. cit., p. 9; also L. Dehio, 'Deutschland und die Weltpolitik im 20. Jahrhundert' (Munich, 1955), pp. 76-90.

10 See above, pp. 39-43, 61, 69.

11 J.C.G. Röhl, 'Germany without Bismarck', pp. 200-40.

12 H. Böhme, 'Deutschlands Weg zur Grossmacht'.

13 J.C.G. Röhl, op. cit., pp. 246-58; D. Stegmann, 'Die Erben Bismarcks', pp. 59-130.

14 J.C.G. Röhl, op. cit., p. 128.

15 Ibid., p. 129f.

16 V.R. Berghahn, 'Tirpitz-Plan', Wirtschaftsinteressen und Flottengesetz, pp. 129-57.

17 For the agitation see also J. Steinberg, 'Yesterday's Deterrent', p. 179f.

18 R.W. Tims, 'Germanizing Prussian Poland'.

19 V.R. Berghahn, op. cit. For a somewhat qualifying criticism of the emerging new orthodoxy see G. Eley, Sammlungspolitik, Social Imperialism and the Navy Law of 1898, Militärgeschichtliche Mitteilungen, 1, 1974, pp. 29-63.

20 A.J. Marder, 'From the Dreadnought to Scapa Flow', 5 vols (London, 1961-70).

21 See below, p. 146f.

22 See below, p. 102.

23 F. Fischer, 'War of Illusions', pp.

24 H.-U. Wehler, op. cit., pp. 464-502.

25 See above, p. 45f.

26 See above, p. 66.

27   W.J. Mommsen, 'Max Weber und die deutsche Politik 1890-1920'
     (Tübingen, 1958), p. 78.
28   F. Fischer, 'War of Illusions', p.
29   Ibid.; for the position of many more university professors
     see also note 23.
30   A. von Tirpitz, 'Erinnerungen' (Leipzig, 1919), p. 52.
31   See above, p. 71.
32   'Reden Kaiser Wilhelms II', II, pp. 78-80; the speech was made
     when seeing off the Kaiser's brother, Admiral Prince Heinrich,
     to a naval mission to the Far East, on 15 December 1897.
33   J.J. Ruedorffer (Kurt Riezler), 'Grundzüge der Weltpolitik',
     p. 102.
34   F. Fischer, 'Krieg der Illusionen', pp. 68-71.
35   J.J. Ruedorffer, op. cit., pp. 23, 32.
36   K. Riezler, 'Tagebücher, Aufsätze, Dokumente', ed. K.D.
     Erdmann (Göttingen, 1972), especially pp. 217, 229, 234, 357,
     360, 478; see also my own critical analysis Kurt Riezler und
     der Erste Weltkrieg, in Geiss and Wendt (eds), 'Deutschland
     in der Weltpolitik des 19. und 20. Jahrhunderts' (Düsseldorf,
     1973), pp. 398-418.
37   See above, pp. 14-16.
38   See above, p. 78.
39   See above, p. 65f; also Document 9.
40   Ibid.
41   J. Steinberg, A German Plan for the Invasion of Holland and
     Belgium, 1897, 'Historical Journal', VI, no. 1 (1963), pp. 107-
     19.
42   See below, p. 101.

CHAPTER 9   THE DIPLOMACY OF 'WELTPOLITIK', 1897-1902

1   See above, p. 70.
2   J.C.G. Röhl, 'Germany without Bismarck', p. 130.
3   See above, p. 70.
4   For sources see above, p. 70, note 40; see also N.R. Rich,
    'Holstein', II, pp. 555-66.
5   GP 3701.
6   See below, p. 96.
7   Still valuable is H. Kantorowicz, 'The Spirit of British
    Policy and the Myth of the Encirclement of Germany' (London,
    1932); also E. Kehr, Englandhass und Weltpolitik, in 'Primat
    der Innenpolitik', pp. 149-75, and Deutsch-englisches Bündnis-
    problem, ibid., pp. 176-83.
8   GP 4398.
9   GP 2641.
10 See above, p. 58.
11 See above, p. 71.
12 N.R. Rich, op. cit., II, pp. 567-82, and for the following;
    for the material from the German side, see GP 3779-805; for
    the British side see C.J. Lowe, 'The Reluctant Imperialists',
    vol. I, 'British Foreign Policy 1878-1902' (London, 1967), in
    this series, p. 234f.
13 N.R. Rich, op. cit., II, p. 574f; C.J. Lowe, op. cit., p. 222.

14   Ibid., pp. 575-82.
15   GP 3806-83; C.J. Lowe, op. cit., I, pp. 218-22; N.R. Rich, op. cit., II, p. 586ff; also R. Langhorne, Anglo-American Negotiations Concerning the Future of the Portugese Colonies, 1911-1914, 'Historical Journal', XVI (1973), pp. 361-87, especially pp. 363-7.
16   See below, p. 478.
17   M. Balfour, 'The Kaiser', p. 216f.
18   W. van Kampen, 'Studien zur deutschen Türkeipolitik unter Wilhelm II', theses (Kiel, 1968).
19   See below, p. 106.
20   U. Trumpener, 'Germany and the Ottoman Empire 1914-1918' (Princeton, 1968).
21   A. Vagts, 'Deutschland und die Vereinigten Staaten in der Weltpolitik', 2 vols (New York, 1935).
22   N.R. Rich, op. cit., II, pp. 590-600; GP 4028-116.   For the latter point see N.R. Rich, op. cit., p. 598.
23   H. Kantorowicz, 'Myth of Encirclement', p. 256.
24   Ibid., p. 257; GP 4255; the material on the whole complex, ibid., 4215-355; GDD, III, pp. 74-81.
25   GP 4256.
26   Ibid., 4281.
27   Ibid., 4294.
28   Ibid., 4300.
29   Ibid., 4310.
30   Ibid., 4320.
31   See above, p. 90.
32   GP 4362; for the whole complex see ibid., 4356-510; GDD, III, pp. 82-126.
33   GP 4472.
34   Ibid., 4475.
35   For this and the following, see N.R. Rich, op. cit., II, pp. 614-16.
36   See above, p. 92.
37   M. Balfour, op. cit., p. 226.
38   GP 4511-698; GDD, III, pp. 127-39.
39   GP 4398, 4979, 4980.
40   N.R. Rich, op. cit., II, p. 613.
41   Ibid., pp. 626-42; GDD, III, pp. 140-52; GP 4979-5035; also for the following.
42   GP 5005; GDD, III, p. 145; C.J. Lowe, op. cit., pp. 233-5.
43   BD, II, no. 94.

CHAPTER 10   THE BEGINNING OF GERMANY'S CONTAINMENT, 1902-6

1   See below, p. 106.
2   I. Geiss, 'Julikrise 1914', II, no. 980.
3   GP 5049, 5050, 5725, 5726.
4   See B. Vogel, 'Deutsche Russlandpolitik', sub-ch. V, 1/, Diplomatische Aktivität zur Herbeiführung des Krieges, pp. 154-61.   The official German version in GP vol. 19; its propaganda character has been shown by B. Vogel.
5   Ibid., sub-ch. II, 5, Der gemeinsame Kampf gegen 'Anarchismus' und 'Revolution', pp. 87-103.

6   Ibid., p. 102.
7   Ibid., p. 116.
8   W.L. Langer, 'The Diplomacy of Imperialism', I, p. 10.   For
    details see C. Andrew, 'Theophile Delcassé and the Making of
    the Entente Cordiale.   A Reappraisal of French Foreign Policy
    1898-1905' (London, 1968).
9   L. Albertini, 'Origins', I, p. 129;   Lowe and Marzari, op. cit.,
    pp. 82-90.
10 F. Fellner, 'Der Dreibund', ch. III, 'Erwerbsgenossenschaft'
    oder 'Versicherungsgesellschaft'?, pp. 36-49.
11 See above, p. 42f.
12 F. Fellner, op. cit., pp. 53-7;   L. Albertini, op. cit., I,
    pp. 118-27;   the sub-ch., The renewal of the Triple Alliance,
    28 June 1902, is mainly based on GP, vol. 18, 5712-823.
13 P.J.V. Rolo, 'Entente Cordiale. The Origins and Negotiations
    of the Anglo-French Agreements of 8 April 1904' (London, 1969);
    C. Andrew, op. cit.;   see also N. Rich, op. cit., II, p. 675f,
    for a glance at the German side of it.
14 N. Rich, ibid., II, pp. 673-5;   Eckardstein's memorandum
    printed in H. Freiherr von Eckardstein, 'Lebenserinnerungen
    und politische Denkwürdigkeiten', 2 vols (Leipzig, 1920), II,
    pp. 422-5;   see also L. Albertini, op. cit., I, pp. 145-8.
15 M. Balfour, 'The Kaiser', p. 247.
16 N. Rich, op. cit., II, p. 681f.
17 For details see B. Vogel, op. cit., ch. IV, Der deutsch-
    russische Handelsvertrag, pp. 124-53, and sub-ch. VI, 1, pp.
    174-89.
18 GP 6118.
19 Ibid., 6120;   see also B. Vogel, op. cit., sub-ch. VII, 1,
    Das erste Bündnisangebot an Russland, pp. 201-16.
20 GP 6127.
21 GP 7349.
22 B. Vogel, op. cit., p. 216f.
23 Ibid.;   see also below, p. 121.
24 Ibid., sub-ch. VII, 2, Das zweite Bündnisangebot an Russland,
    pp. 216-31.
25 Ibid., p. 217f;   also I. Geiss, 'July 1914', sub-ch., The
    German Concept of a Preventive War, pp. 38-48.
26 For a detailed discussion see G. Ritter, 'The Schlieffen Plan:
    Critique of a Myth' (London, 1958).
27 Von Einem, 'Erinnerungen eines Soldaten, 1853-1933' (Leipzig,
    1933), p. 114;   B. Vogel, op. cit., p. 165f.
28 See above, p. 28f.
29 N. Rich, op. cit., II, p. 700f.
30 B. Vogel, op. cit., p. 217f;   for the German material see GP,
    vols 20 and 21, and GDD, III, ch. 18, pp. 219-33.   Also C.
    Andrew, op. cit., ch. 14, The First Moroccan Crisis, pp. 268-
    301;   for Delcassé's fall, see N. Rich, op. cit., II, pp.
    693-706.
31 GP vol. 19, II, ch. 138, Der Vertrag von Björkoe, 6202-58;   the
    draft in GP, 6203;   the text actually signed, GP 6220, annex;
    GP 6220 contains the Kaiser's long and verbose report of the
    event, signed Wisby, 25 July 1905.   See also B. Vogel, op.
    cit., pp. 223-7 (also for the following).

32 GP 6220.
33 GP 6222, 6223.
34 B. Vogel, op. cit., sub-ch. V, 3, Diplomatische Aktivität zur "Hintertreibung einer Mediation" im russisch-japanischen Krieg, pp. 169-73.
35 GP 6227-40.
36 B. Vogel, op. cit., p. 226f.
37 See above, p. 56.
38 The German material in GP vol. 21, 7237-75.
39 See below, pp. 133-5.

CHAPTER 11 TRIPLE ENTENTE AND THE BOSNIAN CRISIS, 1907-9

1 M. Balfour, 'The Kaiser', p. 247.
2 BD, III, annex; see below Document 11.
3 See also I. Geiss, 'July 1914', pp. 28-32. A biography on Crowe by Dr Zara Steiner is in preparation. For British policy towards Germany see Lowe and Dockrill, 'Mirage of Power', I, pp. 29-31.
4 Document 11, p. 199; also I. Geiss, op. cit., p. 31.
5 A.J. Marder, 'From Dreadnought to Scapa Flow', I.
6 V.R. Berghahn, 'Tirpitz-Plan', pp. 448-504.
7 See above, p. 102, and below, p. 136, 143f.
8 GP, vol. 23, 7749-8159; also L. Albertini, 'Origins', I, pp. 184-7.
9 GP vol. 24, chs 174, 175, 178, nos 8160-99, 8212-48; GDD, III, chs 22, 23, pp. 268-98.
10 GP 8225, 8226, of 12-13 August 1908; Hardinge's version in BD IV, 124; see also M. Balfour, op. cit., p. 286.
11 GP 8193, Metternich to Bülow, private letter, 8 March 1908.
12 GP 8220.
13 B. Gebhardt, 'Handbuch der deutschen Geschichte', p. 298, quoting from H.H. Robertz, 'Die deutsch-englischen Flotten-besprechungen im Sommer 1908', thesis, (Berlin, 1938).
14 GP 8219, with many of the Kaiser's profuse and revealing minutes.
15 GP 8226, GDD, III, p. 294.
16 GP 8239.
17 GD 401, concluding minute from the Kaiser to a telegram of the German Ambassador to St Petersburg of 30 July 1914; see also I. Geiss, 'July 1914', p. 294f.
18 See above, pp. 30-4.
19 See above, pp. 39-43.
20 See A.J.P. Taylor, 'The Habsburg Monarchy', for an excellent analysis of the internal weakness and problems of Austria-Hungary at the time, especially pp. 199-229, but also the following chapter, Solution by Violence, 1908-14, pp. 230-50.
21 See above, p. 37f, 42.
22 See below, p. 140, 154f.
23 See above, p. 11f.
24 See F.R. Bridge, 'From Sadowa to Sarajevo', pp. 280-2.
25 A.J.P. Taylor, op. cit., p. 230f; L. Albertini, 'Origins', I, p. 190f; B. Schmitt, 'The Coming of the War', I, p. 121f.

26   See F.R. Bridge, op. cit., pp. 288-92.
27   A.J.P. Taylor, op. cit., p. 231;   V. Dedijer, 'The Road to
     Sarajevo', p. 369.
28   See also Dimitrije Djordjevic, 'La guerre douanière entre
     l'Autriche-Hongrie et la Serbie 1906-1911' (Belgrade, 1962);
     this is the French title of a study in Serbo-Croat, but with a
     lengthy and rather detailed summary in French, see pp. 691-710;
     see also A.J.P. Taylor, op. cit., pp. 225-7.
29   B. Schmitt, 'The Coming of the War', p. 123.
30   See above, p. 33f.
31   L. Albertini, op. cit., I, pp. 193-5.   But see F.R. Bridge,
     op. cit., pp. 300-2 for a very different interpretation.
32   L. Albertini, op. cit., p. 194, with quotations from Conrad von
     Hötzendorf.
33   Ibid., pp. 225-33, sub-ch. England, France and Russia propose a
     European Conference.
34   The German material in GP, vol. 25;   GDD, III, pp. 299-311.
     For Bülow's first reactions on the annexation, see his detailed
     memoranda to the Kaiser and the Auswärtiges Amt, both on 5
     October 1908, GP 8939, 8984.
35   GP 9173.
36   Conrad von Hötzendorf, 'Erinnerungen', I, pp. 631-4;   for the
     whole complex see L. Albertini, op. cit., pp. 268-73.
37   See above, p. 42f.
38   GP 9391.
39   See above on this page.
40   GP 9457.
41   See below, p. 169.
42   L. Albertini, op. cit., p. 277.
43   ÖD, II, 1080.
44   L. Albertini, op. cit., p. 291f;   the Serbian declaration also
     in BD, V, no. 782.
45   See below, pp. 166-8.
46   GP 9437.
47   GP 9460.
48   Von Bülow, 'Memoirs', II, p. 513.
49   V. Dedijer, op. cit., p. 175f.
50   See below, p. 151f.
51   See below, pp. 133-7, 140-2.

CHAPTER 12   'ENCIRCLEMENT' AND GERMANY'S SELF-ISOLATION

1   L. Albertini, 'Origins', I, p. 293f.
2   H. Kantorowicz, 'The Spirit of British Policy', p. 458.
3   First sentence quoted in H. Kantorowicz, ibid.;   the rest of
    the passage was translated by the present author.
4   Quoted in H. Kantorowicz, ibid., p. 461.
5   J. Steinberg, The Copenhagen Complex, 'Journal of Contemporary
    History', 1/3 (1966), pp. 23-46.
6   I. Geiss, 'July 1914', p. 26f;   in greater detail, but un-
    published and unknown to the author then, H. Kantorowicz,
    'Gutachten zur Kriegsschuldfrage 1914', pp. 112-25, 131-3.
    Also 'British Policy', ch. V, The Myth of the Encirclement of
    Germany, pp. 365-475.

7   See above, p. 53.
8   See above, p. 11;   also H.-U. Wehler, Unfähig zur Verfassungs-
    reform: Das 'Reichsland' Elsass-Lothringen von 1870 bis 1918
    in H.-U. Wehler, 'Krisenherde des Kaiserreichs 1871-1918.
    Studien zur deutschen Sozial- und Verfassungsgeschichte'
    (Göttingen, 1970), pp. 17-63.
9   See above, p. 103.
10 H.-U. Wehler, Symbol der halbabsolutistischen Herrschafts-
    systems: Der Fall Zabern von 1913-14 als Verfassungskrise des
    wilhelminischen Kaiserreichs, in Wehler, 'Krisenherde',
    pp. 65-83.
11 GP 12, 522 (10 November 1912), 15, 657 (15 November 1913), 15,
    667 (5 February 1914), 15, 675 (15 June 1914).
12 For a brilliant and more detailed analysis of the material
    available in the late 1920s, see H. Kantorowicz, 'Gutachten
    zur Kriegsschuldfrage 1914'.
13 See above, p. 32.
14 I. Geiss, 'Julikrise 1914', I, p. 42.
15 See below, p. 171f.
16 H. Kantorowicz, 'British Policy', pp. 373-8, 383-5, 390-8.
17 For a more detailed discussion of Britain's relations with the
    other Great Powers see now C.J. Lowe and M.L. Dockrill, 'The
    Mirage of Power', vol. I, British Foreign Policy 1902-14
    (London, 1972), pp. 29-95, 107-41.
18 See below, pp. 175-81.
19 See below, p. 146;   also V.R. Berghahn, 'Tirpitz-Plan', p. 381,
    where he mentions the neurosis of the German Navy to be found
    out and be punished for their secret far-reaching intentions.
20 See below, p. 149.
21 See below, p. 130f, 137f.
22 J.C.G. Röhl, 'Germany without Bismarck', p. 127;   for the
    ollowing, ibid., pp. 128-30.
23 Ibid., p. 130.
24 See above, p. 58.
25 GP 6681;   H. Kantorowicz, 'The Spirit of British Policy', op.
    cit., p. 369, also for the following.
26 E. Jäckh (ed.), 'Kiderlen Wächter. Der Staatsmann und Mensch.
    Briefwechsel und Nachlass', 2 vols (Berlin, Leipzig, 1924),
    vol. II, p. 234f;   the first sentence in H. Kantorowicz, op.
    cit., p. 369.
27 See above, p. 121f.
28 K.D. Erdmann (ed.), 'Kurt Riezler. Tagebücher, Aufsätze,
    Dokumente' (Göttingen, 1972), p. 29.
29 J.J. Ruedorffer, 'Weltpolitik', p. 115f;   also I. Geiss,
    'July 1914', p. 35.
30 This came out strongly in the polemics of conservative German
    historians against Fritz Fischer's book 'Griff nach der Welt-
    macht'.   Their views, in particular on this point, are
    critically discussed by I. Geiss, Dis Fischer-Kontroverse.
    Ein kritischer Beitrag zum Verhältnis zwischen Historiographie
    und Politik in der Bundesrepublik in I. Geiss, 'Studien über
    Geschichte und Geschichtswissenschaft', Edition Suhrkamp 569
    (Frankfurt/Main, 1972), p. 131f, 135, 152f.
31 See below, pp. 146-8.
32 H. Kantorowicz, op. cit., p. 462.

CHAPTER 13   GERMANY'S POLITICAL OFFENSIVE AGAINST 'ENCIRCLEMENT',
             1909-12

1 For material see GP 8249-74;   GDD, III, 312-15;   see also
   M. Balfour, 'The Kaiser', pp. 289-93.
2 P.C. Witt, 'Die Finanzpolitik des Deutschen Reiches von 1903
   bis 1913. Eine Studie zur Innenpolitik des wilhelminischen
   Deutschland' (Lübeck, Hamburg, 1970).
3 See above, p. 76f.
4 For his first full-fledged biography, full of sympathy and
   apologetic tones, see E. von Vietsch, 'Bethmann-Hollweg.
   Staatsmann zwischen Macht und Ethos' (Boppard/Rhein, 1969).
   In a harsher vein, see W. Gutsche, 'Aufstieg und Fall eines
   kaiserlichen Reichskanzlers. Theobald von Bethmann-Hollweg
   1856-1921. Ein politisches Lebensbild' (East Berlin, 1973) ch.13.
5 GP 10, 306;   GDD, III, pp. 352-60;   see also, as for the rest
   of this book, the corresponding and much more detailed treatment of the same subject by Fritz Fischer, 'War of Illusions',
   p. 59f.
6 GP 10, 325;   see also 10, 320, 10, 321.
7 GP 10, 326.
8 See above, p. 125f.
9 See below, p. 141.
10 See below, pp. 163-71.
11 See. F. Fischer, 'War of Illusions', pp. 121-31.
12 K. Riezler, 'Tagebücher', p. 184.
13 E. v. Vietsch, op. cit., p. 121.
14 Formally in a letter to Admiral von Müller, Chief of the
   Imperial Naval Cabinet, in a letter of 8 February 1912;
   Alfred von Tirpitz, 'Politische Dokumente, I, Der Aufbau der
   deutschen Weltmacht' (Stuttgart, Berlin, 1924), p. 282.
15 V.R. Berghahn, 'Der Tirpitz-Plan'.
16 See below, p. 155.
17 See above, p. 19, 29f.
18 The text of the agreement in GP 8490;   the German material on
   the Moroccan problem summer 1907 to early 1909, in GP 8275-
   500.
19 See above, p. 116.
20 See below, pp. 133-5.
21 See above, p. 130f.
22 GP 10, 331-7, 10, 349, 10, 353;   GDD, III, p. 407f.
23 GP 10, 346, 10, 355.
24 GP 10, 355.
25 BD, VII, p. 310, Crowe's minute of 8 November 1909, to Goschen's
   despatch of 21 October, reporting of a conversation with the
   Chancellor.   See Lowe and Dockrill, I, pp. 34-7.
26 GP 9979, 9980.
27 GP 10, 152.
28 GP 10, 155, 10, 156.
29 See above, p. 55f.
30 GP 10, 066, 10, 1067, 10, 071.
31 F. Fischer, op. cit., p. 68, quoting a letter of Bethmann-
   Hollweg to his friend Eisendecher of 27 December 1912, where
   he expected as a result of Russia's 'new rapprochement' to
   Germany that Britain would come with new suggestions.

238 Notes to Chapter 13

32 GP 12, 500-932.
33 For the German material see GP vol. 29, 10, 569-797.   See also
    F. Fischer, op. cit., ch. 5, Morocco Crisis 1911 - The Break-
    through of the National Opposition, pp. 72-94; for German
    public opinion see in particular K. Wernecke, 'Der Wille zur
    Weltgeltung. Aussenpolitik und Öffentlichkeit im Kaiserreich am
    Vorabend des Ersten Weltkrieges' (Düsseldorf, 1970), pp. 26-143.
34 GP 10, 607.
35 GP 10, 608.
36 E. Jäckh, 'Kiderlen-Wächter', II, p. 129; see also F. Fischer,
    'War of Illusions', pp. 76-8.
37 K. Riezler, op. cit., pp. 178-80.
38 GP 10, 621, 10, 623; Lowe and Dockrill, I, pp. 42-3.
39 F. Fischer, op. cit., p. 77f, 81f.
40 Ibid., pp. 84-8; K. Wernecke, op. cit., pp. 75-88.
41 F. Fischer, op. cit., p. 87f.
42 GP 10, 771, 10, 772.
43 See below, pp. 135-7; also F. Fischer, op. cit., pp. 88-94.
44 BD, X, 2, 416; also Lowe and Dockrill, I, pp. 43-6, 54-8.
45 K. Wernecke, op. cit., p. 30f.
46 Ibid., pp. 75-88; 102-30; 139-43.
47 G.W.F. Hallgarten, 'Imperialismus', II, pp. 265-7; also F.
    Fischer, op. cit., p. 89f; K. Wernecke, op. cit., pp. 114-16.
48 Ibid., pp. 288-310.
49 'Deutschland und der nächste Krieg'. It ran through five edi-
    tions in its year of publication, 1912; an English edition,
    'Germany and the Next War' (London, 1914). For an extract see
    J.C.G. Röhl (ed.), 'From Bismarck to Hitler', pp. 65-7; see
    also Barbara Tuchman, 'The Guns of August' (New York, 1962,
    paperback 1963), p. 25f.
50 See above, p. 130.
51 W. Görlitz (ed.), 'Der Kaiser ... Aufzeichnungen des Chefs des
    Marinekabinetts Admiral Georg Alexander v. Müller über die Ära
    Wilhelms II' (Göttingen, 1965), pp. 90-2; see also J.C.G.
    Röhl, Admiral von Müller and the Approach of War, 'Historical
    Journal', XII, 4, (1969), pp. 651-73.
52 Görlitz (ed.), 'Der Kaiser ...', p. 126.
53 See above, pp. 76-8; for the following also see F. Fischer,
    op. cit., ch. 6, The Elections of January 1912 - The Domestic
    Defeat, pp. 95-111.
54 H. Pogge-v. Strandmann, Staatsstreichpläne, Alldeutsche und
    Bethmann-Hollweg, in H. Pogge-v. Strandmann and I. Geiss, 'Die
    Erforderlichkeit des Unmöglichen. Deutschland am Vorabend des
    ersten Weltkrieges' (Frankfurt/Main, 1965), pp. 14-18.
55 Ibid., p. 17f.
56 See above, p. 136.
57 F. Fischer, op. cit., pp. 112-40
58 GP 11, 395; also, and for the following, F. Fischer, op. cit.,
    p. 130; C.J. Lowe and M.L. Dockrill, 'Mirage of Power', I,
    pp. 48-59.
59 GP 11, 403.

CHAPTER 14 THE DECISION TO GO TO WAR, JANUARY TO 8 DECEMBER 1912

1 See above, pp. 85, 90, 135.
2 See above, pp. 111-17.
3 See above, p. 89f.
4 See above, p. 89.
5 F. Fischer, 'War of Illusions', p. 142f.
6 L. Albertini, 'Origins', I, pp. 349-52; F. Fischer, op. cit., pp. 143-5.
7 F. Fellner, 'Dreibund', p. 78f; F. Fischer, op. cit., p. 145f.
8 Ibid., pp. 153-9, especially p. 157f; the German material in GP, vol. 33, 12, 033-499; see also OD, 4, 4959, especially 12, 087-8.
9 F. Fischer, op. cit., p. 158f.
10 F. Fischer, op. cit., pp. 470-3; also the many entries 'neutrality, British, Germany and' in I. Geiss, 'Julikrise und Kriegsausbruch 1914', 2 vols (Hanover, 1963-4) II, p. 844.
11 Also reprinted in GP in footnote to 12, 474.
12 GP 12, 481, 12, 483.
13 GP 15, 612; also F. Fischer, op. cit., p. 160, and for the following, pp. 161-9; also, in even greater detail, A. Gasser, Der deutsche Hegemonialkrieg von 1914, in I. Geiss and B.J. Wendt (eds), 'Deutschland in der Weltpolitik des 19. und 20. Jahrhunderts', pp. 307-20.
14 The Kaiser's minute to GP 15, 621.
15 The following after Müller's Diary, English version in J.C.G. Röhl, Admiral von Müller and the Approach of War; see also Document 18.
16 See above, p. 136.
17 F. Fischer, op. cit., p. 163f; I. Geiss, 'July 1914', p. 42. This is another of those key documents not to be published in 'Die Grosse Politik', because it would have belied the official German apologia.
18 Ibid.
19 Müller, 'Der Kaiser ...', p. 126; see also, above, p. 136.
20 See above, p. 134.
21 F. Fischer, 'War of Illusions', p. 166; A. Gasser, Der deutsche Hegemonialkrieg von 1914, p. 311.
22 Ibid., p. 311f; F. Fischer, op. cit., p. 163.
23 See above, p. 136.

CHAPTER 15 PREPARING FOR WAR

1 See above, p. 144.
2 F. Fischer, 'War of Illusions', pp. 177-282, also for the following.
3 See above, p. 90f, 108.
4 The intensity of the 'August-Erlebnis' may be gauged by the fact that Friedrich Meinecke, the great liberal-conservative German historian, could write, even after the Second World War, in 'Die Deutsche Katastrophe' (1946), a book most critical of the German political tradition:
    When the First World War broke out, it seemed once more

that a kind of Angel might lead the German people back to
the right path.   The exaltation of spirit experienced
during the August days of 1914, in spite of its ephemeral
character, is one of the most precious, unforgettable
memories of the highest sort.   All the rifts which had
hitherto existed in the German people, both within the
bourgeoisie and between the bourgeoisie and the working
classes, were suddenly closed in the fact of the common
danger which snatched us out of the security of the material
prosperity that we had been enjoying.   And more than that,
one perceived in all camps that it was not a matter merely
of the unity of a gain-seeking partnership, but that an
inner renovation of our whole state and culture was needed.
We generally believed indeed that this had already commen-
ced and that it would progress further in the common
experiences of the war, which was looked upon as a war of
defense and self-protection.   Friedrich Meinecke, 'The
German Catastrophe, Reflections and Recollections'.
Translated by Sydney B. Fay (Cambridge, Mass., 1950, 3rd
imp. Boston, 1964), p. 25.

5   P.-C. Witt, 'Finanzpolitik 1903-1913', pp. 356-76.
6   A. Gasser, Deutschlands Entschluss zum Präventivkrieg, in
'Discordia concors, Festgabe für Edgar Bonjour', 2 vols
(Basle, 1968), pp. 171-224.
7   See above, pp. 28, 101, 134-7.
8   I. Geiss, 'July 1914', p. 40.
9   See above, pp. 142-5.
10   For a more technical critique of the plan see G. Ritter, 'The
Schlieffen Plan: Critique of a Myth' (London, 1958).   For a
more fundamental criticism, also in the context of the more
recent research, see Y.L. Wallach, 'Das Dogma der Vernichtungsschlacht. Die Lehren von Clausewitz und Schlieffen und
ihre Wirkungen in zwei Weltkriegen' (Frankfurt/Main, 1967);
see also F. Fischer, op. cit., pp. 389-92.
11   F. Fischer, op. cit., pp. 397-403.
12   C. von Hötzendorf, 'Aus meiner Dienstzeit, 1906-1918', 5 vols
(Vienna, Leipzig, Munich, 1922), III, p. 670.   For a broader
analysis see N. Stone, V. Moltke-Conrad.   Relations between
the Austro-Hungarian and German General Staffs, 1909-1914,
'Historical Journal', IX (1966), pp. 201-28.
13   According to a statement written by Jagow shortly after the
war but brought to light by the present author in September
1965;   see also Document 19.
14   See Bethmann Hollweg's remark to Conrad Haussmann, 24 February
1918, to that effect about the generals' arguments, F.
Fischer, op. cit., p. 468.
15   See below, pp. 150-2.
16   F. Fischer, op. cit., pp. 190-5;   idem, 'German War Aims',
p. 34.
17   K. Wernecke, 'Der Wille zur Weltgeltung', pp. 220-4.
18   Ibid., pp. 208-18;   F. Fischer, op. cit., pp. 190-5.
19   C. von Delbrück, 'Die wirtschaftliche Mobilmachung in Deutschland' (Munich, 1924), p. 99.
20   Reichsarchiv, 'Der Weltkrieg 1914-1918. Kriegsrüstung und

Kriegswirtschaft'. Anlagen zum 1. Band (Berlin, 1930), p. 163; also quoted in F. Fischer, op. cit., p. 180f; K. Wernecke, op. cit., p. 182.

21 F. Fischer, op. cit., p. 167; also F.R. Bridge, 'From Sadowa to Sarajevo', p. 350f.

22 I. Geiss, 'Julikrise 1914', II, p. 575, n. 3; F. Fischer, op. cit., p. 168.

23 GP 15, 560, Chancellor to the Kaiser, 18 December 1912: That a war with Russia will mean for us also a war with France, is certain. But judging from many symptoms it is at least doubtful whether Britain would intervene actively if Russia and France were to appear as the parts provoking war. For then the British Government would have to reckon with their public opinion.

24 GP 12, 489, 12, 561.

25 F. Fischer, op. cit., p. 205f, also for the following.

26 GP 12, 818; see also I. Geiss, 'July 1914', p. 44.

27 C. von Hötzendorf, op. cit., III, p. 144; also I. Geiss, op. cit., p. 43.

28 G. Ritter, 'Staatskunst und Kriegshandwerk. Das Problem des "Militarismus" in Deutschland', 4 vols (Munich, 1954-67), III, p. 311 ('Der Beginn eines Weltkrieges sei sehr wohl zu überlegen').

29 For this and the following see F. Fischer, op. cit., pp. 213-19; L. Albertini, 'Origins', I, pp. 433-87; and the German material in GP 12, 784-932.

30 GP 14, 176.

31 See below, p. 165.

32 C. von Hötzendorf, op. cit., III, p. 470; see also I. Geiss, 'July 1914', p. 45.

33 C. von Hötzendorf, op. cit., p. 477; see also L. Albertini, op. cit., p. 484.

34 OD 8934, for Berchtold's own account of the Kaiser's words; see also F. Fischer, op. cit., pp. 221-3.

35 Ibid., p. 315.

36 See above, p. 37f.

37 F. Fischer, op. cit., p. 223.

38 This is a point forcefully made by G.W.F. Hallgarten, 'Imperialismus', II, pp. 434-48. Unfortunately, Hallgarten overemphasizes his good point if he suggests that the Liman von Sanders mission 'was the beginning of the international trouble which led to war eight months later'; G.W.F. Hallgarten, 'Das Schicksal des Imperialismus im 20. Jahrhundert. Drei Abhandlungen über Kriegsursachen' (Frankfurt/Main, 1969), p. 37. The Straits were certainly a sore point in international relations, but so were many other places (Morocco, Serbia, Alsace-Lorraine, Bosnia-Herzegovina, Anglo-German naval rivalry, etc.). If one wished, events connected with any of them could be seen as 'the beginning of the international trouble which led to war' any given length of time 'later'. For details of the Liman Sanders affair see F. Fischer, op. cit., ch. XXV, pp. 481-514.

39 Ibid., pp. 516-27.

40 See above, p. 153.

41 See above, p. 151f.
42 See above, p. 150.
43 F. Fischer, op. cit., pp. 306-19; and 'Germany's Aims', p. 102f.
44 F. Fischer, 'War of Illusions', p. 311f.
45 Ibid., pp. 302-9.
46 Ibid., p. 307; for the following, p. 308.
47 GP 15, 732.
48 DD 72; also I. Geiss, 'July 1914', p. 122.
49 K. Wernecke, op. cit., pp. 244-73.
50 C. von Hötzendorf, op. cit., p. 670.
51 See below, p. 169.
52 He later published the material, see B. von Siebert (ed.),
    'Diplomatische Aktenstücke zur Geschichte der Ententepolitik
    der Vorkriegsjahre' (Berlin, Leipzig, 1921).
53 DD 3.
54 See below, pp. 165-72.
55 DD 3.
56 E. Zechlin, Deutschland zwischen Kabinettskrieg und Wirt-
    schaftskrieg. Politik und Kriegführung in den ersten Monaten
    des Weltkrieges 1914, 'Historische Zeitschrift', 199/2 (1964),
    pp. 347-458.

CHAPTER 16   THE CRISIS AND THE OUTBREAK OF WAR

1 See below, p. 170f.
2 See above, pp. 115-17, 150-4.
3 For literature see mainly L. Albertini, 'Origins', II and III;
   F. Fischer, 'Germany's Aims', ch. 2, pp. 50-92, and also 'War
   of Illusions', ch. 22.   For the documents see I. Geiss,
   'Julikrise und Kriegsausbruch 1914' and the condensed version
   in English, 'July 1914' with all important documents to be
   found there in chronological order.   For the point in question
   see I. Geiss, 'July 1914', pp. 55-69.
4 OD 9984; DD 13, 14; I. Geiss, 'Julikrise 1914', no. 9.
5 I. Geiss, 'July 1914', p. 54f.
6 Ibid., pp. 67-9; see also above p. 149.
7 For the following see I. Geiss, op. cit., pp. 64-
8 Ibid., p. 64f.
9 Ibid., p. 76f.
10 L. Albertini, 'Origins', II, p. 142.
11 See above, p. 115.
12 K. Riezler, 'Tagebücher', p. 183f.
13 I. Geiss, 'July 1914', p. 87f, 94f, 102f, 105-11, 114-17, 119f,
    124-30.
14 Ibid., pp. 89-81.
15 I. Geiss, 'Julikrise 1914', I, nos 103, 138, 140, 199, 213, 214,
    231, 241; also 'July 1914', p. 127.
16 I. Geiss, 'July 1914', p. 129.
17 See above, p. 165f.
18 I. Geiss, 'Julikrise 1914', no. 43.
19 I. Geiss, 'July 1914', p. 87f, 94f, 102f, 106-9, 120f, 126-30.
20 Ibid., p. 119.
21 Ibid., p. 200f.

22   Ibid., p. 175.
23   Ibid., p. 161f.
24   Ibid., p. 163f, 180, 199f.
25   Ibid., pp. 186-8.
26   Ibid., p. 200f, 155.
27   Ibid., pp. 222, 245;   also BD 264, 281, 329, 677.
28   I. Geiss, 'July 1914', pp. 219, 226-9.
29   Ibid., pp. 266, 244f, 253, 282-4.
30   Ibid., p. 222f.
31   Ibid., p. 223f, 256f, 259.   The great eye-opener on that
     point was L. Albertini, 'Origins', II, pp. 466-74.
32   I. Geiss, 'July 1914', p. 267.
33   Ibid., pp. 268, 300f.
34   Ibid., pp. 291-3.
35   Ibid., pp. 272, 297-9, 309-12.
36   Ibid., pp. 269-71.
37   Ibid., pp. 271;   DD 542, 608.
38   I. Gkiss, 'July 1914', p. 336f, 343.
39   Ibid., p. 274f, 312, 348f, 356.
40   Ibid., p. 339f, 354f, 358-60.
41   Ibid., p. 129.
42   Ibid., p. 150.
43   I. Geiss, 'Julikrise 1914', II, no. 1089, p. 639.
44   Ibid., II, pp. 721-31;   'July 1914', pp. 361-75.   Also
     K. Epstein, Gerhard Ritter and the First World War, 'Journal
     of Contemporary History', 1/3 (1966), pp. 193-210, especially
     p. 197f.
45   See A. Gasser, 'Der deutsche Hegemonialkrieg', p. 338f.

CHAPTER 17   GERMAN WAR AIMS, 1914

1   See above, pp. 135-7.
2   See also above, pp. 13-16.
3   F. Fischer, 'Germany's Aims in the First World War'.
4   BD, III, annex A, see below, Document 11.
5   For example, both Riezler and General Bernhardi expressed the
    same idea.   See B. Tuchman, 'The Guns of August', New York,
    1962, paperback edition 1963, p. 25.
6   K. Wernecke, 'Der Wille zur Weltgeltung', pp. 289-308.
7   See below, pp. 175-80.
8   See above, p. 66.
9   B. Fürst von Bülow, 'Denkwürdigkeiten', 4 vols (Berlin, 1930),
    II, pp. 243-6.   The Kaiser, in the summer of 1906, also pro-
    mised to do something about the Baltic provinces and the German
    element there, if Russia were to disintegrate 'into a number
    of federative republics'.   If Poland were to be resurrected,
    all Polish magnates would have to swear the oath of allegiance
    to the Kaiser.   Those who refused would have to leave Prussia.
10 See below, p. 178.
11 BD, XI, 293;   also I. Geiss, 'July 1914', p. 300f.
12 I. Geiss, 'July 1914', p. 231f.
13 See above, n. 4.
14 This was one of the main arguments of German critics against

1   F. Fischer.   For a critical discussion of their aguments see
    I. Geiss, 'Studien über Geschichte und Geschichtswissenschaft'
    (Frankfurt/Main, 1972), pp. 128-50.
15 For this and the following, see F. Fischer, op. cit., pp. 95-
    119.
16 K. Riezler, 'Tagebücher', p. 198; for the following, ibid.,
    p. 201f.
17 F. Fischer, op. cit., p. 104f; see also Document 26.
18 K. Riezler, op. cit., pp. 200, 217, 229, 234, 271; see also
    F. Fischer, op. cit., the sub-chapter Mitteleuropa as the
    Basis for Germany's World Power Status, pp. 201-8.
19 See also K.D. Erdmann in his introduction to K. Riezler, op.
    cit., p. 62.
20 F. Fischer, op. cit., p. 185; for the whole problem, ibid.,
    pp. 184-8.
21 I. Geiss, 'Der polnische Grenzstreifen 1914-1918. Ein Beitrag
    zur deutschen Kriegszielpolitik im Ersten Weltkrieg' (Hamburg,
    Lübeck, 1960), p. 73; see also F. Fischer, op. cit., pp. 271-3.
22 This was not seen by the uncritical study by H.C. Meyer,
    'Mitteleuropa in German Thought and Action, 1815-1945' (The
    Hague, 1954).
23 K. Riezler, op. cit., pp. 360, 362, 399.
24 For the beginning of discussion on the problem of continuity
    in German history from the First World War to the Second World
    War, see J.C.G. Röhl, 'From Bismarck to Hitler'.

BIBLIOGRAPHY

COLLECTIONS OF DOCUMENTS

BÖHME, H. (ed.), 'Die Reichsgründung' (Munich, 1967), dtv 428.
'British Documents on the Origins of the War, 1898-1914', eds
Gooch, G.P., and Temperley, H.W.V., 11 vols (London, 1926-38).
'German Diplomatic Documents, 1871-1914', selected and translated
by Dugdale, E.T.S., 4 vols (London, New York, 1928, reprinted
1969).
'Documents Diplomatiques Français, 1871-1914', Ministère des
Affaires Etrangères. Commission de Publication des Documents
Relatifs aux Origines de la Guerre de 1914 (Paris, 1929-40).
'Die Grosse Politik der Europäischen Kabinette, 1871-1914'.
Sammlung der diplomatischen Akten des Auswärtigen Amtes, eds
Lepsius, J., Mendellsohn-Bartholdy, A., and Thimme, F., 39 vols
(Berlin, 1922-7).
'Julikrise und Kriegsausbruch 1914. Eine Dokumentensammlung', ed.
Geiss, I., 2 vols (Hannover, 1963-4).
'July 1914. Selected Documents', ed. Geiss, I., (London, 1967, New
York, 1968).
'Die Internationalen Beziehungen im Zeitalter des Imperialismus'.
Dokumente aus den Archiven der Zarischen und der Provisorischen
Regierung. German edition ed. Hoetzsch, O., ser. I, 5 vols (Berlin,
1931-4).
JÄCKH, E. (ed.), 'Kiderlen Wächter. Der Staatsmann und Mensch.
Briefwechsel und Nachlass', 2 vols (Berlin, Leipzig, 1924).
MEDLICOTT, W.N. and COVENEY, Dorothy K. (eds), 'Bismarck and
Europe' (London, 1971).
'Österreich-Ungarns Aussenpolitik von der Bosnischen Krise 1908
bis zum Kriegsausbruch 1914'. Diplomatische Aktenstücke des
Österreich-Ungarischen Ministeriums des Äusseren, eds Bittner, L.,
Pribram, A., Srbik, H. and Uebersberger, H., 8 vols (Vienna,
1930).
RÖHL, J.C.G. (ed.), 'From Bismarck to Hitler. The Problem of Con-
tinuity in German History' (London, 1970).
VON SIEBERT, B. (ed.), 'Diplomatische Aktenstücke zur Geschichte
der Ententepolitik der Vorkriegsjahre' (Berlin, Leipzig, 1921).
STÜRMER, M. (ed.), 'Bismarck und die preussisch-deutsche Politik
1871-1890' (Munich, 1970), dtv 692.

For general accounts see also GOLLWITZER, H., 'The Age of European
Imperialism, 1880-1918' (London, 1969), and MOMMSEN, W.J., 'Das
Zeitalter des Imperialismus' (Frankfurt-am-Main, 1969).   For
students with sufficient knowledge of German, HALLGARTEN, G.W.F.,
'Imperialismus vor 1914. Die soziologischen Grundlagen der Aussen-
politik europäischer Grossmächte vor dem Ersten Weltkrieg', 2 vols,
2nd ed. (Munich, 1963), will always remain stimulating; also JOLL,
J., 'Europe since 1870. An International History' (London, 1973).

BOOKS AND MONOGRAPHS

ALBERTINI, L., 'The Origins of the War of 1914'. Translated and
edited by Massey, Isabella H., 3 vols (London, New York, Toronto,
1952-7, 2nd imp. 1966).
ANDERSON, M.S., 'The Eastern Question' (London, 1966).
ANDREW, C., 'Théophile Delcassé and the Making of the Entente
Cordiale. A Reappraisal of French Foreign Policy 1898-1905' (London,
1968).
BALFOUR, M., 'The Kaiser and His Times' (London, 1964).
BARRACLOUGH, G., 'History in a Changing World' (Oxford, 1957).
BERGHAHN, V.R., 'Der Tirpitz-Plan. Genesis und Verfall einer
innenpolitischen Krisenstrategie unter Wilhelm II' (Düsseldorf,
1971).
BERGHAHN, V.R., 'Rüstung und Machtpolitik. Zur Anatomie des 'Kalten
Krieges' vor 1914' (Düsseldorf, 1973).
BERGHAHN, V.R., 'Germany and the Approach of War in 1914' (London,
1973).
BLEY, H., 'South-West Africa under German Rule, 1894-1914' (London,
1971).
BÖHME, H., 'Deutschlands Weg zur Grossmacht' (Cologne, 1966).
BORCHARDT, K., 'The Industrial Revolution in Germany' (London, 1972).
BÜLOW, B. FÜRST VON, 'Denkwürdigkeiten', 4 vols (Berlin, 1930).
CORNEVIN, R., 'Histoire du Togo' (Paris, 1963).
CROWE, Sybil E., 'The Berlin West Africa Conference' (London, 1942).
DEDIJER, V., 'The Road to Sarajevo' (London, 1966).
DEHIO, L., 'Deutschland und die Weltpolitik im 20. Jahrhundert'
DELBRÜCK, C. VON, 'Die wirtschaftliche Mobilmachung in Deutschland'
(Munich, 1924).
DJORDJEVIC, D., 'Révolutions nationales des peuples balkaniques,
1804-1914' (Belgrade, 1965).
DRECHSLER, H., 'Südwestafrika unter deutscher Kolonialherrschaft'
(East Berlin, 1966).
ECKARDTSTEIN, H. FREIHERR VON, 'Lebenserinnerungen und politische
Denkwürdigkeiten', 2 vols (Leipzig, 1920).
EINEM, VON, 'Erinnerungen eines Soldaten, 1853-1933' (Leipzig,
1933).
FELLNER, F., 'Der Dreibund' (Vienna, 1960).
FISCHER, F., 'Germany's Aims in the First World War' (London, 1967).
FISCHER, F., 'Krieg der Illusionen. Die deutsche Politik von 1911
bis 1914' (Düsseldorf, 1969); English edition: 'War of Illusions.
German Policies 1911-1914' (London, 1975).
GALOS, A., GENTZEN, F.H. and JAKOBCZYK, W., 'Die Hakatisten. Der
deutsche Ostmarkenverein (1894-1934). Ein Beitrag zur Geschichte
der Ostpolitik des deutschen Imperialismus' (East Berlin, 1966).

GEISS, I., 'Der polnische Grenzstreifen 1914-1918. Ein Beitrag zur deutschen Kriegszielpolitik im Ersten Weltkrieg' (Hamburg, Lübeck, 1960).

GIFFORD, P. and LOUIS, R.W. (eds), 'Britain and Germany in Africa' (New Haven, 1967).

GOLLWITZER, H., 'The Age of European Imperialism, 1880-1918' (London, 1969).

GROH, D., 'Negative Integration und revolutionärer Attentismus. Die deutsche Sozialdemokratie am Vorabend des 1. Weltkrieges' (Berlin, 1973).

GUTSCHE, W., 'Aufstieg und Fall eines kaiserlichen Reichskanzlers. Theobald von Bethmann-Hollweg 1856-1921. Ein politisches Lebensbild' (East Berlin, 1973).

HALLGARTEN, G.W.F., 'Imperialismus vor 1914. Die soziologischen Grundlagen der Aussenpolitik europäischer Grossmächte vor dem Ersten Weltkrieg', 2 vols, 2nd ed. (Munich, 1963).

HALLGARTEN, G.W.F., 'Das Schicksal des Imperialismus im 20. Jahrhundert. Drei Abhandlungen über Kriegsursachen' (Frankfurt, 1969).

HAMEROW, T.S., 'Restoration, Revolution, Reaction. Economics and Politics in Germany, 1815-1871' (Princeton, 1958).

HENDERSON, W.D., 'Studies in German Colonial History' (London, 1962).

HERZFELD, H., 'Die Moderne Welt 1789 bis 1945' 2 parts, 3rd ed. (Brunswick, 1961).

HILDEBRAND, K., 'Vom Reich zum Weltreich. Hitler, NSDAP und koloniale Frage 1919-1945' (Munich, 1969).

HILLGRUBER, A., 'Kontinuität und Diskontinuität in der deutschen Aussenpolitik von Bismarck bis Hitler' (Düsseldorf, 1969, 3rd imp. 1971).

HILLGRUBER, A., 'Bismarcks Aussenpolitik' (Freiburg, 1972).

HÖTZENDORF, C. VON, 'Aus meiner Dienstzeit 1906-1918' 5 vols (Vienna, Leipzig, Munich, 1922).

JOLL, J., 'Europe since 1870. An International History' (London, 1973).

KAMPEN, W. VAN, 'Studien zur deutschen Türkeipolitik in der Zeit Wilhelms II', Thesis (Kiel, 1968).

KANN, R.A., 'The Multinational Empire. Nationalism and national reform in the Hapsburg monarchy 1848-1918', 2nd ed. (New York, 1970).

KANTOROWICZ, H., 'The Spirit of British Policy and the Myth of the Encirclement of Germany' (London, 1932).

KANTOROWICZ, H., 'Gutachten zur Kriegsschuldfrage 1914', ed. Geiss, I., foreword by Heinemann, G.W. (Frankfurt, 1967).

KEHR, E., 'Schlachtflottenbau und Parteipolitik 1894-1901. Versuch eines Querschnitts durch die innenpolitischen, sozialen und ideologischen Voraussetzungen des deutschen Imperialismus' (Berlin, 1930, 2nd imp. Vaduz, 1965).

KEHR, E., 'Der Primat der Innenpolitik. Gesammelte Aufsätze zur preussisch-deutschen Sozialgeschichte im 19. und 20. Jahrhundert', ed. Wehler, H.-U., preface by Herzfeld, H. (Berlin, 1965, 2nd imp. 1969).

KENT, G.O., 'Arnim and Bismarck' (Oxford, 1968).

KOLB, E., 'Kriegsausbruch 1970. Politische Entscheidungsprozesse und Verantwortlichkeiten in der Julikrise 1870' (Göttingen, 1970).

KRUCK, A., 'Geschichte des Alldeutschen Verbandes 1890-1939' (Wiesbaden, 1954).

KUMPT-KORTES, S., 'Bismarcks "Draht nach Russland"' (East Berlin, 1968).
LANGER, W.L., 'The Diplomacy of Imperialism 1890-1902', 2 vols (New York, 1935).
LANGER, W.L., 'European Alliances and Alignments 1871-1890' (New York, 2 imp. 1951).
LEIDIGKEIT, K.-H. (ed.), 'Der Leipziger Hochverratsprozess von 1872' (East Berlin, 1960).
LOWE, C.J., 'The Reluctant Imperialists', vol. I, 'British Foreign Policy 1879-1902' (London, 1967).
MARDER, A.J., 'From the Dreadnought to Scapa Flow', 5 vols (London, 1961).
MEINECKE, F., 'The German Catastrophe. Reflections and Recollections' (Cambridge, Mass., 1950), 3rd imp. Boston, 1964).
MEYER, H.C., 'Mitteleuropa in German Thought and Action, 1815-1945' (The Hague, 1954).
MOMMSEN, W.J., 'Max Weber und die deutsche Politik 1890-1920' (Tübingen, 1958).
MOMMSEN, W.J., 'Das Zeitalter des Imperialismus' (Frankfurt/Main, 1969).
MONGER, G., 'The End of Isolation. British Foreign Policy 1900-1907' (London, 1963).
MOSES, J.A. and KENNEDY, P.D. (eds), 'Germany in the Pacific and Far East 1870-1914' (Dublin, 1974).
MÜLLER, F.F., 'Deutschland, Zanzibar, Ostafrika' (East Berlin, 1959).
OLIVER, R. and ATMORE, A., 'Africa since 1800' (Cambridge, 1967).
PENZLER, J. (ed.), 'Reden Kaiser Wilhelms II, 1888-1912' (Leipzig, n.d.).
PFLANZE, O., 'Bismarck and the Development of Germany. The Period of Unification 1815-1871' (Princeton, 1963).
PLEHN, H., 'Deutsche Weltpolitik und kein Krieg' (Berlin, 1913).
PUHLE, H.-J., 'Agrarische Interessenpolitik und preussischer Konservatismus in wilhelminischen Reich (1893-1914). Ein Beitrag zur Analyse des Nationalismus in Deutschland am Beispiel des Bundes der Landwirte und der Deutsch-Konservativen Partei' (Hanover, 1966).
RICH, N., 'Friedrich von Holstein', 2 vols (Cambridge, 1965).
RITTER, G., 'Staatskunst und Kriegshandwerk. Das Problem des "Militarismus" in Deutschland', 4 vols (Munich, 1954-68).
RITTER, G., 'Lebendige Vergangenheit. Beiträge zur historisch-politischen Selbstbesinnung' (Munich, 1958).
RITTER, G., 'The Schlieffen Plan: Critique of a Myth' (London, 1958).
RIEZLER, K., 'Tagebücher, Aufsätze, Dokumente', ed. Erdmann, K.D. (Göttingen, 1972).
RÖHL, J.C.G., 'Germany without Bismarck. The Crisis of Government in the Second Reich, 1890-1900' (London, 1967).
ROLO, P.J.V., 'Entente Cordiale. The Origins and Negotiations of the Anglo-French Agreements of 8 April, 1904' (London, 1969).
ROSENBERG, H., 'Grosse Depression und Bismarckzeit. Wirtschaftsablauf, Gesellschaft und Politik in Mitteleuropa' (Berlin, 1967).
RUDIN, H.F., 'The Germans in the Cameroons, 1884-1914' (London, 1938).
RUEDORFFER, J.J., (= K. Riezler) 'Grundzüge der Weltpolitik (Stuttgart, Berlin, 1914).
RUSSELL, B., 'German Social Democracy' (London, 1896).

SCHRECKER, J.E., 'Imperialism and Chinese Nationalism. Germany in Shantung' (Cambridge, Mass., 1971).

SCHÜCK, R., 'Brandenburg-Preussens Kolonialpolitik' (Leipzig, 1889).

SLADE, Ruth, 'King Leopold's Congo'(London, 1962).

STEGMANN, D., 'Die Erben Bismarcks. Parteien und Verbände in der Spätphase des wilhelminischen Deutschlands. Sammlungspolitik 1897-1918' (Cologne, Berlin, 1970).

STEINBERG, J., 'Yesterday's Deterrent. Tirpitz and the Birth of the German Battle Fleet' (London, 1965).

STÜRMER, M. (ed.), 'Das kaiserliche Deutschland. Politik und Gesellschaft 1870-1918' (Düsseldorf, 1970).

TAYLOR, A.J.P., 'Germany's First Bid for Colonies' (London, 1938).

TAYLOR, A.J.P., 'The Course of German History since 1815. A Survey of the Development of German History since 1815' (London, 1945, reprints 1961, 1964).

TAYLOR, A.J.P., 'The Hapsburg Monarchy 1809-1918. A History of the Austrian Empire and Austria-Hungary' (London, 1948, reprint 1964).

TAYLOR, A.J.P., 'The Struggle for Mastery in Europe, 1848-1918' (Oxford, 1954).

TIMS, R.W., 'Germanizing Prussian Poland. The H-K-T-Society and the Struggle for Eastern Marches in the German Empire, 1894-1919' (New York, 1941).

TIRPITZ, A. VON, 'Erinnerungen' (Leipzig, 1919).

TIRPITZ, A. VON, Politische Dokumente, 2 vols, I, 'Der Aufbau der deutschen Weltmacht' (Stuttgart, Berlin, 1924).

TOWNSEND, Mary E., 'The Rise and Fall of Germany's Colonial Empire' (New York, 1930).

TRUMPENER, U., 'Germany and the Ottoman Empire 1914-1918' (Princeton, 1968).

TUCHMAN, Barbara, 'The Guns of August' (New York, 1962, paperback 1963).

VAGT, A., 'Deutschland und die Vereinigten Staaten in der Weltpolitik' (New York, 1935).

VEBLEN, T., 'Imperial Germany and the Industrial Revolution' (New York, 1915, paperback 1966, 1968).

VEROSTA, S., 'Theorie und Realität von Bündnissen. Heinrich Lannasch, Karl Renner und der Zweibund (1897-1914)' (Vienna, 1971).

VIETSCH, E. VON, 'Bethmann-Hollweg. Staatsmann zwischen Macht und Ethos' (Boppard/Rhein, 1969).

VOGEL, Barbara, 'Deutsche Russlandpolitik. Das Scheitern der deutschen Weltpolitik unter Bülow 1900-1906' (Düsseldorf, 1973).

WALLACH, Y., 'Das Dogma der Vernichtungsschlacht. Die Lehren von Clausewitz und Chlieffen und ihre Wirkungen in zwei Weltkriegen' (Frankfurt/Main, 1967).

WEHLER, H.-U., 'Bismarck und der Imperialismus' (Cologne, 1969, 3rd imp. 1972).

WEHLER, H.-U., 'Krisenherde des Kaiserreiches 1871-1918' (Göttingen, 1970).

WEHLER, H.-U., 'Das deutsches Kaiserreich, 1871-1918' (Göttingen, 1974).

WERNECKE, K., 'Der Wille zur Weltgeltung. Aussenpolitik und Öffentlichkeit im Kaiserreich am Vorabend des Ersten Weltkrieges' (Düsseldorf, 1970).

WITT, P.-C., 'Die Finanzpolitik des Deutschen Reiches von 1903 bis
1913. Eine Studie zur Innenpolitik des wilhelminischen Deutschland'
(Lübeck, Hamburg, 1970).
ZECHLIN, E., 'Bismarck und die Grundlegung der deutschen Grossmacht'
(Stuttgart, Berlin, 1930, 2nd imp. 1960).

ESSAYS AND ARTICLES

BÖHME, H., Politik und Ökonomie in der Reichsgründungszeit und
späten Bismarck-Zeit, in Stürmer, M. (ed.), 'Das kaiserliche
Deutschland. Politik und Gesellschaft 1870-1918' (Düsseldorf, 1970),
pp. 26-50.
ELEY, G., Sammlungspolitik, Social Imperialism and the Navy Law of
1898, 'Militärgeschichtliche Mitteilungen', 1/1974, pp. 29-63.
EPSTEIN, K., Gerhard Ritter and the First World War, 'Journal of
Contemporary History' 1/3 (1966), pp. 193-210.
FLINT, J.E., Chartered Companies and the Scramble for Africa, in
Anene, J.C. and Brown, G.N. (eds), 'Africa in the Nineteenth and
Twentieth Centuries' (Ibadan, London, 1966), pp. 110-32.
GALL, L., Zur Frage der Annexion von Elsass und Lothringen 1870,
'Historische Zeitschrift', 206 (1968), p. 265f.
GALL, L., Das Problem Elsass-Lothringen, in Schieder, T. and
Deuerlein, E. (eds), 'Reichsgründung 1870/71. Tatsachen, Kontra-
versen, Interpretationen' (Stuttgart, 1970), pp. 366-85.
GASSER, A., Deutschlands Entschluss zum Präventivkrieg 1913-14, in
'Discordia concors, Festgabe für Edgar Bonjour', 2 vols (Basle,
1968), pp. 171-224.
GASSER, A., Der deutsche Hegemonialkrieg von 1914, in Geiss, I.
and Wendt, B.J. (eds), 'Deutschland in der Weltpolitik des 19. und
20. Jahrhunderts' (Düsseldorf, 1973), pp. 307-39.
GEISS, I., Weltherrschaft durch Hegemonie. Die deutsche Politik im
1. Weltkrieg nach den Riezler-Tagebüchern, in 'Beilage zu "Das
Parlament"', B 50/72.
GEISS, I., 'Kurt Riezler und der Erste Weltkrieg', in Geiss, I.
and Wendt, B.J. (eds), 'Deutschland in der Weltpolitik des 19. und
20. Jahrhundert', pp. 398-418.
GEISS, I., Reich und Nation. Anmerkungen zu zwei zentralen
Kategorien deutscher Geschichte und Politik, in 'Beilage zu "Das
Parlament"', B 15/73.
HAMEROW,T.S., The Origins of Mass Politics in Germany 1866-1867, in
Geiss, I. and Wendt, B.J. (eds), 'Deutschland in der Weltpolitik
des 19. und 20. Jahrhunderts', pp. 105-20.
HILLGRUBER, A., Die 'Krieg-in-Sicht'-Krise 1875 - Wegscheide der
europäischen Grossmächte in der späten Bismarck-Zeit, in 'Gedenk-
schrift Martin Göhring', ed. Schulin, E. (Wiesbaden, 1968), p. 239f.
HINSLEY, F.H., Bismarck, Salisbury and the Mediterranean Agree-
ments, 'Cambridge Historical Journal' (1958), p. 76f.
KENNEDY, P.M., Bismarck's Imperialism. The Case of Samoa, 1880-
1890, 'Historical Journal', XV (1972), pp. 261-83.
KOLB, E., Bismarck und das Aufkommen der Annexionsforderung 1870,
'Historische Zeitschrift', 209 (1969), pp. 318-56.
LANGHORNE, R., Anglo-German Negotiations Concerning the Future of
the Portuguese Colonies, 1911-1914, 'Historical Journal', XVI
(1973), pp. 361-87.

LIPGENS, W., Bismarck, die öffentliche Meinung und die Annexion von Elsass und Lothringen 1870, 'Historische Zeitschrift', 199 (1964), pp. 31-112.

LIPGENS, W., Bismarck und die Frage der Annexion 1870, (HZ), 206 (1968), pp. 586-617.

RÖHL, J.C.G., A Document of 1892 on Germany, Prussia and Poland, 'Historical Journal', VII 91964), pp. 143-9.

RÖHL, J.C.G., Admiral von Müller and the Approach of War, 'Historical Journal', XII (1969), pp. 651-73.

STEINBERG, J., A German Plan for the Invasion of Holland and Belgium 1897, 'Historical Journal', VI (1963), pp. 107-19.

STEINBERG, J., The Copenhagen Complex, 'Journal of Contemporary History', 1/3 (1966), pp. 23-46.

STONE, N., V. Moltke-Conrad: Relations Between the Austro-Hungarian and German General Staffs, 1909-1914, 'Historical Journal', IX (1966), pp. 201-28.

STRANDMANN, H. POGGE-VON and SMITH, Alison, The German Empire in Africa and British Perspectives: A Historiographical Essay, in Gifford, P. and Louis, W.R. (eds), 'Britain and Germany in Africa' (New Haven, 1967). pp. 709-95.

STRANDMANN, H. POGGE-VON, Domestic Origins of Germany's Colonial Expansion under Bismarck, in 'Past and Present' (1969), pp. 140-59.

STÜRMER, M., Staatsstreichgedanken im Bismarckreich, 'Historische Zeitschrift', 209 (1969), pp. 566-615.

TURNER, H.A., Bismarck's Imperialist Venture. Anti-British in Origin?, in Gifford, P. and Louis, W.R. (eds), 'Britain and Germany in Africa' (New Haven, 1967), pp. 47-82.

WEHLER, H.-U., Bismarck's Imperialism, in 'Past and Present' (1970), pp. 119-55.

WEHLER, H.-U., Bismarck's Imperialismus und späte Russlandpolitik unter dem Primat der Innenpolitik, in Stürmer, M. (ed.), 'Das kaiserliche Deutschland. Politik und Gesellschaft 1870-1918' (Düsseldorf, 1970), pp. 235-64.

ZECHLIN, E., Deutschland zwischen Kabinettskrieg und Wirtschaftskrieg. Politik und Kriegführung in den ersten Monaten des Weltkrieges 1914, 'Historische Zeitschrift' 199 (1964), pp. 347-458.

INDEX

50·301